ADVANCES IN DATA BASE THEORY

Volume 1

ADVANCES IN DATA BASE THEORY

Volume 1

Edited by

Hervé Gallaire

Ecole Nationale Supérieure de l'Aéronautique et de l'Espace
Toulouse, France

Jack Minker

University of Maryland
College Park, Maryland

and

Jean Marie Nicolas

Centre d'Etudes et de Recherches de Toulouse
Toulouse, France

PLENUM PRESS · NEW YORK AND LONDON

ISBN 0-306-40629-2

The content of this volume is based on the proceedings of the Workshop on Formal Bases for Data Bases held at the Centre d'Etudes et de Recherches de l'Ecole Nationale Supérieure de l'Aéronautique et de l'Espace de Toulouse (CERT), Toulouse, France, December 12–14, 1979.

A Division of Plenum Publishing Corporation
227 West 17th Street, New York, N.Y. 10011

Printed in the United States of America

FOREWORD

During the 1970's a theory of data bases began to evolve providing a foundation for some existing tools and techniques. The significance of this theory is beginning to have an impact particularly with respect to the design and implementation of the relational model of data bases.

To further the state of the art in the theory of data bases, a workshop was held in Toulouse, France on December 12-14, 1979. The workshop was a sequel to one held two years previously and entitled, "Logic and Data Base Workshop". As with the earlier workshop, the meetings were conducted at the Centre d'Etudes et de Recherches de l'Ecole Nationale Superieure de l'Aéronautique et de l'Espace de Toulouse (C.E.R.T). We are pleased to acknowledge the financial support received from the Direction des Recherches, Etudes et Techniques d'Armement (D.R.E.T.), and from C.E.R.T. that made the workshop possible.

As a consequence of the first workshop, a book, *Logic and Data Bases* was published. When the 1979 workshop was completed, it was clear that bringing together researchers concerned with the theory of data bases led to a useful interchange of ideas and that finished work should be published in book form in one place. Furthermore, future workshops should be held. We have embedded this concept in the title of the book, *Advances in Data Base Theory — Volume 1*. The book *Logic and Data Bases* should be considered Volume 0 of this series as it describes theoretical aspects of data bases. Its larger focus was to relate the subjects of logic and data bases to each other. As was the case for its predecessor, the chapters of this book are based on substantially revised versions of papers presented at the workshop. Each chapter included in the book was reviewed by at least three experts in the field — both individuals who attended the workshop and others who did not attend the workshop. The list of reviewers is found in the back of the book. We are indebted to them for their efforts on behalf of this undertaking.

This book can be used as the basis of a graduate seminar in

computer science. Students should have a first level course in data base systems and some background in mathematical logic.

The aspects of data base theory developed in this book are:

(1) Data Base Design. The focus of the chapters is on various dependency relationships and their use in designing data base schema.

(2) General Laws: Deduction and Integrity. The chapters continue to describe the relationships between logic and data bases. Emphasis is towards augmenting relational data bases to handle deduction and integrity constraints.

(3) Informative Capabilities for Users. The efforts describe how data base systems may be developed which are "friendly".

The book starts with an introductory chapter which we have written to provide some needed background in logic and data bases, to summarize the achievements in each paper, and to relate the theoretical developments to other work in the literature.

Our grateful appreciation goes to Constance Engle who typed the entire book. We also wish to thank Lynn Brandes, Elizabeth Louie, and Susan Schwab for their assistance with the book and in the development of the subject and name indexes. Support for work on the book was also provided by NASA under NGR21-002-270 and from the NSF under GJ 43632 and MCS 7919418.

H. Gallaire
J. Minker
J. M. Nicolas
September 1980

CONTENTS

INTRODUCTION

BACKGROUND FOR ADVANCES IN DATA BASE THEORY

Hervé Gallaire,[1] Jack Minker[2] and Jean-Marie Nicolas[3]

ENSAE-CERT, Toulouse, France[1]
University of Maryland, College Park, Maryland[2]
ONERA-CERT, Toulouse, France[3]

ABSTRACT

The intent of this chapter is to provide appropriate background for the reader so that he can comprehend more readily the advances in data base theory described in the chapters to follow. Following this introductory chapter there are three major subdivisions in the book: Data Base Design; General Laws: Deduction and Integrity; and Informative Capabilities for Users. For each area we provide background material on the subject matter, related work that has taken place in the particular subject, and provide an overview of the essential aspects of each paper that appears in the section.

INTRODUCTION

The papers collected in this book report on some of the recent theoretical studies concerning data bases. They deal with three main topics: Data base design, general laws: deduction and integrity, and informative capabilities for users.

The purpose of this introductory chapter is twofold: to provide background material for each of the above mentioned topics and to outline the main results presented in each of the papers of the book.

DATA BASE DESIGN

As with many other aspects of data bases, the relational model of data provides a convenient formalism to study data base design. Thus, it is no surprise that all the papers in this book that deal with the design aspect of data bases consider relational databases.

The purpose of this section is to provide an introduction to those papers and to outline their content briefly. We will assume that the reader is familiar with the basic concepts of the relational model such as relation schemes, relations (instances) and decomposition of relations (e.g. see Ullman [1980] or Date [1977]). For a survey of the design aspects of relational data bases the reader is referred to Beeri, Bernstein and Goodman [1978].

Briefly, the design problem for a relational data base consists of choosing, from among different possibilities, some "good" relation schemes for representing information in the world to be modeled. A "good" relation scheme can be characterized broadly as one that is free of data manipulation anomalies and of data redundancy.

For example, consider the relation scheme SUPP(SUPPLIER, TOWN, POPULATION) ; its intended meaning is such that whenever a tuple, say <s,t,p>, occurs in a relation on this scheme it means that "supplier s is located in town t whose population is p". The relation scheme SUPP leads in fact to the following data manipulation anomalies. First, notice that the population of a given town must appear as many times as there are suppliers located in that town (data redundancy). Thus, if the population of a town has to be updated, all the tuples in which it occurs have to be retrieved in order to update consistently the population of the town (updating anomaly). Now, if the last supplier located in a given town is deleted, then the population of this town is lost (deletion anomaly). Conversely, the population of a town can be recorded only when one knows at least one supplier located in that town (insertion anomaly).

It has been shown that data manipulation anomalies are in fact due to the presence of certain dependencies between the attributes of a relation scheme. Thus, the characterization of good relation schemes amounts to characterizing relation schemes free of these dependencies. It was for this purpose that the so-called normal forms of relations were developed.

Returning to the above example, the following dependencies may be found among the attributes in SUPP: A supplier determines a town, a town determines a population, and a supplier determines a population. The undesirable properties of the relation scheme SUPP are due to this latter dependency which is transitive, and because of the presence of this transitive dependency the relation scheme is not in third normal form (3NF).

Several normal forms have been introduced. Each normal form has improved over the previous normal forms with regard to the elimination of data manipulation anomalies. The normal forms called 3NF and Boyce-Codd Normal Form (BCNF) were defined based on the concept of functional dependency, whereas the concept of multivalued dependency was used to define fourth normal form, and the concept of join dependency to define the Projection-Join Normal Form (PJNF) (Fagin [1979]).

Dependencies

The concept of dependency appears to be fundamental to the design of relational data bases, and two chapters in this book are concerned directly with this concept.

In their chapter, Beeri and Vardi study the not yet well understood concept of join dependency. Although both embedded and total join dependencies are considered, the latter are treated more thoroughly. The authors propose a formal system for join dependencies. Most of the results presented are obtained by studying the power of this formal system. The proposed system, which is rather simple in the sense that it consists of only one axiom and two inference rules (for total join dependencies), turns out to be very powerful. Most of the already known inference rules for different special cases of join dependencies (e.g.: multivalued dependencies, first order hierarchical decomposition, cross, etc.) can be derived from this system. As their main result, the system is proved to be complete for deriving the first order hierarchical decompositions implied by a set of join dependencies. By providing many new results as well as simplified proofs of already known results, a more comprehensive understanding of join dependencies is obtained.

In the second chapter devoted to the study of dependencies, Paredaens and Janssens propose a new dependency, called general dependency. General dependencies have to be related to two other new classes of dependencies which have been introduced recently: the class of template dependencies (Sadri and Ullman [1980]) and the class of implicational dependencies (Fagin [1980]) which properly include the preceding one. The concept of general dependency contains two different aspects. On the one hand it says that "if some tuples appear in a relation then some other tuple must also appear in that relation", and, on the other hand, it also says that "if some tuples appear in a relation then some of the components of the tuples have to be equal". Because it combines these two aspects, this concept encompasses both functional dependencies and most of the previously known types of dependencies. It thereby provides a unifying view of these dependencies.

The authors also show by providing a sufficient condition, how their dependencies relate to the nonloss decomposition of relations. Further, they propose a set of inference rules for general dependencies. However, the completeness of the set of rules is only conjectured.

Equivalence of Data Bases

Dependencies are used to define normal forms of relations, but they are also involved in the normalization process. This transformation relies upon the decomposition of a relation scheme (relation) into some of its subsets (projections). But the problem is then to know what constitutes a "good" decomposition. In other words, under what conditions will one consider that the resulting set of relation schemes is equivalent to the initial relation scheme.

Several proposals have been made in the literature to define the concept of an adequate decomposition. One, introduced by Rissanen [1977] relies upon the notion of independent components; another, proposed by Arora and Carlson [1978], requires that decompositions be both lossless and constraint (dependency) preserving. In their chapter, Maier, Mendelzon, Sadri and Ullman study the above two definitions of adequate decomposition and propose a third definition. They show that the three definitions are equivalent when constraints considered on relations are restricted to functional dependencies. However this equivalence does not hold when multivalued dependencies are also considered. In such a case the definition they propose appears to be intermediate between the definition by Arora and Carlson which is the most stringent and the definition by Rissanen which is the least stringent. They also propose necessary and sufficient conditions associated with these definitions and discuss the complexity required to test whether they hold.

Aids for the Data Base Designer

The initial set of dependencies (associated with some relation schemes) that is dealt with in the design process, is provided by the data base designer. However, one must ensure that these dependencies represent correctly the actual constraints on the world being modeled. Obviously there is no way to do so. The correctness of these dependencies rests only on the ability of the data base designer to translate correctly his perception of the world in terms of relation schemes and dependencies. However, one can provide the designer with some tools which will help him in this process.

In their chapter, Silva and Melkanoff propose such a tool which exploits the fact that any set of functional (FDs) and/or multivalued dependencies (MVDs) admits a so-called Armstrong relation (see Fagin [1980]). An Armstrong relation for a given set of dependencies is a relation which obeys all the dependencies and only those dependencies belonging to the closure of the considered set.

Given a relation scheme and a set of FDs and/or MVDs, provided by the data base designer, the tool proposed by Silva and Melkanoff generates an Armstrong relation for that set. Thus the designer can check whether the generated relation is compatible with the understanding he has of the world he wants to model. For example, because the generated relation does not obey any of the dependencies not in the closure of the set of dependencies the designer provided, in view of this relation he could detect some dependencies he possibly forgot to make explicit.

GENERAL LAWS: DEDUCTION AND INTEGRITY

We present here only brief summaries of the material in mathematical logic needed for a consideration of deduction and integrity. For additional material the reader is referred to the predecessor to this book, *Logic and Data Bases* (Gallaire and Minker, Eds.), in which we outlined basic concepts required to comprehend material in chapters that follow (Gallaire, Minker, and Nicolas [1978]). Details concerning mathematical logic may be found in Chang and Lee [1973], Robinson [1965], or Loveland [1978].

Sentences within predicate logic are specified by *well-formed formulae (wffs)*. A wff is built from *terms* and *atomic formulae*. A term is defined recursively as a constant, a variable, or an n-ary function ($n \geq 0$) whose arguments are terms. An atomic formula is defined as an m-ary predicate, $m \geq 0$, whose arguments are terms. Well-formed formulae are defined recursively as follows: atomic formulae are wffs; if A is a wff and x is an individual variable, then $(\forall x)A$ is a wff; if A and B are wffs, then $(\sim A)$ and $(A \rightarrow B)$ are wffs; the only wffs are those formed by finite applications of the above rules. Boolean combinations of wffs and logical equivalence ($\leftrightarrow$) are encompassed by these rules as is the existential quantifier $(\exists x)$.

Given a wff, it can be transformed to a conjunction of *clauses* by eliminating existential quantifiers by the use of Skolem functions (see, for example, Chang and Lee). A clause is a disjunction of *literals*, all of whose variables are universally quantified. By a literal we mean an atomic formula or the negation of an atomic formula. A *ground literal* is a literal that contains no variables (i.e. *an elementary fact*). Thus,

$$\sim P_1(x_1,x_2,x_4) \vee \sim P_2(x_2,x_3) \vee Q_1(x_3,x_1,x_2) \vee Q_2(x_1,x_2,x_3)$$

is a clause. There are several alternate forms used to represent a clause in this book. The above clause may be written equivalently as:

(a) $P_1(x_1,x_2,x_4) \& P_2(x_2,x_3) \rightarrow Q_1(x_3,x_1,x_2) \vee Q_2(x_1,x_2,x_3)$

(b) $Q_1(x_3,x_1,x_2) \vee Q_2(x_1,x_2,x_3) \leftarrow P_1(x_1,x_2,x_4) \& P_2(x_2,x_3)$

(c) $Q_1(x_3,x_1,x_2), Q_2(x_1,x_2,x_3) \leftarrow P_1(x_1,x_2,x_4) \& P_2(x_2,x_3)$

(d) $Q_1(x_3,x_1,x_2), Q_2(x_1,x_2,x_3) \leftarrow P_1(x_1,x_2,x_4), P_2(x_2,x_3)$.

Statements such as the above can be read as "for all x_1, x_2, x_3, x_4 if $P_1(x_1,x_2,x_4)$ and $P_2(x_2,x_3)$ then $Q_1(x_3,x_1,x_2)$ or $Q_2(x_1,x_2,x_3)$".

Using form (c), above, a general clause may be written as,

(1) $Q_1, Q_2, \ldots, Q_m \leftarrow P_1 \& P_2 \& \ldots \& P_n$,

where $n,m \geq 0$, and the P_i and Q_j are atomic formulae. A *general law* is a well-formed formula that is not a ground literal.

When a clause of form (1) has $m = 1$, we refer to the clause as a *definite Horn clause*; when $n = 0$, $m = 1$ we refer to the clause as an assertion; when $m > 1$ we refer to the clause as an *indefinite* (or a *non-Horn clause*).

Data bases are generally considered to be function-free (Reiter [1978], Ullman [1980]) and hence do not need the full power of a theorem prover. The use of function-free forms avoids problems associated with the equality predicate. Throughout the book, the authors of each chapter, although not stating so explicitly, use function-free forms and further assume that there are a finite number of constants in the system. Furthermore, the general laws used are Horn clauses. This means that all answers are definite. An indefinite answer arises when, for example, a system responds "A is located at B or A is located at C", and insufficient information exists to specify at which location A is located. See Reiter [1978] for a treatment of indefinite data bases.

When dealing with Horn clauses that are function-free, given two clauses that have *complementary literals* that can be *unified*, a new clause can be derived. Thus, given the two clauses,

(a) FATHER(A,B)
(b) PARENT(x,y) V ∿FATHER(x,y),

one can deduce

PARENT(A,B).

This is accomplished by noticing that clause (a) and clause (b) have complementary predicate letters, and that one can unify

{FATHER(A,B), FATHER(x,y)}

(that is make the two forms identical) by substituting A for x and B for y, written, $\theta = \{A/x, B/y\}$. The derived clause may then be obtained.

More generally, if we have two Horn clauses,

$$L_1 \vee \sim L_2 \vee \cdots \vee \sim L_r$$

$$M_1 \vee \sim M_2 \vee \cdots \vee \sim M_s ,$$

where L_1 and M_i have the same predicate letter and a unifier θ can be found to make them identical, then one can derive the new clause,

$$(M_1 \vee \sim M_2 \vee \cdots \vee \sim M_{i-1} \vee (\sim L_2 \vee \cdots \vee \sim L_r) \vee \sim M_{i+1} \vee \cdots \vee \sim M_s)\theta.$$

That is, delete the complementary pairs in the two clauses, from the disjunction of the remaining literals, and apply the unifying substitution to the result. The unification algorithm is particularly simple for function-free forms.

The Use of General Laws in Data Bases

General laws have been used in a number of ways in data base technology:

(1) As *integrity constraints* on data.
(2) As *deduction rules*.

Integrity Constraints

Integrity constraints specify restrictions on arguments of relational tuples or between relational tuples. Integrity constraints can be represented as clauses or sets of clauses.

Integrity constraints apply generally to the meaning associated with data. For example, one can restrict the values of arguments of relations to a specified range, or to be in a specific domain. Thus, we might have

$$\text{MALE}(x) \vee \text{FEMALE}(x) \leftarrow \text{PARENT}(x,y) ,$$

which specifies that a parent can be either in the domain male or the domain female. The following integrity constraint,

$$\text{MALE}(x) \leftarrow \text{FATHER}(x,y) ,$$

assumes that the first argument of the FATHER relation is a male. The integrity constraint

$$\text{GREATOREQ}(z,18) \leftarrow \text{FATHER}(x,y) \ \& \ \text{AGE}(x,z)$$

insists that all fathers in the data base be at least 18 years old.

The semantic integrity constraints of this type can be used in two ways: at data entry, or at query entry time. The use of these integrity constraints at data entry time has been discussed in chapters in the books by Gallaire and Minker [1978], Date [1977] and Ullman [1980], where additional references may be found. The use of semantic integrity constraints at query time is intended to reject queries that do not comply with the semantic constraints specified. Such constraints restrict the types to which arguments can belong.

In his chapter, Reiter considers a typed first-order data base in which each quantified variable is constrained to range over some type. With each data base relation is associated an integrity constraint which specifies which types of individuals are permitted to fill the argument positions of that relation. The problem addressed is the detection of violations of these integrity constraints in the case of data base updates with universally quantified formulae. Any such formula is first transformed to its so-called typed normal form, which is a suitably determined set of formulae whose conjunction is equivalent to the original formula. Criteria are then presented which, when applied to this normal form, determines whether that formula violates any of the argument typing integrity constraints. The method handles both definite and indefinite integrity constraints.

Reiter's approach is in some sense more general and in another sense more permissive than that permitted by McSkimin and Minker [1977] who present their results elsewhere. McSkimin and Minker handle, in a similar way formulae that do not involve indefinite integrity constraints. They will reject some updates that deal with integrity constraints that are accepted by Reither's approach.

An important aspect in developing a data base model would be the ability to obtain a specification of a relational data base as an abstract data type in such a way that a computer program can simulate on a small scale the intended use of the data base by generating formal consequences of the data base. The objective would be to achieve such a specification without the existence of the data base. The abstract definition of the data model would not specify any particular representation of a data base, but would only specify the effect of the admissible operations on the data base. This approach is well known in programming languages as has been discussed by Zilles [1974], Goguen [1977] and Guttag [1977]. They use equations to define abstract data types.

Colombetti et al. [1978] proposed that work in programming languages on abstract data types be carried over to data base models. In their chapter, Van Emden and Maibaum show that instead of equations, general laws can be used to define abstract data types. Equations are considered as special cases of clauses and an algorithm is presented to translate equations into logic programs automatically. They compare the equational approach and the clause approach (general laws) with respect to mathematical semantics, computational efficiency and expressiveness. A data model defined by a set of clauses can be given as a program to a clausal processor such as PROLOG (Roussel [1975]) for testing. Their work represents a step in the direction of providing automated tools to aid in the design of a specification. The availability of a predicate logic programming language, such as PROLOG, makes it convenient to implement such a specification. They present an example to illustrate the use of clausal form for the direct axiomatization of a data type.

Deduction Rules

The use of general laws for deduction rules has been discussed by various authors as, for example, in Gallaire and Minker [1978]. Two approaches have been taken to deductive search. These have been referred to as the interpretive and the compiled approaches. Both approaches can yield the same answer to a query. The approaches relate to how a theorem prover interacts between the deduction laws and a relational data base system.

In the interpretive approach as described by Minker [1978] and his colleagues, a theorem prover is used in a top-down search starting from the query. The theorem prover uses heuristics to determine which general laws to select in the deduction process, and retrieval commands are sent to a data base management system to retrieve explicit data in the relational data base. Thus, the control structure associated with the theorem prover guides the search. Using this method, answers and the deductive reasoning steps can be obtained.

The compiled approach separates the theorem proving task from the data base retrieval task. This approach is exemplified by the work of Chang [1978], Kellogg et al. [1978], and Reiter [1978a]. The theorem prover operates only upon general laws and does not intermix search with the relational data base. It transforms a query requiring deduction into a set of queries that do not require deduction, but only require look-ups in a relational data base. Answers to the query can then be extracted. Both the interpreted and the compiled approaches have difficulty with recursively defined general laws.

In the chapter by Grant and Minker, the compiled approach is considered. They develop an optimization algorithm that interfaces between the output of the theorem prover and the data retrieval component and retrieves answers minimizing data access time. Related work on optimizing individual queries may be found in Selinger et al. [1979], Ullman [1980], and references given in Kim [1979]. The approach by Grant and Minker can handle nonrecursively defined axioms and if recursive axioms are specified, they assume a cut-off on recursion and thereby cannot guarantee that all answers are obtained. Their optimization method is based on the method of branch-and bound and applies not only to deductive searches but to batched and complex queries.

Chang in his chapter considers the problem of recursive general laws and conditions for termination. He assumes that a relation is defined either exclusively in extensional form (i.e. by a relational table), or exclusively in intensional form (i.e., by general laws). If recursive axioms are of the form:

$$R \leftarrow A$$

$$R \leftarrow E_1 \;\&\; E_2 \;\&\; \ldots \;\&\; E_n \;\&\; F \;\&\; R,$$

where A and the E_i are extensionally defined relations, F is a relation evaluated by a procedure (for example, equality), and R an intensionally defined relation, then one can find a termination rule for evaluating the relation R. The Chang approach is based on results of language theory (Hopcroft and Ullman [1969]). The set of queries which can be generated from a given query using axioms of the above form is represented by a regular expression which is then used to generate an adequate program in the DEDUCE 2 language developed by Chang. Elsewhere, Reiter [1976] also considers recursive deductive rules and specifies how they might be handled.

If deductive data bases are to become a reality, it must be shown that they can be designed and implemented so as to be as efficient as relational data bases that have no deductive capability, but require that the user perform deduction through a query language. The work by Grant and Minker as described in their chapter attempts to develop an optimizer for a deductive relational data base so as to make deduction faster. It will be of interest to see algorithms such as they develop, incorporated into deductive systems. There do exist experimental deductive relation data base systems. Two such systems that have been implemented are described by Minker [1978] and by Kellogg et al. [1978]. In their chapter, Kellogg and Travis report upon further developments that they have made to their system. They have developed perhaps the most comprehensive deductive relational data base system to date. They provide capabilities for simplified natural language input, a dialogue feature possible between the user and the system, the ability to do deductive planning, and to respond to the user both the answer and the deductive steps used to achieve the answer. Some limited capabilities are provided to handle recursive general laws. As has been the case with relational data base systems, deductive relational systems will be achieved following effective work on experimental systems as described by Kellogg and Travis and by work reported on in the book *Logic and Data Bases*.

INFORMATIVE CAPABILITIES FOR USERS

The title of this section needs some explanation; any information system, such as a data base system, has capabilities to provide information to the user; furthermore, systems such as those described in the previous section, which handle general laws, are in a sense equipped with improved informative capabilities. But the point made in chapters in this section of the book is that all information systems are, in many different ways, not sufficiently "friendly" to the needs of the users. They either

(a) do not allow the user to specify kinds of information in the data base, such as "unknown", or
(b) they do not work properly when given partial information, or
(c) they require queries stated far too precisely than would be strictly necessary from what they already know, or
(d) they provide meaningless answers that could have been turned into meaningful ones provided some additional treatment were performed by the system.

Of course, the above four items are still not well defined. But, information systems model human activity which is prone to the same type of problems and there is no limitation to the extent of these problems nor to the solutions that humans give to them. Typical of the aforementioned difficulties is the classical example of a meaningless answer:

Q: Could you give me the time, please?

A: Yes!

Chapters described in this section cover the above mentioned areas; they are difficult to classify as these areas are quite related to each other. As an example a system which does query interpretation may well result in a system which does answer completion, and vice versa, query interpretation is likely to be a necessary tool for answer completion. In this analysis we shall go from the user querying process to the answer extraction process.

Data Representation

This general term is restricted here to the following: the user should be allowed to express somehow that his data is incomplete,— and in which various ways it is incomplete and the system should be capable of reasoning in this framework. Probably, the first attempt in this direction was made by Codd [1975] who concentrated on the so-called null value, meaning value at present unknown. In his approach, a 3-valued logic is developed for data representation and all relational operators (join, projection, etc.) are given an interpretation in this logic system. Grant [1977], and subsequently, Lipski [1979], show that the logic system defined by Codd is questionable. Indeed Codd's system would assign the null value to an expression 'P and not P' when P is null (i.e. unknown), while a not unreasonable answer could be False. This, in fact, raises the issue of the proper interpretation of a formula when knowledge is incomplete. Lipski studies several interpretations of such formulas, and specifies algorithms for computing these formulas. This subject is far from being settled and other approaches have been developed in other contexts. For instance work in Artificial Intelligence, by Doyle [1979] and Reiter [1980] give partial answers to incomplete world reasoning using modal logic and fixed point operators. Some of their interpretations of formulas coincide with Lipski's, while others do not. In another approach, Vassiliou [1979], who refutes 3-valued logic on the same grounds as does Grant, uses denotational semantics for data base relations: a relation is viewed as a data type including unknown (i.e. "null") and inconsistent values (i.e. not applying attributes); then a query is a continuous function mapping domains, and not a truth-value preserving function as in Codd; this allows Vassiliou to obtain a more precise query interpretation than that of Codd.

In his chapter Biskup provides a different treatment for values expressing some kind of ignorance (null values): the null value $\exists$ which stands for unknown (but it exists), and the null value $\forall$ standing for irrelevant. The "not applying" of Vassiliou is seen as a regular value in the attribute domain, and as such, does not require special treatment. A generalized tuple is given a logic interpretation as seen in the following example:

let R be a generalized relation (i.e. a set of generalized tuples which include values $\exists$ and $\forall$), and r a domain valued relation (without the values $\exists$ and $\forall$); then a tuple

$\mu = (\forall, a, \exists, \forall, b) \in R$ is interpreted with respect to r as

$\exists x_3 \; \forall x_1 \; \forall x_4 \; (x_1, a, x_3, x_4, b) \in r.$

Thus, r is a model of μ (and of R if it is a model of all $\mu \in R$). This kind of interpretation allows a lattice structure to be defined on the class of generalized relations which are compared in terms of their information content. Biskup further gives definitions of operators on generalized relations, which generalize operators on domain valued relations (such as join, union, ...).

All of these definitions are shown to behave properly; i.e. they are both correct and complete with respect to classical operators. Complete means that if $O(R_1,\ldots,R_n)$ corresponds to $o(r_1,\ldots,r_n)$ then $O(R_1,\ldots,R_n)$ is the most informative relation obtained via an operator O correct with respect to o. O is correct with respect to o iff $O(R_1,\ldots,R_n)$ admits $o(r_1,\ldots,r_n)$ as a model for all r_i models of the generalized relations R_i. Not all operators are covered. For instance division, and negation are only sketched. Biskup further refutes another possible treatment of $\exists$ based on Skolem functions. From the diversity of approaches reviewed here briefly, it is clear that the interesting results obtained so far are but a beginning.

Query Interpretation

In the previous section the subject dealt with was that of defining precisely the semantics of relations (in an incomplete world). We now turn to defining precisely the semantics of queries in two cases: natural language, and the first order logic predicate calculus (FOPC).

Dealing with Presuppositions

When expressing a (natural language) query, the user very often makes hidden hypotheses, i.e. presuppositions: "who are the students from Germany who live in Aix" is a query that may presuppose that: there are students or that there are students from Germany. To answer correctly, the system must know the presuppositions, and in case they are false, it should answer that the query is meaningless. Presuppositions can stem from the structure of the query (basically from implication), and from quantifiers used (articles in natural language). For instance, the statement, "a car is blue", presupposes that $\exists$x iscar(x) and isblue(x).

In the logic framework defined by Colmerauer and Pique in their chapter, this would be represented as a(x, car(x), blue(x)) which is equivalent to exist(x, if (car(x), blue(x))) where exist, and if, are defined precisely in a 3-valued logic (true, false, defined). Then, and this is crucial for building a system, a formula q in this logical system is valid (i.e. true in all interpretations in which the data base formulas P_i representing a partially known world are true) iff T(q) is deducible (in FOPC) from $\{T(p_i)\}$, where T is a transformation from the 3-valued system to FOPC. Similarly transformations F and D are given such that q is False (respectively Defined) iff T (not (q)) = F(q) is deducible (respectively D(q)). They have implemented a system which handles all of these aspects. Presuppositions have received less formal treatment, mainly through range restricted variables, in several data base systems (e.g. ILL by Lacroix-Pirotte [1977]). Not covered here, and attacked in other fields such as linguistics are problems such as choosing among all presuppositions in a given query, and in logic, finding the correct logic system.

Dealing with Ill-Defined Queries

A many sorted logic is generally used to restrict the range of variables so as to obtain more meaningful queries and answers. This is insufficient in that one is led either to have wide ranges (Person, ...) which become useless, or restricted ranges which give rise to rejecting interesting queries. See for instance INGRES (Stonebraker et al. [1976]). Other systems, such as MRPPS (Minker [1978]) use domains (or sorts) not at a syntactic level, but in the query analysis process.

Demolombe, in his chapter, proposes a two-fold process: let the user express FOPC queries, without restrictions; then let the system interpret these queries using information about domains. The task for the system is complicated by the fact that many FOPC queries are ill-defined, i.e. the range of the variables are not sufficiently restricted, to obtain significant answers. Demolombe characterizes syntactically a class of well defined queries (extending, for instance, the class described by Pirotte [1976]). Then he defines several transformations on queries which allow an ill-defined query to be transformed to a well-defined query. These transformations represent various ways to assign meaning to an imprecisely defined query and it is not therefore surprising, that they lead to different interpretations of a query.

For example, the domain of the query $R_1 \wedge R_2$ is generally assumed to be $dom(R_1) \cap dom(R_2)$. However, Demolombe correctly notes that one could equally choose the domain to be $dom(R_1 \cup dom(R_2)$. He analyzes and compares the consequences of each choice.

Answer Completion

In his chapter, Janas addresses the problem of building systems which complete an answer that would not be significant enough for a user. For example, when there is no answer to a query, analyzing subqueries of the query may give the user a reason for this "no answer". In a way this involves a query interpretation similar to that described above. To be efficient, the number of subqueries that should be analyzed should be kept to a minimum. Janas presents several means to reduce the number of subqueries to be analyzed. In particular, he describes how to use constraints to eliminate subqueries evaluating to true (due to integrity constraints). The dual notion of false subqueries is not used here. As noted by Janas

a drawback of this method is that one can go from an und
tive system to an over-informative one: a smart user
get information he is not entitled to know. This extra
can be obtained through multiple queries and correlation
This is a problem known in the so-called statistical data base area, where information systems only supply statistical summaries about populations and not about individuals (see Denning and Denning [1979] for a description of statistical data bases). The treatment suggested here is based more on privacy constraints, but the query modification process used in INGRES is refuted and an algorithmic treatment is proposed.

SUMMARY

Based on the developments reported upon in this book and its predecessor, *Logic and Data Bases*, and other work being reported upon in the literature, there is no doubt that a body of theory is being developed for data bases. Scientific progress can be accelerated greatly when theoretical results are available. With a firmer theoretical basis, data base technology will move from the development of ad-hoc systems to ones that are cleanly designed and implemented.

The chapters in the section DATABASE DESIGN provide a comprehensive understanding of join dependencies. The development of the concept of general dependencies places the subject of dependencies in a better perspective. Most known dependencies are encompassed by general dependencies. It is now necessary that these theoretical results be translated into tools for designers of database systems. Work has been started towards this objective with the development of a system that will show a user the functional and multivalued dependencies that exist in a prototype data base system based on inputs from the user. However, much more work is required both in providing methodological formalisms and practical tools for the designer.

An underlying theme in the book, and in particular in the sections GENERAL LAWS: DEDUCTION AND INTEGRITY, is that mathematical logic is an essential element in the theory and practice of data bases. Contributions in this section have shown how logic can be applied to integrity constraints and to assuring that queries are semantically meaningful. The use of logic for abstract data types and for deductive data bases have been described in this section. Methods are described in the book to make deductive systems practical by optimizing searches, and a comprehensive deductive system is reported upon. The use of work in language theory to help develop methods to handle recursive deductive data bases is also a welcome development.

There is still much to be done in applying logic to data bases. Although some progress has been evidenced with the deductive data bases, more work is needed. The predicate logic language PROLOG applied to the field of abstract data types is important for work in the specification of data base schemes. However, additional developments are required to achieve a PROLOG-like language to interface with relational data bases. We can expect logic to be applied to network and hierarchic systems. Work in artificial intelligence, language theory, and data base systems will move closer together based upon the work reported upon in this volume.

The section INFORMATIVE CAPABILITIES FOR USERS discusses a number of important issues. Relational data base systems have been unable to handle null values effectively. The use of logic has been applied here to clarify some of the issues. Additional work is required. However, logic is a mechanism through which one will understand and be able to work with null values. If, as some propound, natural language is to be used as a front end of a data base system, one must be able to deal with many subtle linguistic problems among which is the subject of presuppositions. Again, the use of logic has been demonstrated here, to permit a system to be developed to handle presuppositions. In every day usage of query systems one finds that users tend to make mistakes. It is good to see tools developed here to inform the user as to where the problems might be. More efforts are needed to make query systems more "friendly" to users and easier to work with.

We look forward to additional efforts in data base theory that will continue to place the technology on a firm scientific foundation.

ACKNOWLEDGEMENTS

The authors would like to thank John Grant, Raymond Reiter and Guy Zanon for their helpful comments on this paper.

The work was supported by the DRET with a contribution from the CRNS. It was also supported by the NSF under Grants GJ-43832 and MCS 7919418, and by NASA under Grant 21-002-280.

REFERENCES

1. Arora, A. K. and Carlson, C. R. [1978] "The Information Preserving Properties of Relational Data Base Transformations," *Proc. of the VLDB 78 Conf.*, Berlin, W. Germany, Sept. , 1978, 352-359.

2. Beeri, C., Bernstein, P. A., and Goodman, N. [1978] "A Sophisticate's Introduction to Data Base Normalization Theory," *Proc. of the VLDB 78 Conf.*, Berlin, W. Germany, 1978, 113-124.

3. Chang, C. L. [1978] "DEDUCE 2: Further Investigation of Deductions in Relational Data Bases." In: *Logic and Data Bases* (H. Gallaire and J. Minker, Eds.) Plenum Press, New York, N. Y., 1978, 201-236.

4. Chang, C. L. and Lee, R. C. T. [1973] *Symbolic Logic and Mechanical Theorem Proving*, Academic Press, New York, N. Y., 1973.

5. Codd, E. F. [1975] "Understanding Relations"(Installment #7) *FDT Bulletin of ACM-SIGMOD* 7 (3,4), (1975), 23-28.

6. Codd, E. F. [1979] "Extending the Data Base Relational Model to Capture More Meaning," *ACM-TODS 4,* 4 (Dec. 1979), 397-434.

7. Colombetti, M., Paolini, P. and Pelagatti, G. [1978] "Nondeterministic Languages Used for the Definition of Data Models." In: *Logic and Data Bases* (H. Gallaire and J. Minker, Eds.), Plenum Press, New York, N. Y., 1978, 237-257.

8. Date, C. J. [1977] *An Introduction to Data Base Systems,* Addison-Wesley Pub. Co., Reading, Mass., 1977.

9. Denning, D. E. and Denning, P. J. [1979] "Data Security," *ACM Computing Survey 11,* 3 (Sept. 1979), 227-249.

10. Doyle, J. [1979] "A Truth Maintenance System," *Artificial Intelligence 12,* 3 (Nov. 1979), 231-272.

11. Fagin, R. [1979] "Normal Forms and Relational Data Base Operators," *Proc. of the ACM-SIGMOD 79 Conf.,* Boston, Mass., May 1979, 153-160.

12. Fagin, R. [1980] "Horn Clauses and Data Dependencies," *Proc. of the ACM-SIGACT Symp. on the Theory of Computing,* Los Angeles, California, April 1980.

13. Gallaire, H. and Minker, J. [1978] *Logic and Data Bases,* Plenum Press, New York, N. Y., 1978.

14. Gallaire, H., Minker, J. and Nicolas, J. M. [1978] "An Overview and Introduction to Logic and Data Bases." In: *Logic and Data Bases* (H. Gallaire and J. Minker, Eds.), Plenum Press, New York, N. Y., 1978, 3-30.

15. Goguen, J. A. [1977] "Abstract Errors for Abstract Data Types," *Proc. of IFIP Working Conference on Formal Description of Programming Concepts,* North-Holland, 1977.

17. Guttag, J. V. [1977] "Abstract Data Types and the Development of Data Structures," *CACM 20,* 6 (1977), 396-404.

18. Hopcroft, J. and Ullman, J. [1969] *Formal Languages and Their Relation to Automata,* Addison-Wesley Publ. Co., Reading, Mass., 1969.

19. Kellogg, C., Klahr, P., and Travis, L. [1978] "Deductive Planning and Pathfinding for Relational Data Bases," In: *Logic and Data Bases* (H. Gallaire and J. Minker, Eds.) Plenum Press, New York, N. Y., 1978, 179-200.

20. Kim, W. [1979] "Relational Database Systems" *Computing Surveys 11,* 3 (Sept. 1979) 185-211.

21. Lacroix, M. and Pirotte, A. [1977] "ILL: an English Structured Query Language for Relational Databases, *Proc. IFIP-TC2 Conf. 77,* Nice, France, North-Holland, 1977, 237-260.

22. Lipski, W. [1979] "Incomplete Information Data Bases," *ACM-TODS 4,* 3 (Sept. 1979), 262-296.

23. Loveland, D. [1978] *Automated Theorem Proving: A Logical Basis,* North Holland Publ. Co., New York, 1978.

24. McSkimin, J. R. and Minker, J. [1977] "The Use of a Semantic Network in a Deductive Question-Answering System," *Proceedings IJCAI-77,* Cambridge, Mass, 1977, 50-58.

25. Minker, J. [1978] "An Experimental Relational Data Base System Based on Logic." In: *Logic and Data Bases* (H. Gallaire and J. Minker, Eds.), Plenum Press, New York, N.Y., 1978, 107-147.

26. Pirotte, A. [1976] *Explicit Description of Entities and their Manipulation in Languages for the Relational Data Base Model,* Thèse de doctorat, Université Libre de Bruxelles, Belgique, Décembre 1976.

27. Reiter, R. [1978a] "Deductive Question-Answering on Relational Data Bases" In: *Logic and Data Bases* (H. Gallaire and J. Minker, Eds.) Plenum Press, New York, N. Y., 1978, 149-177.

28. Reiter, R. [1978b] "On Structuring a First Order Data Base, *Proceedings of the Canadian Society for Computational Studies of Intelligence, Second National Conference* (R. Perrault, Ed.), Toronto (July 19-21, 1978).

29. Reiter, R. [1980] "A Logic for Default Reasoning" *Artificial Intelligence 13* (1980), 81-132.

30. Reiter, R. [1981] "On the Integrity of Typed First Order Data Bases," this volume.

31. Rissanen, J. [1977] "Independent Components of Relations," *ACM-TODS 2,* 4 (Dec. 1977), 317-325.

32. Robinson, J. A. [1965] "A Machine Oriented Logic Based on the Resolution Principle," *JACM 12,* 1 (Jan. 1965), 23-41.

33. Roussel, P. [1975] *PROLOG: Manuel de Reference et d'Utilisation,* Groupe d'Intelligence Artificielle, Universite d'Aix-Marseille, Luminy, Sept. 1975.

34. Sadri, F. and Ullman, J. D. [1980] "A Complete Axiomatization for a Large Class of Dependencies in Relational Data Bases," *Proc. of the ACM-SIGACT Conf. on the Theory of Computing,* Los Angeles, California, April 1980.

35. Selinger, P., Astrahan, M. M., Chamberlin, D. D., Lorie, R.A., and Price, T. G. [1979] "Access Path Selection in a Relational Database System," *Proc. ACM SIGMOD 1979,* 23-34.

36. Stonebraker, M. et al. [1976] "The Design and Implementation of INGRES," *ACM-TODS 1,* 3 (Sept. 1976), 189-222.

37. Ullman, J. D. [1980] *Principles of Data Base Systems,* Computer Science Press, Potomac, Maryland, 1980.

38. Vassiliou, Y. [1979] "Null Values in Data Base Management: a Denotational Semantic Approach," *Proc. ACM-SIGMOD 79,* Boston, Mass., May 1980, 162-169.

39. Zilles, S. N. [1974] "Algebraic Specification of Data Types," *Project MAC Progress Report II,* 1974, 28-52.

DATA BASE DESIGN

ON THE PROPERTIES OF JOIN DEPENDENCIES *

C. Beeri and M. Y. Vardi

The Hebrew University

Jerusalem, Israel

ABSTRACT

In this chapter we introduce a formal system for the family of functional and join dependencies. The system contains one axiom and three inference rules. A few additional useful rules are derived. It is shown that various formal systems for subfamilies of the family of join dependencies can be derived from our system. Special attention is paid to the case where the dependencies are total. For this case it is shown that our rules derive the complete system for multivalued dependencies. The concepts of left side and right side of multivalued dependency are generalized to stems and branches of a join dependency. The notion of a dependency basis is also extended. Finally, several completeness results concerning the system are proved, e.g., completeness of a projection rule. The main result is that our system is complete for deriving functional and multivalued dependencies from functional and join dependencies and for deriving branches of join dependencies.

INTRODUCTION

One of the important issues in the design of relational database schemas is the specification of the constraints that the data must satisfy to model correctly the part of the world under consideration. These constraints determine which databases are considered

---

* The research reported in this paper was partially supported by Grant 1849/79 of the U.S.A.-ISRAEL Binational Science Foundation. This research was carried out while the second author was at the Department of Applied Mathematics, The Weizman Instititute of Science, Rehovot, Israel.

meaningful; i.e., a database is meaningful, or legal, only if it satisfies the constraints.

Of particular importance are the constraints, called depen dencies, that influence the schema design process. Examples of such constraints are the functional and multivalued dependencies (Codd [1972a], Fagin [1977], Zaniolo [1976]). Recently a more general dependency called a join dependency was introduced by Rissanen [1978] (following the study of lossless joins by Aho, Beeri, and Ullman [1979]). Its important role in the process of schema design soon became obvious (Beeri, Mendelzon, Sagiv and Ullman [1979], Beeri and Rissanen [1980], Maier, Mendelzon, Sadri and Ullman [1981]).

Functional and multivalued dependencies were thoroughly investigated by Armstrong [1974], Beeri and Bernstein [1979], Beeri, Fagin and Howard [1977], Biskup [1978, 1979] and Mendelzon [1979]. The properties of join dependencies are much less understood, though special cases have been studied by Armstrong and Delobel [1979], Dayal and Bernstein [1978], Delobel [1978], Maier and Mendelzon [1979], Nicolas [1978] and Paredaens [1979]. Only very recently a complete formal system for a class of dependencies that properly contains the join dependencies was presented by Sciore [1979]. See also Paredaens [1980] for a study of a more general class of dependencies.

The purpose of this paper is to study the properties of join dependencies with an emphasis on total join dependencies. We present a formal system for these dependencies and study its power. The system contains one axiom and three simple rules. Despite its simplicity, the system is very powerful. In particular, almost all systems and rules considered in the literature for various special cases of join dependencies are included in or can be derived from our system.

The outline of the paper is as follows. In the section BASIC CONCEPTS we present the basic concepts and definitions of the relational model. In the section INTEGRITY CONSTRAINTS we introduce join dependencies and discuss the concepts of implication and formal system. The formal system for embedded join dependencies is presented in the section A FORMAL SYSTEM FOR JOIN DEPENDENCIES. It includes one axiom and three rules. Several derived rules are also presented.

A main theme of the paper is that join dependencies can be viewed as an extension of multivalued dependencies. This theme is taken up in the sections ON THE POWER OF THE RULES and THE BRANCH BASIS. Thus, the concepts of left and right side of a dependency are generalized to stems and branches of a join dependency and a rule for the manipulation of stems and branches is presented. We conclude the section, ON THE POWER OF THE RULES, by considering the restriction of the system to total join dependencies. In the section THE BRANCH BASIS we show how the concept of a dependency basis of Fagin [1977] and Beeri, Fagin and Howard [1977] can be generalized to join dependencies.

Our main result — that our system is complete for deriving multivalued and functional dependencies from join and functional dependencies is presented in the section BRANCH COMPLETENESS OF THE RULES. One proof is presented in that section. Two additional proofs are presented in the section TABLEAUX AND THE CHASE. These two proofs utilize the concepts of tableau and chase, hence they appear separately with a brief presentation of these concepts. Conclusions and problems are discussed in the section CONCLUSIONS.

BASIC CONCEPTS

The Relational Model

We assume some familiarity with the relational model, e.g., as described by Date [1977]. In this section we define the elements of the model that are used in the chapter.

Attributes are symbols taken from a given finite set $U = \{A_1, \ldots, A_n\}$. The set U is called the *universe*. All sets of attributes are assumed to be subsets of U. Following customary notation, we use the letters A,B,C,... to denote single attributes and R,S,....X,Y,... to denote sets of attributes. We usually do not distinguish between the attribute A and the set {A}. The union of X and Y is denoted by XY. Thus, ABD denotes the set {A,B,D}. The complement of a set X in U is denoted by $\bar{X}$.

We will often deal with collections of attribute sets. For clarity we will use the abbreviation asc (*attribute set collection*). If $\underline{R} = \{R_1, \ldots, R_k\}$ is an asc then the *attribute set* of $\underline{R}$, denoted $ATTR(\underline{R})$, is the set $\cup_i R_i$.

Note that an asc is a set, hence is not ordered.

We assume that with each attribute A there is associated a set, called its domain, denoted by DOM(A). Let $D = \cup_{A \in U} DOM(A)$. For a set X, an X-*value* is a mapping $\mu: X \to D$ such that $\mu(A) \in DOM(A)$ for every A in X. A *relation* on X is a finite set of X-values. The elements of a relation are also called *tuples* or *rows*. We will denote relations by $I, I_1, \ldots$. A relation I on the set X is denoted by I(X) and we write ATTR(I) = X. For an arbitrary relation I, unless explicitly stated otherwise, ATTR(I) = U.

Relational Algebra Operators

We will use two operations of the relational algebra (Codd [1972b]). For an X-value ν and a set $Y \subset X$, we denote by $\nu[Y]$ the restriction of ν to Y. Let I be a relation on X and let Y be a subset of X. The *projection* of I on Y, denoted by $\pi_Y(I)$ (or by I[Y]) is the set

$$\{\pi_Y(I) \triangleq \{\nu \mid \text{for some } \mu \in I,\ \nu = \mu[Y]\}.$$

The projection $\pi_Y(I)$ is a relation on Y whose elements are the restrictions of the mappings in I to the domain Y. In more intuitive terms, $\pi_Y(I)$ is obtained from I by deleting all columns labeled with attributes in Y-X and identifying duplicate rows.

Let $I_1(X_1),\ldots,I_k(X_k)$ be relations. The *join* of $I_1,\ldots,I_k$, denoted by $I_1 * \ldots * I_k$ or by $\overset{k}{\underset{j=1}{*}} I_j$, is the relation on $\bigcup_{j=1}^{k} X_j$ denoted by

$$\overset{k}{\underset{j=1}{*}} I_j \triangleq \{\mu \mid \mu \text{ is a tuple on } \bigcup_{j=1}^{k} X_j \text{ such that for all } j,\ \mu[X_j] \text{ is in } I_j\}$$

Each tuple μ in the join is generated from tuples $\mu_j \in I_j$ such that every two of them agree on the attributes common to them. The join is commutative and associative. In general, the projection of $\overset{k}{\underset{j=1}{*}} I_j(X_j)$ on some X_ℓ may be a proper subset of I_ℓ. In this chapter, however, we deal only with joins of collections of relations that are projections of a single relation. In such a case, $(\underset{j}{*} I_j)[X_\ell] = I_\ell$ for all ℓ.

Using the projection and the join we can form relational expressions. We are interested only in a restricted class of expressions with a single argument. *Restricted relational expressions* (abbr. rre) are defined as follows.

(1) $\underline{1}_X$, the identity operator on relations on X, is an rre and its associated attribute set is X, $ATTR(\underline{1}_X) = X$.

(2) Let E_1 be an rre, $ATTR(E_1) = X$ and let $\underline{R} = \{R_1,\ldots,R_k\}$ be an asc, $ATTR(\underline{R}) = R \subseteq X$, then $E_2 = \overset{k}{\underset{i=1}{*}} \pi_{R_i} \circ E_1$ is an rre and $ATTR(E_2) = R$ (where $\circ$ denotes the composition operator).

(3) No expression is an rre unless it so follows by 1 and 2 above.

In the following we will usually omit the identity operator from rre's. In the special case that E_1 in case 2 above is an identity operator, E_2 is called a project join expression and denoted by $m_{\underline{R}}$; i.e., $m_{\underline{R}} = \mathop{*}\limits_{i=1}^{k} \pi_{R_i}$. For a relation I(X) and an asc $\underline{R}$ such that $\text{ATTR}(\underline{R}) \subseteq X$, we have

$$m_{\underline{R}}(I) = \{\mu \mid \mu \text{ is a tuple on ATTR}(\underline{R}) \text{ and for all } j, \text{ there is a tuple } \mu_j \text{ in I such that } \mu[R_j] = \mu_j[R_j]\}.$$

Every rre is either an identity operator or a composition of project join mappings. In the following, we assume that the arguments for rre's are relations on U and we regard each rre as defining a map on the set of relations on U (i.e., we use only $\underline{1}_U$).

Project-join mappings were studied in Beeri, Mendelzon, Sagiv and Ullman [1979]. We mention some properties.

(1) $\pi_{\text{ATTR}(\underline{R})}(I) \subseteq m_{\underline{R}}(I)$

(2) $m_{\underline{R}}(m_{\underline{R}}(I)) = m_{\underline{R}}(I)$ (idempotence)

(3) $I \subseteq J \Rightarrow m_{\underline{R}}(I) \subseteq m_{\underline{R}}(J)$ (monotonicity)

Let E_1 and E_2 be expressions denoting mappings on relations such that $\text{ATTR}(E_1) = \text{ATTR}(E_2)$. ($E_1$ and E_2 can be rre's or expressions in any other formalism for denoting mappings). We say that E_1 is *contained* in E_2, denoted $E_1 \leq E_2$, if $E_1(I) \subseteq E_2(I)$ for all relations I. They are *equivalent* denoted $E_1 \equiv E_2$, if $E_1(I) = E_2(I)$ for all I, i.e., if both $E_1 \leq E_2$ and $E_2 \leq E_1$.

Lemma 1 (Beeri, Mendelzon, Sagiv and Ullman [1979])

Let $\underline{R} = \{R_i\}$ and $\underline{S} = \{S_j\}$ be two asc's such that $\text{ATTR}(\underline{R}) = \text{ATTR}(\underline{S})$. Then $m_{\underline{R}} \leq m_{\underline{S}}$ if and only if for each $S_j \in \underline{S}$ there exists an $R_i \in R$ such that $S_j \subseteq R_i$. □

INTEGRITY CONSTRAINTS

Dependencies

For any given application, only a subset of all possible relations is usually of interest. This subset is defined by constraints that are specified for the application. Formally, a constraint is a predicate expressed in a suitable notation, that assigns to each relation either the value T (i.e., it is *satisfied* by the relation), or the value F (i.e., it is not satisfied by the relation). It may also be undefined for some relations. For a set of constraints C, we denote by SAT(C) the set of relations on U that satisfy C.

A class of constraints that was extensively studied is the class of dependencies. A *functional dependency* (fd or fds for plural) is a statement $X \rightarrow Y$. It is satisfied by a relation I, if for all $t_1, t_2 \in I$, if $t_1[X] = t_2[X]$ then $t_1[Y] = t_2[Y]$. A *join dependency* (jd or jds for plural) is a statement $*[\underline{R}]$ or $*[R_1, \ldots, R_k]$, where $\underline{R} = \{R_1, \ldots, R_k\}$ is an asc. It is satisfied by a relation I if $m_{\underline{R}}(I) = \pi_{ATTR(\underline{R})}(I)$. The set $ATTR(\underline{R})$ is the *attribute set* of the $\underline{R}$ jd. Note that if $ATTR(\underline{R}) = R$, then the jd $*[\underline{R}]$ is satisifed by I if and only if it is satisfied by $\pi_R(I)$.

Fds and their properties have been extensively studied (Armstrong [1974], Codd [1972a] and Beeri and Bernstein [1979]). Jds have been introduced only recently (Aho, Beeri and Ullman [1979], Rissanen [1978] and Nicolas [1978]). However, several special cases of jds were studied in detail earlier. A jd $*[R_1, \ldots, R_k]$ is called a *first order hierarchical decomposition* (fohd or fohds for plural) if there exists a set X such that $R_i \cap R_j = X$ for all $i \neq j$. Fohds and their properties were studied by Delobel [1978]. We will use the notation $*[XY_1, \ldots, XY_k]$ to denote the fohd above, where $Y_i = R_i - X$ (i.e., the Y_i's are pairwise disjoint and X is the common set).

A *cross* is a jd $*[R_1, \ldots, R_k]$ where the R_i's are pairwise disjoint. Binary crosses have been studied by Paredaens [1979].

A binary jd is always an fohd. Binary jds have been studied by Armstrong and Delobel [1979] and Paredaens [1979]. They have also been studied extensively in a different form. A *multivalued dependency* (mvd) is a statement $X \rightarrow\rightarrow Y(R)$. It is equivalent to the binary jd $*[XY, X(R-Y)]$. Its attribute set is R. When $R = U$, the mvd is usually written $X \rightarrow\rightarrow Y$. Mvds were studied by Fagin [1977], Beeri, Fagin and Howard [1977] and Zaniolo [1976].

A constraint is *total* if its attribute set is U, it is *embedded* otherwise. The difference between total and embedded constraints is the following. In order to ascertain that a given total constraint is satisfied in a relation I(U), all of I has to be examined. If, however, the constraint is embedded, then only the projection of the relation I on the attribute set of the constraint needs to be checked. Properties of embedded constraints seem to be quite different from those of total constraints (see Maier, Mendelzon and Sagiv [1979] and Beeri and Rissanen [1979]).

It turns out that there is no essential difference between embedded and total fds. Therefore, in this chapter we regard all fds as being total, i.e., $X \rightarrow Y$ is regarded as $X \rightarrow Y(U)$.

A Formal System for Constraints

A set of constraints C *implies* a constraint c, denoted $C \models c$, if, for every relation on U, if the constraints of C are satisfied in it then c is also satisfied in it. Note that $C \models c$ if and only if $SAT(C) \subseteq SAT(c)$.

Two approaches to deciding implication have been considered in the literature. One approach is based on the concept of formal system which will be discussed below. The second approach is semantic in nature. It is based on the chase process developed by Aho, Sagiv and Ullman [1979] and Maier, Mendelzon and Sagiv [1979] and will be discussed in the section TABLEAUX AND THE CHASE.

Much effort has been devoted to the development of formal systems for dependencies. Formal systems enjoy several advantages over the semantic approach that uses the chase. A formal system allows us to infer new dependencies from given dependencies using the rules of the system, whereas the chase only allows us to check if a dependency is implied by given dependencies but it does not tell us how to generate new dependencies. Therefore, formal systems offer more insight into the properties of the family of dependencies under consideration. They can also be used to develop decision procedures that are more efficient than the chase. (E.g., the procedure developed by Beeri et al. [1977] and Sagiv [1979] is more efficient than the chase).

A *formal system* for a family of constraints consists of *axioms* (i.e., constraints that are always satisfied) and *inference rules* that specify how to generate new constraints from given constraints in the family. A *derivation* of a constraint c from a set C is a sequence of constraints $c_1, c_2, \ldots, c_n = c$, where each c_i is either an axiom, or a member of C, or is inferred from preceding constraints in the sequence by an inference rule. If c is derivable from C in a system Γ, we write $C \vdash_\Gamma c$. A system Γ is *sound* if $C \vdash_\Gamma c$ implies $C \models c$. It is *complete* if $C \models c$ implies $C \vdash_\Gamma c$. (We will also encounter restricted completeness, where a subset of a formal system is powerful enough to derive a subset of the family of dependencies under consideration).

Various sound and complete systems for families of dependencies have been studied extensively; for fds in Armstrong [1974]; for mvds in Beeri, Fagin and Howard [1977], Biskup [1978, 1979] and Mendelzon [1979]; for binary decompositions in Armstrong and Delobel [1979] and for binary decompositions and crosses in Paredaens [1979]. Very recently, a system for dependencies called full jds was presented by Sciore [1979]. This system is similar to the system presented in this chapter but the two systems were developed independently. Systems that are sound but not known to be complete have also been studied, e.g., for fohds in Delobel

[1978].

The system for jds that we present in this chapter contains some rules that can be considered as generalizations of rules for mvds. It will be useful to compare our rules to the mvd rules. In addition, we often use rules for fds and mvds. For completeness, we include here the sound and complete system for fds and mvds as developed in Beeri, Fagin and Howard [1977], Biskup [1978, 1979] and Mendelzon [1979]. The set of rules we present is not minimal, i.e., some rules can be derived from other rules. For details see the references above. In the following, X,Y,Z,W are arbitrary subsets of U.

FD1 (Reflexivity axiom). $\vdash X \to Y$ if $Y \subseteq X$.

FD2 (Augmentation rule). $X \to Y \vdash XW \to YZ$ if $Z \subseteq W$.

FD3 (Transitivity rule). $X \to Y,\ Y \to Z \vdash X \to Z$.

FD4 (Union rule). $X \to Y,\ X \to Z \vdash X \to YZ$.

FD5 (Decomposition rule). $X \to Y \vdash X \to A$ for all $A \in Y$.

(Because of rules FD4, FD5, it can be assumed that fds are given in the *canonical form* $X \to A$ where A is a single attribute. This justifies the definition of the F-rule in the chase.)

MVD0 (Complementation axiom). $\vdash X \twoheadrightarrow \bar{X}$.

MVD1 (Reflexivity axiom). $\vdash X \twoheadrightarrow Y$ if $Y \subseteq X$.

MVD2 (Augmentation rule). $X \twoheadrightarrow Y \vdash XW \twoheadrightarrow YZ$ if $Z \subseteq W$.

MVD3a (Subset rule). $X \twoheadrightarrow Y,\ W \twoheadrightarrow Z \vdash X \twoheadrightarrow Y \cap Z$,

$X \twoheadrightarrow Y-Z$ if $Y \cap W = \emptyset$

MVD3b (Transitivity rule). $X \twoheadrightarrow Y,\ W \twoheadrightarrow Z \vdash X \twoheadrightarrow Z-Y$,

$X \twoheadrightarrow ZY$ if $W \subseteq XY$.

MVD4 (Boolean rules).

MVD4a (Union rule). $X \twoheadrightarrow Y,\ X \twoheadrightarrow Z \vdash X \twoheadrightarrow YZ$.

MVD4b (Decomposition rule). $X \twoheadrightarrow Y,\ X \twoheadrightarrow Z \vdash X \twoheadrightarrow Y-Z$,

$X \twoheadrightarrow Y \cap Z,\ X \twoheadrightarrow Z-Y$.

FD-MVD1 (Translation rule). $X \to Y \vdash X \twoheadrightarrow Y$.

FD-MVD2 (Mixed subset rule). $X \twoheadrightarrow Y,\ W \to Z \vdash X \to Y \cap Z$

if $W \cap Y = \emptyset$.

As remarked above, this set is redundant. It is known that the set (FD1, FD2, FD3) is complete for fds. The set {MVD0, MVD2. MVD3a} is complete for mvds (Vardi [1980a]). The union of these two sets and the set {FD-MVD1, FD-MVD2} is complete for fds and mvds. There are other sets of rules that are complete.

A FORMAL SYSTEM FOR JOIN DEPENDENCIES

In this section we present our formal system for jds. We start by presenting rules that can be applied to jds in general, whether they are total or embedded. Then we restrict our attention to total jds and consider the rules and their consequences for this special case.

An Axiom

For both fds and mvds, the formal systems contain axioms, i.e., dependencies that are always satisfied. We present here an axiom for jds. Since $\pi_R(I) = \pi_R(I)$ holds trivially, the constraint $*[R]$ is satisfied in every relation. Thus we have:

EJD0 (EJ-axiom).

$\vdash *[R]$ for every $R \subseteq U$.

The Rule of Covering

Let $\underline{R}$ and $\underline{S}$ be two asc's such that $ATTR(\underline{R}) = ATTR(\underline{S})$. We say that $\underline{R}$ *covers* $\underline{S}$, denoted $\underline{R} \geq S$, if for every $S_j \in \underline{S}$ there exists an $R_i \in \underline{R}$ such that $S_j \subseteq R_i$.

EJD1 (Covering rule).

$*[\underline{S}] \vdash *[\underline{R}]$ if $ATTR(\underline{R}) = ATTR(\underline{S})$ and $\underline{R} \geq \underline{S}$.

The covering rule is sound. In proof, note that, by Lemma 1 of the subsection Relational Algebra Operators $m_{\underline{R}} \leq m_{\underline{S}}$ if and only if $\underline{R} \geq \underline{S}$. Suppose that $ATTR(\underline{R}) = ATTR(\underline{S})$, that $\underline{R} \geq \underline{S}$ holds, and let I be in $SAT(*[\underline{S}])$. Then

$$\pi_{ATTR(\underline{S})}(I) = \pi_{ATTR(\underline{R})}(I) \subseteq m_{\underline{R}}(I) \subseteq m_{\underline{S}}(I) = \pi_{ATTR(\underline{S})}(I) .$$

Thus, I is also in $SAT(*[\underline{R}])$.

To simplify the use of the covering rule, we present four special cases.

EJD1a $*[S_1,\ldots,S_k] \vdash *[S_1,\ldots,S_k,\emptyset]$ (add a set)

EJD1b $*[S_1,\ldots,S_k] \vdash *[S_1A,S_2,\ldots,S_k]$ (add an attribute to a set)

EJD1c $*[S_1,\ldots,S_k] \vdash *[S_1,\ldots,S_{k-1}]$ if $S_k \subseteq S_j$ for some $j \neq k$

EJD1d $*[S_1,\ldots,S_k) \vdash *[S_1S_2, S_3,\ldots,S_k]$ (replace sets by their union)

The first rule allows us to add a new attribute set to a jd, and the second rule allows us to add an attribute to an existing attribute set. The last two rules are implied by the second rule. Since an asc is a set where two identical elements are considered the same element, if $S_i \subseteq S_j$ then we can add attributes to S_i until it becomes identical to S_j. Thus rule c is implied by rule b. A similar argument holds for rule d. It is easy to see that $\underline{R} \geq \underline{S}$ iff $\underline{R}$ can be obtained from $\underline{S}$ by using the first two rules.

Proposition 1

Let $*[\underline{R}]$ and $*[\underline{S}]$ be two jds such that $ATTR(\underline{R}) = ATTR(\underline{S})$. Then the following statements are equivalent.

(a) $\underline{R} \leq \underline{S}$.

(b) $*[\underline{R}] \vdash *[\underline{S}]$, where only EJD1 is used in the derivation.

(c) $*[\underline{R}] \models *[\underline{S}]$.

Proof: The implication of (b) by (a) is obvious and the implication of (c) by (b) follows from the soundness of EJD1. We prove only the implication of (a) by (c).

For an arbitrary relation I, $\pi_{ATTR(\underline{R})}(I) \subseteq m_{\underline{R}}(I)$, hence $m_{\underline{S}}(I) = m_{\underline{S}}(\pi_{ATTR(\underline{R})}(I)) \subseteq m_{\underline{S}}(m_{\underline{R}}(I))$. However, $m_{\underline{R}}(I)$ satisfies $*[\underline{R}]$, hence it also satisfies $*[\underline{S}]$. Therefore $m_{\underline{S}}(m_{\underline{R}}(I)) = m_{\underline{R}}(I)$ and it follows that $m_{\underline{S}}(I) \subseteq m_{\underline{R}}(I)$, i.e., $m_{\underline{S}} \leq m_{\underline{R}}$. By Lemma 1 (cf. the section Relational Algebra Operator) $\underline{S}$ covers $\underline{R}$. □

This proposition characterizes the jds that are implied by a single jd (without changing the attribute set) and it states that rule EJD1 is complete for this restricted case. We can apply it to obtain a characterization of the jds implied by the empty set of jds. A jd is *trivial* if it holds in every relation, i.e., it is implied by Ø. Let $*[\underline{R}]$ be a jd. Then $*[ATTR(\underline{R})]$ is a trivial jd that has the same attribute set as $*[\underline{R}]$. This jd is covered by $*[\underline{R}]$ if and only if $ATTR(\underline{R}) \in \underline{R}$, and $*[\underline{R}]$ is derivable from it using EJD1 if and only if $*[\underline{R}]$ is derivable from Ø using EJD0 and EJD1. We have proved the following:

Corollary 1

Let $\underline{R}$ be an asc. The following are equivalent.

(a) $ATTR(\underline{R}) \in \underline{R}$.

(b) $\vdash *[\underline{R}]$, where only EJD0 and EJD1 are used in the derivation.

(c) $*[\underline{R}]$ is a trival jd, i.e., $\models *[\underline{R}]$. □

The corollary states that {EJD0, EJD1} is complete for deriving the trivial dependencies.

When binary jds are considered, we obtain, as special cases, the complementation and reflexivity axioms of the subsection A Formal System for Constraints. Similarly, rule EJD1 yields the augmentation rule for mvds.

We can now prove easily a theorem of Nicolas [1978]. Define a relation to be *decomposable* if it satisfies a nontrivial total jd.

Theorem 1

Let $\tilde{U} = \{A \mid A \in U\}$. A relation I is decomposable if and only if $I \in SAT(*[\tilde{U}])$.

Proof: Since $ATTR(U) = U \notin \tilde{U}$, $*[\tilde{U}]$ is a nontrivial jd, which proves the if direction. To prove the only if direction, assume that I satisfies the nontrivial total jd $*[\underline{R}]$. Since $U = ATTR(\underline{R}) \notin \underline{R}$, it follows that $\underline{R} \leq \tilde{U}$ so by rule EJD1, I satisfies $*[\tilde{U}]$. □

The Rule of Projection

Let c be a constraint, ATTR(c) = R, and let S be a subset of R. Intuitively, a projection of c on S, is a constraint c', ATTR(c') = S, such that whenever $I \in SAT(c)$, then $I \in SAT(c')$. In other words, if $\pi_R(I)$ satisfies c then $\pi_S(I)$ satisfies c'. Usually, if such a c' exists, then it is not unique since other constraints can be obtained from it by applying rule EJD1. In such a case, the minimal such constraint on S (with respect to covering) is called the projection of c.

Projection rules are known for fds and mvds. If I satisfies $X \rightarrow Y$ and $X \subseteq R$ then $\pi_R(I)$ satisfies $X \rightarrow Y \cap R$. Similarly, if I satisfies $X \twoheadrightarrow Y(R)$ and $X \subseteq S \subseteq R$, then I satisfies $X \twoheadrightarrow Y \cap S(S)$ (Fagin [1977]). Projected dependencies are extremely important in the process of decomposition of schemes. A projection rule for jds was presented recently in Beeri and Rissanen [1979]. We now present the rule and prove that it is sound and complete.

For an asc $\underline{R}$, define $MANY(\underline{R})$ to be the set of attributes that appear in at least two sets in $\underline{R}$, and $ONCE(\underline{R}) = ATTR(\underline{R}) - MANY(\underline{R})$ to be the set of attributes each of which belongs to exactly one set in $\underline{R}$. For a set S, define the *projection* of $\underline{R}$ on S, denoted by $\underline{R} \cap S$, to be $\{R \cap S \mid R \in \underline{R}\}$.

EJD2 (Projection rule)

Let $\underline{R}$ be an asc and S be a set such that $\mathrm{MANY}(\underline{R}) \subseteq S$, then

$$*[\underline{R}] \vdash *[R_i \cap S,\ldots,R_k \cap S] = *[\underline{R} \cap S] .$$

In proof of soundness of the rule, assume that $I \in \mathrm{SAT}(*[\underline{R}])$, but $I \notin \mathrm{SAT}(*[\underline{R} \cap S])$. Then there exists an S-value w_S and rows $w_1,\ldots,w_k$ in I such that $w_S[R_i \cap S] = w_i[R_i \cap S]$ but $w_S \notin \pi_S(I)$. Extend w_S to an $\mathrm{ATTR}(\underline{R})$-value w as follows. For each $A \in \mathrm{ATTR}(\underline{R})-S$ add to w_S the A-value $w_i[A]$, where R_i is the unique element of $\underline{R}$ such that $A \in R_i$. Obviously w is well defined and $w[R_i] = w_i[R_i]$. Since I satisfies $*[\underline{R}]$, $w \in \pi_{\mathrm{ATTR}(\underline{R})}(I)$, hence $w_S = w[S] \in \pi_S(I)$ -- a contradiction.

The following example, shows that the condition $\mathrm{MANY}(\underline{R}) \subseteq S$ is essential. (This also follows from the completeness of the rule stated below.)

Example

Let $U = \{A,B,C,D,E\}$, $\underline{R} = \{ABE, ACD, BCD\}$, $S_1 = \{A,B,C,D\}$ and $S_2 = \{A,B,C,E\}$. Let I be the relation

I =

A	B	C	D	E
1	1	2	1	1
1	2	1	2	2
2	1	1	3	2

The reader can verify that I satisfies $*[\underline{R}]$ and $*[\underline{R} \cap S_1]$ but not $*[\underline{R} \cap S_2]$. □

The projection rule is complete for projections of total dependencies. By completeness we mean that if C is a set of fds and total jds and c is an embedded jd implied by C, then there exists a total jd that is implied by C and projects to c.

Theorem 2 (Completeness of the projection rule)

Let C be a set of fds and total jds and suppose that $C \models *[\underline{R}]$, where $\mathrm{ATTR}(\underline{R}) \subsetneq U$. Then there exists an asc $\underline{Q}$ such that $\mathrm{ATTR}(\underline{Q}) = U$, $\mathrm{MANY}(\underline{Q}) = \mathrm{MANY}(\underline{R})$, $C \models *[\underline{Q}]$ and $\underline{R} = \underline{Q} \cap \mathrm{ATTR}(\underline{R})$.

Proof: The proof will be presented in the section TABLEAUX AND THE CHASE.

The following corollary generalizes a result of Aho, Beeri and Ullman [1979].

Corollary 3

Let C be a set of fds and total jds. Then, C implies an embedded mvd $X \twoheadrightarrow Y(S)$ if and only if there exists a total mvd $X \twoheadrightarrow Y'$ such that $C \models X \twoheadrightarrow Y'$ and $Y' \cap S = Y$. □

The Rule of Substitution

The rules EJD1 and EJD2 both allow us to infer from one given dependency another dependency that is less informative than the one that is given. EJD0 is an axiom that allows us to infer only trivial dependencies. We now present a rule that will allow us to combine two dependencies to yield a third dependency that is more informative than either one of the given dependencies.

EJD3 (Substitution rule).

Let $\underline{R}$ and $\underline{S}$ be ascs such that $\mathrm{ATTR}(\underline{S}) \in \underline{R}$, then $*[\underline{R}], *[\underline{S}] \vdash *[\underline{R} - \{\mathrm{ATTR}(\underline{S})\} \cup \underline{S}]$.

The rule is sound. Indeed, assume that $\underline{R} = \{R_1,\ldots,R_k\}$, $\underline{S} = \{S_1,\ldots,S_\ell\}$, $\mathrm{ATTR}(\underline{S}) = R_j$, and let I be in $\mathrm{SAT}(*[\underline{R}],*[S])$. Then $\pi_{\mathrm{ATTR}(\underline{R})}(I) = \overset{k}{\underset{i=1}{*}} \pi_{R_i}(I)$ and $\pi_{R_j}(I) = \overset{\ell}{\underset{i=1}{*}} \pi_{S_i}(I)$. Substituting the right side of the second equality for the occurrence of $\pi_{R_j}(I)$ in the first equality we obtain

$$\pi_{\mathrm{ATTR}(\underline{R})}(I) = (\underset{i\neq j}{*} \pi_{R_i}(I)) * (\overset{\ell}{\underset{h=1}{*}} \pi_{S_h}(I)),$$

which concludes the proof.

Mixed Rules

Up to now we have considered only jds. If fds are also considered then *mixed rules*, similar to the FD-MVD rules are needed. We present two rules.

FD-EJD1 (translation rule)

$X \rightarrow Y \vdash *[XY, X\bar{Y}]$

FD-EJD2 (mixed subset rule)

$*[X,Y], S \rightarrow A \vdash X \cap Y \rightarrow A$, if $(X-Y) \cap S = \emptyset$, $S \subseteq XY$ and $A \in X-Y$.

These two rules are translations of the rules FD-MVD1 and FD-MVD2 of Beeri, Fagin and Howard [1977], so, in particular, they are sound. The first states that each fd is also a total mvd, i.e., a total binary jd. Note that by using EJD2 we may derive from $*[XY, X\bar{Y}]$ the embedded jd $*[XY, XZ]$, where Z is any set of attributes. The second rule states that if an attribute in the right side of an mvd functionally depends on a set that is disjoint to that right side, then it functionally depends on the left side of the mvd.

The second rule applies only to binary jds. It seems that a rule for the interaction of fds and general jds is needed. Generalizations of the rule will be presented later. However, they will be shown to be derivable from FD-EJD2 and EJD1. Further, from the completeness results proved in the section BRANCH COMPLETENESS OF THE RULES it follows that the rules as presented here are sufficient for the formal treatment of the interaction of fds and jds.

Completeness for Crosses

In spite of their simplicity, the rules we have presented so far are very powerful. Thus, we will see that the rules that will be presented later, some of which seem to be quite different, can be derived from them. Also, the inference rules for jds presented in Armstrong and Delobel [1979], Delobel [1978] and Paredaens [1979] are all consequences of our rules. As an example, consider the formal system for binary crosses of Paredaens [1979]:

(i) $*[X,Y] \vdash *[X',Y]$ if $X' \subseteq X$

(ii) $*[X,Y],\ *[X',Y'] \vdash *[X \cap X',\ (YY') \cap (XY)]$

(In these rules, disjointness of the components of each binary jd is assumed.) Now rule (i) is a special case of rule EJD2. Rule (ii) can be obtained from our rules as follows: First project $*[X,Y]$ to $*[X \cap X'Y',Y]$. Next, project $*[X',Y']$ to $*[X \cap X', X \cap Y']$ and substitute into the previous jd, obtaining $*[X \cap X',\ X \cap Y',\ Y]$. By EJD1 obtain $*[X \cap X',\ (X \cap Y')Y] = *[X \cap X',\ (YY') \cap (XY)]$.

Proposition 2

The system {EJD0, EJD1, EJD2, EJD3} is complete for general (not necessarily binary) crosses.

Proof: A general cross has the form $*[X_1,\ldots,X_k]$ where the X_is are pairwise disjoint. With a general cross as above we can associate the set of binary crosses $\{*[X_j,\ \bigcup_{i \neq j} X_i]\}$. By the rules EJD1, EJD2, EJD3, the general cross above implies each binary cross in this set and is implied by the set. Thus, every general k-ary cross is equivalent to a collection of k binary crosses.

It follows that a general cross c is implied by a set C of general crosses if and only if the binary crosses associated with c are implied by the binary crosses associated with the crosses of C. The rules (i) and (ii) above are complete for binary crosses (Paredaens [1979]). Since these rules are derived from our EJD rules, and since our EJD rules can transform a general cross into the set of its associated binary crosses and vice versa, the Proposition follows. □

ON THE POWER OF THE RULES

In this section we consider the rules we have introduced so far, explain how they can be used and illustrate their power. Some concepts pertaining to mvds are generalized and several additional derived rules are presented. Finally, the restriction of the system to total jds is considered.

ONCE Versus MANY

Consider first the rule of projection. For a jd $*[\underline{R}]$ the rule allows us to project it on a set S provided that $\text{MANY}(\underline{R}) \subseteq S \subseteq \text{ATTR}(\underline{R})$. Thus, the minimal projection of this jd is $*[\underline{R} \cap \text{MANY}(\underline{R})]$. Note, however, that several elements of $\underline{R}$ may project to the same element of $\underline{R} \cap \text{MANY}(\underline{R})$. In particular, it may happen that $\text{MANY}((\underline{R}) \cap \text{MANY}(\underline{R})) \subsetneq \text{MANY}(\underline{R})$. In such a case we can project again. This chain of possible projections terminates when a jd is obtained whose set of attributes is equal to its MANY set.

There may be cases where we need to project out an attribute in $\text{MANY}(\underline{R})$. E.g., suppose that we are given $*[\underline{R}]$ and $*[\underline{S}]$. We would like to refine $*[\underline{S}]$ by projection $*[\underline{R}]$ onto some member of $\underline{S}$ and substituting the result into $*[\underline{S}]$. It may often be the case that no member of $\underline{S}$ contains $\text{MANY}(\underline{R})$. Are we prevented from using $*[\underline{R}]$ to refine $*[\underline{S}]$ in such a case?

Our first observation is that by applying our rules we can transfer attributes from MANY to ONCE and vice versa. Indeed, assume that $A \in \text{ONCE}(\underline{R})$. By rule EJD1, $*[\underline{R}] \vdash *[\underline{R} \cup \{A\}]$ and obviously $A \in \text{MANY}(\underline{R} \cup \{A\})$. Conversely, assume $A \in \text{MANY}(\underline{R})$. We can replace in $\underline{R}$ the sets that contain A by their union. If the resulting collection is $\underline{Q}$, then $*[\underline{R}] \vdash *[\underline{Q}]$ (again by EJD1) and $A \in \text{ONCE}(\underline{Q})$.

Let us return now to the problem of projecting $*[\underline{R}]$ on a set S where $\text{MANY}(\underline{R}) \not\subseteq S$. The discussion above suggests the following method. For an attribute $A \in \text{MANY}(\underline{R}) - S$, replace in $\underline{R}$ the sets that contain A by their union, thus effectively transferring A from MANY to ONCE. Repeat the process until the resulting jd can be projected on S. This method is formalized below.

Given a set S, define a binary relation on 2^U, denoted by $\sim_S$, as follows.

(a) $X \sim_S X$

(b) If $X \cap Y \not\subseteq S$ then $X \sim_S Y$

(c) If $X \sim_S Y$ and $Y \sim_S Z$ then $X \sim_S Z$

(d) $X \sim_S Y$ only if it so follows from (a), (b) and (c).

Clearly $\sim_S$ is an equivalence relation. For a jd $*[\underline{R}]$ and a set $S \subseteq \text{ATTR}(\underline{R})$, $\sim_S$ induces a partition of $\underline{R}$ into equivalence classes. The equivalence class of R_i in $\underline{R}$ will be denoted by $[R_i]_S$. The *reduction* of $\underline{R}$ by $\sim_S$, denoted by $\underline{R}/\sim_S$, is the collection obtained from $\underline{R}$ by replacing the elements of each equivalence class of $\sim_S$ in $\underline{R}$ by their union, i.e., $\underline{R}/\sim_S = \{\cup[R_i]_S \mid R_i \in \underline{R}\}$.

Proposition 3

For a collection $\underline{R}$ and a set $S \subseteq \text{ATTR}(\underline{R})$, the following are true.

1) $*[\underline{R}] \vdash *[\underline{R}/\sim_S]$

2) $\text{MANY}(\underline{R}/\sim_S) \subseteq S$

3) If $*[\underline{R}] \models *[\underline{Q}]$, $\text{ATTR}(\underline{R}) = \text{ATTR}(\underline{Q})$, and $\text{MANY}(\underline{Q}) \subseteq S$ then $\underline{Q}$ covers $\underline{R}/\sim_S$.

Proof: Obviously $*[\underline{R}] \vdash *[\underline{R}/\sim_S]$ by EJD1. Next, assume that there exists an attribute A in $\text{MANY}(\underline{R}/\sim_S) - S$. For some i and j, A belongs to $[R_i]$ and $[R_j]$ and these two equivalence classes are distinct. Without loss of generality we may assume that $A \in R_i$ and $A \in R_j$. But then $R_i \sim_S R_j$ — a contradiction. Hence $\text{MANY}(\underline{R}/\sim_S) \subseteq S$.

To prove the third property, we first note that by Proposition 1, if $*[\underline{R}] \models *[\underline{Q}]$, $\text{ATTR}(\underline{R}) = \text{ATTR}(\underline{Q})$ then $\underline{Q}$ covers $\underline{R}$. If $\text{MANY}(\underline{Q}) \subseteq S$, then it follows that if $R_i \cap R_j \not\subseteq S$ then R_i and R_j are contained in the same element of $\underline{Q}$. It follows easily that for every $R_i \in \underline{R}$, $\cup[R_i]_S$ is contained in a single element of $\underline{Q}$, hence $\underline{Q}$ covers $\underline{R}/\sim_S$. □

By the proposition, $*[\underline{R}/\sim_S]$ is the most informative jd implied by $*[\underline{R}]$ that can be projected on S. Let us define, for an asc $\underline{R}$ and a set $S \subseteq \text{ATTR}(\underline{R})$, the *extended projection* of $\underline{R}$ on S, denoted by $\pi_S(\underline{R})$, to be $\underline{R}/\sim_S \cap S$. Note that if $\text{MANY}(\underline{R}) \subseteq S$ then $\pi_S(\underline{R}) = \underline{R} \cap S$. We will continue to use the notation $\underline{R} \cap S$ when $\text{MANY}(\underline{R}) \subseteq S$. Note also that for $S_1 \subset S_2$, $\pi_{S_1}(\pi_{S_2}(\underline{R})) = \pi_{S_1}(\underline{R})$. We can now extend rule EJD2.

EJD2' (Extended projection rule)

Let $\underline{R}$ be an asc and let $S \subseteq \text{ATTR}(\underline{R})$, then $*[\underline{R}] \vdash *[\pi_S(\underline{R})]$.

Example 2

Let $U = \{A,B,C,D,E,F,G\}$ and $\underline{R} = \{ABCD, CDEF, EFG\}$. $MANY(\underline{R}) = \{C,D,E,F\}$. Let $S = \{A,B,E,F,G\}$. Then $\underline{R}/\sim_S = \{ABCDEF, EFG\}$, $MANY(\underline{R}/\sim_S) = \{E,F\}$ and $\pi_S(\underline{R}) = \{ABEF, EFG\}$. □

Now, given jds $*[\underline{R}]$ and $*[\underline{S}]$ we can combine rules EJD2' and EJD3 to refine $*[\underline{S}]$ as follows. For any $S_i \in \underline{S}$, we can substitute $\pi_{S_i}(\underline{R})$ for S_i in $*[\underline{S}]$. This combination of projection-substitution is very powerful, as will be illustrated later.

Stems and Branches

The projection rule indicates the important role of the sets $MANY(\underline{R})$ and $ONCE(\underline{R})$. It turns out to be useful to regard each R_i in $\underline{R}$ as consisting of two components, the attributes that appear only in R_i and the attributes that appear also in some other elements of $\underline{R}$. We now define these components. The usefulness of this viewpoint is illustrated by a characterization theorem for jds.

Let $\underline{R} = \{R_1,\ldots,R_k\}$ be an asc and X be a set such that $MANY(\underline{R}) \subseteq X \subseteq ATTR(\underline{R})$. The *X-stem* of R_i, denoted by $ST_X(R_i)$, is the set $R_i \cap X$; the *X-branch* of R_i, denoted by $BR_X(R_i)$, is the set $R_i - X$. We will sometimes use the notation $\underline{R} = \{(ST_X(R_i), BR_X(R_i))\}$ to make explicit the fact that each R_i consists of two components — a stem and a branch. It should be borne in mind that $(ST_X(R_i), BR_X(R_i))$ stands for the set $ST_X(R_i) \cup BR_X(R_i)$. When $X = MANY(\underline{R})$, we write simply $ST(R_i)$ and $BR(R_i)$ and call them the *stem* and the *branch* of R_i, respectively. In the following, when X-stems and X-branches are mentioned, it is assumed that X contains the MANY sets of all the relevant jds. We use $ST_X(\underline{R})$ for $\{ST_X(R) \mid R \in \underline{R}\}$ and $BR_X(\underline{R})$ for $\{BR_X(R) \mid R \in \underline{R}\}$.

Example 3

Let $U = \{A,B,C,D,E,F,G,H,I,J\}$, $\underline{R} = \{ABCD, BEFG, EHIJ\}$. Then $MANY(\underline{R}) = \{BE\}$. Let $X = \{BDE\}$, then $\underline{R} = \{(BD, AC), (BE, FG), (E, HIJ)\}$. □

By the definition, for a set X and elements R_i and R_j of $\underline{R}$, $BR_X(R_i) \cap BR_X(R_j) = \emptyset$ (since $MANY(\underline{R}) \subseteq X$). Further, if R and S are any two sets, from the same jd or from different jds, then $ST_X(R) \cap BR_X(S) = BR_X(R) \cap ST_X(S) = \emptyset$. Therefore, $S \cap R = (ST_X(R) \cap ST_X(S)) \cup (BR_X(S) \cap BR_X(R))$. This fact will be useful later.

The concepts of stem and branch can be viewed as generalizations of the concepts of left side and right side of an mvd. Indeed, when $X \twoheadrightarrow Y$ is viewed as a binary jd, then X is the stem and Y-X,

$\bar{Y}$-X are the branches. An mvd or an fohd is, therefore, a jd with a degenerate collection of stems — it has only one stem.

A word of explanation is due here as to why we choose to define stems and branches relative to an arbitrary set X. For one thing, we want to present rules where two (or more) jds are treated simultaneously. Since the jds do not necessarily have the same MANY sets, it is convenient to use a set X that contains all the relevant MANY sets. Consider also the following situation. Suppose that we have an asc $\underline{X} = \{X_i\}$, $\bigcup_i X_i = X$. We can create various jds by partitioning U-$\bar{X}$ and attaching the elements of the partition as branches to the X_i's. Now, if we attach, say, two branches to each X_i we obtain a jd with X as its MANY set, and the X_is are its stems. However, if we attach only a single branch to each X_i we may obtain a jd with MANY set properly contained in X. The relativization of stems and branches to X allows us to treat this collection of jds uniformly as one family.

As an illustration of the use of the new concepts, we present here a generalization of a theorem of Maier and Mendelzon [1979]. This theorem is used later for proving the completeness results given in BRANCH COMPLETENESS OF THE RULES.

Theorem 3

Let $\underline{R} = \{R_1,\ldots,R_k\}$ be an asc, ATTR($\underline{R}$) = R, and let S be a set such that MANY($\underline{R}$) $\subseteq$ S $\subseteq$ R. Then

$$*[\underline{R}] \vdash\dashv \{*[\underline{R} \cap S]\} \cup \{*[R_i,\ R-(R_i-S)]\}_{i=1}^{k}$$

$R_i - S = BR_S(R_i)$, so the binary jd $*[R_i,\ R-(R_i-S)]$ is equivalent to the mvd $ST_S(R_i) \twoheadrightarrow BR_S(R_i)(R)$. We thus obtain the following equivalent formulation of the theorem.

Theorem 4

Let $\underline{R} = \{R_i\}_{i=1}^{k}$ be an asc, and let S be a set, MANY($\underline{R}$) $\subseteq$ S $\subseteq$ ATTR($\underline{R}$). Then

$$*[\underline{R}] \vdash\dashv *[ST_S(\underline{R})] \cup \{ST_S(R_i) \twoheadrightarrow BR_S(R_i)(R)\}_{i=1}^{k}.$$

Proof: ($\vdash$) By rule EJD2, $*[\underline{R}] \vdash *[\underline{R} \cap S]$. By rule EJD1,

$$*[\underline{R}] \vdash *[R_i,\ \bigcup_{j\neq i} R_j] \vdash *[R_i\ (\bigcup_{j\neq i} R_j) \cup S].\ \text{But}$$

$$(\bigcup_{j\neq i} R_j) \cup S = R - (R_i - S) = R - BR_S(R_i).$$

($\dashv$) We prove, using induction, that for every ℓ, $0 \leq \ell \leq k$, there exists a derivation of the jd $h_\ell = *[R_1,\ldots,R_\ell,\ S \cup (\bigcup_{j>\ell}(R_j-S))]$ from the set $*[\underline{R} \cap S] \cup \{*[R_i,\ R-(R_i-S)]\}_{i=1}^{k}$.

For $\ell = 0$, $S \cup (\bigcup_{j>0} (R_j - S)) = R$ and by EJD0 $\vdash *[R]$. Assuming that the claim holds for $\ell < k$, we show that it also holds for $\ell+1$. By the induction hypothesis, we have a derivation from the given premises of the jd h_ℓ. Let us project the jd $*[R_{\ell+1}, R-(R_{\ell+1}-S)]$ that is included in the premises on $S \cup (\bigcup_{j>\ell} R_j - S))$. The result is $*[R_{\ell+1}, S \cup (\bigcup_{j>\ell+1} R_j - S))]$. When this jd is substituted for the last component of h_ℓ, we obtain the desired $h_{\ell+1}$.

It follows that there exists a derivation from the premises of the jd $h_k = *[R_1,\ldots,R_k,S]$. Substituting $*[\underline{R} \cap S]$ for S in h_k we obtain $*[\{R_1,\ldots,R_k\} \cup (\underline{R} \cap S)]$. However, each component of $\underline{R} \cap S$ is covered by some R_i, so by applying EJD1 we obtain the desired jd $*[\underline{R}]$. □

<u>Corollary 4</u> (Equivalence of fohds and mvds)

Let $*[\underline{R}]$ be an fohd, $S = \mathrm{MANY}(\underline{R})$. Then

$$*[\underline{R}] \vdash\dashv \{S \twoheadrightarrow BR_S(R_i)(R)\}.$$

Proof: Under the given conditions, $*[\underline{R} \cap S] = *[S]$ is a trivial jd which can be eliminated. Also, $ST_S(R_i) = S$, so all left sides are equal to S. □

The Intersection Rule

As branches and stems of jds are important, it is useful to have a rule for their manipulation. Note that several such rules exist for mvds, namely, the transitivity/subset rule and the Boolean rules. We now present such a rule for jds.

<u>EJD4</u> (Branch intersection rule)

Let $\underline{R}$ and $\underline{S}$ be ascs and let X be a set such that $\mathrm{MANY}(\underline{R}) \cup \mathrm{MANY}(\underline{S}) \subseteq X \subseteq \mathrm{ATTR}(\underline{R}) \cap \mathrm{ATTR}(\underline{S})$. Then $*[\underline{R}], *[\underline{S}] \vdash *[\underline{Q}]$, provided that the following conditions hold:

(a) $\mathrm{ATTR}(\underline{Q}) = \mathrm{ATTR}(\underline{R}) \cap \mathrm{ATTR}(\underline{S})$

(b) $\underline{Q}$ contains a subcollection $\{Q_{ij}\}$ such that

1) $BR_X(Q_{ij}) = BR_X(R_i) \cap BR_X(S_j)$.

2) $ST_X(Q_{ij})$ contains $ST_X(R_i) \cap ST_X(S_j)$. In addition, $ST_X(Q_{ij})$ contains either $ST(R_i)$ or $ST(S_j)$.

(c) For each i, if for some j, $ST_X(Q_{ij})$ does not contain $ST(R_i)$ (in which case it must contain $ST(S_j)$ by (b2)), then for this i and all j, $ST(S_j) \cup (ST_X(R_i) \cap ST_X(S_j))$ is contained in some $Q \in \underline{Q}$.

Intuitively, the rule allows us to intersect the X-branches of $\underline{R}$ with the X-branches of $\underline{S}$ and connect each of these intersected X-branches to a new X-stem. The new X-stem is not arbitrary. Rather, it must contain the intersection of the appropriate X-stems from $\underline{R}$ and $\underline{S}$ and, in addition, it must contain one of the non-relativized stems. While condition (b) deals with each component separately, condition (c) deals with the collection as a whole. The need for this condition becomes clear when one tries to prove the rule (see below). Note that the rule is not symmetric in $\underline{R}$ and $\underline{S}$. Thus, if we exchange the roles of $\underline{R}$ and $\underline{S}$, we may derive a different jd.

Rule EJD4 is the most complex rule we have presented so far. The following simpler version is usually sufficient for our needs.

<u>EJD4'</u>

Let $\underline{R}$, $\underline{S}$ and X be as in EJD4. Then $*[\underline{R}], *[\underline{S}] \vdash *[\underline{Q}]$, provided that the following conditions hold:

(a) $ATTR(\underline{Q}) = ATTR(\underline{R}) \cap ATTR(\underline{S})$.

(b) $\underline{Q}$ contains a subcollection $\{Q_{ij}\}$ such that

1) $BR_X(Q_{ij}) = BR_X(R_i) \cap BR_X(S_j)$

2) $ST_X(Q_{ij}) = ST_X(R_i)$, or
$ST_X(Q_{ij}) = ST_X(S_j)$.

(c) $ST_X(\underline{Q})$ contains either $ST_X(\underline{R})$ or $ST_X(\underline{S})$.

The reader can verify that rule EJD4' is implied by rule EJD4. We now prove the soundness of rule EJD4'. The proof of rule EJD4 is similar (though more difficult) and is left to the reader. The proof is by showing how to derive the rule from rules EJD1, EJD2 and EJD3. Thus, these rules are not independent.

We first note that by the conditions on $\underline{R}$, $\underline{S}$ and X we can project $*[\underline{R}]$ and $*[\underline{S}]$ on $ATTR(\underline{R}) \cap ATTR(\underline{S})$; $*[\underline{Q}]$ can still be derived from the projected dependencies by the rule. Therefore, without loss of generality, we assume that $ATTR(\underline{R}) = ATTR(\underline{S})$. Next, let us augment both $\underline{R}$ and $\underline{S}$ by X, that is, using EJD1 we have $*[\underline{R}] \vdash *[\underline{R}'] = *[XR_1,\ldots,XR_k]$ and $*[\underline{S}] \vdash *[\underline{S}'] = *[XS_1,\ldots,XS_\ell]$. Projecting $*[\underline{R}']$ on each element of $*[\underline{S}']$ and substituting in $*[\underline{S}']$ (or vice versa) we obtain $*[\underline{P}] = *[\{P_{ij}\}_{i=1,j=1}^{k,\ell}]$, where

$P_{ij} = (X, BR_X(R_i) \cap BR_X(S_j))$. Now, for a pair i, j, if $ST_X(Q_{ij}) = ST_X(R_i)$, we project $*[\underline{R}]$ on P_{ij} and substitute in $\underline{P}$. Thus, P_{ij} is replaced by a collection containing $(ST_X(R_i), BR_X(R_i) \cap BR_X(S_j))$ and all other X-stems of $\underline{R}$ connected to empty X-branches. Similarly, if $ST_X(Q_{ij}) = ST_X(S_j)$, we project $*[\underline{S}]$ and substitute. In either case, the resulting jd $*[\underline{P}']$ contains either $ST_X(\underline{R})$ or $ST_X(\underline{S})$. The conditions on $*[\underline{Q}]$ imply that $*[\underline{P}'] \vdash *[\underline{Q}]$ by EJD1. This concludes the proof.

The reader should note that, except for the projection of R and S on $ATTR(\underline{R}) \cap ATTR(\underline{S})$, rules EJD2 and EJD3 are used in the proof only in the combination of projection-substitution. This fact will prove to be significant later.

Example 3 (Continued)

Let $\underline{S}$ = {ADGI, CDEF, BEHJ}, $MANY(\underline{S})$ = DE. Let X = $MANY(\underline{R}) \cup MANY(\underline{S})$ = {BDE}. Then $\underline{S}$ = {(D, AGI), (DE, CF), (BE, HJ)}. Applying EJD4 to $*[\underline{R}]$ and $*[\underline{S}]$ we obtain

$$*[\underline{Q}] = *[(BD, A), (BD, C), (BE, G), (DE, F), (D,I), (E,HJ)].$$

□

A Rule with an Unbounded Number of Premises

The next rule we present is different from all previous rules in that it may have an arbitrary number of premises.

EJD5

Let $\underline{R} = \{R_1,\ldots,R_k\}$ and $\underline{S}^i = \{S_1,\ldots,S_{m_i}\}$, $1 \le i \le k$, be ascs such that, for all i, $R_i \subseteq ATTR(\underline{S}^i)$ and $MANY(\underline{S}^i) \subseteq ATTR(\underline{R})$. Then $*[\underline{R}], \{*[\underline{S}^i]\}_{i=1}^{k} \vdash *[\underline{Q}] = *[\{Q_j\}_{j=1}^{\max(m_i)}]$, where

$$Q_j = \bigcup_{i=1}^{k} ((R_i \cap S_j^i) \cup ST(S_j^i)), \quad 1 \le j \le \max(m_i).$$

The soundness of the rule is proved as follows. First we use EJD1 to replace each $R_i \in \underline{R}$ by $R_i \cup MANY(\underline{S}^i)$. Then we use EJD2 and EJD3 to replace each $R_i \cup MANY(\underline{S}^i)$ by $\underline{S}^i \cap (R_i \cup MANY(\underline{S}^i))$. Thus the jd $*[\{(R_i \cap S_j^i) \cup ST(S_j^i) \mid 1 \le i \le k, 1 \le j \le m_i\}]$ is derived. Now use EJD1 and for each j replace all elements indexed by this j and all i, $1 \le i \le k$, by their union to obtain $*[\underline{Q}]$.

Note that the $\underline{S}^i$'s are treated in this rule as sequences of length m_i rather than as sets. If the order of some elements in some $\underline{S}^i$ is changed, the derived jd may be different. Note also that for each i and j such that S^i_j does not exist, it is assumed to be empty. Correspondingly, $R_i \cap S^i_j$ and $ST(S^i_j)$ are taken to be the empty set. Thus, we can assume all $\underline{S}^i$ are sequences of the same length $m = \max(m_i)$. Further, we can permute these sequences such that the empty sets appear anywhere we like, and the rule remains valid.

The rule is particularly simple when all the $*[\underline{S}^i]$s are fohds with a common left side, i.e., for some set Y, $MANY(\underline{S}^i) = Y \subseteq ATTR(\underline{R})$. Then $ST(S^i_j) = Y$. In this case we can make all sequences to be of the same length by adding occurrences of Y. Thus we have that $\bigcup_{i=1}^{k} (R_i \cap S^i_j)$ contains Y and we obtain the following.

EJD5a

Let $*[\underline{R}] = *[R_1,\ldots,R_k]$ be a jd and let $*[\underline{S}^i]$, $1 \leq i \leq k$, be fohds such that $MANY(\underline{S}^i) = Y \subseteq ATTR(\underline{R})$. For each i and j such that S^i_j does not exist define $S^i_j = Y$. Then $*[\underline{R}], \{*[\underline{S}^i]\}_{i=1}^{k} \vdash *[\{\bigcup_{i=1}^{k} (R_i \cap S^i_j)\}_{j\geq 1}]$.

More on the Mixed Rules

The mixed rule FD-EJD2 applies only to a binary jd. We show now how it can be generalized.

FD-EJD3

$*[\underline{R}], S \rightarrow A \vdash ST_X(R_i) \rightarrow A$, if $A \in BR_X(R_i)$, $S \subseteq ATTR(\underline{R})$ and $S \cap BR_X(R_i) = \emptyset$.

In words, if an attribute in an X-branch is functionally dependent on a set that is disjoint to that X-branch, then it also depends on the corresponding X-stem. It turns out, however, that this rule is derivable from FD-EJD2 and EJD1. Indeed, by EJD1,

$*[\underline{R}] \vdash *[R_i, \bigcup_{j\neq i} R_j] \vdash *[R_i, ST_X(R_i) \cup (\bigcup_{j\neq i} R_j)]$. In the latter binary jd, the common stem is $ST_X(R_i)$ and one of the branches is $BR_X(R_i)$. Application of FD-EJD2 yields the desired fd $ST_X(R_i) \rightarrow A$.

We can generalize even further. Let $*[\underline{R}]$, $S \rightarrow A$ and a set Z be given. If $ST(R_i) \not\subseteq Z$, where $A \in R_i$, then FD-EJD3 is not sufficient to derive $Z \rightarrow A$. However, $Z \rightarrow A$ may still be derivable from the given jd and fd.

Proposition 4

Let $*[\underline{R}]$, $S \rightarrow A$ and a set Z be given $Z \subseteq A \subseteq ATTR(\underline{R})$. Let R_A be the element of $\underline{R}/\sim_Z$ that contains A. If $R_A \cap S = \emptyset$ then

$*[\underline{R}], S \rightarrow A \vdash Z \rightarrow A.$

Proof: Let R_S be the union of the elements of $R/\sim_Z$ that intersect S, and let R_S' be the union of all other elements of $R/\sim_Z$. Then $*[\underline{R}] \vdash *[R_S, R_S']$, $S \cap BR(R_S') = \emptyset$ and $A \in BR(R_S')$, hence $R_S \cap R_S' \rightarrow A$ is derivable. The claim now follows since $R_S \cap R_S' \subseteq Z$. □

In the following, we use only rules FD-EJD1 and FD-EJD2.

A System for Total Join Dependencies (jds)

From now on, we restrict our attention to total jds. Our goal is to determine the power of our rules when they are applied to total jds. We will use JD_i to denote rule EJD_i restricted to total jds.

Some changes are needed in our rules. In JD0, the J-axiom, we have $\vdash *[U]$. Rule JD1 is the same as EJD1. Rules EJD2 and EJD3 pose a problem since each one of them necessarily deals with embedded jds. However, as we have already noted, they can be combined to form a rule for total jds.

<u>JD2-3</u> (Projection-substitution rule)

$*[\underline{R}], *[\underline{S}] \vdash *[(\underline{R} - \{R_i\}) \cup \pi_{R_i}(\underline{S})].$

Rules JD4 and JD4' are the same as rules EJD4 and EJD4', except that the assumption that X is contained in $ATTR(\underline{R}) \cap ATTR(\underline{S})$ is redundant. The following special cases are of interest.

<u>JD4a</u> (Generalized transitivity/subset rule)

Let $\underline{R} = \{R_i\}_{i=1}^{k}$ and $\underline{S} = \{S_j\}_{j=1}^{\ell}$ be total ascs and assume that, for some i, $MANY(\underline{S}) \cap BR(R_i) = \emptyset$. Then $*[\underline{R}], *[\underline{S}] \vdash *[\underline{Q}]$, where where $\underline{Q}$ is obtained from $\underline{R}$ by replacing R_i by the collection $\{(ST(R_i), BR(R_i) \cap BR(S_j))\}_j$.

To see that this is a special case of JD4, choose $X = \overline{BR(R_i)}$. Then, for $k \neq i$, $ST_X(R_k) = R_k$ and $BR_X(R_k) = \emptyset$. Also, $ST_X(R_i) = ST(R_i)$ and $BR_X(R_i) = BR(R_i)$. Since $MANY(\underline{S}) \subseteq X$, $BR_X(R_i) \cap BR_X(S_j) = BR(R_i) \cap BR(S_j)$. Thus $*[\underline{Q}]$ satisfies the conditions of JD4.

Consider now the transitivity and subset rules for mvds. Obviously, applying transitivity to $X \twoheadrightarrow Y$ and $W \twoheadrightarrow Z$ is the same as applying the subset rule to $X \twoheadrightarrow Y$ and $W \twoheadrightarrow \overline{Z}$. In terms of binary jds, the two rules are the same: if $*[XY, X\overline{Y}]$ and $*[WZ, W\overline{Z}]$ are given and $W \cap Y = \emptyset$, then $*[X(Z \cap Y), \overline{X(Z \cap Y)}]$ is derivable.

Clearly the same result is obtained by applying JD4a followed by JD1 (since the result has to be a binary jd).

Rule JD4' is, similarly, a generalization of the mvd decomposition rules. The interesting case here is when $ST_X(\underline{R}) = ST_X(\underline{S})$. The rule allows us to intersect the X-branches of $\underline{R}$ and $\underline{S}$ to connect each such intersection either to its X-stem in $\underline{R}$ or to its X-stem in $\underline{S}$, provided that the set of X-stems is preserved. Since rule JD1 generalizes the union rule, we have generalized the Boolean mvd rules. An immediate consequence is that the concept of a dependency basis can also be generalized. This subject will be taken up in the next section.

Rules JD5 and JD5a are the same as rules EJD5 and EJD5a, except that the assumptions on the attribute and MANY sets are redundant. The mixed rules are also essentially the same.

We conclude this section with some observations about the relationships between the different rules.

Proposition 5

The sets of rules {JD1, JD2-3} and {JD1, JD4} are equivalent.

Sketch of proof: We have seen that EJD4' is derivable from EJD1, EJD2 and EJD3. As we remarked there, if the jds are total then only the combination JD2-3 is used. Rule JD4 can be derived similarly. It remains to prove that JD2-3 is derivable from JD1 and JD4.

Let $*[\underline{R}]$ and $*[\underline{S}]$ be given. We will show how $*[\underline{R} - \{R_i\} \cup \pi_{R_1}(\underline{S})]$ can be derived. Since JD1 can be used, we assume without loss of generality that $MANY(\underline{S}) \subseteq R_1$, so $\pi_{R_1}(\underline{S}) = \underline{S} \cap R_1$. Choose $X = MANY(\underline{R}) \cup MANY(\underline{S})$ and apply JD4 to $*[\underline{R}]$ and $*[\underline{S}]$ to obtain the jd $*[\underline{Q}]$, where $\underline{Q} = \{Q_{ij}\}$, and the following holds:

1) $BR_X(Q_{ij}) = BR_X(R_i) \cap BR_X(S_j)$

2) For $i > 1$, $ST_X(Q_{ij}) = ST_X(R_i)$

3) For $i = 1$, $ST_X(Q_{ij}) = (ST_X(S_j) \cap ST_X(R_i)) \cup ST(S_j)$.

Obviously, $*[\underline{Q}]$ satisfies the conditions required for its being derivable from $*[\underline{R}]$ and $*[\underline{S}]$ by JD4.

Now using JD1 we replace the collection $\{Q_{ij}\}$ for each fixed $i > 1$ by its union over all j. This union can be shown to be equal to R_i. As for Q_{ij}, it can be shown that it is equal to $S_j \cap R_1$, since $ST(S_j) \subseteq R_1$. We have thus obtained the required jd. □

We now consider the power of our rules when applied to mvds. We first introduce rules to translate from mvds to binary jds and back.

MVD-JD $\quad X \twoheadrightarrow Y \vdash *[XY, X\bar{Y}]$

JD-MVD $\quad *[X,Y] \vdash X \cap Y \twoheadrightarrow Y'$, if $Y-X \subseteq Y' \subseteq Y$

Proposition 6

Each one of the sets {JD0, JD1, JD2-3, MVD-JD, JD-MVD} and {JD0, JD1, JD4, MVD-JD, JD-MVD} is complete for mvds. If the mixed rules are added to either one, a complete system for fds and mvds is obtained.

Proof: We already know that the two systems are equivalent. Now, from JD0 and JD1 we obtain $*[X,U]$ and using the translation rule JD-MVD we obtain the complementation and reflexivity axioms for mvds. The translation rules and JD1 derive the augmentation rule for mvds. Finally JD4 with the other rules yields the subset and transitivity rules. Thus, our rules derive a set of rules that is known to be complete for mvds (Beeri, Fagin and Howard [1977]). That the addition of mixed rules yields a complete system for fds and mvds has also been proven there.

Additional relationships between the rules, especially concerning JD5, are presented in Vardi [1980].

THE BRANCH BASIS

Before presenting the completeness theorems, we study in this section the structure of X-branches of total jds implied by a given set C of fds and total jds, for an arbitrary set $X \subseteq U$. In the following we use for convenience mvds instead of binary jds. We use Theorem 4 which was proven using our system and mvd rules that are also implied by our system.

For C and X as above, we define

$$DEP_C(X) = \{Y \mid \phi \neq Y \subseteq \bar{X},\ C \models X \twoheadrightarrow Y \text{ and for all nonempty } Y' \subset Y,\ C \not\models X \twoheadrightarrow Y'\}.$$

In words, $DEP_C(X)$ is the collection of minimal subsets of $\bar{X}$ whose dependence on X is implied by C. From the rules it follows that $DEP_C(X)$ is a partition of $\bar{X}$ and, for $Y \subseteq \bar{X}$, $C \models X \twoheadrightarrow Y$ if and only if Y is a union of elements of $DEP_C(X)$. (See also Beeri, Fagin and Howard [1977], but note that they include in $DEP_C(X)$ also the collection of singleton subsets of X.)

The following two propositions connect $DEP_C(X)$ to the X-branches of jds.

Proposition 7

Let $DEP_C(X) = \{W_1,\ldots,W_m\}$. If $C \models *[\underline{R}]$ and $MANY(\underline{R}) \subseteq X$, then for all R_i in $\underline{R}$ and W_j in $DEP_C(X)$ either $W_j \subseteq BR_X(R_i)$ or $W_j \cap BR_X(R_i) = \emptyset$. In either case, $C \models ST_X(R_i) \twoheadrightarrow W_j \cap BR_X(R_i)$.

Proof: By Theorem 4, $*[\underline{R}] \models ST_X(R_i) \twoheadrightarrow BR_X(R_i)$, hence by rule MVD2 $*[\underline{R}] \models X \twoheadrightarrow BR_X(R_i)$. The first claim now follows by well known properties of $DEP_C(X)$. Applying rule MVD3a to the mvds above that are implied by C proves the second claim. □

For an asc $\underline{X}$, $ATTR(\underline{X}) = X$, define $J_C(\underline{X})$ to be the collection of all jds implied by C whose set of X-stems is $\underline{X}$. Note that $J_C(\underline{X})$ may be empty.

Proposition 8

If $J_C(\underline{X}) \neq \emptyset$, then there exists a jd $*[\underline{R}] \in J_C(X)$ such that $BR_X(\underline{R}) = DEP_C(X) \cup \{\emptyset\}$.

Proof: Let $X = ATTR(\underline{X})$. From the definition of $DEP_C(X)$, the fohd $*[XW_1,\ldots,XW_m]$ is implied by C. Let $*[\underline{S}]$ be in $J_C(\underline{X})$. Applying the intersection rule to $*[\underline{S}]$ and the fohd above we can replace each $S \in \underline{S}$ by the collection $\{(ST_X(S), BR_X(S) \cap W_i)\}_{i=1}^m$. The claim now follows from the previous proposition. □

By the intersection rule, given any two jds with MANY sets contained in X, we can intersect their X-branches, preserving the X-stems collection of the one or the other. The propositions above state that the smallest X-branches that may thus be obtained are the empty set and the elements of $DEP_C(X)$. Further, if $J_C(\underline{X})$ is not empty then it contains a jd whose set of nonempty X-branches is exactly $DEP_C(X)$. Obviously, the mere knowledge of the set of X-branches is not sufficient to characterize $J_C(\underline{X})$ uniquely, since it is always either empty (if $J_C(\underline{X})$ is empty) or $DEP_C(X) \cup \{\emptyset\}$. We need also to know how the X-branches are connected to the X-stems. Define the *branch basis* of $\underline{X}$ (with respect to C), denoted by $BRAN_C(\underline{X})$ as follows. If $J_C(\underline{X})$ is empty then so is $BRAN_C(\underline{X})$. If it is not empty then

$$BRAN_C(\underline{X}) = \{(W_i,\underline{X}^i) \mid W_i \in DEP_C(X) \text{ and } X_i \in \underline{X}^i \text{ iff, for some } *[\underline{R}] \text{ in } J_C(\underline{X}) \text{ and } R \in \underline{R},\ ST_X(R) = X_i \text{ and } BR_X(R) = W_i\}.$$

That is, $BRAN_C(\underline{X})$ is a set of pairs, a typical pair consisting of a member of $DEP_C(ATTR(\underline{X}))$ and the collection of X-stems from $\underline{X}$ which can be attached to it. Obviously $\underline{X}^i \subseteq \underline{X}$. Notice also that

$J_C(\underline{X}) \neq \emptyset$ if and only if $\underline{X}^i \neq \emptyset$ for all i.

We show that $BRAN_C(\underline{X})$ uniquely characterizes $J_C(\underline{X})$. Assume that $J_C(\underline{X}) \neq \emptyset$ and let $BRAN_C(\underline{X}) = \{(W_i, \underline{X}^i)\}_{i=1}^m$. We define $J_C'(\underline{X})$ as the set of all jds that can be constructed from $BRAN_C(\underline{X})$, i.e., $J_C'(\underline{X}) = \{*[\underline{X} \cup \{X_1W_1,\ldots, X_mW_m\}] \mid X_i \in X^i\}$. That is, an element of $J_C'(\underline{X})$ is obtained by attaching each W_i to some element of $\underline{X}^i$ and adding $\underline{X}$ to ensure that the collection of X-stems is indeed $\underline{X}$.

Proposition 9

Assume that $J_C(\underline{X})$ is not empty. Then

a) $J_C'(\underline{X}) \subseteq J_C(\underline{X})$

b) If $*[\underline{S}] \in J_C(\underline{X})$ then there exists some $*[\underline{R}]$ in $J_C'(\underline{X})$ such that $\underline{S} \geq \underline{R}$.

Proof: a) Let $*[\underline{R}]$ be in $J_C'(\underline{X})$. By the definition of $BRAN_C(\underline{X})$ and Theorem 4, $C \models X_i \twoheadrightarrow W_i$ for all i. Now $ST_X(\underline{R}) = \underline{X}$ and since $J_C(\underline{X})$ is not empty, using Theorem 4 again we obtain that $C \models *[\underline{X}]$. Now, using Theorem 4 in the opposite direction, we obtain $C \models *[\underline{R}]$.

b) Let $*[\underline{S}]$ be in $J_C(\underline{X})$. As in the proof of the previous proposition, we can refine the X-branches of $*[\underline{S}]$ to be elements of $DEP_C(X)$. We thus obtain a jd $*[\underline{R}]$ in $J_C'(\underline{X})$ and obviously $\underline{S} \geq \underline{R}$. □

We now consider what happens to the branch basis when some elements are removed from $\underline{X}$ without changing its attribute set.

Proposition 10

Let $\underline{Z} \subseteq \underline{X}$ such that $ATTR(\underline{Z}) = ATTR(\underline{X}) = X$. If $J_C(\underline{X}) \neq \emptyset$ then $BRAN_C(\underline{Z}) = \{W_i, \underline{X}^i \cap \underline{Z}) \mid (W_i, \underline{X}^i) \in BRAN_C(\underline{X})\}$.

Proof: By Theorem 4 and rule JD1, for Z_i in $\underline{Z}$ and W_j in $DEP_C(X)$ there is a jd in $J_C(\underline{Z})$ containing (Z_i, W_j) as a member if and only if $C \models Z_i \twoheadrightarrow W_j$ if and only if there is a jd in $J_C(\underline{X})$ containing that member. The claim follows. □

Corollary 6

Assume that $J_C(\underline{X})$ is not empty and let $BRAN_C(\underline{X}) = \{(W_i, \underline{X}^i)\}_{i=1}^m$. Then $X_i \in \underline{X}^i$ if and only if $W_i \in DEP(X_i)$. □

Note that it is quite possible that $J_C(\underline{X})$ is empty even though $DEP_C(X_i)$ is not empty for each X_i in $\underline{X}$. Compare this to Theorem 4.

BRANCH COMPLETENESS OF THE RULES

In this section we show that our rules are sufficient for deriving all information about branches of jds implied by any given set of fds and total jds. In particular, they allow us to derive all fds and fohds implied by such a set. This result will be proved using three distinct approaches. Each one of these approaches allows us to gain some understanding of the structure of the jds from a specific viewpoint and we feel that it is instructive to study each one of them. In this section we present one proof. The other two approaches require the use of tableaux and the chase and will be presented in the section, TABLEAUX AND THE CHASE.

In the following, all jds are assumed to be total.

The Branch Completeness Theorems

Let Γ be a formal system, i.e., a set of axioms and inference rules, and let α and β be families of dependencies. We say that Γ is (α,β)-*complete* if, for every set C of dependencies of family α, every constraint of family β that is implied by C can be derived from C using Γ. This is an extension of the concept of completeness defined in the section INTEGRITY CONSTRAINTS, which is essentially (α,α)-completeness.

Let Γ be the set of JD rules of the subsection A System for Total Join Dependencies and let Φ be the union of Γ, the FD rules of the section INTEGRITY CONSTRAINTS and the mixed rules of the subsection Mixed Rules. We denote by JD the family of jds, by FOHD the family of fohds and by FD the family of fds. (Mvds are considered as a special case of fohds). The notation $\alpha+\beta$ denotes the union of the families α and β. We can now state our first completeness theorem.

<u>Theorem 5</u> (First FOHD completeness theorem)

The set Γ is (JD, FOHD)-complete.

We will prove the theorem in the following sections. We proceed here to examine corollaries and generalizations. Our first goal is the inclusion of the FD family. For an fd $f: X \to A$, let us denote by $\bar{f}$ the binary jd $*[XA,X\bar{A}]$. For a set F of fds, $\bar{F} = \{\bar{f} \mid f \in F\}$.

<u>Lemma 2</u>

Let F be a set of fds, J be a set of jds and $*[\underline{R}]$ be an fohd. Then $F \cup J \models *[\underline{R}]$ if and only if $\bar{F} \cup J \models *[\underline{R}]$. □

A similar claim is proved in Beeri [1977] for the case that J contains only mvds and $*[\underline{R}]$ is also an mvd. Actually, the claim is valid even if $*[\underline{R}]$ is not an fohd, but a proof of that is outside the scope of the chapter. We will prove the lemma in the end of this section.

Corollary 7 (Second FOHD completeness theorem)

The set Φ is (FD+JD, FOHD)-complete.

Proof: Let F be a set of fds and let J be a set of jds. By Lemma 3, for an fohd $*[\underline{R}]$, $F \cup J \models *[\underline{R}]$ if and only if $\bar{F} \cup J \models *[\underline{R}]$. However, each f in F derives $\bar{f}$ in $\bar{F}$ by the translation rule FD-JD1 which is in Φ. That is $F \cup J \vdash_{\Phi} \bar{F} \cup J$. Also, by Theorem 5, $\bar{F} \cup J \models *[\underline{R}]$ implies $\bar{F} \cup J \vdash_{\Phi} *[\underline{R}]$. Thus, $F \cup J \models_{\Phi} *[\underline{R}]$. □

Corollary 8

The set Φ is (FD+JD, FD+FOHD)-complete.

Proof: It suffices to prove that Φ is (FD+JD, FD)-complete. That is, for every set C of fds and jds and for every fd f, if $C \models f$ then $C \vdash_{\Phi} f$.

Without loss of generality, assume that f is the fd $X \to A$, $A \notin X$. If $C \models X \to A$, then by rule FD-JD1, $C \models *[XA, X\bar{A}]$ and by the previous corollary, $C \vdash_{\Phi} *[XA, X\bar{A}]$. Now, this jd has $\{A\}$ as one of its X-branches and X is the corresponding X-stem. Therefore, it suffices to show that C contains an fd $S \to A$, $A \notin S$. For if C contains such an fd, then an application of rule FD-JD2 yields the desired fd $X \to A$. That C contains such an fd will be proved in the next section. □

Corollary 9

(a) Let C be a set of jds and let $*[\underline{R}]$ be an fohd. Then $C \models *[\underline{R}]$ if and only if $C \vdash_{\Gamma} *[\underline{R}]$.

(b) Let C be a set of fds and jds and let d be an fd or an fohd. Then $C \models d$ if and only if $C \vdash_{\Phi} d$.

Proof: The only if direction is a rephrasing of the completeness theorems. The if direction follows from the soundness of the rules. □

The rules above imply more than completeness of our rules for deriving fds and fohds. Let $\underline{X}$ be an asc, $ATTR(\underline{X}) = X$. By Theorem 4 and the results of the section THE BRANCH BASIS, a set W is an X-branch of a jd in $J_C(\underline{X})$ with X-stem X_i if and only if W is the right side of an mvd with left side X_i. Thus, the derivation of X-branches of jds is a special case of the derivation of X-branches of fohds. In a sense, we may therefore claim that our rules are *branch complete* for jds, that is, they can be used to derive all information about X-branches and how they can be attached to X-stems, for jds implied by a given set C.

Corollary 10 (Branch completeness theorem)

Let C be a set of fds and jds and let X be a set. For a jd $*[\underline{R}]$, $C \models *[\underline{R}]$ if and only if $C \models *[ST_X(\underline{R})]$ and $C \vdash_\Phi \{ST_X(R_i) \twoheadrightarrow BR_X(R_i) \mid R_i \in R\}$.

Proof: The claim is an immediate result of Theorem 4 and the FOHD completeness theorems. Note that by Theorem 2, $C \models *[ST_X(\underline{R})]$ if and only if $J_C(ST_X(\underline{R})) \neq \emptyset$.

The First Approach — a Counter-Example Relation

The first approach to proving completeness is to show that if $C \not\vdash_\Gamma c$ then $C \not\models c$, where C and c are from the appropriate families. This is done by providing a counterexample relation I such that $I \in SAT(C)$ but $I \notin SAT(c)$. This method is used in Beeri, Fagin and Howard [1977] to prove (FD+MVD, FD+MVD)-completeness. We will show below how the proof can be extended to cover jds as well. Since the extension is quite straightforward, the presentation will be brief.

For a given set X, consider the collection $D_C^\Gamma(X)$

$$D_C^\Gamma(X) = \{Y \mid Y \text{ is an X-branch of an fohd } *[\underline{R}],\ MANY(\underline{R}) = X, \text{ such that } C \vdash_\Gamma *[\underline{R}]\}.$$

This collection is closed under union and intersection, by rules JD1 and JD4, and it covers $\bar{X}$ since $C \vdash *[X,U]$. Denote by $DEP_C^\Gamma(X)$ the collection of nonempty minimal sets in $D_C^\Gamma(X)$. $DEP_C^\Gamma(X)$ has the same properties as $DEP_C(X)$ defined previously. The only difference is that the definition here uses $\vdash_\Gamma$ instead of $\models$. Thus, it can be seen easily that $DEP_C^\Gamma(X)$ is a partition of $\bar{X}$, and that, for $Y \neq \emptyset$, $Y \in D_C^\Gamma(X)$ if and only if Y is a union of elements of $DEP_C^\Gamma(X)$. It follows that $C \vdash_\Gamma *[XY_1,\ldots,XY_m]$ if and only if each Y_i is such a union. In particular, let $DEP_C^\Gamma(X) = \{W_1,\ldots,W_k\}$; then $C \vdash_\Gamma *[XW_1,\ldots,XW_k]$.

Let now $*[\underline{R}] = *[XY_1,\ldots,XY_m]$ be an fohd such that $C \not\vdash_\Gamma *[\underline{R}]$. Then for some Y_i and some $W \in BRAN_C^\Gamma(X)$, $Y_i \cap W$ is a proper nonempty subset of W. Let I_W be a relation containing two tuples t_1 and t_2 that agree on $\bar{W}$ and disagree on W. We claim that $I_W \in SAT(C)$ and $I_W \notin SAT(*[\underline{R}])$. That $I_W \notin SAT(*[\underline{R}])$ is obvious since it does not contain the tuple t that agrees with t_1 on XY_i and with t_2 on $X\bar{Y}_i$. It remains to prove that $I_W \in SAT(\bar{C})$.

Let $*[\underline{S}]$ be a jd in C and let $t \in m_{\underline{S}}(I_W)$. That is, for each $S_i \in \underline{S}$ there is a row t_i in I_W, such that $t[S_i] = t_i[S_i]$. Now, each t_i is either t_1 or t_2. Let $\underline{Q} = \{\bigcup_{t_i=t_1} S_i, \bigcup_{t_i=t_2} S_i\} = \{Q_1, Q_2\}$. Clearly $t \in m_{\underline{Q}}(I_W)$, and $t[Q_1] = t_1[Q_1]$, $t[Q_2] = t_2[Q_2]$. It follows that $Q_1 \cap Q_2 \subseteq \bar{W}$, since t_1 and t_2 do not agree on any attribute of W. By the intersection rule, $W \cap Q_1$ and $W \cap Q_2$ are in $D_C^{\Gamma}(X)$. Hence, by the minimality of W, either $W \subseteq Q_1$ or $W \subseteq Q_2$. In either case $t \in I_W$, so $I_W \in SAT(*[\underline{S}])$.

The proof above can be generalized easily to include fds in C (Corollary 7), or to derive fds from C (Corollaries 8 and 9). If C contains fds, it can be easily shown that I_W above satisfies these fds. If we are given an fd $X \to A$ such that $C \not\models X \to A$, we choose $W = \{A\}$ and proceed as above. □

We conclude this section by showing how Lemma 2 can be proved using this approach.

Proof of Lemma 2:

Let $C = F \cup J$ and $\bar{C} = \bar{F} \cup J$. Assume that for an fohd $*[\underline{R}]$, $\bar{C} \not\models *[\underline{R}]$. We show that $C \not\models *[\underline{R}]$.

Let $*[\underline{R}] = *[XY_1,\ldots,XY_m]$. Since $\bar{C} \not\models *[\underline{R}]$, for some Y_i and some $V \in DEP_{\bar{C}}(X)$, $Y_i \cap V$ is a nonempty proper subset of V. Construct the two tuple relation I_V. Using the same proofs as above, we can show that $I_V \in SAT(\bar{C})$ but $I_V \notin SAT(*[\underline{R}])$. It suffices to show that $I_V \in SAT(C)$ also holds.

Clearly, each jd in C is also in $\bar{C}$, hence is satisfied in I_V. Let $S \to A \in C$. If $S \cap V \neq \emptyset$ or $S \subseteq \bar{V}$ and $A \in \bar{V}$ then $S \to A$ is satisfied in I_V, so assume $S \subseteq \bar{V}$ and $A \in V$. Now, $*[SA, S\bar{A}]$ is in $\bar{C}$. Also, by the properties of $DEP_{\bar{C}}(X)$, $\bar{C} \models *[XV, X\bar{V}]$. By applying JD4 to the $\bar{V}$-stems and $\bar{V}$-branches of these jds, we obtain that $\bar{C} \models *[X(V \cap \{A\}), X(V \cap \bar{A}), X\bar{V}]$. This contradicts the fact that $V \in DEP_{\bar{C}}(X)$ and V contains at least two elements. Hence $S \subseteq \bar{V}$ and $A \in V$ is impossible.

It follows that I_V satisfies C. Since it does not satisfy $*[\underline{R}]$, $C \not\models *[\underline{R}]$. We have proved the only if direction of the lemma. The if direction is obvious, since $C \models \bar{C}$. □

TABLEAUX AND THE CHASE

In this section we present two additional proofs of the branch completeness theorems. These proofs are important since they can be generalized easily to other types of dependencies. They also offer some insight about the problem of whether our system is complete for jds in general, though that problem is still open.

In the proofs we rely heavily on the concept of tableaux introduced in Aho, Sagiv and Ullman [1979] and the chase process of Maier, Mendelzon and Sagiv [1979]. Using these we will supply the missing proof of Theorem 2 — the completeness of the projection rule.

Tableaux

Relational expressions define mappings on sets of relations. Therefore, they can be used to specify retrieval queries where the result of the query is obtained by applying the expression to the given relation. Indeed, the relational algebra was introduced by Codd to serve as a retrieval language. Codd also introduced another query language, based on the predicate calculus (Codd [1972b]). Two formalizations of this language have been studied recently — the conjunctive queries of Chandra and Merlin [1977] and the tableaux of Aho, Sagiv and Ullman [1979]. We use tableaux in this paper.

Let us associate with each attribute A a set of variables, denoted by VAR(A). (For clarity, we will use the same letter for attributes and their variables. Thus, $VAR(A) = \{a,a_1,a_2,\ldots\}$, $VAR(B) = \{b,b_1,b_2,\ldots\}$, etc.) There is no essential difference between variables and values (except for the use we make of them), so we can have relations whose elements are variables instead of values from D. A *tableau* $\underline{T}$ is an ordered pair $\langle w_0,T\rangle$ where T is a relation with variables as elements and w_0 is an X-value (for some X) such that for each $A \in X$, $w_0[A] \in T[A]$, i.e., $w_0[A]$ appears in the A-column of T. The attribute set of $\underline{T}$ is X, $ATTR(\underline{T}) = X$. We call the variables that appear in w_0 *distinguished* and all the other variables in T *nondistinguished*. If T contains m rows, they will be denoted by $w_1,\ldots,w_m$. The row w_0 is called the *summary* of $\underline{T}$.

In this chapter, we will use the convention that distinguished variables are unsubcripted and the other variables are subscripted.

An *interpretation* is a mapping $\rho\colon \bigcup_{A\in U} VAR(A) \to D$ such that ρ maps VAR(A) into DOM(A) for each A. The mapping ρ is extended to tuples and relations in the obvious way, i.e., $\rho(A_1\ldots A_k) = \rho(A_1)\ldots\rho(A_k)$. Let $\underline{T} = \langle w_0,T\rangle$ be a tableau, $ATTR(\underline{T}) = X$. Then

$\underline{T}$ defines a mapping from relations on U to relations on X as follows:

$$\underline{T}(I) = \{\rho(w_0) \mid \rho \text{ is an interpretation and } \rho(T) \subseteq I\}$$

That is, $\underline{T}(I)$ is the set of images of the summary under every interpretation that maps every row of T to a row of I. Considered as a predicate calculus query, the variables of T are the variables used to express the query and the distinguished variables are the output variables of the query. It can be seen easily that the first and the third properties of project-join mappings hold for tableaux as well. The second property — idempotence — does not hold for general tableaux.

Clearly, it is the structure of $\underline{T}$ that determines the mapping and not the specific variables it uses. Thus, we have the following:

Lemma 3 (Aho, Sagiv and Ullman [1979])

Let $\underline{T} = \langle w_0, T\rangle$ be a tableau and let ψ be a one to one mapping from the set of variables into itself such that ψ: VAR(A) $\rightarrow$ VAR(A) for each A, then $\underline{T}$ and $\psi(\underline{T}) = \langle\psi(w_0), \psi(T)\rangle$ defines the same mapping. □

An effective method for testing containment and equivalence of tableaux was presented in Chandra and Merlin [1977] and in Aho, Sagiv and Ullman [1979]. Let $\underline{T}^1 = \langle w_0^1, T^1\rangle$ and $\underline{T}^2 = \langle w_0^2, T^2\rangle$ be tableaux, ATTR($\underline{T}^1$) = ATTR($\underline{T}^2$). A *containment mapping* from $\underline{T}^1$ to $\underline{T}^2$ is a mapping ρ from the variables of $\underline{T}^1$ to the variables of $\underline{T}^2$ such that

(a) $\rho(w_0^1) = w_0^2$

(b) $\rho(T^1) \subseteq T^2$

Note that if τ is an interpretation of the variables of T^2, then $\tau \circ \rho$ is an interpretation of the variables of T^1, and $\tau(w_0^2) = \tau \circ \rho(w_0^1)$. This proves one direction of the following lemma. For a full proof, see Aho, Sagiv and Ullman [1979].

Lemma 4

For tableaux $\underline{T}^1$ and $\underline{T}^2$ such that ATTR($\underline{T}^1$) = ATTR($\underline{T}^2$), $\underline{T}^2 \le \underline{T}^1$ if and only if there exists a containment mapping from $\underline{T}^1$ to $\underline{T}^2$. (Note the reversal of the order.) □

In Aho, Sagiv and Ullman [1979] it is shown how one can construct for any rre E a tableau $\underline{T}$ such that for any relation I, $\underline{T}(I) = E(I)$. We say that $\underline{T}$ *represents* E. We describe now this construction. For a proof of its correctness refer to the paper above.

Consider first the identity operator $\underline{1}_X$. The tableau that represents $\underline{1}_X$ is $\underline{T}_X$ = <w[X],w>, where w is an arbitrary tuple of variables. Next, let us consider the projection operator. Let $\underline{T}_E = \langle w_0, T_E\rangle$ be the tableau of some relational expression E, $ATTR(\underline{T}_E) = X$ and let Y be a subset of X. The tableau $\underline{T}$ for $\pi_Y \circ E$ is $\langle w_0[Y], T_E\rangle$. That is, we omit from the summary row the values for the attributes of X-Y. The relation T_E is not changed; however, some variables in it change their status from distinguished to nondistinguished. (Recall that a variable is distinguished if it appears in the summary.)

Next, let us consider the join. For simplicity, assume we have $\underline{T}_1 = \langle w_0^1, T_1\rangle$ and $\underline{T}_2 = \langle w_0^2, T_2\rangle$, where $\underline{T}_i$ represents E_i and $ATTR(\underline{T}_i) = X_i$, i = 1,2. Without loss of generality we assume that $w_0^1[X_1 \cap X_2] = w_0^2[X_1 \cap X_2]$ but all other values in the two tableaux are distinct. The tableau $\underline{T}$ that represents $E_1 * E_2$ is $\langle w_0, T_1 \cup T_2\rangle$, where w_0 is obtained by pasting (i.e., joining) w_0^1 and w_0^2 together. (This is why they need to have the same values on the common attributes.) $T_1 \cup T_2$ is the union of T_1 and T_2 , that is, it contains the rows of both T_1 and T_2.

Now, let $\underline{T}_E = \langle w_0^E, T_E\rangle$ represent the rre E and let $\underline{R}$ be an asc, $ATTR(\underline{R}) = R \subseteq ATTR(E)$. The tableau $\underline{T} = \langle w_0, T\rangle$ for $m_{\underline{R}} \circ E$ is constructed as follows. We first construct the tableau $\langle w_0^E[R_i], T_E\rangle$ for $\pi_{R_i} \circ E$, for each $R_i \in \underline{R}$. Then we perform the "join" of these tableaux as described above. That is, in the tableau for $\pi_{R_i} \circ E$, we replace all the variables, except those of $w_0^E[R_i]$, by new variables, not used in the tableau of $\pi_{R_j} \circ E$ for any $j \neq i$. Let the result be $\langle w_0^E[R_i], T_i\rangle$. The tableau I is $\langle w_0^E[R], \bigcup_i T_i\rangle$, since $*_i\, w_0^E[R_i] = w_0^E[R]$.

Example 4 Let U = {A,B,C,D}, $\underline{S}_1$ = {AB, ACD}, $\underline{S}_2$ = {BC, ABD}. The tableaux $\underline{T}_{AB}$, $\underline{T}_{\underline{S}_1}$ and $\underline{T}_{\underline{S}_2} \circ \underline{T}_{\underline{S}_1}$ are presented below.

$\underline{T}_{AB}$ =

	A	B	C	D
ω_0	a	b		
	a	b	c_1	d_1

, $\underline{T}_{\underline{S}_1}$ =

	A	B	C	D
w_0	a	b	c	d
	a	b	c_1	d_1
	a	b_1	c	d

$T_{\underline{S}_2} \circ T_{\underline{S}_1} =$

	A	B	C	D	
w_0	a	b	c	d	
	a_1	b	c_1	d_1	Copy for BC
	a_1	b_1	c	d_2	
	a	b	c_2	d_3	Copy for ABD
	a	b_2	c_3	d	

We now describe in detail the construction of a tableau that represents a project-join expression.

Let $R = \{R_1,\ldots,R_k\}$, $ATTR(\underline{R}) = R$. A tableau $\underline{T}_{\underline{R}} = \langle w_0, T_{\underline{R}}\rangle$ such that $\underline{T}_{\underline{R}}$ represents $m_{\underline{R}}$ is constructed as follows: w_0 is an arbitrary variable R-value. $T_{\underline{R}}$ consists of k tuples $w_1,\ldots,w_k$ such that $w_i[R_i] = w_0[R_i]$ and $w_i[A]$ is a variable which has a unique occurrence in $T_{\underline{R}}$, for any $A \in R_i$. That is, w_i and w_j agree exactly on $R_i \cap R_j$ and disagree elsewhere. As an example, refer to $T_{\underline{S}_1}$ in Example 4.

Consider now the following problem. Given a tableau $\underline{T} = \langle w,T\rangle$, under what condition is $\underline{T}$ a tableau which represents some project-join expression $m_{\underline{R}}$? Let us examine $T_{\underline{R}} = \langle w_0, T_R\rangle$. First notice that in any attribute A, there is at most one variable which appears more than once in the corresponding column of T_R , i.e., for $w_i, w_j, w_k, w_\ell \in T$, $i \neq j$, $k \neq \ell$, if $w_i[A] = w_j[A]$ and $w_k[A] = w_\ell[A]$ then $w_i[A] = w_k[A]$. Such a variable is called a repeated variable, REP(A). A variable relation A, having the property that for any attribute A, REP(A) is either undefined or unique is called a *simple variable relation*. Furthermore, in $\underline{T}_{\underline{R}}$ if REP(A) is defined then $w_0[A] = REP(A)$. Finally we have that $w_0[R_i] = w_i[R_i]$. Thus we get:

<u>Fact</u>. Let $\underline{T} = \langle w,T\rangle$ be a tableau. Then $\underline{T}$ represents a project-join mapping if and only if T is a simple variable relation and, for each A such that REP(A) is defined, $w[A] = REP(A)$. If $\underline{T}$ satisfies this condition and $T = \{w_1,\ldots,w_k\}$, then the project-join mapping of $\underline{T}$ is $m_{\underline{R}}$, where $\underline{R} = \{R_1,\ldots,R_k\}$, $R_i = \{A \mid w_i[A] = w[A]\}$.

The Chase

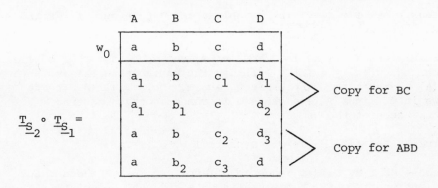

The chase is a process by which a relation is "forced" to satisfy a given set of dependencies. Though it is applicable to any relation, it is useful (and meaningful) especially when applied to tableaux. Let $\underline{T} = \langle w_0, T\rangle$ be a tableau and C be a set of fds and *total* jds. The following rules are used.

F-rule: Let $X \to A$ be in C and let w_i and w_j be two rows of T such that $w_i[X] = w_j[X]$. Identify the variables $w_i[A]$ and $w_j[A]$ whenever they appear in w_0 and T. Delete all duplicate rows in T (since T is a set and it cannot contain several occurrences of the same row).

J-rule: Let $*[\underline{R}]$ be in C. Replace T by $m_{\underline{R}}(T)$.

A *chase* of $\underline{T}$ by C is a sequence of applications of these rules to $\underline{T}$, in any order, until a tableau is obtained that cannot be changed by applying any of the rules. Obviously, a relation cannot be changed by the rules if and only if it satisfies C. It is proved in Maier, Mendelzon and Sagiv [1979] that every chase of $\underline{T}$ by C terminates and the result is unique, up to a renaming of variables. For simplicity, we will henceforth assume that, when two variables are equated, the larger subscript is replaced by the smaller subscript. An unsubscripted variable will be regarded as having the smallest subscript. Under this assumption, the row w_0 is not affected by the chase and this result is stated as follows.

Theorem 6

All chases of $\underline{T}$ by C terminate and yield a unique result $chase_C(\underline{T}) = \langle w_0, chase_C(T)\rangle$. The relation $chase_C(T)$ satisfies C. □

The following theorem is an extended version of the main result of Maier, Mendelzon and Sagiv [1979].

Theorem 7

Let C be a set of fds and total jds.

(a) If $*[\underline{R}] = *[R_1,\ldots,R_k]$ is a jd (not necessarily total), $\underline{T}_{\underline{R}} = \langle w_0, T_{\underline{R}}\rangle$, then $C \models *[\underline{R}]$ if and only if for some $w_0' \in chase_C(T_{\underline{R}})$, $w_0 = w_0'[ATTR(\underline{R})]$.

(b) For a set X, let T_X be a relation (of variables) consisting of two rows that agree on the attributes of X and disagree elsewhere. Then $C \models X \to A$ if and only if $chase_C(T_X)$ contains a single value in its A-column.

Proof: A proof of part (b) can be found in Maier et al. [1979]. Part (a) is proved there for the case that $\underline{R}$ is total. We present here an outline of the proof for the general case.
(if) Let I be a relation satisfying C and suppose that I contains

rows $r_1,\ldots,r_k$ such that r_i and r_j agree on $R_i \cap R_j$. Let $T_{\underline{R}} = \{w_1,\ldots,w_k\}$. Define an interpretation for the variables of $T_{\underline{R}}$ by $\rho(w_i[A]) = r_i[A]$. The compatibility conditions that the rows $r_1,\ldots,r_k$ are assumed to satisfy guarantee that ρ is well defined. Obviously, ρ maps row w_i of T_R onto row r_i of I. Since the chase does not introduce new values, ρ is defined on $chase_C(T_{\underline{R}})$. We claim that ρ maps each row of $chase_C(T_{\underline{R}})$ to a row of I. The proof of the claim is by induction on the number of steps in the case. For details, see Maier et al. [1979].

Now, the row w_0 is $w_0'[ATTR(\underline{R})]$ for some $w_0' \in chase_C(T_{\underline{R}})$. It follows that for the row $r_0 = \rho(w_0')$ in I, $r_0[ATTR(\underline{R})] = \rho(w_0)$. Since w_0 agrees with the row w_i of $T_{\underline{R}}$ on R_i, $\rho(w_0) = r_0[ATTR(\underline{R})]$ agrees with $\rho(w_i) = r_i$ on R_i. Thus the row in $T_{\underline{R}}(I)$ that is generated by the interpretation ρ is in $\pi_{ATTR(\underline{R})}(I)$. Since $r_1,\ldots,r_k$ were arbitrary rows of I that satisfy the compatibility conditions needed to generate a row of $T_{\underline{R}}(I)$, it follows that $m_{\underline{R}}(I) = T_{\underline{R}}(I) \subseteq \pi_{ATTR(\underline{R})}(I)$. Since inclusion in the other direction always holds, I satisfies $*[\underline{R}]$.

(only if) Assume that $w_0 \notin \pi_{ATTR(\underline{R})}(chase_C(T_{\underline{R}}))$. Then $chase_C(T_{\underline{R}})$ is in SAT(C) but not in SAT($*[\underline{R}]$), hence $C \not\models *[\underline{R}]$. □

We can now prove Theorem 2.

Proof (of Theorem 2):

Consider the tableau $\underline{T}_{\underline{R}} = \langle w_0, T_{\underline{R}}\rangle$. Since $C \models *[\underline{R}]$, we have by Theorem 1 that $w_0 \in (chase_C(T_{\underline{R}}))[ATTR(\underline{R})]$. Choose a tuple w in $chase_C(T_{\underline{R}})$ such that $w[ATTR(\underline{R})] = w_0$. Obviously, $\langle w, T_{\underline{R}}\rangle$ is the tableau of some total jd $*[\underline{Q}]$. Further, since $w \in chase_C(T_{\underline{R}})$, $C \models *[\underline{Q}]$. Now, $\langle w, T_{\underline{R}}\rangle$ is obtained from $\langle w_0, T_{\underline{R}}\rangle$ simply by changing one nondistinguished variable to a distinguished variable in each column of $ATTR(\underline{R})$. Since in these columns each variable appears only once, that means that $\underline{Q}$ is obtained from $\underline{R}$ by adding each attirubte of $ATTR(\underline{R})$ to exactly one set of $\underline{R}$. Thus $R = Q \cap ATTR(\underline{R})$ and $*[\underline{R}]$ is obtained from $*[\underline{Q}]$ by EJD2. □

We can now also prove that a set C implies an fd only if it contains an fd with the same right side.

Corollary 11

If $C \models X \rightarrow A$, where C is a set of fds and total jds then C contains an fd $S \rightarrow A$ where A is not in S.

Proof: If $C \models X \to A$ then $chase_C(T_X)$ contains a single value in its A-column. Since T_X contains two distinct values in this column, this is possible only if the values in this column are equated by applying some fd $S \to A$ from C. □

From now on we deal only with total project-join mappings. Hence, the associated tableaux have summaries that are defined on U.

The Second Approach — The Chase as a Test for Containment Mapping

The key to our second proof is the next proposition that relates the concepts of implication and containment mapping.

Proposition 10

Let C be a set of total jds and let $*[\underline{R}]$ be a total jd. Then $C \models *[\underline{R}]$ if and only if either $*[\underline{R}]$ is a trivial jd or there is a sequence $*[\underline{S}_1],\ldots,*[\underline{S}_n]$ of jds from C (not necessarily distinct) such that $m_{\underline{S}_n} \circ \cdots \circ m_{\underline{S}_1} \geq m_{\underline{R}}$.

Proof: (if) That C implies every trivial jd is obvious, so assume $*[\underline{R}]$ is nontrivial. Let I be a relation in SAT(C). Since $m_{\underline{S}_n} \circ \ldots \circ m_{\underline{S}_1}(I) = I$, it follows that $m_{\underline{R}}(I) \subseteq I$. Thus $I \in SAT(*[\underline{R}])$ and $C \models *[\underline{R}]$.

(only if) Let $\underline{T}_{\underline{R}} = \langle w_0, T_{\underline{R}}\rangle$ and assume that $*[\underline{R}]$ is nontrivial, so $w_0 \notin T_{\underline{R}}$. However, $C \models *[\underline{R}]$ implies that $w_0 \in chase_C(T_{\underline{R}})$. Let $*[S_1]$, ..., $*[S_n]$ be the sequence of jds applied in the chase and let $\underline{T} = \langle w,T\rangle$ be the tableau of $m_{\underline{S}_n} \circ \cdots \circ m_{\underline{S}_1}$. Then $chase_C(T_{\underline{R}}) = m_{\underline{S}_n}(\ldots(m_{\underline{S}_1}(T_{\underline{R}})\ldots) = m_{\underline{S}_n} \circ \cdots \circ m_{\underline{S}_1}(T_{\underline{R}}) = \underline{T}(T_{\underline{R}})$. But $w_0 \in \underline{T}(T_{\underline{R}})$ means that there is a mapping $\rho: T \to T_{\underline{R}}$ such that $\rho(T) \subseteq T_{\underline{R}}$ and $\rho(w) = w_0$. This ρ is a containment mapping from $\underline{T}$ to $\underline{T}_{\underline{R}}$, hence $\underline{T}_{\underline{R}} \leq \underline{T}$, i.e., $m_{\underline{R}} \leq m_{\underline{S}_n} \circ \cdots \circ m_{\underline{S}_1}$. □

Note that if $*[\underline{R}]$ is trivial, then for every jd $*[\underline{S}]$, $m_{\underline{R}} \leq m_{\underline{S}}$. In particular, $m_{\underline{R}} \leq \underline{1}_U$. The mapping $\underline{I}_U$ can be viewed as a composition of 0 (zero) project-join mappings. Thus, we can express the proposition as follows: $C \models *[\underline{R}]$ if and only if $m_{\underline{R}}$ is covered by a composition of $n \geq 0$ project-join mappings corresponding to jds in C. We use this form below.

The following lemma provides a further simplification of the proof. For an asc $\underline{S}$ and a set X, denote by $\underline{S} \cup X$ the asc $\{S \cup X \mid S \in \underline{S}\}$. For a set C of jds, denote by C_X the set of jds $\{*[\underline{S} \cup X] \mid *[\underline{S}] \in C\}$.

Lemma 5

Let C be a set of jds and let $*[\underline{R}]$ be an fohd, MANY($\underline{R}$) = X. Then $C \models *[\underline{R}]$ if and only if $C_X \models *[\underline{R}]$.

Proof: (if) This direction follows immediately from the fact that $C \models C_X$.
(only if) Let $\underline{T}_{\underline{R}} = \langle w_0, T_{\underline{R}} \rangle$. By the assumption about $\underline{R}$, $T_{\underline{R}}$ contains a single X-value, that is, $T_{\underline{R}}[X] = \{w_0[X]\}$. Since the chase does not introduce new values, this is also true for $\text{chase}_C(T_{\underline{R}})$ and $(\text{chase}_C(T_{\underline{R}}))[X] = \{w_0[X]\}$.

Consider now the application of a jd $*[\underline{S}]$ in C to an intermediate relation during the chase. If this application adds a row w, then for some set of rows $\{w_j\}$ that are already in the relation, $w[S_j] = w_j[S_j]$ for each $S_j \in \underline{S}$. However, w and $\{w_j\}$ all agree on X, so $w[XS_j] = w_j[XS_j]$. It follows that the applications of $*[\underline{S}]$ or of $*[\underline{S} \cup X]$ to the relation add the same rows. By induction on the length of the chase we obtain $\text{chase}_C(T_{\underline{R}}) = \text{chase}_{C_X}(T_{\underline{R}})$.

Now, by Theorem 7, $C \models *[\underline{R}]$ if and only if $w_0 \in \text{chase}_C(T_{\underline{R}})$, and similarly for C_X. The claim follows. □

Proof (of the FOHD Completeness Theorem): Let C be a set of total jds and let $*[\underline{R}]$ be a total fohd, MANY($\underline{R}$) = X. Assume that $C \models *[\underline{R}]$. Then $m_{\underline{R}}$ is covered by the composition of $n \geq 0$ project-join mappings corresponding to jds in C. We prove that $C \vdash_T *[\underline{R}]$ by induction on n.

Basis (n = 0). In this case $*[\underline{R}]$ is trivial and $C \vdash_T *[\underline{R}]$ by Proposition 1 of the subsection The Rule of Covering.

Induction. Let $\underline{T} = \langle w,T \rangle$ represent $m_{\underline{S}_n} \circ \cdots \circ m_{\underline{S}_1}$, and let $\underline{T}' = \langle w',T' \rangle$ represent $m_{\underline{S}_{n-1}} \circ \cdots \circ m_{\underline{S}_1}$. (If n-1 = 0, then $T' = \langle w',\{w'\} \rangle$ the tableau of $\underline{1}_U$.) Let $\underline{S}_n = \{S_1,\ldots,S_k\}$. By the construction of tableaux as described in the previous section, T is the union of k isomorphic copies of T', $\psi_1(T'),\ldots,\psi_k(T')$, such that ψ_i and ψ_j agree on $w'[S_i \cap S_j]$ and disagree elsewhere. The summary w is the join of the rows $\{\psi_i(w'[S_i])\}$.

By Proposition 10, there exists a containment mapping $\rho: \underline{T} \to \underline{T}_{\underline{R}}$, i.e., $\rho(T) \subseteq T_{\underline{R}}$ and $\rho(u) = w_0$. Denote by $\underline{T}_i$ the tableau $\langle \rho \circ \psi_i(w'), \rho \circ \psi_i(T') \rangle = \langle w_i, T_i \rangle$. Note that even though $\{\psi_i(T')\}$ are pairwise disjoint subsets of T, their images are not necessarily disjoint. It can be verified easily that $\underline{T}_i$ is the tableau of a project-join mapping (cf. the subsection Tableaux), which we denote by $m_{\underline{P}_i}$. Further, since T_i is a subset of $T_{\underline{R}}$, any two rows of T_i agree on X and disagree elsewhere. It follows that if $|T_i| = 1$ then $\underline{P}_i = \{U\}$ and if $|T_i| > 1$ then $*[\underline{P}_i]$ is an fohd such that $\text{MANY}(\underline{P}_i) = X$. We now proceed to show that $C \vdash_\Gamma *[\underline{P}_i]$ for all i and that $\{*[\underline{P}_i]\}_i \cup \{*[\underline{S}_n]\} \vdash_\Gamma *[\underline{R}]$.

To prove the first claim, we observe that $\rho \circ \psi_i$ is a containment mapping from $\underline{T}'$ to $\underline{T}_i$. Since $\underline{T}'$ represents $m_{\underline{S}_{n-1}} \circ \cdots \circ m_{\underline{S}_1}$, we have $m_{\underline{S}_{n-1}} \circ \cdots \circ m_{\underline{S}_1} \geq m_{\underline{P}_i}$ (where n-1 = 0 if and only if $*[\underline{P}_i]$ is trivial). The claim follows by Proposition 10 and the induction hypothesis.

Consider now the tableau of $m_{\underline{P}_i}$, $\underline{T}_i = \langle w_i, T_i \rangle = \langle \rho \circ \psi_i(w'), \rho \circ \psi_i(T') \rangle$. Even though $T_i \subseteq T_{\underline{R}}$, ρ is not a containment mapping from $\langle \psi_i(w'), \psi_i(T') \rangle$ to $\underline{T}_{\underline{R}}$. The reason is that $\rho \circ \psi_i(w') = w_i$ agrees with w_0, the summary of $\underline{T}_{\underline{R}}$, exactly on S_i.

Indeed, w, the summary of $\underline{T}$, agrees with $\psi_i(w')$ exactly on S_i; hence $w_0 = \rho(w)$ agrees with $\rho \circ \psi_i(w')$ exactly on S_i. Therefore $\langle w_i, T_i \rangle$ cannot be considered a "subtableau" of $\underline{T}_{\underline{R}}$. However, if we choose from each T_i only the S_i-columns, we can join this tableau to obtain a subtableau of $\underline{T}_{\underline{R}}$. Formally, the construction proceeds as follows.

By Lemma 5, we assume that $C = C_X$, so for each $S_i \in \underline{S}_n$, $X \subseteq S_i$. We can therefore project each $*[\underline{P}_i]$ on S_i. By repeated applications of JD2-3, we obtain $*[\underline{P}] = *[\bigcup_{i=1}^{k} (\underline{P}_i \cap S_i)]$ and $C \vdash_\Gamma *[\underline{P}]$.

Let $\underline{P}_i = P_i^j$. The set P_i^j corresponds to a row $w_i^j \in T_i \subseteq T_{\underline{R}}$. In this row, if $A \in P_i^j$, then w_i^j and w_i agree on A. If A is also in S_i, then w_i and w_0 agree on A, so $w_i^j[A]$ is distinguished in $\underline{T}_{\underline{R}}$. Now, if row w_i^j corresponds to $R_k \in \underline{R}$, then for every A such that $w_i^j[A]$ is distinguished in $\underline{T}_{\underline{R}}$, $A \in R_k$. It follows that $R_k \supseteq P_i^j \cap S_i$. Thus $\underline{R}$ covers $\underline{P} = \bigcup_i (\underline{P}_i \cap S_i)$, so $*[\underline{P}] \vdash_\Gamma *[\underline{R}]$, which concludes the proof. □

Example 4 (Continued)

Let R = {AB, AC, AD}. $*[\underline{R}]$ is an fohd, $\text{MANY}(\underline{R}) = \{A\}$ and let $C = \{*[\underline{S}_1], *[\underline{S}_2]\}$. It can be verified by computing $\text{chase}_C(T_{\underline{R}})$, that $C \models *[\underline{R}]$. In fact, the chase consists of the sequence $*[\underline{S}_1]$, $*[\underline{S}_2]$. We modify $\underline{S}_2$ to $\underline{S}_2' = \{ABC, ABD\}$. Now,

		A	B	C	D
$\underline{T}_{\underline{R}}$ =	w_0	a_0	b_0	c_0	d_0
	ε	a_0	b_0	c_1	d_1
	η	a_0	b_1	c_0	d_2
	θ	a_0	b_2	c_2	d_0

	A	B	C	D
$\underline{T}' = \underline{T}_{\underline{S}_i} = w'$	a'	b'	c'	d'
	a'	b'	c_1'	d'_1
	a'	b_1'	c'	d'

(We have changed the notation in $\underline{T}_{\underline{S}_1}$ to conform to the notation used in the proof.)

		A	B	C	D	
$\underline{T} = \underline{T}_{\underline{S}_2'} \circ \underline{T}_{\underline{S}_1}$ =	w	a	b	c	d	
	α	a	b	c_3	d_3	copy for ABC
	β	a	b_3	c	d_4	
	γ	a	b	c_4	d_5	copy for ABD
	δ	a	b_4	c_5	d	

(Compare the first column here to the first column of $\underline{T}_{\underline{S}_2} \circ \underline{T}_{\underline{S}_1}$.) The reader can verify that there exists a map ρ such that $\rho(w) = w_0$, $\rho(\alpha) = \rho(\gamma) = \varepsilon$, $\rho(\beta) = \eta$ and $\rho(\delta) = \theta$. The tableau for $\underline{P}_1$ is obtained from $\{\alpha,\beta\}$ by adding the summary row (a_0,b_0,c_0,d_2) and $\underline{T}_{\underline{P}_2}$ is obtained from $\{\gamma,\delta\}$ by adding the summary row (a_0,b_0,c_2,d_0). Thus $\underline{P}_1 = \underline{P}_2 = \{AB, ACD\} = \underline{S}_1$, and by projection $\underline{P}_1$ on ABC and $\underline{P}_2$ on ABD we obtain $\underline{P} = \{AB, AC, AD\} = R$. □

The Third Approach — Assigning Meaning to Tuples

Up to now we have not payed much attention to the meaning of the tuples generated in the chase. It turns out, however, that some of these tuples can be viewed as representing jds; as a matter of fact, we used this meaning implicitly in the proof of Theorem 2.

We consider the case that C contains only jds. Let $\underline{R} = \{R_1,\ldots,R_k\}$ be an asc, MANY($\underline{R}$) = X, and let $\underline{T}_{\underline{R}} = \langle w_0, T_{\underline{R}}\rangle$. The relation $T_{\underline{R}}$ has k rows, where row w_i corresponds to R_i. For an attribute A, the A-column of $T_{\underline{R}}$ contains distinct variables, each appearing exactly once, if $A \in \overline{X}$. If $A \in X$, then the A-column contains exactly one variable that appears more than once.

We have already considered the requirements that a row w needs to satisfy in order that $\langle w, T_{\underline{R}}\rangle$ be a tableau of a project-join mapping. These are, first, that only variables of $T_{\underline{R}}$ appear in w, and, second, that for $A \in X$, w[A] is the unique variable in $T_{\underline{R}}[A]$ that appears more than once. Let us denote the X-value consisting of these variables that appear more than once by x_0.

Now, let w be such a row, i.e., $w[X] = x_0$, and let $\langle w, T_{\underline{R}}\rangle$ represent $m_{\underline{S}}$. Since $T_{\underline{R}}$ has k rows, $\underline{S} = \{S_1,\ldots,D_k\}$. By the requirement that $w[X] = x_0$, $ST_X[R_i] = ST_X[S_i]$. Thus, $\underline{S}$ and $\underline{R}$, when regarded as sequences (of length k), must have the same subsequence of X-stems. (This is more restrictive than the set equality $ST_X(\underline{R}) = ST_X(\underline{S})$). The X-branches of $\underline{S}$ are not, however, constrained in any way. For $A \in \overline{X}$, A is in $BR_X(S_i)$ if and only if w[A] is taken from row w_i of $T_{\underline{R}}$, $w[A] = w_i[A]$.

By Theorem 2, $C \models *[\underline{R}]$ if and only if $w_0 \in \text{chase}_C(T_{\underline{R}})$. However, $\text{chase}_C(T_{\underline{R}})$ is independent of w_0. Thus, for any row w such that $\langle w, T_{\underline{R}}\rangle$ represents $m_{\underline{S}}$, $C \models *[\underline{S}]$ if and only if $w \in \text{chase}_C(T_{\underline{T}})$.

In summary

Proposition 11

Each row w in $\text{chase}_C(T_{\underline{R}})$ such that $w[X] = x_0$ represents a jd $\underline{S}_w$ that is implied by C. $\underline{S}_w = \{S_1,\ldots,S_k\}$, where $ST_X(S_i) = ST_X(R_i)$ and $BR_X(S_i) = \{A \in \overline{X} \mid w[A] = w_i[A]\}$. Distinct rows represent distinct jds. A jd $S = \{S_1,\ldots,S_k\}$ such that $ST_X(S_i) = ST_X(R_i)$ is implied by C if and only if it is S_w for some $w \in T_{\underline{R}}$. □

We now restrict our attention to the case that $*[\underline{R}]$ is an fohd, and prove the completeness theorem.

Proof (of the FOHD Completeness Theorem): Since $*[\underline{R}]$ is an fohd, $T_{\underline{R}}[X] = (\text{chase}_C(T_{\underline{R}}))[X] = \{x_0\}$, so that every row in $\text{chase}_C(T_{\underline{R}})$, including the original rows of $T_{\underline{R}}$, represents an fohd with MANY set X and the same number of X-branches as $*[\underline{R}]$, implied by C. Note that since empty X-branches are allowed, these rows actually represent all fohds with MANY set X that have the same number of X-branches as $*[\underline{R}]$ or less and are implied by C. We prove, using induction on the number of steps in the chase that each row in

$chase_C(T_{\underline{R}})$ represents an fohd derivable from C.

Basis (n = 0). In this case we consider one of the original rows of $T_{\underline{R}}$, say w_i. This row represents an fohd in which the X-branch $\bar{X}$ is attached to $X_i = X$, and the other X-stems (all equal to X) have empty X-branches. This fohd is simply $*[X,U]$, and clearly, $C \vdash_{\Gamma} *[X,U]$.

Induction. Assume that $*[\underline{S}] \in C$ was the last jd applied and row w was generated. Let $\underline{S} = \{S_1,\ldots,S_m\}$ and let $u_1,\ldots,u_m$ be the rows that existed before $*[\underline{S}]$ was applied, such that $w[S_i] = u_i[S_i]$. Let u_i represent the fohd $*[\underline{Q}^i]$, where $\underline{Q}^i = \{XY^i_j\}^k_{j=1}$. Since $w[S_i] = u_i[S_i]$, we have that $w[Y_j] = w_j[Y_j]$ for $Y_j = \bigcup_i (S_i \cap Y^i_j)$. That is, w represents the fohd $*[\underline{P}]$, where $\underline{P} = \{XY_j\}_j$ $= \{X \cup (\bigcup_i (S_i \cap Y^i_j))\}_j = \{\cup_i (S_i \cap XY^i_j)\}_j$. But then $*[\underline{S}], *[\underline{Q}^1], \ldots, *[\underline{Q}^m] \vdash *[\underline{P}]$ by rule JD5.

We have thus proved that $C \vdash_{\Gamma} *[S_w]$ for every row $w \in chase_C(T_{\underline{R}})$. It follows that $C \models *[\underline{R}] \Leftrightarrow w_0 \in chase_C(T_{\underline{R}}) \Leftrightarrow C \vdash_{\Gamma} *[\underline{R}]$. □

<u>Corollary 12</u>

If rules JD0 and JD5 are restricted to fohds, then they are (FOHD,FOHD)-complete. □

We conclude with a few additional observations on the meaning of tuples. First, suppose C contains fds also. Then during the chase, variables are equated. Hence a row may represent more than one jd. To make this representation simpler, let us consider an alternative form of the chase. Let the values in the relation be sets, where initially every value is a singleton set. Whenever two values (= sets) are equated by an F-rule, they are replaced by their union. The reader can easily check that nothing is really changed in the chase if this view is adopted. However, upon termination, each row contains values that are sets and can be expanded to a set of rows. The advantage of this view is that now each row obtained by the expansion represents a unique distinct jd, according to the correspondence between rows and jds described above. Further, Theorem 2 can be applied to these expanded rows.

As an application, it is now easy to prove Lemma 3. Just prove by induction that the chase of $T_{\underline{R}}$ by $\bar{F} \cup J$ contains exactly the same rows as the chase of $T_{\underline{R}}$ by $F \cup J$, after its rows are expanded. Details are left to the reader.

We have seen that $chase_C(T_{\underline{R}})$ represents some jds with the set of X-stems as $\underline{R}$ that are implied by C, but not necessarily all of them. If $\underline{R} = \{R_1,\ldots,R_k\}$, then only jds with the sequence of X-stems $ST_X(R_1),\ldots,ST_X(R_k)$ can be represented. Can this restriction be lifted? The answer is yes.

For an asc $\underline{X} = \{X_i\}_{i=1}^{k}$, $ATTR(\underline{X}) = X$, consider the set of jds $\{*[\underline{S}] \mid ST_X(\underline{S}) = \underline{X}\}$. If $*[\underline{S}]$ is in this set, then X_i may appear in $\underline{S}$ with several nonempty X-branches, and it may appear at most once with an empty X-branch (since $\underline{S}$ is a set). The nonempty X-branches of $\underline{S}$ are a partition of $\bar{X}$. It follows that X_i can appear in $\underline{S}$ at most m+1 times, where m denotes the size of $\bar{X}$.

Let $T(\underline{X})$ be a relation of variables, $T(X) = \{w_{ij}\}_{i=1\ldots k}^{j=1\ldots m+1}$ such that w_{ij} and $w_{k\ell}$ agree on $X_i \cap X_k$ and disagree elsewhere. Thus, row $w_{i1},\ldots,w_{im+1}$ represent m+1 occurrences of the stem X_i. Then $chase_C(T(\underline{X}))$ contains rows that represent every jd $*[\underline{S}]$ such that $ST_X(\underline{S}) = \underline{X}$ and $C \models *[\underline{S}]$. The construction of $chase_C(T(\underline{X}))$ serves as a universal test of implication by C of all jds with set of X-stems $\underline{X}$.

CONCLUSIONS

We have presented in this chapter a simple yet powerful set of rules for manipulating jds. The rules can be applied to embedded jds, but our main interest here was their use for total jds. All the rules known to us from the literature for manipulating jds or special cases of jds are consequences of our rules. Our set of rules is complete for special cases, e.g., for crosses and fohds and for inferring fds or fohds from fds and jds. It is also complete for jds for which no more than one jd is given.

We have also extended the concepts of left side and right side of an mvd to stems and branches of a jd. This extension proved to be very useful in the characterization of the power of our rules. The rules enable us to manipulate both stems and branches. However, we only know how to use them to manipulate branches in a meaningful way. That is, given a set C and a collection of stems, we can apply the rules to C to derive the branches that can be attached to stems. This is expressed formally in the Branch completeness theorem. We do not seem to know how to manipulate stems so as to derive a desired collection of stems.

Are the rules complete for jds? If not, can the rules be augmented to a complete set for jds? A clue to the answer can be found in the results of the subsection, The Third Approach — Assigning Meaning to Tuples. There, we have not assigned meaning to rows in $chase_C(T_{\underline{R}})$ that contain nondistinguished values for some attributes in $\bar{}$ MANY$(\underline{R}) = X$. If we could make each such row also represent a jd then all the rows of $chase_C(T_{\underline{R}})$ would be representations of jds and we could try to simulate $\bar{}$ the chase by an inference rule as we actually did for fohds.

There are two ways to generate a jd from such a row w. The first is that if $w[A] = w_i[A]$ is nondistinguished and $A \in X$, then add A to $ST_X(R_i)$ but do not delete it from other X-stems. This jd has a set of X-stems different from that of $\underline{R}$. The second method is to add such an A to $ST_X(R_i)$ and at the same time delete it from all other X-stems. This jd also has a different set of X-stems. However, for both methods, examples can be found of rows in the chase that "represent" jds that are not implied by C. Thus, both methods fail.

There exists a third way to assign meaning to such rows. However, the meaning is not a jd but a more general type of constraint. Thus, surprisingly, the answer seems to be not the extension of the set of rules for jds, but rather the extension of the type of dependencies to include more than jds. It turns out that a natural extension of the family of jds does exist, and the rules generalize to a complete set of rules for this extension. This subject will be treated in a forthcoming paper. See also Sciore [1979].

REFERENCES

1. Aho, A. V., Beeri, C., and Ullman, J. D. [1979] "The Theory of Joins in Relational Databases", *ACM Trans. on Database Systems 4*, 3 (Sept. 1979), 297-314.

2. Armstrong, W. W. [1974] "Dependency Structures of Data Base Relationships", *Proc. IFIP 74,* North Holland, 1974, 580-583.

3. Armstrong, W. W., and Delobel, C. [1979], " Decomposition and Functional Dependencies in Relations", publication #271, Dept. d'Informatique et de Recherche Operationnelle, Universite de Montreal, Oct. 1977, Rev. Sept. 1979.

4. Aho, A. V., Sagiv, Y., and Ullman, J. D. [1979] "Equivalences Among Relational Expressions", *SIAM J. on Computing 8*, 2 (May 1979), 218-246.

5. Beeri, C. [1977] "On the Membership Problem for Multivalued Dependencies in Relational Databases", TR-229, Dept. of Elec. Engr. and Computer Sci., Princeton University, Princeton, N.J. (Sept. 1977), to appear in *ACM Trans. on Database Systems.*

6. Beeri, C. and Bernstein, P. A. [1979] "Computational Problems Related to the Design of Normal Form Relational Schemas", *ACM Trans. on Database Systems 4,* 1 (March 1979), 30-59.

7. Beeri, C., Fagin, R., and Howard, J.H. [1977] "A Complete Axiomatization for Functional and Multivalued Dependencies in Database Relations", *Proc. 3rd ACM-SIGMOD Int'l. Conf. on Management of Data,* Toronto, August 1977, 47-61.

8. Beeri, C., Mendelzon, A. O., Sagiv, Y., and Ullman, J. D. [1979] "Equivalence of Relational Database Schemes", *Proc. 11th Annual ACM Symp. on Theory of Computing,* May 1979, 319-329.

9. Beeri, C., and Rissanen, J. [1980] "Faithful Representations of Relational Database Schemes", IBM Research Report, San Jose, California, 1980.

10. Biskup, J. [1978] "On the Complementation Rule for Multivalued Dependencies in Database Relations", *Acta Informatica 10,* 3 (1978), 297-305.

11. Biskup, [1979] "Inferences of Multivalued Dependencies in Fixed and Undetermined Universes", June 1978, *Theoretical Computer Science 10,* 1 (1980), 93-106.

12. Chandra, A. K., and Merlin, P. M. [1977] "Optimal Implementation of Conjunctive Queries in Relational Databases", *Proc. 9th Annual ACM Symp. on Theory of Computing,* May 1977, 77-90.

13. Codd, E. F. [1970] "A Relational Model for Large Shared Data Bases", *CACM 13,* 6 (June 1970), 377-387.

14. Codd, E. F. [1972a] "Further Normalization of the Data Base Relational Models" In: *Date Base Systems* (R. Rustin, Ed.), Prentice-Hall, Englewood Cliffs, N. J. 1972, 33-64.

15. Codd, E. F. [1972b] "Relational Completeness of Data Base Sublanguages", In: *Data Base Systems* (R. Rustin, Ed.), Prentice-Hall, Englewood Cliffs, N. J., 1972, 65-98.

16. Dayal, U., and Bernstein, P. A. [1978] "The Fragmentation Problem: Lossless Decomposition of Relations into Files", *Technical Report CCA-78-13,* Computer Corp. of America, Cambridge, Mass., Nov. 1978.

17. Date, C. J. [1977] *An Introduction to Database Systems* (2nd Ed.), Addison-Wesley, Reading, Mass., 1977.

18. Delobel, C. [1978] "Semantics of Relations and Decomposition Process in the Relational Data Model", *ACM Trans. on Database Systems 3,* 3 (Sept. 1978), 201-222.

19. Fagin, R. [1977] "Multivalued Dependencies and a New Normal Form for Relational Databases", *ACM Trans. on Database Systems 2*, 3 (Sept. 1977), 262-278.

20. Mendelzon, A. O. [1979] "On Axiomatizing Multivalued Dependencies in Relational Databases", *JACM 26*, 1 (Jan. 1979), 37-44.

21. Maier, D., Mendelzon, A. O., and Sagiv, Y. [1979] "Testing Implication Dependencies", *ACM Trans. on Database Systems 4*, 4 (Dec. 1979), 455-469.

22. Maier, D., Nendelzon, A. O., Sadri, F., and Ullman, J. D. [1981] "Adequacy of Decompositions of Relational Databases", *this volume*.

23. Maier, D., and Mendelzon, A. O. [1979] "Generalized Mutual Dependencies and the Decomposition of Database Relations", *Proc. 5th Int'l. Conf. on Very Large Data Bases,* Rio de Janeiro, Octo. 1979, 75-82.

24. Nicolas, J. M. [1978] "Mutual Dependencies and Some Results on Undecomposable Relations", *Proc. 4th Int'l. Conf. on Very Large Data Bases,* Berlin, Sept. 1978, 360-367.

25. Paredaens, J. [1979] "The Interaction of Integrity Constraints in an Information System", to appear, *J. of Computer and System Sciences*.

26. Paredaens, J. and Janssens, D. [1980] "Decompositions of Relations: A Comprehensive Approach", *in this volume*.

27. Rissanen, J. [1978] "Theory of Relations for Databases — A Tutorial Survey", *Proc. 7th Symp. on Foundations of Computer Science,* Poland, 1978, Lecture Notes in Computer Science 64, Springer-Verlag, 537-551.

28. Sagiv, Y. [1979] "An Algorithm for Inferring Multivalued Dependencies with an Application to Propositional Logic", *JACM 27,* 2 (April 1980), 250-262.

29. Sciore, E. [1979] "A Complete Axiomatization of Full Join Dependencies", *TR #279,* Dept. of EECS, Princeton U., July 1979.

30. Vardi, M. Y. [1980a] "Axiomatization of Functional Multivalued Dependencies — a Comprehensive Study", to appear.

31. Vardi, M. Y. [1980] "On the Properties of Join Dependencies in Relational Databases", M.Sc. Thesis, The Weizman Inst. of Sci., May 1980.

32. Zaniolo, C. [1976] "Analysis and Design of Relational Schemata for Database Systems", *Tech. Rep. UCLA-ENG-7769*, Dept. of Comp. Sci., UCLA, July 1976.

DECOMPOSITIONS OF RELATIONS: A COMPREHENSIVE APPROACH

J. Paredaens and D. Janssens

University of Antwerp
Antwerp, Belgium

ABSTRACT

In this paper a new integrity constraint, called general dependencies, is introduced. It generalizes a number of well-known types of constraints. A corresponding decomposition property is given and a set of inference rules is presented.

A characterization of trivial general dependencies and of unique disjoint general dependencies (a restricted type of general dependencies) is also included. The proofs of these characterizations show that the given set of inference rules is complete for these classes of dependencies.

INTRODUCTION

Since the introduction of the relational database model (Codd [1970]), many constraints and "dependencies" have been studied. Functional dependencies were first introduced by Codd [1971]. Inference rules for functional dependencies can be found in Armstrong [1974] and algorithms to decompose relations are derived in Bernstein [1976]. They are generalized to multivalued dependencies (Fagin [1977], Zaniolo [1976]), which give a characterization of the decompositions of a relation. Their inference rules are explained in Beeri et al. [1977]. Multivalued dependencies have been extended to generalized multivalued dependencies and to first order hierarchic decompositions by Delobel [1978]. Their relationship to decompositions has also been given, but a complete set of inference rules is unknown to the authors. Dependencies called crosses form a subclass of the first order hierarchical decompositions for which a complete set of inference rules is known (Paredaens [1980]). Mutual dependencies, introduced by Nicolas [1978], describe a more general decomposition but their inference rules are again not known. Many of the above dependencies can be expressed in terms of transitive dependencies (Paredaens [1979]). Another attempt to generalize some dependency classes are interdependencies, defined in Dayal and Bernstein [1978], and also generalized mutual dependencies defined in Maier and Mendelzon [1979]. Their relationship to decomposition is also discussed there. Finally join dependencies were introduced by Rissanen [1978].

The aim of this paper is to introduce general dependencies, a new formalism in terms of which all the above dependencies can be expressed. Another generalization of the same sort is described by Sadri and Ullman [1980]. The generalization provides a unifying view of dependencies, and gives rise to a new and very general decomposition property for relations. Finally, trivial general dependencies are characterized and some inference rules and properties are discussed in the hope that this will help us to find a complete set of inference rules for general dependencies.

GENERAL DEPENDENCIES

Before we give the definition of general dependencies, we specify the notation used in this paper.

A *relation scheme* $\mathcal{R}$ is a system (Ω,Δ,w,b,B) where Ω is a finite set, called the set of *attributes*, Δ is a finite set, called the set of *domains*, w is a function associating a domain to each attribute, b is a description of the meaning of $\mathcal{R}$ (b will not be discussed here) and B is a set of *constraints*. In the sequel, we assume that Ω has an arbitrary but fixed ordering: $\Omega = \{A_1,A_2,\ldots,A_n\}$ and if we use a subset H of Ω, then we assume that the ordering on H is the one, induced by the ordering of Ω. By $\mathcal{P}(\Omega)$ we denote the set of subsets of Ω. If $\Omega = \{A_1,A_2,\ldots,A_n\}$ then a *relation instance* R of $\mathcal{R}$ is a subset of $w(A_1)\times w(A_2)\times\ldots\times w(A_n)$ that satisfies the constraints of B. An element of R is called a tuple.

Let R be a relation instance and let $H = \{A_{i_1},A_{i_2},\ldots,A_{i_r}\}$ be a subset of Ω. Then the projection of R onto $w(A_{i_1}) \times w(A_{i_2}) \times \ldots \times w(A_{i_r})$ is called the *projection of* R *on* H and denoted by R[H]. If u is a tuple of R then by u[H] we denote the projection of u on H. We say that an element v of $w(A_{i_1}) \times w(A_{i_2}) \times \ldots \times w(A_{i_r})$ *occurs in* R, iff there exists a tuple u in R such that u[H] = v.

If R is an instance of $\mathcal{R}$ and S is an instance of $\mathcal{S}$ and if we denote the sets of attributes of $\mathcal{R}$ and $\mathcal{S}$ by $\Omega_{\mathcal{R}}$ and $\Omega_{\mathcal{S}}$ respectively, then the *join of* R *and* S, denoted by R * S, is the set of tuples $\{z | z[\Omega_{\mathcal{R}}] \in R, z[\Omega_{\mathcal{S}}] \in S\}$ over $\Omega_{\mathcal{R}} \cup \Omega_{\mathcal{S}}$.

We end this section by introducing the notion of "evaluation". Let $\mathcal{R}$ be a relation scheme. If $X = \{A_{i_1}, A_{i_2}, \ldots, A_{i_r}\}$ is a subset of Ω, then an *evaulation of* $\mathcal{R}$ is an element of $w(A_{i1}) \times w(A_{i2}) \times \ldots \times w(A_{ir})$. If $X_1, X_2, \ldots, X_r \subseteq \Omega$ and $x_1, x_2, \ldots, x_r$ are evaluations of $X_1, X_2, \ldots, X_r$ respectively, then by $x_1 x_2 \ldots x_r$ we mean the evaluation x of $X_1 \cup X_2 \cup \ldots \cup X_r$ with for each i, $x[X_i] = x_i$. Observe that $x_1 x_2 \ldots x_r$ is only defined in the case that for $1 \leq i,j \leq r$ either $X_i \cap X_j = \emptyset$ or $x_i[X_i \cap X_j] = x_j[X_i \cap X_j]$.

Definition of the General Dependency

Let $\mathcal{R} = (\Omega, \Delta, w, b, B)$ be a relation scheme. The *general dependency structure* of $\mathcal{R}$ is a triple (Σ, S, G) where Σ is a set, called the set of *names*, S is a surjective function from Σ onto $\mathcal{P}(\Omega)$, associating to every name a set of attributes, and G is a set of expressions of the form

$$\frac{\begin{matrix} X_1^1 \ldots X_{n_1}^1 \\ \vdots \\ X_1^k \ldots X_{n_k}^k \end{matrix}}{Y_1 \ldots Y_m} \qquad (1)$$

- where each X_j^i and each Y_j belongs to Σ.
- where, for each Y_j, there exist indices p,q such that $Y_j = X_q^p$.

These expressions are called *general dependencies*. The general dependency structure is a part of the specification of B. The first k rows of (1) are called *the inputlines*, the last row is called the *outputline*. If (Σ, S, G) is the general dependency structure of $\mathcal{R}$, and $X \in \Sigma$, then by an evaluation of X we mean an evaluation of S(X). Hence from now on we consider evaluations as being defined on names. We still have to define what it means for a relation scheme $\mathcal{R}$ to satisfy such a dependency. We say that $\mathcal{R}$ *satisfies* the general dependency

$$\frac{\begin{matrix} X_1^1 \ldots X_{n_1}^1 \\ \vdots \\ X_1^k \ldots X_{n_k}^k \end{matrix}}{Y_1 \ldots Y_m}$$

if and only if for every instance R of $\mathcal{R}$ the following holds: if for each $X \in \Sigma$ an evaluation e(X) is given such that for each inputline, $e(X_1^i)e(X_2^i) \ldots e(X_{n_i}^i)$ is defined and it occurs in R, then $e(Y_1)\,e(Y_2) \ldots e(Y_m)$ is defined and it occurs in R.

(1). Observe that the order of the inputlines and the order of the names in a line are irrelevant in the expression

$$\frac{\begin{matrix} X_1^1 & \cdots & X_{n_1}^1 \\ \vdots & & \vdots \\ X_1^k & \cdots & X_{n_k}^k \end{matrix}}{Y_1 \quad \cdots \quad Y_m}$$

(2). Of course, by saying that the general dependency structure of $\mathcal{R}$ is (Σ,S,G) we mean that $\mathcal{R}$ satisfies every general dependency of the set G.

(3). If $\mathcal{R}$ satisfies a general dependency d and we change Σ and S in such a way that the names, occurring in d are not affected (e.g., we add new names to Σ) then the resulting relation scheme still satisfies d. More formally, if $\mathcal{R}$ and $\bar{\mathcal{R}}$ are relation schemes that differ only in Σ and S, if S and $\bar{S}$ agree on $\Sigma \cap \bar{\Sigma}$ and if d is a dependency with names in $\Sigma \cap \bar{\Sigma}$ only, then $\mathcal{R}$ satisfies d if and only if $\bar{\mathcal{R}}$ satisfies d.

<u>Example 1</u>.

Let $\Omega = \{A_1,A_2,A_3,A_4,A_5\}$ and $X,\bar{X},Y,\bar{Y},Z \in \Sigma$ with $S(X) = S(\bar{X}) = \{A_1\}$, $S(Y) = S(\bar{Y}) = \{A_2,A_3\}$ and $S(Z) = \{A_3,A_4\}$. Consider the general dependency

$$d = \frac{\begin{matrix} XYZ \\ \bar{X}Z \\ \bar{X}\bar{Y} \end{matrix}}{Y\bar{Y}}$$

In the following relation instance, this dependency is satisfied because $e(Y)$ must be equal to $e(\bar{Y})$ (small letters with distinct indices denote distinct values).

Rel	A_1	A_2	A_3	A_4	A_5
	a_1	b_1	c_1	d_1	e_1
	a_2	b_1	c_1	d_2	e_2
	a_2	b_1	c_1	d_1	e_3

The following instance, however, does not satisfy the dependency, because the Y-value of the second tuple is different from the Y-value of the first tuple but the X-value of the second tuple occurs together with the Z-value of the first tuple.

Rel	A_1	A_2	A_3	A_4	A_5
	a_1	b_1	c_1	d_1	e_1
	a_2	b_2	c_1	d_2	e_2
	a_2	b_1	c_1	d_1	e_3

GENERAL DEPENDENCIES AS A UNIFYING FORMALISM

In this section we prove that several kinds of well-known dependencies can be expressed by means of general dependencies. Throughout this section $\mathcal{R} = (\Omega, \Delta, w, b, B)$ denotes an arbitrary relation scheme.

(a). Functional Dependency (Codd [1971])

Let A,B be subsets of Ω. Then the relation scheme $\mathcal{R}$ satisfies the *functional dependency* $A \to B$ if and only if for every instance R of $\mathcal{R}$ and for every two arbitrary tuples u,v in R we have $u[A] = v[A]$ implies $u[B] = v[B]$.

It is easily seen that we have the following property: if $\mathcal{R}$ is a relation scheme and $X, Y, \bar{Y}$ are elements of Σ such that $S(Y) = S(\bar{Y})$ and $Y \neq \bar{Y}$, then $\mathcal{R}$ satisfies $\begin{array}{c} XY \\ X\bar{Y} \\ \hline Y\bar{Y} \end{array}$ iff $\mathcal{R}$ satisfies $S(X) \to S(Y)$.

(b). Multivalued Dependency (Beeri, Fagin, and Howard [1977])

Let $\mathcal{R}$ be a relation scheme. For each subset U of Ω, for each subset V of Ω and for each evaluation v of V we define $U_R(v) = \{u \mid \text{for some tuple } r \in R,\ r[V] = v \text{ and } r[U] = u\}$.

Let $A, B \subseteq \Omega$ and let C be the complement of $A \cup B$ with respect to Ω, written as $C = \Omega \setminus (A \cup B)$. Then $\mathcal{R}$ satisfies the *multivalued dependency* (MVD) $A \twoheadrightarrow B$ if and only if for every instance R of $\mathcal{R}$ and for every AC-evaluation ac that appears in R, we have $B_R(ac) = B_R(a)$. (In Paredaens [1980], this type of dependency is called "decomposition").

It is easily seen that we have the following property. Let $\mathcal{R}$ be a relation scheme and let $X, Y, Z \in \Sigma$ with $S(Z) = \Omega \setminus (S(X) \cup S(Y))$. Then $\mathcal{R}$ satisfies the general dependency $\begin{array}{c} XY \\ XZ \\ \hline XYZ \end{array}$ iff $\mathcal{R}$ satisfies $S(X) \twoheadrightarrow S(Y)$.

(c). Generalized Multivalued Dependency (Delobel [1978])

Let $\mathcal{R}$ be a relation scheme. If $A, B_1, B_2, \ldots, B_n$ $(n \geq 2)$ are pairwise disjoint nonempty subsets of Ω such that $A \cup B_1 \cup B_2 \ldots \cup B_n = \Omega$, then $\mathcal{R}$ satisfies the *generalized multivalued dependency* (GMVD) $A \twoheadrightarrow B_1|B_2|\ldots|B_n$ if and only if for every instance R of $\mathcal{R}$ we have $R = R[A,B_1]*R[A,B_2]*\cdots*R[A,B_n]$.

We obviously have the following property. Let $X,Y_1,Y_2,\ldots,Y_n$ be elements of Σ that $S(X),S(Y_1),S(Y_2),\ldots,S(Y_n)$ are pairwise disjoint, nonempty subsets of Ω such that $S(X) \cup S(Y_1) \cup S(Y_2) \cup \ldots \cup S(Y_n) = \Omega$. Then $\mathcal{R}$ satisfies the general dependency

$$\frac{\begin{array}{c} XY_1 \\ XY_2 \\ \vdots \\ XY_n \end{array}}{XY_1Y_2\ldots Y_n}$$

iff $\mathcal{R}$ satisfies $S(X) \twoheadrightarrow S(Y_1)|S(Y_2)|\ldots|S(Y_n)$.

(d). First-Order Hierarchical Decomposition (Delobel [1978])

Let $\mathcal{R}$ be a relation scheme. If $A,B_1,B_2,\ldots,B_n$ are disjoint subsets of Ω (it is not needed that $A \cup B_1 \cup B_2 \cup \ldots \cup B_n = \Omega$), then $\mathcal{R}$ satisfies the *first-order hierarchical decomposition* (FOHD) $A\colon B_1|B_2|\ldots|B_n$ if and only if for every instance R of $\mathcal{R}$ we have

$R[A,B_1,B_2,\ldots,B_n] = R[A,B_1]*R[A,B_2]*\cdots*R[A,B_n]$.

We obviously have the property:

Let $X,Y_1,Y_2,\ldots,Y_n$ be elements of Σ such that $S(X),S(Y_1),S(Y_2),\ldots,S(Y_n)$ are disjoint subsets of Ω. Then $\mathcal{R}$ satisfies the general dependency

$$\frac{\begin{array}{c} XY_1 \\ XY_2 \\ \vdots \\ XY_n \end{array}}{XY_1Y_2\ldots Y_n}$$

iff $\mathcal{R}$ satisfies $S(X)\colon S(Y_1)|S(Y_2)|\ldots|S(Y_n)$.

(e). Cross (Paredaens [1980])

Let $\mathcal{R}$ be a relation scheme. If A,B are disjoint nonempty subsets of Ω, then $\mathcal{R}$ satisfies the cross CR(A,B) if and only if for every instance R of $\mathcal{R}$ we have $R[A,B] = R[A]*R[B]$.

We have the property:

If $X,Y \in \Sigma$ such that $S(X)$ and $S(Y)$ are disjoint and nonempty, then $\mathcal{R}$ satisfies $\frac{X \quad Y}{XY}$ iff $\mathcal{R}$ satisfies $CR(S(X),S(Y))$.

(f). Mutual Dependency (Nicolas [1978])

Let $\mathcal{R}$ be a relation scheme and let A,B be two disjoint subsets of Ω. Let $C = \Omega \setminus (A \cup B)$. Then $\mathcal{R}$ satisfies the *mutual dependency* $A \leftrightsquigarrow B$ if and only if for every instance R of $\mathcal{R}$ and for every pair abc, ab_oc_o of tuples in R, we have $bc_o \in R[BC] \Rightarrow abc_o \in R$ and $b_oc \in R[BC] \Rightarrow ab_oc \in R$. We easily deduce the following property:
If $X,Y,Z \in \Sigma$ such that $S(X) \cap S(Y) = \emptyset$ and $S(Z) = \Omega \setminus (S(X) \cup S(Y))$, then $\mathcal{R}$ satisfies $\frac{XY \quad XZ \quad YZ}{XYZ}$ iff $\mathcal{R}$ satisfies $S(X) \leftrightsquigarrow S(Y)$.

(g). Transitive Dependency (Paredaens [1979])

Let $\mathcal{R}$ be a relation scheme and let A,B,C be subsets of Ω. $\mathcal{R}$ satisfies the *transitive dependency* A(B,C) if and only if for every instance R of $\mathcal{R}$ we have

$$\left.\begin{array}{l} ab \in R[AB] \\ ac \in R[AC] \end{array}\right\} \Rightarrow bc \in R[BC] .$$

It is easy to see that we have the property:

If X,Y,Z are distinct elements of Σ, then $\mathcal{R}$ satisfies $\frac{XY \quad XZ}{YZ}$, iff $\mathcal{R}$ satisfies $S(X)(S(Y),S(Z))$.

(h). Interdependency (Delobel and Pichat [1978])

Let A be a finite set.
A *partial covering* of A is a family of subsets of A.
A *covering* of A is a family $G = \{A_1, A_2, \ldots, A_k\}$ of subsets of A such that $\bigcup_{i=1}^{k} (A_i) = A$.

A covering or partial covering $\{A_1, A_2, \ldots, A_k\}$ is called *reduced* if for each i,j with $1 \leq i \neq j \leq k$ we have $A_i \not\subseteq A_j$ and $A_j \not\subseteq A_i$.
Let $\mathcal{R}$ be a relation scheme and let $\mathcal{C} = \{U_1, U_2, \ldots, U_k\}$ be a partial covering of Ω. Let R be an instance of $\mathcal{R}$ and let $v \in R$.

Then $R[\mathcal{C}]$ denotes the relation $R[U_1]*R[U_2]*\cdots*R[U_n]$ and analogously, $v[\mathcal{C}] = v[U_1] * v[U_2] * \cdots *v[U_n]$.
Now let A,B,C be disjoint subsets of Ω with $A \cup B \cup C = \Omega$ and $A \neq \emptyset$. Then $\mathcal{R}$ satisfies the *interdependency* $C \to A|B$ if and only if there exists a reduced partial covering $\mathcal{C}$ of Ω such that $\mathcal{C} \cup \{A \cup C, B \cup C\}$ is a reduced covering of Ω and such that for each instance R of $\mathcal{R}$ and for each pair abc, $a_o b_o c$ of tuples of R we have:

$$ab_oc[\mathcal{C}] \in R[\mathcal{C}] \quad \text{implies} \quad ab_oc \in R \quad \text{and}$$

$$a_obc[\mathcal{C}] \in R[\mathcal{C}] \quad \text{implies} \quad a_obc \in R .$$

We have the following property:

Theorem 1. If X,Y,Z are elements of Σ such that $S(X)$, $S(Y)$, $S(Z)$ are disjoint, $S(X) \cup S(Y) \cup S(Z) = \Omega$ and $S(X) \neq \emptyset$, then there exists a subset $\{U_1,U_2,\ldots,U_k\}$ of Σ such that $\mathcal{C} = \{S(U_1),S(U_2),\ldots,S(U_k)\}$ is a reduced partial covering from Ω, $\mathcal{C} \cup \{S(X) \cup S(Z), S(Y) \cup S(Z)\}$ is a reduced covering of Ω, and such that $\mathcal{R}$ satisfies

$$\begin{array}{c} XZU_1 \\ XZU_2 \\ \vdots \\ XZU_k \\ XZU_1 \\ XZU_2 \\ \vdots \\ XZU_k \\ \hline XZU \end{array}$$

iff $\mathcal{R}$ satisfies $S(Z) \to S(Z)|S(Y)$.

Proof:

"IF".

If $\mathcal{R}$ satisfies $S(Z) \to S(X)|S(Y)$ then there exists a subset $\{U_1,U_2,\ldots,U_k\}$ of Σ such that $\mathcal{C} = \{S(U_1),S(U_2),\ldots,S(U_k)\}$ is a reduced covering of Ω and $\mathcal{C} \cup \{S(X) \cup S(Z), S(Y) \cup S(Z)\}$ is a reduced covering of Ω. Now let R be an arbitrary instance of $\mathcal{R}$ and for each $T \in \Sigma$ choose an arbitrary evaluation e(T) such that for $1 \leq i \leq k$, $e(X)\ e(Z)\ e(U_i)$ and $e(Y)\ e(Z)\ e(U_i)$ are defined and occur in R. Since $S(X)$, $S(Y)$ and $S(Z)$ are disjoint, $e(X)\ e(Y)\ e(Z)$ is defined. Moreover, for each i with $1 \leq i \leq k$, $e(X)\ e(Y)\ e(Z)[S(U_i)] = e(U_i)$ (and hence, it occurs in R) since $e(U_i)[S(U_i) \cap (S(X) \cup S(Z))] = e(X)e(Z)[S(U_i) \cap (S(X) \cup S(Z))]$, $e(U_i)[S(U_i) \cap (S(Y) \cup S(Z))] = e(Y)\ e(Z)[S(U_i) \cap (S(Y) \cup S(Z))]$ and $S(X) \cup S(Y) \cup S(Z) = \Omega$. If we now let $a = e(X)$, $b_o = e(Y)$ and $c = e(Z)$ then it follows easily from the definition of interdependency and from the fact that a c and $b_o c$ occur in R that a $b_o c$ = e(X) e(Y) e(Z) occurs in R.

"ONLY IF".

Again let R be an arbitrary instance of $\mathcal{R}$ for each $T \in \Sigma$, let e(T) be the projection a $b_o c$ [S(T)]. Since a $b_o c$ $[\mathcal{C}] \in R[\mathcal{C}]$ we have for each i with $1 \leq i \leq k$ that e(X) e(Z) $e(U_i)$
and e(Y) e(Z) $e(U_i)$
both occur in R, and thus, if $\mathcal{R}$ satisfies

$$\begin{array}{c} X\ Z\ U_1 \\ \vdots \\ X\ Z\ U_k \\ \hline X\ Y\ Z \end{array}$$

, we have

a b_o $c \in R$. □

(i). Join Dependency (Rissanen [1978], Fagin [1979])

Let $\mathcal{R}$ be a relation scheme.
If $A_1,\ldots,A_r$ $(r \geq 1)$ are nonempty subsets of Ω (not necessarily disjoint) such that $\bigcup_{i=1}^{r} A_i = \Omega$, then $\mathcal{R}$ satisfies the join dependency (JD) $A_1 \times \ldots \times A_r$ if and only if for every instance R of $\mathcal{R}$ we have $R = \mathop{*}_{i=1}^{r} R[A_i]$.

We obviously have the following property:

Let $X_1,\ldots,X_n$ be elements of Σ such that $S(X_i) = \{B_i\}$ where $\Omega = \{B_1,\ldots,B_n\}$.
Consider the general dependency that has r inputlines, and one outputline. The inputline, associated with A_i , contains those X_j for which $S(X_j) \in A_i$. The outputline contains all X_j.
$\mathcal{R}$ satisfies this general dependency iff $\mathcal{R}$ satisfies $A_1 \times\ldots\times A_r$.
The join dependencies are sometimes called the interdependencies (Dayal and Bernstein [1978]).

(j). Summary

Figure 1 depicts the relations between the different types of dependencies described in this section. An arrow

$$\begin{array}{c} \boxed{A} \\ \downarrow \\ \boxed{B} \end{array}$$

means that the dependencies of type B can be described in terms of dependencies of type A.

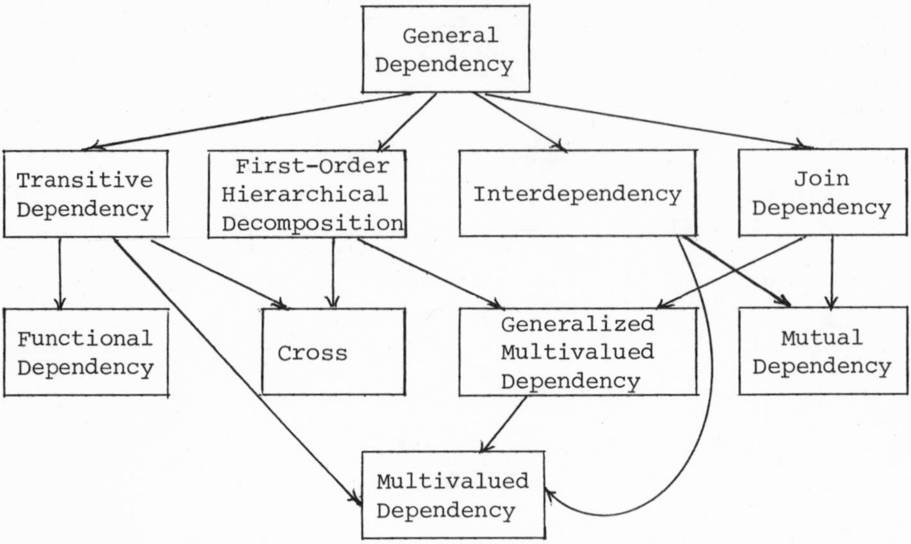

Figure 1. Relationships between Different Dependencies

INFERENCE RULES FOR GENERAL DEPENDENCIES

Let $\mathcal{R} = (\Omega,\Delta,w,b,B)$ be a relation scheme and let (Σ,S,G) be its general dependency structure: G is a set of general dependencies, given together with $\mathcal{R}$. However, the fact that $\mathcal{R}$ satisfies the dependencies of G will usually imply that $\mathcal{R}$ also satisfies other dependencies which are not in G.

Now let G^* denote the set of general dependencies, satisfied by any relation scheme that satisfies G. *Trivial general dependencies* are general dependencies that belong to G^* for every relation scheme $\mathcal{R}$ with a given Ω, Σ and S. We will also give inference rules for general dependencies: rules that describe how, starting from one or more general dependencies, satisfied by a relation scheme $\mathcal{R}$, other general dependencies can be derived that also will be satisfied by $\mathcal{R}$. Let G^A denote the set of general dependencies that can be derived by the inference rules given below from the set $G \cup T$ where G is a set of general dependencies and T is the set of trivial general dependencies. Our conjecture (that is still open) is that for an arbitrary G, $G^A = G^*$.

(1) Trivial General Dependencies

The following types of general dependencies are always satisfied, by any relation scheme $\mathcal{R}$. This follows directly from the definition.

(T1)

$$\begin{array}{c} X_1^1 \ldots X_{n_1}^1 \\ \vdots \\ X_1^i \ldots X_{n_i}^i \\ \vdots \\ X_1^k \ldots X_{n_k}^k \\ \hline X_1^i \ldots X_{n_i}^i \end{array}$$

(T2)

$$\begin{array}{c} X_1 \ldots X_i \ldots X_s \\ \hline X_1 \ldots X_i \end{array}$$

(T3)

$$\begin{array}{l} X_1 \ldots X_i \ldots X_s \\ X_1 Y \\ X_2 Y \\ \vdots \\ X_i Y \\ \hline YX_1 \quad \ldots \quad X_s \end{array} \qquad \text{with } S(Y) \subseteq S(X_1) \cup \ldots \cup S(X_i).$$

(2) Theorem 2.

(R1)

$$\text{If } \mathcal{R} \text{ satisfies } \begin{array}{ccc} X_1^1 & \ldots & X_{n_1}^1 \\ & \vdots & \\ X_1^i \ldots & X_j^i & \ldots X_{n_i}^i \\ & \vdots & \\ X_1^k & \ldots & X_{n_k}^k \\ \hline Y_1 & \ldots & Y_m \end{array} \quad \begin{array}{l} \text{where } X_j^i \text{ occurs} \\ \text{only once in} \\ \text{this expression} \end{array}$$

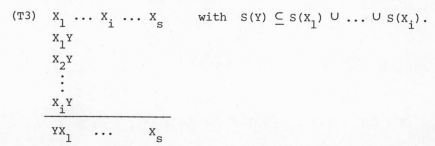

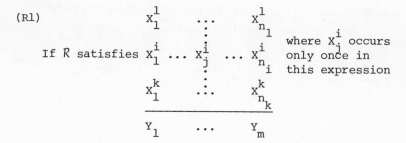

then $\mathcal{R}$ satisfies

$$\frac{\begin{matrix} X_1^1 & \cdots & & X_{n_1}^1 \\ & \vdots & & \\ X_1^i \cdots X_{j-1}^i & & X_{j+1}^i \cdots & X_{n_i}^i \\ & \vdots & & \\ X_1^k & \cdots & & X_{n_k}^k \end{matrix}}{Y_1 \quad \cdots \quad Y_m} .$$

Proof:

Let R be an arbitrary instance of $\mathcal{R}$, and let for each $X \in \Sigma$, e(X) be an evaluation of X in $\mathcal{R}$, such that:

$$\begin{matrix} e(X_1^1)\ e(X_2^1) & \cdots & e(X_{n_1}^1)\ , \\ & \vdots & \\ e(X_1^i)\ \cdots\ e(X_{j-1}^i) & e(X_{j+1}^i)\ \cdots & e(X_{n_i}^i)\ , \\ & \vdots & \\ e(X_1^k)\ e(X_2^k) & \cdots & e(X_{n_k}^k) \end{matrix}$$

are defined and occur in R. Then there exists a tuple u in R with

$$u[S(X_1^i) \cup \ldots \cup S(X_{j-1}^i) \cup S(X_{j+1}^i) \cup \ldots \cup S(X_{n_i}^i)]$$
$$= e(X_1^i) \ \ldots \ e(X_{j-1}^i) \ e(X_{j+1}^i) \ \ldots \ e(X_{n_i}^i) .$$

Now for each $X \in \Sigma$ define the evaluation $\bar{e}$ as follows:

$$\bar{e}(X) = e(X) \qquad \text{if} \quad X \neq X_j^i$$
$$\bar{e}(X) = u[S(X_j^i)] \quad \text{if} \quad X = X_j^i$$

Then it follows from the fact that $\mathcal{R}$ satisfies

$$\frac{\begin{matrix} X_1^1 & \cdots & X_{n_1}^1 \\ & \vdots & \\ X_1^k & \cdots & X_{n_k}^k \end{matrix}}{Y_1 \ \cdots \ Y_m}$$

that $\bar{e}(Y_1)\ \bar{e}(Y_2)\ \ldots\ \bar{e}(Y_m)$ is defined and occurs in R. But because X_j^i occurs only once in the whole expression, it does not occur in the outputline and hence, $e(Y_1)\ldots e(Y_m)$ $= \bar{e}(Y_1)\ldots\bar{e}(Y_m)$ and thus $e(Y_1)\ldots e(Y_m)$ is defined and it occurs in R. □

(R2) If $\mathcal{R}$ satisfies

$$\frac{\begin{matrix} X_1^1 \dots X_{n_1}^1 \\ \vdots \\ X_1^k \dots X_{n_k}^k \end{matrix}}{Y_1^1 \dots Y_{m_1}^1}, \quad \frac{\begin{matrix} X_1^1 \dots X_{n_1}^1 \\ \vdots \\ X_1^k \dots X_{n_k}^k \end{matrix}}{Y_1^2 \dots Y_{m_2}^2} \quad \dots \quad \frac{\begin{matrix} X_1^1 \dots X_{n_1}^1 \\ \vdots \\ X_1^k \dots X_{n_k}^k \end{matrix}}{Y_1^s \dots Y_{m_s}^s} \quad \text{and} \quad \frac{\begin{matrix} Y_1^1 \dots Y_{m_1}^1 \\ \vdots \\ Y_1^s \dots Y_{m_s}^s \end{matrix}}{Z_1 \dots Z_r}$$

then $\mathcal{R}$ satisfies

$$\frac{\begin{matrix} X_1^1 \dots X_{n_1}^1 \\ \vdots \\ X_1^k \dots X_{n_k}^k \end{matrix}}{Z_1 \dots Z_r}$$

This follows immediately from the definition of general dependencies. In the sequel, when no confusion is possible, we will often use "dependency" instead of "general dependency".

(T1), (T2), (T3), (R1), (R2) are independent:

(a). (T1): there exists a relation scheme $\mathcal{R}$ and general dependencies of type (T1) in $\mathcal{R}$ that cannot be obtained from the types (T2) or (T3) by (R1) and (R2).
Indeed, let $\mathcal{R}$ and Σ be such that $X_1, X_2, \dots, X_6$ are elements of Σ. Then

$$\frac{\begin{matrix} X_1 \; X_2 \; X_3 \\ X_4 \; X_5 \; X_6 \end{matrix}}{X_1 \; X_2 \; X_3} \quad \text{is of type (T1)}, \tag{1}$$

and it is clear that no dependency of types (T2) or (T3) has two or more inputlines of length bigger than two. It is also easily seen that by (R1) and (R2) no dependency with this property can be derived from a set that does not contain at least one such dependency. However, (1) has the mentioned property, and thus we conclude that (1) cannot be derived by (R1) and (R2) from the set of all dependencies of types (T2) and (T3).

(b). (T2): Now, consider the dependency

$$\frac{X_1 \; X_2}{X_1} . \tag{2}$$

It is of type (T2). Clearly, the set of all dependencies of types (T1) and (T3) does not contain a dependency which has the property that the outputline is shorter than the shortest inputline. It is also clear that no dependency with this property can be obtained by (R1) and (R2) from a set of dependencies that does not contain at least one such dependency. However, (2) has the property. Therefore, it cannot be derived by (R1) and (R2) from the set of all dependencies of types (T1) and (T3).

(c) (T3): Now let X_1, X_2, X_3 be names of Σ such that $S(X_1) = S(X_2) \neq S(X_3)$. Then

$$\frac{\begin{array}{c} X_1\ X_3 \\ X_1\ X_2 \end{array}}{X_1\ X_2\ X_3} \qquad (3)$$

is of type (T3). The set of all dependencies of types (T1) and (T2) does not contain a dependency d with the property that names Y and Y' occur in the outputline such that there exists no inputline of d in which both Y and Y' occur. It is clear that no dependency with this property can be derived by (R1) and (R2) from a set that does not contain such a dependency. However, (3) has the property and therefore, it cannot be derived from the set of all dependencies of types (T1) and (T2) by (R1) and (R2).

(d) (R1). Let R be a relation scheme such that $X,Y,Z \in \Sigma$ and $S(X)$, $S(Y)$ and $S(Z)$ are disjoint. Let $d = \frac{\begin{array}{c} XY \\ Z \end{array}}{YZ}$. Then clearly by (R1) we can derive the general dependency

$$\frac{\begin{array}{c} Y \\ Z \end{array}}{YZ} \qquad (1)$$

We show that this dependency cannot be derived by (R2) alone from the set D where $D = \{d\} \cup \{g \mid g$ is a general dependency of one of the types (T1), (T2) or (T3)$\}$. For each integer n, recursively define the set D_n by $D_o = D$ and $D_{i+1} = D_i \cup \{g \mid g$ is a general dependency that can be derived by (R2) from the dependencies of $D_i\}$. We show by induction on n that no such D_n contains (1). Clearly, (1) $\notin D_o$. Assume that (1) $\notin D_i$, (1) $\in D_{i+1}$. This means that there exist dependencies of the form

$$\frac{\begin{matrix} Y \\ Z \end{matrix}}{\alpha^1}, \frac{\begin{matrix} Y \\ Z \end{matrix}}{\alpha^2}, \ldots \frac{\begin{matrix} Y \\ Z \end{matrix}}{\alpha^k}, \frac{\begin{matrix} \alpha^1 \\ \alpha^2 \\ \vdots \\ \alpha^k \end{matrix}}{YZ} \quad \text{in } D_i .$$

Since each α^j equals either Y or Z or YZ this means that (1) $\in D_i$, a contradiction.

(e) (R2). Now let X,Y,Z be elements of Σ.
Then clearly $\frac{\begin{matrix} TX \\ X \end{matrix}}{T}$ can be derived by (R2) from trivial dependencies of the forms (T1) and (T2). However, it clearly cannot be derived by (R1) alone from dependencies of the forms (T1), (T2) or (T3).

GENERAL DECOMPOSITIONS

As mentioned in the introduction, most of the dependencies are related to decompositions of relations. It is typical that functional dependencies are "stronger" than decompositions (these only give a sufficient condition) while all other dependencies are equivalent to some decomposition statements. We will see that general dependencies are also stronger than decompositions, though they cover a very general decomposition statement. This is stated in the following theorem:

<u>Theorem 3</u>. Let $\mathcal{R}$ be a relation scheme and let (Σ,S,G) be the general dependency structure of $\mathcal{R}$.

(1) If $\mathcal{R}$ satisfies $\frac{\begin{matrix} X_1^1 \ldots X_{n_1}^1 \\ \vdots \\ X_1^k \ldots X_{n_k}^k \end{matrix}}{Y_1 \ldots Y_m}$, then for every instance R of $\mathcal{R}$

we have $\left(\overset{k}{\underset{i=1}{*}} R\left[\bigcup_{j=1}^{n_i} S(X_j^i)\right]\right)\left[\bigcup_{p=0}^{m} S(Y_p)\right] = R\left[\bigcup_{p=0}^{m} S(Y_p)\right]$.

(2) If the sets $S(X_j^i)$ are pairwise disjoint then the inverse of (1) also holds.

Proof:

(1) Assume that $\mathcal{R}$ satisfies the dependency. Let R be an arbitrary instance of $\mathcal{R}$. We have to prove that

$(\overset{k}{\underset{i=1}{*}} R[\cup_{j=1}^{n_i} S(X_j^i)])[\cup_{p=1}^{m} S(Y_p)] \subseteq R[\cup_{p=1}^{m} S(Y_p)]$ holds.

Indeed, the inverse inclusion always holds. Let y be a tuple of the left member. Then there exists a tuple $\bar{y}$ of $\overset{k}{\underset{i=1}{*}} R[\cup_{j=1}^{n_i} S(X_j^i)]$ whose projection on $\cup_{p=1}^{m} S(Y_p)$ equals y. Hence for every i there is a tuple y_i in R for which $y_i[\cup_{j=1}^{n_i} S(X_j^i)] = \bar{y}[\cup_{j=1}^{n_i} S(X_j^i)]$. Now for each $X \in \Sigma$ define an evaluation x such that for every X_j^i occurring in the dependency, $x_j^i = y_i[S(X_j^i)]$. Since the dependency is satisfied, it follows that y occurs in $R[\cup_{p=1}^{m} S(Y_p)]$, which proves (1).

(2) Assume that the decomposition statement is satisfied in $\mathcal{R}$ and that the sets $S(X_j^i)$ are pairwise disjoint. If x_j^i are evaluations of the X_j^i such that for each $1 \leq i \leq k$, $x_1^i x_2^i \ldots x_{n_i}^i$ is defined and occurs in R, then $x_1^i x_2^i \ldots x_{n_i}^i \in R[\cup_{j=1}^{n_i} S(X_j^i)]$ for each i. Hence the combination $x_1^1 x_2^1 \ldots x_{n_1}^1 x_1^2 x_2^2 \ldots x_{n_k}^k$ of all the x_j^i is in $\overset{k}{\underset{i=1}{*}} R[\cup_{j=1}^{n_i} S(X_j^i)]$ (it is defined because the $S(X_j^i)$ are disjoint). Therefore the combination $y_1 \ldots y_n$ of the evaluations of the Y_j belongs to the left side of the decomposition statement, hence it also belongs to $R[\cup_{p=1}^{m} S(Y_p)]$, proving (2). □

Generally the inverse of (1) does not hold. This can be seen by the following example:

Let $\Omega = \{A,B\}$, $\Sigma = \{\alpha,\beta_1,\beta_2\}$, $S(\alpha) = \{A\}$; $S(\beta_1) = S(\beta_2) = \{B\}$.

The instance

R	A	B
	0	0
	0	1

satisfies (R[AB] * R[AB])[B] = R[B] but does not satisfy

$$\frac{\begin{matrix}\alpha & \beta_1 \\ \alpha & \beta_2\end{matrix}}{\beta_1 \quad \beta_2}$$

Hence the concept of general dependency contains two completely different aspects:

1. It says that if some combinations of values appear in a relation instance then a new combination of these values must also appear in the instance. This aspect is formalized in the first part of Theorem 3, and is as such an extension of all the dependencies studied before, except for the functional dependencies.

2. It says that if some combinations of values appear in a relation instance then some of these values have to be equal. This aspect is a generalization of functional dependency. It has to be formalized and studied in detail.
   If the $S(Y_i)$ are all disjoint, this aspect vanishes, which is formalized in the second part of Theorem 3.

TRIVIAL AND DISJOINT GENERAL DEPENDENCIES

The first problem to be investigated in this section is how to decide whether a given general dependency is trivial or not: we give a characterization for the class of trivial dependencies. To this aim we define equivalence relations on Σ as follows: let

$$\begin{array}{c} X_1^1 \ldots X_{n_1}^1 \\ \vdots \\ X_1^k \ldots X_{n_k}^k \\ \hline Y_1 \ldots Y_m \end{array}$$

be a given general dependency and let $A \in \Omega$.

We define $\overset{A}{\sim}$ to be the reflexive and transitive closure of the relation RA where Z RA T iff

(1) $A \in S(Z) \cap S(T)$, and

(2) There is an inputline in which both Z and T occur.

<u>Example 2</u>

Given $\Omega = \{A,B,C,D\}$, $\Sigma = \{X,Y,Z\}$

$S(X) = \{A,B\}$, $S(Y) = \{A,C\}$, $S(Z) = \{A,D\}$

$$\begin{array}{c} XY \\ XZ \\ \hline XYZ \end{array}$$

then for $\overset{A}{\sim}$ all elements of Σ are equivalent and for $\overset{B}{\sim}$, $\overset{C}{\sim}$, $\overset{D}{\sim}$ they are all inequivalent.

Theorem 4. Given $\mathcal{R} = (\Omega,\Delta,w,b,B)$ and a general dependency structure (Σ,S,G) on $\mathcal{R}$. The general dependency

$$\frac{\begin{array}{ccc} X_1^1 & \cdots & X_{n_1}^1 \\ & \vdots & \\ X_1^k & \cdots & X_{n_k}^k \end{array}}{Y_1 \cdots Y_m}$$

is trivial, if and only if there exists an inputline (say the ith) such that for every attribute A of an arbitrary $S(Y_r)$ of the outputline holds that there is a name in the ith inputline (say X_j^i) with $X_j^i \overset{A}{\sim} Y_r$.

Proof:

"IF".

If the condition is satisfied we prove that the given general dependency is trivial. Actually we prove, by induction on s, that for each $0 \leq s \leq m$,

$$\frac{\begin{array}{ccc} X_1^1 & \cdots & X_{n_1}^1 \\ & \vdots & \\ X_1^i & \cdots & X_{n_i}^i \\ & \vdots & \\ X_1^k & \cdots & X_{n_k}^k \end{array}}{X_1^i \cdots X_{n_i}^i \; Y_1 \cdots Y_s} \qquad (1)$$

is trivial, where i is the number of the inputline from the condition.

For s = 0 this statement clearly holds (the dependency is of the form (T1)). Now assume that

$$\frac{\begin{array}{ccc} X_1^1 & \cdots & X_{n_1}^1 \\ & \vdots & \\ X_1^i & \cdots & X_{n_i}^i \\ & \vdots & \\ X_1^k & \cdots & X_{n_k}^k \end{array}}{X_1^i \cdots X_{n_i}^i \; Y_1 \cdots Y_{s-1}} \qquad (2)$$

is trivial and that $S(Y_s) = \{A_1,\ldots,A_r\}$.

Let $\bar{A}_1,\ldots,\bar{A}_r$ be names of Σ that do not occur among the X_j^i or the Y_j and assume that $S(\bar{A}_i) = A_i$ then we prove by induction that

$$\begin{array}{l} X_1^1 \ldots X_{n_1}^1 \\ \vdots \\ X_1^i \ldots X_{n_i}^i \quad \bar{A}_1 \ldots \bar{A}_r \\ \vdots \\ X_1^k \ldots X_{n_k}^k \\ \hline X_1^i \ldots X_{n_i}^i \; Y_1 \ldots Y_{s-1} \; \bar{A}_1 \ldots \bar{A}_r \end{array} \text{ is trivial.}$$

Let $1 \leq j \leq r$.
Because the condition is satisfied for (1), there exists an X_t^i with $X_t^i \overset{A_j}{\sim} Y_s$. From $A_j \in S(Y_s)$ it follows that $A_j \in S(X_t^i)$ and hence $S(\bar{A}_j) \subseteq S(X_t^i)$.

Now by (T1)

$$\begin{array}{l} X_1^1 \ldots X_{n_1}^1 \\ \vdots \\ X_1^i \quad X_{n_i}^i \quad \bar{A}_1 \ldots \bar{A}_r \\ \vdots \\ X_1^k \ldots X_{n_k}^k \\ \hline X_1^i \ldots X_{n_i}^i \quad \bar{A}_1 \ldots \bar{A}_r \end{array}$$

is trivial, by (T2),

$$\begin{array}{l} X_1^i \ldots X_{n_i}^i \quad \bar{A}_1 \ldots \bar{A}_r \\ \hline X_t^i \; \bar{A}_j \end{array} \tag{3}$$

is trivial and using r times (T3) we see that

$$\begin{array}{ll} X_1^i \ldots X_{n_i}^i \; Y_1 \ldots Y_{s-1} & \\ X_{t_1}^i \; \bar{A}_1 & \text{with } S(\bar{A}_1) \subseteq S(X_{t_1}^i) \\ \vdots & \\ X_{t_r}^i \; \bar{A}_r & \text{with } S(\bar{A}_r) \subseteq S(X_{t_r}^i) \\ \hline X_1^i \ldots X_{n_i}^i \; Y_1 \ldots Y_{s-1} \; \bar{A}_1 \ldots \bar{A}_r & \end{array} \tag{4}$$

is trivial.

Hence, combining (2), (3) and (4) by (R2) we see that

$$\frac{\begin{array}{l} X_1^1 \dots X_{n_1}^1 \\ \quad\vdots \\ X_1^i \dots X_{n_i}^i \quad \bar{A}_1 \dots \bar{A}_r \\ \quad\vdots \\ X_1^k \dots X_{n_k}^k \end{array}}{X_1^i \dots X_{n_i}^i \; Y_s \dots Y_{s-1} \; \bar{A}_1 \dots \bar{A}_r} \quad \text{is trivial.} \tag{5}$$

We now prove that for any $1 \le j \le r$,

$$\frac{\begin{array}{l} X_1^1 \dots X_{n_1}^1 \\ \quad\vdots \\ X_1^i \dots X_{n_i}^i \quad \bar{A}_1 \dots \bar{A}_r \\ \quad\vdots \\ X_1^k \dots X_{n_k}^k \end{array}}{X_s \; \bar{A}_j} \quad \text{is trivial.}$$

Because the condition is satisfied in (1) there exists an X_t^i in the ith inputline such that $X_t^i \overset{A_j}{\sim} Y_s$. This implies that there exist $N_1, \dots, N_q \in \Sigma$ that each occur in at least two different inputlines and

$$\begin{array}{l} N_1 \; RA_j \; X_k^i \quad , \\ N_2 \; RA_j \; N_1 \quad , \\ \quad\vdots \\ N_q \; RA_j \; N_{q-1} \; , \\ Y_s \; RA_j \; N_q \quad . \end{array}$$

This implies that

$$A_j \in S(N_1) \cap S(X_k^i) \text{ and } S(\bar{A}_j) \subseteq S(N_1)$$

and there is an inputline i in which both N_1 and X_k^i occur.

$$A_j \in S(N_1) \cap S(N_2) \text{ and } S(\bar{A}_j) \subseteq S(N_2)$$

and there is an inputline k_1 in which both N_2 and N_1 occur

$$\vdots$$

$$A_j \in S(Y_s) \cap S(N_q)$$

and there is an inputline k_q in which both Y_s and N_q occur.

Now

$$\begin{array}{l} X_1^i \dots X_{n_i}^i \quad \bar{A}_1 \dots \bar{A}_r \\ \hline \end{array}$$

and

$$\begin{array}{l} \bar{A}_j \; N_1 \\ X_1^k \dots X_{n_{k_1}}^{k_1} \\ \bar{A}_j \; N_1 \\ \hline X_1^{k_i} \dots X_{n_{k_1}}^{k_1} \quad \bar{A}_j \end{array}$$ are trivial (by (T2) and (T3)),

$$\begin{array}{l} X_1^{k_1} \dots X_{n_{k_1}}^{k_1} \quad \bar{A}_j \\ \hline N_2 \; \bar{A}_j \end{array}$$

and

$$\begin{array}{l} X^{k_2} \dots X_{n_{k_1}}^{k_2} \\ N_2 \; \bar{A}_j \\ \hline X_1^{k_2} \dots X_{n_{k_2}}^{k_2} \quad \bar{A}_j \end{array}$$ are trivial,

$$\begin{array}{ll} \vdots & \vdots \end{array}$$

$$\begin{array}{l} X^{k_1} \dots X_{n_{k_q}}^{k_q} \\ N_q \; \bar{A}_j \\ \hline X_1^{k_1} \dots X_{n_{k_q}}^{k_1} \quad \bar{A}_j \end{array}$$ is trivial.

Thus, because Y_s occurs in the k_q-th inputline,

$$\begin{array}{l} X_1^1 \dots X_1^1 \\ \vdots \\ X_1^i \dots X_{n_i}^i \quad \bar{A}_1 \dots \bar{A}_r \\ \vdots \\ X_1^k \dots X_{n_k}^k \\ \hline Y_s \; \bar{A}_j \end{array}$$ is trivial.

Using r times that (T3) we see that

$$\frac{\begin{array}{l} X_1^i \ldots X_{n_i}^i \quad Y_1 \ldots Y_{s-1} \quad \bar{A}_1 \ldots \bar{A}_r \\ Y_s \, \bar{A}_1 \\ \vdots \\ Y_s \, \bar{A}_r \end{array}}{X_1^i \ldots X_{n_i}^i \quad Y_1 \ldots Y_{s-1} \quad \bar{A}_1 \ldots \bar{A}_r \quad Y_s} \text{ is trivial.} \qquad (6)$$

Combining (5) and (6) and using (R2) we see that

$$\frac{\begin{array}{l} X_1^1 \ldots X_{r_1}^1 \\ \vdots \\ X_1^i \ldots X_{n_i}^i \quad \bar{A}_1 \ldots \bar{A}_r \\ \vdots \\ X_1^k \ldots X_{n_k}^k \end{array}}{X_1^i \ldots X_{n_i}^i \quad Y_1 \ldots Y_s \quad \bar{A}_1 \ldots \bar{A}_r} \quad \text{is trivial.}$$

Now we can use subsequently (T3)

$$\left(\frac{X_1^i \ldots X_{n_i}^i \quad Y_1 \ldots Y_s \quad \bar{A}_1 \ldots \bar{A}_r}{X_1^i \ldots X_{n_i}^i \quad Y_1 \ldots Y_s} \quad \text{is trivial} \right)$$

and (R2) to conclude that (1) is trivial. Choosing s = m and using the fact that

$$\frac{X_1^i \ldots X_{n_i}^i \quad Y_1 \ldots Y_m}{Y_1 \ldots Y_m}$$

is trivial (T2), we finish the proof.

"ONLY IF"

Assume that the condition is not satisfied. We shall prove that then the general dependency is not trivial, i.e. that there is a scheme R and at least one instance of R where the general dependency is not satisfied. If the condition is not satisfied then for every inputline i, there is an attribute A of some output element Y_r with for each X_j^i of the ith line:

$$X_j^i \overset{A}{\not\approx} Y_r \; .$$

To construct the relation instance, for every attribute A of Ω and for every $X \in \Sigma$, we define an evaluation e(X) as follows: Let the domain of A be $\{0,1,\ldots \ell\}$ where $\ell = \#(\Sigma/\overset{A}{\sim})$, and let $X \in \Sigma$ and $A \in S(X)$. $\overset{A}{\sim}$ defines equivalence classes $H_1,\ldots,H_\ell$ on Σ. Let $X \in H_t$. Then we let the A-projection of e(X) be equal to t. For example, let $S(X) = \{A_1,A_2,A_3\}$ and $X \in H_{t_1}$, an equivalence class defined by A_1, $X \in H_{t_2}$, an equivalence class defined by A_2, $X \in H_{t_3}$, an equivalence class defined by A_3 then $e(X) = (t_1,t_2,t_3)$.

We define an instance with at most R tuples:
By the definition of the relation $\overset{A}{\sim}$ we know that $e(X_1^i)\ldots e(X_n^i)$ is defined:

— If $S(X_1^i) \ldots S(X_n^i)$ are disjoint then it is clear that $e(X_1^i) \ldots e(X_n^i)$ is defined,

— Else let $A \in S(X_j^i) \cap S(X_k^i)$. Then X_j^i RA X_k^i and thus, $X_j^i \overset{A}{\sim} X_k^i$. Therefore the A-projection of $e(X_j^i)$ equals the A-projection of $e(X_k^i)$. Hence $e(X_1^i) \ldots e(X_n^i)$ is defined also in this case.

Now for each inputline i, we define a tuple u_i by

$$u_i[\bigcup_{j=1}^{n_i} S(X_j^i)] = e(X_1^i) \ \ldots \ e(X_{n_i}^i)$$

and

$$u_i[\Omega \setminus \bigcup_{j=1}^{n_i} S(X_j^i)] = (0,\ldots,0) ,$$

that means, we fill up the "empty places" of u_i (corresponding to attributes that do not belong to $\bigcup_{j=1}^{n_i} S(X_j^i)$) by zeros.

The instance contains only the so constructed tuples. Then we prove that the given general dependency is not satisfied in this instance. Observe that if $X_j^i \overset{A}{\not\sim} Y_r$ then X_j^i and Y_r belong to different classes defined by $\overset{A}{\sim}$ and the A-projections of $e(X_j^i)$ and $e(Y_r)$ are different. We have to prove that the evaluation $e(Y_1) \ldots e(Y_m)$ does not occur in the above defined instance.

Assume $e(Y_1) \ldots e(Y_m)$ occurs in the instance. Then there exists an i such that

$$u_i[\bigcup_{j=1}^{m} S(Y_j)] = e(Y_1) \ \ldots \ e(Y_m).$$

But because the condition is not satisfied, there exists an attribute A in some $S(Y_s)$ such that there is no X_t^i in the i-th inputline with $X_t^i \overset{A}{\sim} Y_s$. Thus, either $A \in \bigcup_{j=1}^{n_i} S(X_j^i)$ and then

$$u_i[A] \neq e(Y_1) \ldots e(Y_m)[A] \quad \text{or} \quad A \not\in \bigcup_{j=1}^{n_i} S(X_j^i)$$

and then

$$u_i[A] = 0 \neq e(Y_1) \ldots e(Y_m)[A] .$$

In both cases, we have a contradiction. □

The second problem to be discussed is:
Given a set of general dependencies, decide whether or not another general dependency is a consequence of the given set. This problem is solved in the special case of disjoint unique general dependencies.

Definition 1. A general dependency d is called *disjoint* iff $S(X) \cap S(Y) = \emptyset$ for all names $X \neq Y$ occurring in d. It is called *unique* iff no X figures in two different inputlines.

Theorem 5. Given a set of disjoint unique general dependencies, Another disjoint unique general dependency

$$\frac{\begin{matrix} X_1^1 \ldots X_{n_1}^1 \\ \vdots \\ X_1^k \ldots X_{n_k}^k \end{matrix}}{Y_1 \ldots Y_m} \qquad (1)$$

is a consequence of the given set iff for each V such that

$$[V \subseteq \bigcup_{j=1}^{m} S(Y_j) \text{ and for each inputline } i,\ V \not\subseteq \bigcup_{j=1}^{n_i} S(X_j^i) \qquad (2)$$

it holds that there is a general dependency (denoted by ') in the given set with $V \subseteq \bigcup_{j=1}^{m'} S(Y_j')$ and for each inputline i, $V \not\subseteq \bigcup_{j=1}^{n_i'} S(X_j'^i)$.

Proof:

"IF".

We prove this theorem by induction on the length of the output $Y_1 \ldots Y_m$.

(1).

$$\frac{\begin{matrix} X_1^1 \ldots X_{n_1}^1 \\ \vdots \\ X_1^k \ldots X_{n_k}^k \end{matrix}}{Y_i} \quad \text{for each } 1 \leq i \leq m$$

is trivial by (T_1) and (T_2) since Y_i occurs in at least one inputline.

(2). If all

$$\frac{\begin{matrix} X_1^1 \ldots X_{n_1}^1 \\ \vdots \\ X_1^k \ldots X_{n_k}^k \end{matrix}}{\alpha_s}$$

(with α_s an arbitrary subline of $Y_1 \ldots Y_m$ of length s) are consequences of the given set then we prove that

$$\frac{\begin{matrix} X_1^1 \ldots X_{n_i}^1 \\ \vdots \\ X_1^k \ldots X_{n_k}^k \end{matrix}}{\alpha_{s+1}} \qquad (3)$$

(with α_{s+1} an arbitrary subline of $Y_1 \ldots Y_m$ of length s+1) are consequences.

We assume that (1) satisfies the condition. Now let $V = \bigcup_{Y \in \alpha_{s+1}} S(Y)$. If there is an inputline i such that $V \subseteq \bigcup_{j=1}^{n_i} S(X_j^i)$, then since the $S(X_j^i)$'s are disjoint this means that every name of α_{s+1} occurs in the i-th inputline and thus, (3) is trivial. If there is no such inputline, then by the condition there is a general dependency

$$\frac{\begin{matrix} X'_1 \ldots X'_{n_1} \\ \vdots \\ X'^{k'}_s \quad X'^{k'}_{n_k} \end{matrix}}{Y'_1 \ldots Y'_{m'}} \qquad (4)$$

in the given set with $V \subseteq \bigcup_{j=1}^{m'} S(Y'_j)$ and for each inputline i, $V \subseteq \bigcup_{j=1}^{n'_i} S(X'^i_j)$.

As a consequence, the inputlines of (4) contain sublines of α_{s+1} of length at most s.

Since (4) is unique we can use (R1) to obtain the dependency

$$\frac{\begin{matrix}\alpha^1\\ \vdots\\ \alpha^p\end{matrix}}{\alpha_{s+1}} \tag{5}$$

where the α^i are sublines of α_{s+1} of length at most s. By induction we know that

$$\frac{\begin{matrix}X_1^1 \dots X_{n_1}^1\\ \vdots\\ X_1^k \dots X_{n_k}^k\end{matrix}}{\alpha^1}, \quad \frac{\begin{matrix}X_1^1 \dots X_{n_1}^1\\ \vdots\\ X_1^k \dots X_{n_k}^k\end{matrix}}{\alpha^2}, \quad \dots, \quad \frac{\begin{matrix}X_1^1 \dots X_{n_1}^1\\ \vdots\\ X_1^k \dots X_{n_k}^k\end{matrix}}{\alpha^p}$$

are consequences of the given set, and by using (5) and (R2) we see that

$$\frac{\begin{matrix}X_1^1 \dots X_{n_1}^1\\ \vdots\\ X_1^k \dots X_{n_k}^k\end{matrix}}{\alpha_{s+1}}$$

is also a consequence of the given set.

"ONLY IF"

Assume that the condition of the theorem is not satisfied for (1). Then we construct a relation (instance) in which all the dependencies of the given set hold, while (1) does not hold.

Since the condition is not satisfied for (1), there exists a set of attributes V, satisfying (2) and such that for each general dependency d' (with outputline $Y_1', \dots, Y_{m'}'$, and inputlines $X_1'^i \dots X_{n_i'}'^i$) in the given set we have either $V \not\subseteq \bigcup_{j=1}^{m'} S(Y_j')$ there is an inputline with $V \subseteq \bigcup_{j=1}^{n_i'} S(X_j'^i)$. We construct the instance R as follows:

let all domains equal {0,1}, and let the instance consist of all the tuples u such that $\sum_{A \in V} u[A] = 0 \bmod 2$. Observe that for any $N_1, N_2, \dots, N_r \in \Sigma$ with $V \not\subseteq \bigcup_{j=1}^{r} S(Y_j')$, any tuple over $\bigcup_{j=1}^{r} S(N_j)$ occurs in R(*). Therefore, if $V \not\subseteq \bigcup_{j=1}^{m'} S(Y_j')$, d' holds in R.

On the other hand, if there is an inputline (the i-th) with $V \subseteq \bigcup_{j=1}^{n_i'} S(X_j'^{\,i})$ then it follows from the fact that d' is disjoint that every $X_j'^{\,i}$ with $V \cap S(X_j'^{\,i}) \neq \emptyset$ occurs in the outputline of d'. Hence, d' holds also in this case. However, the dependency (1) does not hold in this case: for each $X \in \Sigma$, let e(X) be an evaluation of X in such a way that $\sum_{A \in V} e(Y_1) \ldots e(Y_m)[A] = 1 \bmod 2$.

Then it follows from (*) that for each i with $1 \leq i \leq k$, $e(X_1^i) \ldots e(X_{n_i}^i)$ is defined and it occurs in R. □

CONCLUSION

It seems that the general dependencies enclose the intuitive concept of "dependencies" whatever that may be, and starting from our experience we hope that the set of inference rules given in the section, General Decompositions, is complete. The section on Trivial and Disjoint General Dependencies gives some directions towards proving this conjecture. In any event, the rules given in the section, General Decompositions, provide a better insight into the inference rules of the other dependencies.

Finally the general decompositions need to be studied in more detail, in order to see whether they contain applicable aspects, that are not covered by former decompositions.

REFERENCES

1. Armstrong, W. W. [1974] "Dependency Structures of Data Base Relationships", *Proc. IFIP 74*, North Holland, 1974, 580-583.

2. Bernstein, P. A. [1976] "Synthesizing Third Normal Form Relations from Functional Dependencies," *ACM TODS 1*, 4 (Dec. 1976), 277-298.

3. Beeri, C., Fagin, R., and Howard, J. H. [1977] "A Complete Axiomatization for Functional and Multivalued Dependencies in Relational Data BAses", *Proc. ACM SIGMOD 3rd Conf. on Management of Data*, Toronto, Canada, August 1977, 47-61.

4. Codd, E.F. [1970] "A Relational Model for Large Shared Data Bases," *CACM 13*, 6 (June 1970), 377-387.

5. Codd, E. F. [1971] "Further Normalization of the Data Base Relational Model", In: Data Base Systems, *Courant Com. Sc. Symp. Series* 6 (R. Rusin, Ed.), Prentice-Hall, 1971, 33-64.

6. Dayal, U., Bernstein, P. [1978] "The Fragmentation Problem: Lossless Decomposition of Relations into Files", *TR. CCA-78-13*, Computer Corporation of America, Cambridge, Mass., 1978.

7. Delobel, C. [1978] "Normalization and Hierarchical Dependencies in the Relational Data Model", *ACM TODS 3,* 3 (Sept. 1978), 201-222.

8. Delobel, C. and Pichat, E. [1978] "Application de l'algèbre aux modèles de données relationnels", *Congres AFCET-SMF,* 1978.

9. Fagin, R. [1977] "Multivalued Dependencies and a New Normal Form for Relational Databases", *ACM TODS 2,* 3 (Sept. 1977) 262-278.

10. Fagin, R. [1979] "Normal Forms and Relational Database Operators," *ACM SIGMOD*, Boston, May 30-June 1, 1979, 153-160.

11. Maier, D. and Mendelzon, A. [1979] "Generalized Mutual Dependencies and the Decomposition of Database Relations," *Proc. 5th Intl. Conf. on VLDB*, Rio de Janeiro, Oct. 1979, 75-82.

12. Nicolas, J. M. [1978] "Mutual Dependencies and Some Results on Undecomposable Relations", *Proceedings of VLDB*, 1978.

13. Paredaens, J. [1980] "The Interaction of Integrity Constraints in an Information System", to appear in *JCSS*, 1980.

14. Paredaens, J. [1979] "Transitive Dependencies in a Database Scheme," *MBLE*, R387, 1979, to appear in *RAIRO Informatique/ Computer Science 14,* 2, (1980).

15. Rissanen, J. [1978] "Theory of Relations for Databases — A Tutorial Survey", *Proc. 7th Symp. on Math. Found. of Comp. Sci., Lecture Notes in Comp. Science 64*, Springer-Verlag, 1978, 537-551.

16. Sadri, F., and Ullman, J. [1980] "Template Dependencies", unpubl. manuscript, Stanford Univ., 1980.

17. Zaniolo, C. [1976] "Analysis and Design of Relational Schemata for Databse Systems," *UCLA-ENG-7669*, University of California, Los Angeles, 1976.

ADEQUACY OF DECOMPOSITIONS OF RELATIONAL DATABASES †,††

David Maier,[1] Alberto O. Mendelzon,[2] Fereidoon Sadri,[3] and Jeffrey D. Ullman[4]

SUNY, Stony Brook, N.Y.,[1] IBM T.J. Watson Research Center,[2] Princeton University, N.J.,[3] and Stanford University, CA[4]

ABSTRACT

We consider conditions that have appeared in the literature with the purpose of defining a "good" decomposition of a relation scheme. We show that these notions are equivalent in the case that all constraints in the database are functional dependencies. This result solves an open problem of Rissanen. However, for arbitrary constraints the notions are shown to differ.

BASIC DEFINITIONS

We assume the reader is familiar with the relational model of data as expounded by Codd [1970], in which data is represented by tables called *relations*. Rows of tables are *tuples*, and the columns are named by *attributes*. The notation used in this paper is that found in Ullman [1980].

A frequent viewpoint is that the "real world" is modeled by a *universal* set of attributes R and constraints on the set of relations that can be the "current" relation for scheme R (see Beeri, Bernstein and Goodman [1978], Aho, Beeri and Ullman [1979], Beeri, Mendelzon, Sagiv and Ullman [1979]). The *database scheme* represent-

---

† From *Journal of Computer and System Sciences, Volume 21,* Number 2, October 1980; copyright Academic Press, Inc.; reprinted with permission.

†† Work partially supported by NSF grant MCS-76-15255. D. Maier and A. O. Mendelzon were also supported by IBM fellowships while at Princeton University, and F. Sadri by a scholarship from Isfahan University of Technology.

ing the real world is a collection of (nondisjoint) subsets of the universal relation scheme R; each of these subsets is called a *relation scheme*. The *database* is an assignment of *relations* (sets of tuples) to the relation schemes. The *database design* problem is to pick a database scheme $\rho = (R_1,\ldots,R_k)$ with $\bigcup_{i=1}^{k} R_i = R$, such that informally:

1. The "current" relation for R, which does not really exist in the database, can be discovered from the "current" values of the R_i's, which do exist in the database.
2. The constraints on the legal relations for scheme R can be enforced by constraints on the relations for the R_i's.
3. The R_i's have certain desirable properties, usually connected with the constraints, such as lack of redundancy.

While the above notions are informal, precise definitions have been given; Beeri, Bernstein and Goodman [1978] survey these ideas. Briefly, (1) is formalized as the lossless join property of Aho, Beeri and Ullman [1979], which we shall define. Item (2) is usually taken to mean embedability of dependencies (also to be defined) as in Bernstein [1976], while (3) is taken to refer to certain "normal forms", as defined for example by Codd [1972], Fagin [1977, 1979].

Projections and Joins

The key assumption on which our theory of database design rests is the formalization of "representation" by the algebraic operation of projection (see Rissanen [1977], e.g.). If r is a relation over set of attributes R, $S \subseteq R$, then $\pi_S(r)$ is the set of tuples of r with components in columns for attributes in R-S removed. For example, if R = {A,B,C}, and r is

A	B	C
0	1	2
2	1	3
0	3	2

Then $\pi_{AC}(r)$ is:

A	C
0	2
2	3

If $\rho = (R_1,\ldots,R_k)$ is a database scheme for universal relation scheme R, and r is a relation for R, then we use $\pi_\rho(r)$ to stand for the list $(\pi_{R_1}(r),\ldots,\pi_{R_k}(r))$.

If t is a tuple, t[S] is the components of t for the attributes in set S. The *(natural) join* of relations $r_1,\ldots,r_k$, whose schemes are $R_1,\ldots,R_k$ respectively, is the relation r over scheme $R = \bigcup_{i=1}^{k} R_i$ such that tuple t is in r if and only if for each i, $1 \le i \le k$, $t[R_i]$ is in r_i. We use symbol × for the join operation. Thus, if r_1 and r_2 are

A	B
0	1
1	2
2	1

B	C
3	1
1	2
2	0

then $r_1\ r_2$ is

A	B	C
0	1	2
1	2	0
2	1	2

Constraints and Dependencies

Often, the real world is not modeled by an arbitrary relation over the universal scheme R, but only by a subset of the possible relations chosen to represent some "physical constraints". The most common sorts of constraints are functional (Codd [1970, 1972], Armstrong [1974]) and multivalued (Fagin [1977], Beeri, Fagin and Howard [1977], Zaniolo [1976], Delobel [1978]) dependencies. If X and Y are subsets of universal scheme R, we say that *functional dependency* $X \to Y$ holds if every relation r that is allowable as a "current" relation for scheme R has the property that if t_1 and t_2 are tuples in r, and $t_1[X] = t_2[X]$, then $t_1[Y] = t_2[Y]$. The *multivalued dependency* $X \to\to Y$ holds if for each two tuples t_1 and t_2 in r, where $t_1[X] = t_2[X]$, there is a tuple t_3 in r such that $t_3[X] = t_1[X] = t_2[X]$, $t_3[Y] = t_1[Y]$, and $t_3[R - X - Y] = t_2[R - X - Y]$.

For example, if r is

A	B	C	D
0	1	2	3
0	2	3	2
0	2	2	2
0	1	3	3

then the functional dependencies $D \to B$, $BC \to D$, and $C \to A$ are seen to hold, as do the multivalued dependencies $A \to\to C$ and $B \to\to CD$. We show $A \to\to C$, e.g., by observing that for each A-value (0 is the only one) the possible C-values (2 and 3) are paired with the possible BD-values (1 3 and 2 2) in all possible ways in r.

In this paper we shall assume that for each relation scheme R there is an associated set L of legal relations for R. If we are given a set of functional and/or multivalued dependencies, D, then we let SAT(D) be the set of relations that satisfy all the dependencies in D, and we take L = SAT(D). We use $\pi_S(L)$ for $\{\pi_S(r) \mid r \text{ is in } L\}$ and we use $\pi_\rho(L)$, where ρ is the database scheme $(R_1,\ldots,R_k)$, for $\{\pi_\rho(r) \mid r \text{ is in } L\}$.

Lossless Joins

Often, the condition that a database scheme $\rho = (R_1,\ldots,R_k)$ represent the universal relation, i.e., that any legal universal relation be "represented" by its projections, is equated with the *lossless join condition:*

$$\text{for all } r \text{ in } L, \quad \mathop{\text{X}}_{i=1}^{k} \pi_{R_i}(r) = r$$

A test for this condition, when L = SAT(D) for a set of functional and multivalued dependencies D, was given by Aho, Beeri and Ullman [1979].

Preservation of Constrants under Projection

The second desired property of database schemes is that if r is a relation over universal scheme R, and $\rho = (R_1,\ldots,R_k)$ is a database scheme, then whenever the list of relations $\pi_\rho(r)$ satisfies "projected constraints", it follows that r satisfies the constraints themselves. The notion of "projected constraint" is well defined for functional and multivalued dependencies. If D is a set of such dependencies, let D^+ be the *closure* of D, that is, the set of dependencies that follow logically from D in the sense that in every relation r for which D holds, D^+ also holds. The computation of D^+ was explained by Beeri, Fagin and Howard [1977]. If $S \subseteq R$, then $\pi_S(D)$, the dependencies that hold in $\pi_S(R)$ for every relation r that satisfies D, consists of those $X \to Y$ and $X \to\to Y$ such that

1. There is some $X \to Z$ or $X \to\to Z$ in D^+.
2. $X \subseteq S$, and
3. $Y = Z \cap S$.

(Aho, Beeri and Ullman [1979].)

For functional dependencies, we can always assume Y = Z.

For functional dependencies only, the dependencies in $\pi_{R_i}(D)$ may be taken to hold in R, rather than R_i, and the question of logical implication can be decided by the techniques of Bernstein

[1976], for example. However, the projection of a multivalued dependency onto S becomes an "embedded dependency", which, while it holds in S, is not the same as having the same dependency hold in R. Properties of embedded dependencies are not well understood, and it is not clear how to test for logical implications.

In the most general case, the formalization of the condition that the projected constraints logically imply the original constraints is as follows. Let L be the set of legal relations for universal scheme R, and let $\rho = (R_1, \ldots, R_k)$ be a database scheme. Then we say ρ *preserves constraints* if whenever for all i, $\pi_{R_i}(r)$ is in $\pi_{R_i}(L)$, it follows that r is in L.

NOTIONS OF ADEQUATE REPRESENTATION

We now turn to several conditions that appear to combine the notions of representability and constraint preservation.

Rissanen's Approach

The first is the condition called *independent components* (IC) of Rissanen [1977]. Let L be the set of legal relations for universal scheme R and let $\rho = (R_1, \ldots, R_k)$ be a database scheme. Let P be the set of databases $\sigma = (r_1, \ldots, r_k)$ such that

1. For some relation r (not necessarily in L), $\sigma = \pi_\rho(r)$.
2. For $1 \leq i \leq k$, r_i is in $\pi_{R_i}(L)$.

Obviously $\pi_\rho(L) \subseteq P$, but the inclusion could be proper. Figure 1 shows the relationship between these sets.

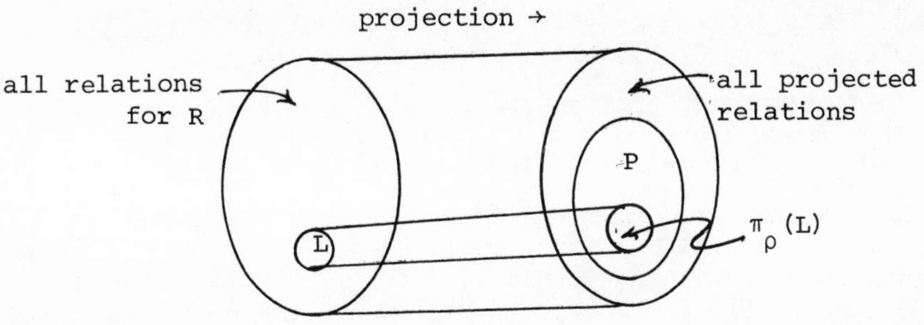

Figure 1. Diagram of relevant sets of relations and projections.

We say ρ is a *decomposition into independent components* if the following hold.

(IC1) If σ is in P, then there is at most one r in L such that $\pi_\rho(r) = \sigma$.

(IC2) If σ is in P, then there is at least one r in L such that $\pi_\rho(r) = \sigma$.

Obviously (IC1) and (IC2) could be combined into the single statement "π_ρ is a bijection from L onto P", but we choose to write them this way for comparisons with other definitions to be made later. The motivation behind the IC conditions is that a unique universal relation in L is represented by every member of P. In turn, P is the set of databases that might arise in practice if we assume the database is always the projection of a universal instance and check constraints in the relations individually, as updates to the relations are made. That is to say, the databases that we expect to occur are in one-to-one correspondence with the universal instances we expect to occur, so the former can be fairly said to represent the latter.

Arora and Carlson's Approach

A second point of view regarding adequate representation was expressed by Arora and Carlson [1978]. Their approach (suitably generalized to arbitrary constraints) is to take the lossless join and constraint preservation conditions together as the definition of an adequate decomposition. We shall relate the Arora-Carlson conditions to independent components by showing equivalence of the above to the following two conditions.

(AC1) = (IC1)

(AC2) If σ is in P, and $\pi_\rho(r) = \sigma$, then r is in L.

Theorem 1

Conditions (AC1) and (AC2) hold if and only if the lossless join and constraint preservation properties hold.

Proof: (If) Suppose (AC1), which is the same as (IC1), does not hold. Then there are r_1 and r_2 in L such that for some σ in P, $\pi_\rho(r_1) = \pi_\rho(r_2) = \sigma$. Let $\sigma = (r_1, \ldots, r_k)$, and $\mathop{\times}\limits_{i=1}^{k} r_i = r$. Then r must be both r_1 and r_2 by the lossless join condition. Thus (AC1) holds. Now suppose (AC2) does not hold, that is, there is a relation r, not in L, such that $\pi_\rho(r) = \sigma$ is in P. We then directly contradict the assumption that ρ preserves constraints.

(Only if) Suppose the lossless join condition is violated. Then there is a relation r in L such that $r' = \mathop{\times}\limits_{i=1}^{k} \pi_{R_i}(r) \neq r$.

It is easy to show that $\pi_{R_i}(r') = \pi_{R_i}(r)$. Thus, $\pi_\rho(r') = \pi_\rho(r)$. Since r is in L, $\pi_\rho(r)$ must be in P. If r' is not in L, we violate (AC2), while if r' is in L, we violate (AC1). Last, if constraints are not preserved, then there is r not in L such that $\pi_\rho(r)$ is in P, immediately contradicting (AC2). □

Corollary

The lossless join and constraint preservation conditions imply the IC conditions.

Proof: (AC1) is (IC1). Suppose (AC2) holds, while (IC2) does not. For each σ in P there must be some r such that $\pi_\rho(r) = \sigma$. If r is in L, then (IC2) holds; if r is not in L, then (AC2) is violated. □

The equivalence of IC and AC was shown by Rissanen [1977] for the case that ρ consists of two relation schemes, and L = SAT(D) for a set of functional dependencies D. We shall generalize this result to arbitrary numbers of relation schemes.

An Intermediate Condition

Let us now introduce a condition that lies between the AC and IC conditions. While the IC conditions guarantee that every database in P represents a unique universal relation in L, we might not be able to find that relation conveniently, given σ in P. Probably the most natural way to go from $\sigma = (r_1,\ldots,r_k)$ in P to the instance that it represents is to take the join of the r_i's. However, it is conceivable that $r = \mathop{\times}_{i=1}^{k} r_i$ is not in L, yes there is still some unique r' in L such that $\pi_\rho(r') = \sigma$. We therefore propose that a more realistic definition of adequacy for decompositions is the following. (The same proposal was made independently by Beeri and Rissanen [1979].)

(J1) = (IC1) = (AC1)

(J2) If $\sigma = (r_1,\ldots,r_k)$ is in P, then $\mathop{\times}_{i=1}^{k} r_i$ is in L.

The *join condition* above has the following factors in its favor.

1. We shall show that in some cases it is more general than AC.

2. The universal instance represented by a database σ in P is effectively constructible from σ, while for IC, this may not be the case.

We shall now explore some of the elementary properties of condition J.

Theorem 2

(AC) implies (J) implies (IC).

Proof: Suppose (AC2) holds, but (J2) does not. Then there is $\sigma = (r_1,\ldots,r_k)$ in P such that $r = \overset{k}{\underset{i=1}{\times}} r_i$ is not in L. But $\pi_\rho(r) = \sigma$, so (AC2) is violated. Now suppose (J2) holds. Then $r = \overset{k}{\underset{i=1}{\times}} r_i$ is in L, and $\pi_\rho(r) = \sigma$, so (IC2) holds. □

Theorem 3

Suppose D is a set of functional dependencies, and L = SAT(D). Then (IC), (AC) and (J) are equivalent.

Proof: By Theorems 1 and 2 it suffices to show that if either the lossless join or constraint preservation properties fail to hold, then (IC) fails. Suppose first that the set of functional dependencies D is not preserved by the decomposition $\rho = (R_1,\ldots,R_k)$. This means that there exists some relation r not in SAT(D) such that $\pi_{R_i}(r)$ is in π_{R_i}**(SAT**(D)) for all i, and hence r satisfies all the dependencies $\pi_{R_i}(D)$. It follows that $E = (\bigcup_{i=1}^{k} \pi_{R_i}(D))^+$ does not contain D^+. In particular, let $X \to A$ be a dependency in D^+ that is not in E. Let Y be the set of attributes B such that $X \to B$ is in E. Surely $X \subseteq Y$ and S is not in Y.

Let r_0 be a universal relation with exactly two tuples. These tuples agree on all attributes of Y and disagree on all other attributes. Then $X \to A$ does not hold in r_0 , so r_0 is not in L = SAT(D). However, $\sigma = \pi_\rho(r_0)$ is in P, since r_0 is easily seen to satisfy all the dependencies in E. We now claim that σ cannot be $\pi_\rho(r)$ for any r in L, thus violating (IC2). For any such r must have only one symbol appearing in the column of any attribute in Y, and it must also have two different symbols for those attributes not in Y. It follows that r must violate $X \to A$. This shows that (IC) implies constraint preservation.

Now suppose the lossless join condition fails. Let r be a relation in L such that $\sigma = \pi_\rho(R)$ and $\times\, \sigma = r' \neq r$. If r' is in L, IC1 is violated. If r' is not in L, constraint preservation is violated, since σ satisfies all the projected dependencies $\pi_\rho(D)$. As we just showed, this implies IC fails. □

Corollary

There is a polynomial time algorithm to test if condition (IC) is satisfied, if L is determined by functional dependencies.

Proof: By Theorems 1 and 3, we have only to test the lossless join and constraint preservation conditions. The lossless join condition can be tested in polynomial time by the algorithm of

Aho, Beeri and Ullman [1979]. Preservation of functional dependencies is testable in polynomial time by the algorithm of Beeri and Honeyman [1979]. □

We have mentioned that the proof of Theorem 3 does not generalize to multivalued dependencies. In fact, we can say more: the theorem is false in this case.

Consider $R = \{A,B,C\}$, and let D consist of the one multivalued dependency $A \to\to B$ (which implies $A \to\to C$ by the complementation rule of Beeri, Fagin and Howard [1977]. If $\rho = (AB,AC)$, then ρ has the lossless join property (Fagin [1977]), and hence, as in the proof of Theorem 1, ρ satisfies (AC1). However, the projected dependencies $A \to\to B$ in AB and $A \to\to C$ in AC are trivial embedded dependencies and do not imply $A \to\to C$ in ABC. Put another way, if $L = SAT(D)$, then any relation whatsoever is in $\pi_{AB}(L)$ and $\pi_{AC}(L)$. Thus membership of $\pi_{AB}(r)$ and $\pi_{AC}(r)$ in P surely does not imply that r is in L. We therefore have an example where $\rho = (AB,AC)$ does not satisfy (AC). However, the join $\pi_{AB}(r) \times \pi_{AC}(r)$ must satisfy $A \to\to B$ for any relation r over ABC, so ρ satisfies (J).

Weak Constraint Preservation

The example above suggests that the lossless join and constraint preservation conditions may be too strong to characterize all desirable decompositions. In fact, if we assume that the instance represented by a database is the join of the relations in the database, then we should take into account the fact that there are other constraints that must necessarily hold in the join, besides those implied by the projected constraints.

Given a decomposition $\rho = (R_1,\ldots,R_k)$, let FIXPT(ρ) be the set of relations r such that $\overset{k}{\underset{i=1}{\times}} \pi_{R_i}(r) = r$. We relax the constraint preservation condition as follows. †

Given the set of legal relations L for universal scheme R, we say that ρ *weakly preserves constraints* if whenever r is in FIXPT(ρ) and for all i, $\pi_{R_i}(r)$ is in $\pi_{R_i}(L)$, it follows that r is in L. We can now show that, for arbitrary L, the (J) condition is equivalent to lossless join and weak preservation.

<u>Theorem 4</u>

Conditions (J1) and J2) hold if and only if the lossless join and weak constraint preservation properties hold.

---

† The same proposal was made independently by Beeri and Rissanen [1979], who also proved results similar to Theorems 3 and 4.

Proof: (If) We have seen in the proof of Theorem 1 that the lossless join property implies (J1). Now suppose that $\pi_\rho(r)$ is in P. Let $r' = \underset{i}{\times} \pi_{R_i}(r)$. Since r' is in FIXPT(ρ), and $\pi_\rho(r') = \pi_\rho(r)$ is in P, weak constraint preservation implies r' is in L, proving (J2).

(Only if) Suppose ρ satisfies (J), and let r be in L. By (J2), $r' = \times \pi_\rho(r)$ is in L. Since $\pi_\rho(r) = \pi_\rho(r')$, (J1) implies r = r', proving the lossless join property. Now let r be in FIXPT(ρ) and let $\pi_\rho(r)$ be in P. By (J2), $\times \pi_\rho(r)$ is in L. Since r is in FIXPT(ρ), we have $r = \times \pi_\rho(r)$, proving weak preservation.

□

Adequacy of 4NF Decompositions

The literature shows that certain undesirable anomalies in the updating of the database can be avoided when the database scheme is in a *normal form* with respect to the given dependencies. Progressively more general formulations of the normal form concept are third normal form (Codd [1972]), fourth normal form (4NF) (Fagin [1977,1979]) and project-join normal form (Fagin [1979]). We shall define 4NF and show that the J and IC conditions are equivalent for 4NF decompositions. We shall also show how to test for the J or IC conditions on a 4NF decomposition.

Suppose the set of legal relations L is defined by a set of fd's D and mvd's M. Let $D_i = \pi_{R_i}(D)$, $M_i = \pi_{R_i}(M)$. A relation scheme R_i is in 4NF if every mvd $m \in M_i$ is implied (in the context of R_i) by an fd of the form $X \rightarrow R_i \in D_i$. A database scheme ρ is in 4NF if every $R_i \in \rho$ is in 4NF.

We shall need some preliminary results for the proof of our theorem. The next theorem is due to Sagiv and Fagin [1979].

Theorem 5

Let D be a set of fd's, M a set of mvd's, and d a functional or multivalued dependency. If $SAT(D \cup M) \not\subseteq SAT(d)$, then there exists a relation r with only two tuples in it such that $r \in SAT(D \cup M) - SAT(d)$.

We define M_ρ as the set of all mvd's that must be satisfied by every relation in FIXPT(ρ). For example, for ρ = {AB,BC,CD}, it can be seen that $M_\rho = \{B \rightarrow\rightarrow A,\ C \rightarrow\rightarrow D\}^+$.

Lemma 1

Let r be a relation containing only two tuples. If $r \in SAT(M_\rho)$, then $r \in FIXPT(\rho)$.

Proof: Let $r = \{t_1,t_2\}$ and $\rho = \{R_1,\ldots,R_k\}$. Suppose $r \notin FIXPT(\rho)$. Let $r' = \times_i (\pi_{R_i}(r))$. Say $t \in r' - r$. Assume without loss of generality that $t[R_i] = t_1[R_i]$ for $1 \leq i \leq j$, $t[R_i] = t_2[R_i]$ for $j < i \leq k$. Let $S_1 = \bigcup_{i=1}^{j} R_i$, $S_2 = \bigcup_{i=j+1}^{k} R_i$. Then $t \in \pi_{S_1}(r) \times \pi_{S_2}(r)$. It follows that $r \notin FIXPT\{S_1,S_2\}$, and hence (Fagin [1977]) $r \notin SAT(S_1 \cap S_2 \rightarrow\rightarrow S_1)$. However, it is shown in Mendelzon and Maier [1979] that $S_1 \cap S_2 \rightarrow\rightarrow S_1$ is in M_ρ, contradicting our assumption that $r \in SAT(M_\rho)$. □

Lemma 2 †

Let D be a set of fd's and d a functional or multivalued dependency. If $FIXPT(\rho) \cap SAT(D) \not\subseteq SAT(d)$, then there exists a relation $r \in FIXPT(\rho) \cap SAT(D) - SAT(d)$ such that r contains only two tuples.

Proof: Let M be the set of mvd's defined above. Since $FIXPT(\rho) \subseteq SAT(M_\rho)$, $SAT(M_\rho \cup D) \not\subseteq SAT(d)$. By Theorem 5, it follows that there is a relation $r = \{t_1,t_2\} \in SAT(M_\rho \cup D) - SAT(d)$. Since r contains only two tuples and satisfies M_ρ, it follows from Lemma 1 that $r \in FIXPT(\rho)$. □

Theorem 6

In any 4NF database scheme, J holds iff IC holds.

Proof: By Theorem 2, J implies IC. We shall prove that for 4NF schemes, IC implies lossless join and weak constraint preservation.

Suppose first that ρ is a 4NF database scheme satisfying IC but not weak constraint preservation. Then there exists a relation $s \in FIXPT(\rho)$ such that $\pi_{R_i}(s)$ satisfies $\pi_{R_i}(D)$ for all i, but $s \notin SAT(M,D)$.

Let $D' = \pi_\rho(D)$. The existence of relation s implies that there exits a functional or multivalued dependency $d \in M \cup D$ such that $FIXPT(\rho) \cap SAT(D') \not\subseteq SAT(d)$. By Lemma 2, there must exist a relation $r = \{t_1,t_2\} \in FIXPT(\rho) \cap SAT(D') - SAT(d)$.

Let $\sigma = \pi_\rho(r)$. Note that σ satisfies all the projected fd's D'. Since ρ is a 4NF scheme, σ must also satisfy the projected mvd's $\pi_\rho(M)$.

---

† This lemma was proved independently by Vardi [1979].

We claim that there is no relation $r' \in SAT(M \cup D)$ such that $\pi_\rho(r') = \sigma$, violating IC2. In proof, suppose there existed such a relation. Since r is in FIXPT(ρ), $\times\ \rho = r$. Thus it must be the case that $r' \subseteq r$. Hence r' has no more than two tuples. On the other hand, if r' contains only one tuple, then so does $\times\ \rho$, which equals r. But this contradicts the fact that r violates dependency d, since a one-tuple relation satisfies every fd and mvd. It follows that r' = r, so r' cannot satisfy M and D.

Now suppose that lossless join fails. Let $r \in SAT(D \cup M)$ be such that $\sigma = \pi_\rho(r)$, $\times\ \sigma = r' \neq r$. If $r' \in SAT(D \cup M)$, then IC1 is violated. If $r' \notin SAT(D \cup M)$, then weak constraint preservation fails, since $r' \in FIXPT(\rho)$ and r' satisfies all the projected dependencies. By the first part of the proof, since weak constraint preservation fails, IC fails.

□

To test whether J holds in a 4NF decomposition, we need to determine whether $D \cup M$ guarantee a lossless join and weak constraint preservation for ρ. The lossless join condition can be tested by the method of Aho, Beeri and Ullman [1979]. Weak constraint preservation, for a 4NF scheme, reduces to the question of whether $FIXPT(\rho) \cap SAT(\pi_\rho(D)) \subseteq SAT(D \cup M)$. In the terminology of Rissanen [1978] (see also Beeri and Vardi [1980], Sciore [1979]), this is the same as testing whether certain fd's and mvd's are implied by a "join dependency" and a set of fd's. An exponential time algorithm for this problem was given by Maier, Mendelzon and Sagiv [1979], and a polynomial time algorithm by Maier, Sagiv and Yannakakis [1980] and Vardi [1979]. Note that the best known test for the lossless join in the presence of mvd's is still exponential in time and space (Aho, Beeri and Ullman [1979]). Also, the computation of the D_i's seems to require exponential time. However, if we assume that the database scheme is the result of the decomposition process of Fagin [1977], and covers for the projected dependencies are given, the test can be done in polynomial time by the algorithm mentioned above, since this process always yields lossless decompositions.

OPEN QUESTIONS

There are a variety of problems suggested by the foregoing results that appear to be quite difficult. Among these are:

1. Is (J) different from (IC) in general? We now know they are the same if the legal relations are determined by functional dependencies, or if ρ is a 4NF scheme. Also, it is easy to show that there exist contrived L's for which they are different. What if L is determined by a set of multivalued dependencies, or by another type of dependency with which we are familiar?

2. Is there an effective test for (IC) for any case but the special cases noted in (1) above?

3. How do we test (AC) if the legal relations are determined by multivalued dependencies? This is a special case of the more general problem of deciding when embedded and full multivalued dependencies determine a full multivalued dependency, where a *full* dependency is one that applies to the universal set of attributes.

REFERENCES

1. Aho, A. V., Beeri, C. and Ullman, J. D. [1979] "The Theory of Joins in Relational Databases," *TODS* 4, 3, (1979) 297-314.

2. Armstrong, W. W. [1974] "Dependency Structures of Database Relationships," *Proc. 1974 IFIP Congress*, North Holland, 1974, 580-583.

3. Arora, A. K., and Carlson, C. R. [1978] "The Information Preserving Properties of Certain Relational Database Transformations," *Proc. 4th Intl. Conf. on Very Large Databases*, 1978, 352-359.

4. Beeri, C., Bernstein, P. A. and Goodman, N. [1978] "A Sophisticate's Introduction to Database Normalization Theory," *Proc. 4th Intl. Conf. on Very Large Databases*, 1978, 113-124.

5. Beeri, C., Fagin, R. and Howard, J. H. [1977] "A Complete Axiomatization for Functional and Multivalued Dependencies," *Proc. ACM-SIGMOD Intl. Conf. on Management of Data*, 1977, 47-61.

6. Beeri, C., and P. Honeyman [1979] "Preserving Functional Dependencies," submitted for publication.

7. Beeri, C., Mendelzon, A. O., Sagiv, Y., and Ullman, J. D. [1979] "Equivalence of Relational Database Schemes," *Proc. 11th ACM Symp. on Theory of Computing*, 1979, 319-329.

8. Beeri, C. and Rissanen, J. [1980] "Faithful Representation of Relational Database Schemes," IBM Research Report RJ2722, 1980.

9. Beeri, C. and Vardi, M. Y. [1980] "On the Properties of Join Dependencies," *Advances in Data Base Theory, Vol. I*, Plenum Press, this volume.

10. Bernstein, P. A. [1976] "Synthesizing Third Normal Form Relations from Functional Dependencies," *TODS 1*, 4 (1976) 277-298.

11. Codd, E. F. [1970] "A Relational Model for Large Shared Data Banks," *CACM 13*, 6 (1970) 377-387.

12. Codd, E. F. [1972] "Further Normalization of the Data Base Relational Model" In: *Data Base Systems* (R. Rustin, Ed.), Prentice Hall, Englewood Cliffs, N. J., 1972, 33-64.

13. Delobel, C. [1978] "Normalization and Hierarchical Dependencies in the Relational Data Model," *TODS 3*, 3 (1978) 201-222.

14. Fagin, R. [1977] "Multivalued Dependencies and a New Normal Form for Relational Databases," *TODS 2*, 3 (1977) 262-278.

15. Fagin, R. [1979] "Normal Forms and Relational Database Operators," *Proc. ACM-SIGMOD Intl. Conf. on Management of Data*, 1979, 153-160.

16. Maier, D., Mendelzon, A. O., and Sagiv, Y. [1979] "Testing Implications of Data Dependencies," *TODS 4*, 4 (1979) 455-469.

17. Maier, D., Sagiv, Y. and Yannakakis, M. [1979] "On the Complexity of Testing Implication of Functional and Join Dependencies," unpublished manuscript, 1979.

18. Mendelzon, A. O. and Maier, D. [1979] "Generalized Mutual Dependencies and the Decomposition of Database Relations," *Proc. 5th Intl. Conf. on Very Large Databases*, 1979, 75-82.

19. Rissanen, J. [1977] "Independent Components of Relations," *TODS 2*, 4 (1977) 317-325.

20. Rissanen, J. [1978] "Theory of Relations for Databases — a Tutorial Survey," *Proc. Symp. on Mathematical Foundations of Computer Science*, Springer-Verlag, Zakopane, Poland, 1978, 536-551.

21. Sagiv, Y. and Fagin, R. [1979] "An Equivalence between Relational Database Dependencies and a Subclass of Propositional Logic," IBM Research Report RJ2500, 1979.

22. Sciore, E. [1979] "A Complete Axiomatization of Full Join Dependencies," Princeton Univ., Dept. of EECS TR#279, July 1979.

23. Ullman, J. D. [1980] *Principles of Database Systems*, Computer Science Press, Potomac, Md. 1980.

24. Vardi, M.Y. [1979] "Inferring Multivalued Dependency from Functional and Join Dependencies," submitted for publication.

25. Zaniolo, C. [1979] "Analysis and Design of Relational Schemata for Database Systems," doctoral dissertation, UCLA, 1976.

A METHOD FOR HELPING DISCOVER THE DEPENDENCIES OF A RELATION

Antonio M. Silva and Michael A. Melkanoff

University of California, Los Angeles

ABSTRACT

One of the problems plaguing a data base designer is the inherent difficulty of extracting from a user the complete semantics of the relations utilized to define the conceptual model of a data base.

The purpose of this paper is to describe an approach for obtaining the functional dependencies (FDs) and the multivalued dependencies (MDs) characterizing a relation by presenting iteratively to the user a contrived instance of each relation. To this effect we have constructed a program which is utilized as follows:

(1) Input for a given relation the following information obtained from preliminary analyses and discussions with the user (this is usually called the universal relation schema):

   (a) the attributes of the relation including (if available) the set of values defined in each domain.

   (b) the FDs and MDs of the relation.

(2) Decomposition of the relation into atomic components following the algorithm developed by Zaniolo and Melkanoff (Zaniolo and Melkanoff [1980], Melkanoff and Zaniolo [1980]).

(3) Construction of a contrived instance for the universal relation schema obtained by joining atomic relational instances for the atomic components derived in step (2). This relation extension contains the tuples needed to illustrate the depen-

dency set input in step (1b).

(4) Display of the relational instance to the user.

The process may be iterated until the user feels that the contrived instance provides a satisfactory illustration of the relation schema.

INTRODUCTION

In order to help a data base designer obtain the dependencies (functional and multivalued) of a relation from the user we propose (and have constructed) a program which:

(1) Given the attribute set of a relation and the dependencies among these attributes decomposes this universal relation schema, yielding the A- and Z-covers[1] by execution of the Zaniolo-Melkanoff algorithm, as shown in Figure 1.

(2) Given the A- and Z-covers and the attribute domains constructs an instance for the universal relation schema by joining the instances constructed for each atomic component as shown in Figure 2.

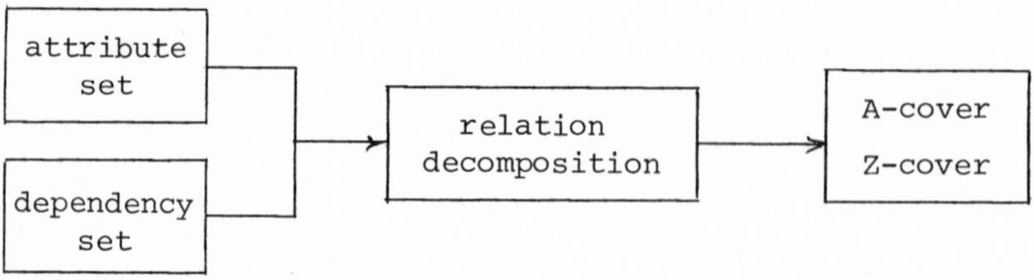

Figure 1. Relation Decomposition.

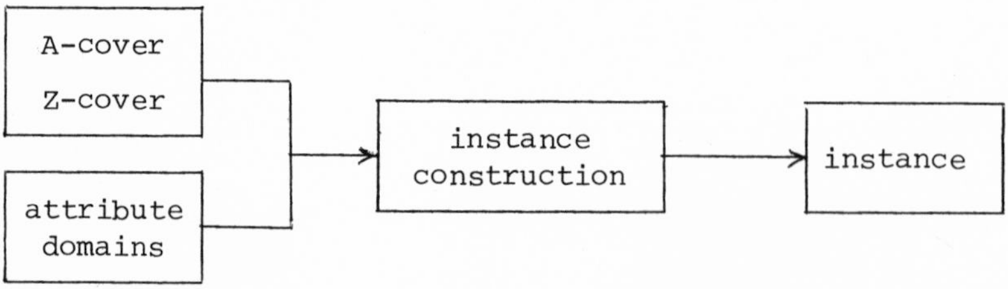

Figure 2. Instance Construction.

[1] These two sets constitute what is usually called the final schema.

We assume that the user is able to recognize whether the constructed instance exhibits all the relationships he knows to exist among the relation attributes. This would usually occur when he sees two or more tuples which cannot exist simultaneously. Having been appraised of this fact the database designer will conclude that a dependency is missing or is wrong, and the dependency set must be changed and a new instance constructed and displayed to the user until the correct dependency set is realized.

We present in this paper a method to generate an instance for a universal relation schema that shows all the relationships implied by the dependency set and no other. An instance for each atomic component is constructed and the instance for the universal relation schema is obtained by joining the instances for the atomic components.

A detailed example is presented in the APPENDIX.

DEFINITIONS AND NOTATION

We shall follow the definitions and notations introduced in Zaniolo and Melkanoff [1980] and in Melkanoff and Zaniolo [1980], relating these to other notations and definitions whenever possible.

Relations and Dependencies

Attributes will be denoted by the letters A,B,... and the letters X,Y,... will be used for sets of attributes, which are also called *combinations*. The cardinality of combination X will be denoted by $|X|$.

The *domain* associated with each attribute will be denoted by DOM(A). The values in DOM(A) will be denoted A1,A2,... . We will use the letters a,b,... or $|DOM(A)|$, $|DOM(B)|$, ... to denote the cardinality of DOM(A), DOM(B), ... For a combination X an *X-value* is an assignment of values to the attributes of X from their domain. The X-values will be denoted X1,X2,... .

A *relation* on the set of attributes {A,B,...} will be denoted by R(A,B,...). Similarly if R is a relation over the union of the disjoint combinations X,Y,..., then we will use the notation R(X,Y,...). The elements of a relation are called *tuples*. The letters u,v,... will be used to denote single tuples. The cardinality of R(X) will be denoted by $|R(X)|$. The *projection* of R on Y will be denoted by R[Y].

The *functional dependency* (FD) of Y on X will be denoted by X ->Y. If Y is not functionally dependent on X the notation X -/-> Y will be used.

The *multivalued dependency* (MD) of Y on X will be denoted by X->>Y.

A- and Z-Covers

The A- and Z-covers are obtained as the result of the execution of the Zaniolo-Melkanoff decomposition algorithm which decomposes a universal relation schema yielding a final schema, in the form of A- and Z-covers, satisfying the requirements of representation, separation and minimal redundancy of Beeri et al. [1978].

The A-*cover* is the set of *atomic components*, the attribute sets of the projections of the universal relation which may be joined together to reconstruct the universal relation. Its elements have the form n: Z where Z is the attribute set of the projection, and n is its label.

The Z-*cover* is the set of FDs associated with the atomic components. Its elements have the form n: X->Y where X->Y is an FD of a minimal cover for the FDs in the universal relation schema, and n is its label. Both the FD and the atomic component have the same label when they are associated.

For example, the following relation which is described in detail in the APPENDIX

FIELD(CUST#,CUSTN,MODEL,MODQ,TEC#,TECN)

with the following set of dependencies

CUST#->CUSTN
CUST#->>{MODEL,MODQ}
CUST#->>{TEC#,TECN}
{CUST#,MODEL}->MODQ
TEC#->TECN
TEC#->>{CUST#,CUSTN,MODEL,MODQ}

is decomposed into the following final schema:

A-COVER:	Z-COVER:
1: CUST#,CUSTN	1: CUST#->CUSTN
2: CUST#,MODEL,MODQ	2: {CUST#,MODEL}->MODQ
3: TEC#,TECN	3: TEC#->TECN
4: CUST#,TEC#	

Note that the FDs in the Z-cover are the original FDs but there is no MD in the Z-cover. The original MDs disappear during the decomposition but are regenerated during the reconstruction of the universal relation schema by joining the atomic components in the

A-cover.

Relationships

There is a *one-to-one relationship* between combinations X and Y when every different X-value corresponds to a different Y-value, that is, X->Y and Y->X.

There is a *many-to-one relationship* between combinations X and Y when one or more X-values may correspond to the same Y-value, but no X-value corresponds to more than one Y-value, that is, X->Y and Y-/->X.

There is a *many-to-many relationship* between combinations X and Y when one or more X-values may correspond to the same Y-value and one or more Y-values may correspond to the same X-value, that is, X-/->Y and Y-/->X.

When a decomposition is carried out following the Zaniolo-Melkanoff algorithm it may happen that the scope of an FD, {X,Y}->Z, is equal to the attribute set of an intermediate relation in the process of being decomposed. In that special case the FD is added to the Z-cover and, if there still exist nontrivial MDs Z->>X or Z->>Y the decomposition continues leaving the FD in the Z-cover without any corresponding atomic component in the A-cover. In order to generate an instance for this special case we need to define the following:

We shall say that a *combined relationship* exists among three combinations X, Y, and Z when {X,Y}->Z and one of the following cases occurs:

(i) Z->>X and Z->>Y
(ii) Z->X and Z->>Y
(iii) Z->>X and Z->Y .

REARRANGEMENTS IN THE A- AND Z-COVERS

We recall that the decomposition algorithm yields the sets A-cover and Z-cover, the latter consisting of FDs of the form X->A where X is a combination and A a single attribute (see the example in the APPENDIX). Now the instances created for the atomic components in the A-cover must eventually be joined to form an instance of the original relation. If there exist several FDs with the same left side, say X->A and X->B whereas A and B belong to different atomic components, joining the two atomic instances will generally not reflect the many-to-many relationship existing between A and B. In order that this relationship be made explicit within the final instance it is necessary that FDs with the same left side be merged into a single FD. This merging is called here rearrangement[1] and we shall describe it now for various special cases (see also the example described in the APPENDIX).

Rearrangements Due to One-to-One Relationships

If there is a one-to-one relationship between two combinations X and Y, that is X->Y and Y->X, and $|X| > 1$ or $|Y| > 1$, then there may be an FD X->Y or Y->X in the Z-cover without associated atomic component, and $|X|$ or $|Y|$ additional FDs in the Z-cover with associated atomic components. The A- and Z-covers must be rearranged so that only one atomic component appears with two FDs with equal inverted left- and right-hand sides.

Rearrangements Due to Many-to-One Relationships

If there is a many-to-one relationship between two combinations X and Y, that is X->Y, and $|Y| > 1$, then there may be $|Y|$ FDs in the Z-cover. The A- and Z-covers must be rearranged so that only one atomic component with one associated FD appears.

If X->Y is an FD associated with atomic component R[X,Y], Z->W is another FD associated with atomic component R[Z,W] and X contains Z, the A- and Z-covers must be rearranged so that only one atomic component R[X,(Y ∪ W)] appears with the FDs X->{Y ∪ W} and Z->>W.

Rearrangements Due to Combined Relationships

If there is a combined relationship among combinations X, Y, and Z, then there is an FD {X,Y}->Z in the Z-cover with no associated atomic component and 2 atomic components R[X,Z] and R[Y,Z] which belong to one of these three cases:

(i) R[X,Z] and R[Y,Z] have no FDs.
(ii) R[X,Z] has no FD and R[Y,Z] has the FD Z->Y.
(iii) R[X,Z] has the FD Z->X and R[Y,Z] has no FDs.

The A- and Z-covers must be rearranged so that only one atomic component appears associated with the FD {X,Y}->Z. The MD Z->>X is added to the Z-cover if there is no FD Z->X, while the MD Z->>Y is added to the Z-cover if there is no FD Z->Y. This can be done because in case (i) the MDs Z->>X and Z->>Y must exist so that R[X,Y,Z] is decomposable into R[X,Z] and R[Y,Z]. In case (ii) the MD Z->>X is obtained by complementing Z->Y. In case (iii) the MD Z->>Y is obtained by complementing Z->X.

---

[1] This process is related to the merging of equivalent keys described in Bernstein's algorithm (Bernstein [1976]).

CONSTRUCTION OF INSTANCES

We use the rearranged A- and Z-covers to determine the scope and nature of the relationships between combinations of attributes in each atomic component.

Based on the types of the relationships between combinations of attributes, the algorithm presented in the section Computation of the Attribute Domain Sizes, below, computes for each attribute the minimum domain size necessary to construct the instance in such a way as to display the given dependencies only.

The actual elements for each domain may be supplied by the data base designer or default-wise automatically generated by the program.

Construction of Instances with Many-to-Many Relationships

Based on the definition of a many-to-many relationship, in an atomic component R[A,B,...] there is a many-to-many relationship among the attributes A,B,... if there is no FD associated with this atomic component in the Z-cover.

An instance showing this many-to-many relationship is constructed by generating the relation R1(A,B) with a many-to-many relationship between A and B, using unary relations corresponding to A and B, then generating the relation R2(A,B,C) with a many-to-many relationship between A, B, and C, using R1(A,B) and the unary relation corresponding to C, and so on.

Given a relation R(X) with a many-to-many relationship among the attributes in X and a unary relation S(A), a relation T(X,A) with a many-to-many relationship among all attributes in X and A is constructed by concatenating the first tuple of R(X) with all tuples of S(A) and the remaining tuples of R(X) with the first tuple of S(A) as shown in Figure 3. Let r be $|R(X)|$ and a be $|S(A)|$. We must have $r \geq 2$ and $a \geq 2$. There is a many-to-many relationship between X and A because r X-values correspond to A1 and a A-values correspond to X1.

For example, let DOM(MAKE)={FORD,GM,FIAT}, DOM(MODEL)={CAPRI,NOVA,128}, and DOM(YEAR)={1972,1975,1973}. The construction of an instance showing a many-to-many relationship among MAKE, MODEL and YEAR is shown in Figure 4. The construction is done in two steps. First R(MAKE,MODEL) with a many-to-many relationship between MAKE and MODEL is constructed from P(MAKE) and Q(MODEL) and then T(MAKE,MODEL,YEAR) is constructed from R(MAKE,MODEL) and S(YEAR).

R(X):	S(A):	T(X, A):
X1	A1	X1 A1
X2	A2	X1 A2
...	...	...
Xr	Aa	X1 Aa
		X2 A1
		...
		Xr A1

Figure 3. Construction of an Instance with a Many-to-Many Relationship between X and A,

P(MAKE):	Q(MODEL):	R(MAKE,MODEL):
FORD	CAPRI	FORD CAPRI
GM	NOVA	FORD NOVA
FIAT	128	FORD 128
		GM CAPRI
		FIAT CAPRI

R(MAKE,MODEL):	S(YEAR):	T(MAKE,MODEL,YEAR):
FORD CAPRI	1972	FORD CAPRI 1972
FORD NOVA	1975	FORD CAPRI 1975
FORD 128	1973	FORD CAPRI 1973
GM CAPRI		FORD NOVA 1972
FIAT CAPRI		FORD 128 1972
		GM CAPRI 1972
		FIAT CAPRI 1972

Figure 4. Construction of an Instance with a Many-to-Many Relationship among MAKE, MODEL and YEAR.

Construction of Instances with a One-to-One Relationship

In an atomic component R[X,Y] there is a one-to-one relationship between the combinations X and Y if there are two FDs X->Y and Y->X associated with R[X,Y] in the Z-cover.

An instance showing this one-to-one relationship is constructed by generating a relation T(X,Y) from a relation R(X) corresponding to combination X, and relation S(Y) corresponding to combination Y. If $|X| = 1$ the relation R(X) is the unary relation constructed from the domain of the attribute in X. If $|X| > 1$ we obtain R(X) by generating a relation with a many-to-many relationship among the attributes in X. In the same way we obtain S(Y).

We must have $|R(X)| = |S(Y)|$ because for each different X-value must correspond a different Y-value. In order that the following algorithm enforces a many-to-many relationship between each attribute A in X and each attribute B in Y we must have $|DOM(A)| > |Y|$ and $|DOM(B)| > |X|$. The construction of T(X,Y) is done in the following way:

1) Set T(X,Y) to the empty set. Remove the first tuple of R(X) and the first tuple of S(Y), concatenate them and insert the resulting tuple into T(X,Y).
2) If $|X| = 1$ or $|Y| = 1$ repeat step 3 until R(X) and S(Y) become empty. If $|X| > 1$ and $|Y| > 1$, for each attribute A in X and each attribute B in Y execute step 4. If some tuples still remain in R(X) and S(Y), repeat step 3 until R(X) and S(Y) become empty.
3) Remove a tuple of R(X) and a tuple of S(Y), concatenate them and insert the resulting tuple into T(X,Y).
4) If T(X,Y) does not contain two tuples with A-values = A1 (first value in DOM(A)) but different B-values, execute step 5. If T(X,Y) does not contain two tuples with different A-values but with B-values = B1 (first value in DOM(B)), execute step 6.
5) Remove a tuple from R(X) with A-value equal to A1 and a tuple from S(Y) with B-value different from B1, concatenate them, and insert the resulting tuple into T(X,Y).
6) Remove a tuple from R(X) with A-value different from A1 and a tuple from S(Y) with B-value equal to B1, concatenate them, and insert the resulting tuple into T(X,Y).

For example, let X={A,B,C}, Y={D,E}, DOM(A)={A1,A2,A3,A4}, DOM(B)={B1,B2,B3}, DOM(C)={C1,C2,C3}, DOM(D)={D1,D2,D3,D4,D5}, and DOM(E)={E1,E2,E3,E4}. The construction of an instance with a one-to-one relationship between {A,B,C} and {D,E} is shown in Figure 5.

R(A, B, C):	S(D, E):	T(A, B, C, D, E):
A1 B1 C1 (1)	D1 E1 (1)	A1 B1 C1 D1 E1 (1)
A1 B1 C2 (2)	D1 E2 (3)	A1 B1 C2 D2 E1 (2)
A1 B1 C3 (4)	D1 E3 (4)	A2 B1 C1 D1 E2 (3)
A1 B2 C1 (6)	D1 E4 (6)	A1 B1 C3 D1 E3 (4)
A1 B3 C1 (7)	D2 E1 (2)	A3 B1 C1 D3 E1 (5)
A2 B1 C1 (3)	D3 E1 (5)	A1 B2 C1 D1 E4 (6)
A3 B1 C1 (5)	D4 E1 (7)	A1 B3 C1 D4 E1 (7)
A4 B1 C1 (8)	D5 E1 (8)	A4 B1 C1 D5 E1 (8)

Figure 5. Construction of an Instance with a One-to-One Relationship between {A,B,C} and {D,E}.

In T(X,Y) there is a one-to-one relationship between X and Y because all X-values are unique and correspond to unique Y-values. Let X' and Y' be proper subsets of X and Y respectively. There is a many-to-one relationship between X and Y' and Y and X' because all X- and Y-values are unique but some of the X'- and Y'-values are not unique. There is a many-to-many relationship between X' and Y' because the algorithm above enforces this relationship between any two attributes in X and Y.

Construction of Instances with Many-to-One Relationships

In an atomic component R[X,Y] there is a many-to-one relationship between the combinations X and Y if there is an FD X->Y associated with R[X,Y] in the Z-cover.

An instance T(X,Y) showing this many-to-one relationship is constructed from a relation R(X) corresponding to combination X and a relation S(Y) corresponding to combination Y. If $|X| = 1$ the relation R(X) is the unary relation constructed from the domain of the attribute in X. If $|X| > 1$ the relation R(X) is obtainted by generating a relation with a many-to-many relationship among the attributes in X. The same applies to S(Y). In order to have a many-to-many relationship between each attribute A in X and each attribute in Y we must have $|DOM(A)| > |S(Y)|$. T(X,Y) is constructed in the following way:

1) Concatenate the first tuple of R(X) to the first tuple of S(Y).

2) For each attribute A in X (from right to left) do the following, where s is $|S(Y)|$, a is $|DOM(A)|$ (we must have a > s), and A1 is the first value in DOM(A):

   a) Concatenate the first s-1 tuples of R(X) with A-value different from A1 to the second to sth tuples of S(Y).

   b) Concatenate the a-s remaining tuples of R(X) with A-value different from A1 to the first tuple of S(Y).

For example, in the atomic component FIELD[CUST#,MODEL,CUSTN, MODQ] we have a many-to-one relationship between {CUST#,MODEL} and {CUSTN,MODQ}. Let DOM(CUST#)={351, 552, 667, 866}. DOM(MODEL)={A,B,C,D}, DOM(CUSTN)={WOODMS,HOUSUP} and DOM(MODQ)= {3,1}. Figure 6 shows the construction of the instance with a many-to-one relationship between {CUST#,MODEL} and {CUSTN,MODQ}.

In T(X,Y) there is a many-to-one relationship between X and each attribute B in Y because the X-values are unique and the B-values are repeated. There is a many-to-many relationship between Y and each attribute A in X because a-s+1 A-values correspond to the first tuple of S(Y) and s Y-values correspond to A1.

R(CUST#,MODEL):

351	A
351	B
351	C
351	D
552	A
667	A
866	A

S(CUSTN,MODQ):

WOODMS	3
WOODMS	1
HOUSUP	3

T(CUST#,MODEL,CUSTN,MODQ):

351	A	WOODMS	3
351	B	WOODMS	1
351	C	HOUSUP	3
351	D	WOODMS	3
552	A	WOODMS	1
667	A	HOUSUP	3
866	A	WOODMS	3

Figure 6. Construction of an Instance with a Many-to-One Relationship between {CUST#,MODEL} and {CUSTN,MODQ}.

If there is more than one FD in the Z-cover associated with the same atomic component R[X,Y] then one of these FDs necessarily has the scope (X,Y) as per the section Rearrangements Due to Many-to-One Relationships; in that case we first construct an instance showing the FD X->Y with scope equal to the attribute set of the atomic component. Then for every other FD Z->W, $Z \subset X$ and $W \subset Y$, we modify this instance. In every tuple where, for each attribute A in Z, the A-value is equal to A1 (first value in DOM(A)), for each attribute B in W the B-value is changed to B1 (first value in DOM(B)).

For example, in the atomic component FIELD[CUST#,MODEL,CUSTN, MODG] besides the FD {CUST#, MODEL}->{CUSTN,MODQ} we have the FD CUST#->CUSTN. The instance showing the first FD with scope equal to the attribute set of the atomic component is constructed as shown in Figure 6. The modified instance with a many-to-one relationship between CUST# and CUSTN is shown in Figure 7. In the tuples where the CUST#-value = 351 the CUSTN-value was changed to WOODMS (only the third tuple was changed).

T(CUST#,MODEL,CUSTN,MODQ):

351	A	WOODMS	3
351	B	WOODMS	1
351	C	WOODMS	3
351	D	WOODMS	3
552	A	WOODMS	1
667	A	HOUSUP	3
886	A	WOODMS	3

Figure 7. The Instance of Figure 6 is Modified to Show the Many-to-One Relationship between CUST# and CUSTN.

Construction of Instances with a Combined Relationship

In an atomic component R[X,Y,Z] there is a combined relationship among X, Y and Z if there is in the Z-cover, associated with this atomic component, one FD {X,Y}->Z and two dependencies belonging to one of the following cases:

(i) Z->>X and Z->>Y.
(ii) Z->X and Z->>Y.
(iii) Z->>X and Z->Y.

An instance T(X,Y,Z) showing this combined relationship is constructed from the relations R(X,Y) and S(Z). We construct R(X,Y) by adding to an instance with a many-to-many relationship between X and Y a tuple obtained by concatenating the last tuples of P(X) and Q(Y) which are the relations corresponding to X and Y. If $|X| = 1$, then P(X) is the unary relation constructed from the domain of the attribute in X. If $|X| > 1$, then P(X) is obtained by generating a relation with a many-to-many relationship among the attributes in X. In the same way we obtain Q(Y) and S(Z).

Let p be $|P(X)|$, q be $|Q(Y)|$, and s be $|S(Z)|$. We must have $p \geq 3$, $q \geq 3$ and $s = p + q - 3$.

T(X,Y,Z) is generated in the following way, as shown in Figure 8.

1) Concatenate the first tuple of R(X,Y) with the first tuple of S(Z).
2) Concatenate the 2nd, 3rd, ..., q-1th tuples of R(X,Y) with the 2nd, 4th, ..., s-1th tuples of S(Z) respectively.
3) If there exists an MD Z->>Y in the Z-cover, concatenate the qth tuple of R(X,Y) with the 1st tuple of S(Z).
4) Concatenate the q+1th, q+2th, ..., q+p-2th tuples of R(X,Y) with the 3rd, 5th, ..., sth tuples of S(Z) respectively.
5) If there exists an MD Z->>X in the Z-cover, concatenate the p+q-1th tuple of R(X,Y) with the first tuple of S(Z).
6) If there exist MDs Z->>X and Z->>Y in the Z-cover, concatenate the last tuple of R(X,Y) with the 1st tuple of S(Z).

There is a many-to-one relationship between {X,Y} and Z because the XY-values are unique and Z1 is repeated. M[Y](Z1,X1) [1] = {Y1,Yq}, M[Y](Z1,Xp) = {Y1,Yq} which shows that Z->>Y. M[X](Z1,Y1) = {X1,Xp}, M[X](Z1,Yq) = {X1,Xp} which shows that Z->>X.

---

[1] In accordance with the definitions of MDs given in Zaniolo and Melkanoff [1980], M[Y](Z1,X1) denotes the set of Y-values found in the tuples of T(X,Y,Z) whose X-value is X1 and Z-value is Z1.

```
R(X, Y):    S(Z):      T(X,   Y,    Z):
  X1 Y1       Z1         X1   Y1    Z1
  X1 Y2       ...        X1   Y2    Z2
   ...        Zs         X1   Y3    Z4
  X1 Yq                       ...
  X2 Y1                  X1   Yq-1  Zs-1
   ...                   X1   Yq    Z1    (if Z->>Y)
  Yp Y1                  X2   Y1    Z3
  Yp Yq                  X3   Y1    Z5
                              ...
                         Yp-1 Y1    Zs
                         Xp   Y1    Z1    (if Z->>X)
                         Xp   Yq    Z1    (if Z->>X , Z->>Y)
```

Figure 8. Construction of an Instance with a Combined Relationship among X, Y and Z.

For example, in relation WS(DAY,TIME,GROUP) we have the FD {DAY,TIME}->GROUP and the MDs GROUP->>DAY and GROUP->>TIME. Let DOM(DAY)={MO,TU,WD}, DOM(TIME) ={8 AM,9 AM,10 AM} and DOM(GROUP)={G1,G2,G3}. The construction of an instance with a combined relationship among DAY, TIME and GROUP is shown in Figure 9.

Computation of the Attribute Domain Sizes

We recall that in the section Construction of Instances with Many-to-Many Relationships we require that an attribute A participating in a many-to-many relationship satisfy $|DOM(A)| \geq 2$. In the section Construction of Instances with a One-to-One Relationship we require that an attribute A participating in a one-to-one relationship satisfy $|DOM(A)| \geq k+1$, where k is the number of attributes in a combination, that is, k is a constant. In the section Construction of Instances with Many-to-One Relationships we require that an attribute A in a combination X in a many-to-one relationship

S(DAY,	TIME):	R(GROUP):	T(DAY,	TIME,	GROUP):
MO	8 AM	G1	MO	8 AM	G1
MO	9 AM	G2	MO	9 AM	G2
MO	10 AM	G3	MO	10 AM	G1
TU	8 AM		TU	8 AM	G3
WD	8 AM		WD	8 AM	G1
WD	10 AM		WD	10 AM	G1

Figure 9. Construction of an Instance with a Combined Relationship among DAY, TIME and GROUP.

X->Y, satisfy |DOM(A)|≥ s+1 where s is the size of the relation constructed with a many-to-many relationship among the attributes in Y. In the section Construction of Instances with a Combined Relationship we require that an attribute A participting in a combined relationship satisfy |DOM(A)|≥3. Note that all these conditions are of the form |DOM(A)|≥ some value. The following algorithm will initialize the domain size for each attribute as 2, thus satisfying the condition for the domain size of an attribute participating in a many-to-many relationship. The algorithm then checks whether the domain size of each attribute is big enough to satisfy all the conditions for the relationships in which the attribute participates. If not, the domain size is increased by the smallest value until all conditions are satisfied. Therefore the final domain size values will be the minimum values which satisfy all conditions. In all the conditions except the condition for many-to-one relationship, the domain size must be greater than a constant. But in a many-to-one relationship the domain size of an attribute depends on the domain sizes of other attributes. The algorithm would not stop if we had a circularity like {A,C}->B and {B,D}->A where the domain sizes of A and B will depend on each other. However in this case the Zaniolo-Melkanoff algorithm reports failure indicating the circularity, and an instance cannot be generated.

In the following algorithm F is a boolean variable which indicates if the computation is to be done again. For each attribute A in relation R(V) there is a variable CT(A) which will contain the minimum domain size when the algorithm is over. When processing an atomic component R[X,Y], X and Y are respectively the left and right side of an FD X->Y associated with R[X,Y]. SX and SY are respectively the cardinalities of relations R(X) and S(Y) corresponding to the left and right sides of the FD with many-to-many relationships among their attributes. LX and LY are respectively the indices of the last attributes (from left to right) of X and Y.

1. [Initialization] F<-TRUE. For each attribute A in V, CT(A)<-2.

2. [Repeat or terminate] If F = TRUE then F<-FALSE and execute step 3, otherwise terminate the algorithm.

3. [Process atomic component] For each atomic component R[X,Y] determine which relationship exists among its attributes:

   If there are two FDs in the Z-cover with equal inverted left- and right-hand sides, then there is a one-to-one relationship; execute step 4 and step 6.

   If there is an MD in the Z-cover, then there is a combined relationship; execute step 4 and step 7.

If there is one or more FDs with different alternated sides and no MD in the Z-cover, then there is a many-to-one relationship; execute step 4 and step 5.

If there is no FD in the Z-cover then there is a many-to-many relationship; do nothing.

Return to step 2 after all atomic components have been processed.

4. [Compute SX, SY, LX, and LY] Let X->Y be an FD in the Z-cover associated with the atomic component R[X,Y].

   SX<-1. For each attribute A in X, SX<-SX+CT(A)-1.
   SX<-1. For each attribute B in Y, SY<-SY+CT(B)-1.
   LX<-last attribute in X.
   LY<-last attribute in Y.

5. [Many-to-one relationship]

   For each attribute A in X, if CT(A)≤SY then CT(A)<-SY+1, F<-TRUE.

6. [One-to-one relationship]

   For each attribute A in X if CT(A)≤ |Y| then CT(A)<-|Y|+1, F<-TRUE.

   For each attribute B in Y if CT(B)≤ |X| then CT(B)<-|X|+1, F<-TRUE.

   If SX<SY then CT(LX)<- CT(LX)+SY-SX, F<-TRUE.

   If SY<SX then CT(LY)<- CT(LY)+SX-SY, F<-TRUE.

7. [Combined relationship]

   For each attribute A of the atomic component R[X,Y], if CT(A)<3 then CT(A)<-3, F<-TRUE.

   If SY<SX-2 then CT(LY)<-CT(LY)+SX-SY-2, F<-TRUE.

   If SX<SY+2 then CT(LX)<-CT(LX)+SY+2-SX, F<-TRUE.

For example, the rearranged A- and Z-covers of relation FIELD presented in the section A- and Z-covers are:

A-COVER:	Z-COVER:
1: CUST#,CUSTN,MODEL,MODG	1: {CUST#,MODEL}->{CUSTN,MODQ}
	1: CUST#->CUSTN
3: TEC#,TECN	3: TEC#->TECN
4: CUST#, TEC#	

Applying the above algorithm, after execution of step 1 we have F=TRUE, CT(CUST#)=2, CT(CUSTN)=2, CT(MODEL)=2, CT(MODQ)=2,

CT(TEC#)=2 and CT(TECN)=2. At step 2, F becomes FALSE and step 3 is to be executed next. In atomic component #1 there are two FDs with different alternated sides, thus there is a many-to-one relationship and steps 4 and 5 are executed. At step 4, the FD {CUST#,MODEL}->{CUSTN,MODQ} is used. SX becomes 1+CT(CUST#)-1 +CT(MODEL)-1=3. SY becomes 1+CT(CUSTN)-1+CT(MODQ)-1=3. LX becomes MODEL and LY becomes MODQ. At step 5, CT(CUST#) is less than SY then CT(CUST#) becomes 4, F becomes TRUE. CT(MODEL) is less than SY then CT(MODEL) becomes 4 and F becomes TRUE. In atomic component #3 there is one FD, thus there is a many-to-one relationship and steps 4 and 5 are executed. At step 4 the FD TEC#->TECN is used. SX becomes 1+CT(TEC#)-1=2. SY becomes 1+CT(TECN)-1=2. LX becomes TEC# and LY becomes TECN. At step 5, CT(TEC#) is less than SY then CT(TEC#) becomes 3, F becomes TRUE. Returning to step 2, F is TRUE, thus F becomes FALSE and the computation is done again. No domain size is changed this time and the algorithm is terminated. The final values are CT(CST#)=4, CT(CUSTN)=2, CT(MODEL)=4, CT(MODQ)=2, CT(TEC#)=3, and CT(TECN)=2.

CONCLUSION

We have developed and implemented an algorithm for constructing and displaying to the prospective user instances of relations embodying the FDs and MDs obtained from the user's knowledge of his conceptual model. It is hoped that such displays can help the database designer obtain the actual FDs and MDs by permitting the user to recognize erroneous instances.

Since the implementation includes the decomposition algorithm developed by Zaniolo and Melkanoff it also yields the A- and Z-covers.

The program was written in PPL and runs on the DEC PDP-10 computer.

REFERENCES

1. Beeri, C., Bernstein, P. A., and Goodman, N. [1978] "A Sophisticate's Introduction to Database Normalization Theory," *Proc. 4th Int. Conf. on VLDB,* Berlin, 1978, 113-124.

2. Bernstein, P. A. [1976] "Synthesizing Third Normal Form Relations from Functional Dependencies," *ACM TODS, 1,* 4 (December 1976), 277-298.

3. Melkanoff, M. and Zaniolo, C. [1980] "Decomposition of Relations and Synthesis of Entity-Relationship Diagrams," In: *Entity-Relationship Approach to Systems Analysis and Design* (P. Chen, Ed.), North-Holland, Amsterdam, 1980, 277-294.

4. Zaniolo, C. and Melkanoff, M. [1980] "On the Design of Relational Database Schemas," to appear in ACM TODS.

APPENDIX

Example Illustrating the Construction of Contrived Instances

We assume an initial universal schema described by the relation FIELD which characterizes the database of a computer maintenance company whose customers are described by customer names (CUSTN) and unique customer numbers (CUST#). The customers operate a certain quantity (MODQ) of computers of a given model (MODEL). Maintenance is provided by technicians whose names (TECN) may not be unique though their technician number (TEC#) is indeed unique. Each technician assigned to a customer must be able to service all the computer models operated by the customer.

```
FIELD(CUST#,CUSTN,MODEL,MODQ,TEC#,TECN)
CUST#->CUSTN
CUST#->>{MODEL,MODQ}
CUST#->>{TEC#,TECN}
{CUST#,MODEL}->MODQ
TEC#->TECN
TEC#->>{CUST#,CUSTN,MODEL,MODQ}
```

Step 1: Decomposition (see INTRODUCTION and Zaniolo and Melkanoff [1980]).

The Zaniolo-Melkanoff algorithm decomposes the universal schema into the following final schema:

A-COVER	Z-COVER
1: CUST#,CUSTN	1: CUST#->CUSTN
2: CUST#,MODEL,MODQ	2: {CUST#,MODEL}->MODQ
3: TEC#,TECN	3: TEC#->TECN
4: CUST#,TEC#	

Step 2: Rearrangement (see the section REARRANGEMENTS IN THE A- AND Z-COVERS)

An examination of the A- and Z-covers indicates that there are many-to-one relationships in atomic components #1, #2 and #3, and a many-to-many relationship in atomic component #4. Therefore we need only follow the construction described in the section Rearrangements Due to Many-to-One Relationships. Furthermore all FDs have different left sides, thus the first part of the construction may be skipped. Applying now the second part of the construction to the FDs in atomic components #1 and #2, rearrangement yields the following schema:

(rearranged) A-COVER		(rearranged) Z-COVER	
1:	CUST#,CUSTN,MODEL,MODQ	1:	{CUSTN,MODEL}->{CUSTN,MODQ}
		1:	CUST#->CUSTN
3:	TEC#,TECN	3:	TEC#->TECN
4:	CUST#,TEC#		

Step 3: Computation of domain sizes (see the section Computation of the Attribute Domain Sizes).

The result of this computation yields the following domain sizes:

Attribute	Domain Size	Domain Elements (given by the user)
CUST#	4	351,552,667,866
CUSTN	2	WOODMS,HOUSUP
MODEL	4	A, B, C, D
MODQ	2	1, 3
TEC#	3	3333,5276,8271
TECN	2	SMITH,FISHER

Step 4: Construction of contrived instance (see the section CONSTRUCTION OF INSTANCES).

We now construct an individual contrived instance for each of the atomic components which appears in the rearranged A-cover.

Substep 4.1: Contrived instance for atomic component #1.

Since the corresponding Z-cover element indicates the presence of a many-to-one relationship we need follow the section Construction of Instances with Many-to-One Relationships where this example is discussed in detail. Thus we obtain the instance presented in Figure 7 which we reproduce below.

T1(CUST#, MODEL, CUSTN, MODQ)

351	A	WOODMS	3
351	B	WOODMS	1
351	C	WOODMS	3
351	D	WOODMS	3
552	A	WOODMS	1
667	A	HOUSUP	3
866	A	WOODMS	3

Substep 4.2: Contrived instance for atomic component #3.

This situation is similar to the one above but much simpler; it yields the following contrived instance:

```
T3(TEC#,  TECN)
   3333   SMITH
   5276   FISHER
   8271   SMITH
```

Substep 4.3: Contrived instance for atomic component #4.

In this case we have a many-to-many relationship between CUST# and TEC#, therefore we need follow the construction given in the section Construction of Instances with Many-to-Many Relationships. This yields the following contrived instance:

```
T4(CUST#,  TEC#)
    351    3333
    351    5276
    351    8271
    552    3333
    667    3333
    866    3333
```

Substep 4.4: Joining the contrived instances into a single final instance (see INTRODUCTION, step 2).

We now join the contrived instances of the atomic components in the reverse order in which they were decomposed. Joining T4 and T3 yields:

```
T43(CUST#,  TEC#,  TECN)
     351    3333   SMITH
     351    5276   FISHER
     351    8271   SMITH
     552    3333   SMITH
     667    3333   SMITH
     866    3333   SMITH
```

Finally joining T43 and T1 yields:

```
T431(CUST#,  CUSTN,  MODEL,  MODQ,  TEC#,  TECN)
      351    WOODMS    A       3    3333   SMITH
      351    WOODMS    A       3    5276   FISHER
      351    WOODMS    A       3    8271   SMITH
      351    WOODMS    B       1    3333   SMITH
      351    WOODMS    B       1    5276   FISHER
      351    WOODMS    B       1    8271   SMITH
      351    WOODMS    C       3    3333   SMITH
      351    WOODMS    C       3    5276   FISHER
      351    WOODMS    C       3    8271   SMITH
      351    WOODMS    D       3    3333   SMITH
      351    WOODMS    D       3    5276   FISHER
      351    WOODMS    D       3    8271   SMITH
      552    WOODMS    A       1    3333   SMITH
      667    HOUSUP    A       3    3333   SMITH
      866    WOODMS    A       3    3333   SMITH
```

GENERAL LAWS: DEDUCTION AND INTEGRITY

ON THE INTEGRITY OF TYPED FIRST ORDER DATA BASES

Raymond Reiter

The University of British Columbia

Vancouver, British Columbia

ABSTRACT

A typed first order data base is a set of first order formulae, each quantified variable of which is constrained to range over some type. Formally, a type is simply a distinguished monadic relation, or some Boolean combination of these. Assume that with each data base relation other than the types is associated an integrity constraint which specifies which types of individuals are permitted to fill the argument positions of that relation. The problem addressed in this paper is the detection of violations of these integrity constraints in the case of data base updates with universally quantified formulae. The basic approach is to first transform any such formula to its so-called reduced type normal form, which is a suitably determined set of formulae whose conjunction turns out to be equivalent to the original formula. There are then simple criteria which, when applied to this normal form, determine whether that formula violates any of the argument typing integrity constraints.

1. INTRODUCTION

It is difficult to conceive of a naturally occurring relation which is unconstrained with respect to the kinds of individuals which may legitimately satisfy that relation.[1] Thus, in speaking about the relation "x is the husband of y" we all of us understand that x must be a male human, and y a female human. At best there

[1] The equality relation appears to be the only exception to this observation.

is something peculiar about the statement "Mary is the husband of Susan", presumably because the individual "Mary" violates the universally accepted constraint that the first argument of the husband relation must be male.

This simple example illustrates what appears to be a universal characteristic of such argument constraints on relations and that is that each such constraint is itself either a simple unary relation, for example MALE(·), or a Boolean combination of such simple unary relations, for example [MALE ∧ HUMAN](·). Given a suitable stock of such simple unary relations, it is now straightforward to formally represent the argument constraints of the husband relation as a first order formula:

$$(x\ y)\,[\text{HUSBAND-OF}(x,y) \supset \text{MALE}(x) \wedge \text{HUMAN}(x) \wedge \text{FEMALE}(y) \wedge \text{HUMAN}(y)] \tag{1.1}$$

In this paper we shall view such formulae as integrity constraints of a particular kind; they specify the allowable arguments to a relation. Any attempt to update a data base with a fact which violates such integrity constraints, for example an attempted update with HUSBAND-OF (Mary, Susan), will be rejected. For the example at hand it is not difficult to see why the update must be rejected since to accept it is to accept, by (1.1), the fact MALE (Mary). Of course, in order that a data base detect the inconsistency of MALE (Mary) it must have available some facts about MALEs, Mary, etc. At the very least, it must know ∿ MALE (Mary) or, what is more likely, it has available the specific fact FEMALE (Mary) as well as the general fact (x) ∿ [MALE(x) ∧ FEMALE(x)] from which ∿MALE (Mary) can be deduced. Accordingly, the entire data base must contain as a subcomponent a data base consisting of both specific and general facts about the unary relations which enter into the integrity constraints of the form (1.1). We refer to this sub-data base as the type data base.

In addition to this type data base, there will be information about the remaining relations. In a conventional relational data base (Date [1977]) this information can be viewed as a set of ground atomic formulae in a first order theory, and the domains associated with a given relation R are simply those unary relations which restrict the allowable arguments of R. In the deductive first order data bases of the kind treated in Kellog et al. [1978], Kowalski [1979], Minker [1978], Reiter [1978] general facts about data base relations are also allowed so that one is permitted to store, for example:

$$(x\ y)\,[\text{HUSBAND-OF}(x,y) \supset \text{WIFE-OF}(y,x)] \tag{1.2}$$

Answers to queries are then obtained by a process of deduction from the first order data base. In Minker [1978], Reiter [1977, 1978] the class of formulae permitted in a first order data base is generalized to admit typed variables so that, in the notation of Reiter [1978] and of this paper, (1.2) would be represented by:

$$(x/\mathrm{MALE} \wedge \mathrm{HUMAN})(y/\mathrm{FEMALE} \wedge \mathrm{HUMAN})[\mathrm{HUSBAND\text{-}OF}(x,y) \supset \mathrm{WIFE\text{-}OF}(y,x)] \tag{1.3}$$

Here the universally quantified variables x and y are restricted to range over instances of the unary relations (or types as we shall henceforth call them) MALE $\wedge$ HUMAN and FEMALE $\wedge$ HUMAN respectively.

For first order data bases containing general facts of the form (1.2) or (1.3) the enforcement of suitable relational argument typing is not as straightforward as it is in the case of conventional nondeductive relational data bases. As an example, consider the integrity constraints:

$$\left.\begin{array}{l}(x\ y)[\mathrm{OFFSPRING}(x,y) \supset \mathrm{HUMAN}(x) \wedge \mathrm{HUMAN}(y)] \\ (x\ y)[\mathrm{MOTHER}(x,y) \supset \mathrm{HUMAN}(x) \wedge \mathrm{FEMALE}(x) \wedge \mathrm{HUMAN}(y)] \\ (x\ y)[\mathrm{FATHER}(x,y) \supset \mathrm{HUMAN}(x) \wedge \mathrm{MALE}(x) \wedge \mathrm{HUMAN}(y)]\end{array}\right\} \quad (1.4)$$

together with a type data base:

$$\left.\begin{array}{l}(x)[\mathrm{HUMAN}(x) \supset \mathrm{MALE}(x) \vee \mathrm{FEMALE}(x)] \\ (x)\sim[\mathrm{MALE}(x) \wedge \mathrm{FEMALE}(x)]\end{array}\right\} \quad (1.5)$$

Now consider an update of this kinship data base with the general fact:

$$(x/\mathrm{HUMAN})(y/\mathrm{HUMAN})[\mathrm{OFFSPRING}(x,y) \supset \mathrm{MOTHER}(y,x) \vee \mathrm{FATHER}(y,x)] \tag{1.6}$$

Should this update be accepted? One possible intuition (which we shall see turns out to be wrong) is that the variable y is constrained by the MOTHER relation to be FEMALE and by the FATHER relation to be MALE so the update should be rejected. Another possible intuition (which turns out to be right) holds that (1.6) is equivalent to the two formulae

$$(x/\mathrm{HUMAN})(y/\mathrm{HUMAN} \wedge \mathrm{FEMALE})[\mathrm{OFFSPRING}(x,y) \supset \mathrm{MOTHER}(y,x)]$$

$$(x/\mathrm{HUMAN})(y/\mathrm{HUMAN} \wedge \mathrm{MALE})[\mathrm{OFFSPRING}(x,y) \supset \mathrm{FATHER}(y,x)]$$

so the update should be accepted. Either way, the example hopefully indicates that the enforcement of correct argument typing poses some difficulties in the case of first order data bases.

The purpose of this paper is to show, in the case of first order data bases, how a type data base, representing the known specific and general facts about types, can be used to enforce integrity constraints of the form (1.4) thereby ensuring that all arguments to a relation will be of the right type. The method is not completely general. First, as it is described in this paper, it applies only to function free data bases, although the approach will generalize to first order data bases with function signs. Secondly, it applies only to ground literals, or to formulae whose prenex normal forms involve only universal quantifiers. Since universally quantified prenex form formulae (e.g. (1.2), (1.6)) are extremely common in first order data base applications, the method is of some practical consequence.

2. FORMAL PRELIMINARIES

We shall be dealing with a first order language *without* function signs. Hence, assume given the following:

1. Constant Signs: $c_1, c_2, \ldots,$

In the intended interpretation, constant signs will denote individual entities, e.g., part-33, John-Doe, etc.

2. Variables: $x_1, x_2, \ldots,$

3. Logical Connectives: $\wedge$ (and), $\vee$ (or), $\sim$ (not), $\supset$ (implies), $\equiv$ (equivalence)

4. Predicate Signs: P, Q, R, ...

With each predicate sign P is associated an integer $n \geq 0$ denoting the number of arguments of P. P will be called an *n-ary predicate sign*. We assume the predicate signs to be partitioned into two classes:

(i) A class of unary predicate signs, which will be called *simple types*. Not all unary predicate signs, need be simple types. In the intended interpretation, simple types (e.g. MALE, HUMAN) as well as various Boolean combinations of these, called types (e.g. MALE $\wedge$ HUMAN) will be used to restrict the allowable ranges of variables occurring in data base formulae as well as to specify integrity constraints on the allowable arguments of predicates.

(ii) The class of remaining predicate signs, which will be called *common predicate signs*. In the intended interpretation, common predicate signs will denote data base relations, e.g., FATHER, HUSBAND-OF.

The set of *types* is the smallest set satisfying the following:

(a) A simple type is a type.
(b) If τ_1 and τ_2 are types, so also are $\tau_1 \wedge \tau_2$, $\tau_1 \vee \tau_2$, $\sim\tau_1$.

We shall have occasion to view types as predicates taking arguments. Accordingly, we make the following definition: If t is a variable or constant sign, τ a nonsimple type, and τ_1 and τ_2 types then

(i) If τ is $\tau_1 \wedge \tau_2$, $\tau(t)$ is $\tau_1(t) \wedge \tau_2(t)$

(ii) If τ is $\tau_1 \vee \tau_2$, $\tau(t)$ is $\tau_1(t) \vee \tau_2(t)$

(iii) If τ is $\sim\tau_1$, $\tau(t)$ is $\sim\tau_1(t)$,

5. Quantifiers:

If x is a variable then (x) is a *universal quantifier* and (Ex) is an *existential quantifier*.

2.1 The Syntax of Data Base Formulae

We define the following syntactic objects:

1. Terms

A *term* is either a variable or constant sign.

2. Common Literals

If P is an n-ary common predicate sign and $t_1, \ldots, t_n$ terms, then $P(t_1, \ldots, t_n)$ is a *common atomic formula*. Both $P(t_1, \ldots, t_n)$ and $\sim P(t_1, \ldots, t_n)$ are *common literals*.

3. Typed Well Formed Formulae (Twffs)

The set of twffs is the smallest set satisfying:

(i) A common literal is a twff.

(ii) If W_1 and W_2 are twffs, so also are $\sim W_1$, $W_1 \wedge W_2$, $W_1 \vee W_2$, $W_1 \supset W_2$.

(iii) If W is a twff, and τ a type, then $(x)[\tau(x) \supset W]$ and $(Ex)[\tau(x) \wedge W]$ are twffs. These will be denoted by $(x/\tau)W$ and $(Ex/\tau)W$ respectively. (x/τ) is a *restricted universal quantifier* and (Ex/τ) is a *restricted existential quantifier*.

Examples of twffs are (1.3) and (1.6). In this paper we consider only closed twffs, i.e. twffs with no free variables.

2.2 The Type Data Base

The type data base is where all information about types resides. Formally, we define a *type data base* (TDB) to be any finite set of closed first order formulae all of whose predicate signs are simple types and which satisfies the following τ-*completeness* property:

For each simple type τ and each constant c, either TDB $\vdash \tau(c)$ [1] or TDB $\vdash \sim\tau(c)$.

This τ-completeness property is the appropriate formalization of the requirement that for each data base individual and for all simple types, we know to which type that individual belongs and to which it does not belong. For the TDB (1.5) of Section 1, if HUMAN (Maureen) were all we are given about Maureen then the TDB would not be τ-complete since neither TDB $\vdash$ FEMALE (Maureen) nor TDB $\vdash$ ∼FEMALE (Maureen). If instead we were given FEMALE (Maureen) then the TDB would be τ-complete since HUMAN (Maureen), FEMALE (Maureen) and ∼MALE (Maureen) are all derivable.

We are not seriously proposing that, in an implementation of a question-answering system, the TDB be represented as a set of first order formulae. There are far more efficient and perspicuous representations of the same facts. One such representation involving semantic networks is thoroughly discussed in McSkimin [1976], McSkimin and Minker [1977]. A different approach is described in Bishop and Reiter [1980]. Since such representations, and their associated procedures, are beyond the intended scope of this paper, we do not discuss them here. Regardless of how the information of the TDB is represented, there is one central observation which can be made:

Formally, the TDB is a set of formulae of the monadic predicate calculus. As is well known (Hilbert and Ackermann [1950]), the monadic predicate calculus is decidable i.e. there exists an algorithm which determines, for any formula W, whether or not TDB $\vdash$ W. This must remain true regardless of how the TDB is represented. Henceforth, we shall assume the availability of such a decision procedure for the TDB. An efficient decision procedure for a large and natural class of TDB's is described in Bishop and Reiter [1980].

If τ is a type, define $|\tau|_{TDB} = \{c \mid c$ is a constant sign and TDB $\vdash \tau(c)\}$. When the TDB is clear from context, we shall write $|\tau|$ instead of $|\tau|_{TDB}$.

---

[1] In general, if A is a set of first order formulae and W is a first order formula, then A $\vdash$ W means that W is provable from the formulae of A.

The notion of a type data base as applied to deductive question-answering has been independently proposed in McSkimin [1976], McSkimin and Minker [1977]. What we have been calling simple types and types, McSkimin and Minker call primitive categories and Boolean category expressions respectively. While McSkimin and Minker do not explicitly make the τ-completeness assumption it appears to be implicit in the ways they use the type data base.

2.3 Predicate Argument Type Constraints

We shall assume that with each n-ary common predicate sign P there is an associated *predicate argument type constraint* of the form:

$$(x_1,\ldots,x_n)[P(x_1,\ldots,x_n) \supset \tau_P^1(x_1) \wedge \ldots \wedge \tau_P^n(x_n)] \qquad (2.1)$$

where $\tau_P^1,\ldots,\tau_P^n$ are types. This will be viewed as an integrity constraint specifying that the i-th argument of P must always satisfy the type τ_P^i. The formulae (1.4) of Section 1 are examples of such constraints.

3. UPDATES WITH UNIVERSALLY QUANTIFIED TWFFS

Our objective in this section is to show how a universally quantified prenex normal form twff may be tested for integrity with respect to the set of predicate argument type constraints of the form (2.1).

3.1 The Formula INT(W)

We begin by noting that

$$\vdash (2.1) \supset (\vec{x})[P(\vec{x}) \equiv P(\vec{x}) \wedge \tau_P^1(x_1) \wedge \ldots \wedge \tau_P^n(x_n)]$$

Hence, if W is a twff, and INT(W) is obtained from W by replacing each common atomic formula $P(t_1,\ldots,t_n)$ by $P(t_1,\ldots,t_n) \wedge \tau_P^1(t_1) \wedge \ldots \wedge \tau_P^n(t_n)$ then

$$\text{PATC} \vdash W \equiv \text{INT}(W)$$

where PATC is the set of all predicate argument type constraints of the form (2.1) associated with the common predicate signs of the data base. This means that instead of updating the data base with a twff W, we can choose instead to update with the equivalent (as far as the integrity constraints are concerned) formula INT(W).

Example 3.1

(i) With reference to the predicate argument type constraints

(1.4), if W is MOTHER (Mary, John) then INT(W) is

$$\text{HUMAN (Mary)} \wedge \text{FEMALE (Mary)} \wedge \text{HUMAN (John)} \wedge \text{MOTHER(Mary,John)}.$$

If W is ∿MOTHER (Bill,Mary) then INT(W) is

$$\sim[\text{HUMAN (Bill)} \wedge \text{FEMALE (Bill)} \wedge \text{HUMAN (Mary)} \wedge \text{MOTHER(Bill,Mary)}].$$

(ii) If W is

$$(x/\tau)(y/\theta)[P(x,y) \supset \sim Q(a,y) \vee R(x,x)]$$

then INT(W) is

$$(x/\tau)(y/\theta)[\tau_P^1(x) \wedge \tau_P^2(y) \wedge P(x,y) \supset \sim[\tau_Q^1(a) \wedge \tau_Q^2(y) \wedge Q(a,y)] \vee [\tau_R^1(x) \wedge \tau_R^2(x) \wedge R(x,x)]] .$$

Clearly, INT(W) imposes on W the integrity constraint that each predicate argument satisfy the corresponding argument types for that predicate. Our approach to data base integrity will be to consider the effects of updating the data base with INT(W). This update will be rejected if the addition of INT(W) to the data base

(i) leads to an inconsistency with respect to the TDB or
(ii) provides no new information, in a sense to be defined below.

On the other hand, if INT(W) leads to no integrity violations, then the data base will be updated with INT(W).[1] Thus, in the process of creating or updating a data base, the user will enter a twff W. A subsystem responsible for maintaining the integrity of the data base will transform W to INT(W). If INT(W) violates no integrity constraints, the data base will be updated with INT(W). There is a strong analogy here between our proposal for data base integrity and compilers for strongly typed programming languages like PASCAL or ALGOL 68. In such languages, all variables must be typed, just as all variables in twffs are assigned types. Furthermore, in typed programming languages, the formal parameters of a procedure must be typed, and any attempt to bind an argument of conflicting type to a formal parameter will be rejected by the compiler. Under our approach to integrity, predicates correspond to prcoedures, and predicate argument types to parameter types. At "compile time" i.e. when an attempted update of the data base is made, the integrity "compiler" will seek out conflicting "argument-parameter" types. Should any be found, the update will be rejected.

---

[1] Actually, as we shall see, the data base is not updated with INT(W), but with a set of simpler, but logically equivalent formulae.

3.2 Updates Involving Constants

With no loss in generality, assume that the data base is to be updated with a twff I in prenex normal form, so that I has the form $(\vec{x}/\vec{\tau})W$,[1] where W is quantifier free. Assume further that W is in conjunctive normal form. Thus I is of the form

$$(\vec{x}/\vec{\tau})[C_1 \wedge C_2 \wedge \ldots \wedge C_m]$$

where each C_i is a disjunct of common literals. This, in turn, is equivalent to

$$(\vec{x}/\vec{\tau})C_1 \wedge (\vec{x}/\vec{\tau})C_2 \wedge \ldots \wedge (\vec{x}/\vec{\tau})C_m \ .$$

Thus, the original update is equivalent to the m updates $(\vec{x}/\vec{\tau})C_i$, $i = 1,\ldots,m$. Our position will be that if any of these m twffs violates an integrity constraint, then the original twff I will be rejected. Thus, again with no loss in generality, we consider updates of the form $(\vec{x}/\vec{\tau})C$ where $C = L_1 \vee \ldots \vee L_k$ is a disjunct of common literals. By virtue of the discussion of section 3.1 we can equivalently consider the effects of updating the data base with

$$\begin{aligned} INT(\vec{x}/\vec{\tau})C &= (\vec{x}/\vec{\tau})INT(C) \\ &= (\vec{x}/\vec{\tau})[INT(L_1) \vee \ldots \vee INT(L_k)] \ . \end{aligned}$$

We consider first the case where some literal, say L_1, contains a constant c.

<u>Case 1</u>. L_1 is positive, say L_1 is $P(c,t_2,\ldots,t_m)$ for terms $t_2,\ldots,t_m$. Then

$$\begin{aligned} INT(C) = [&\tau_P^1(c) \quad \tau_P^2(t_2) \wedge \ldots \wedge \tau_P^m(t_m) \wedge P(c,t_2,\ldots,t_m)] \\ &\vee INT(L_2) \vee \ldots \vee INT(L_k) \ . \end{aligned}$$

Suppose $TDB \vdash \sim\tau_P^1(c)$. Then

$$TDB \vdash INT(C) \equiv [INT(L_2) \vee \ldots \vee INT(L_k)]$$

i.e. the information about L_1 in C is irrelevant! We interpret this as an integrity violation. Notice in particular the case $k = 1$, namely when C is a single literal L_1. In that case $TDB \vdash INT(C) \equiv$ false so that an attempted update with $(\vec{x}/\vec{\tau})INT(C)$ would lead to

---

[1] $(\vec{x}/\vec{\tau})W$ denotes $(x_1/\tau_1)\ldots(x_n/\tau_n)W$. We admit the case $n = 0$ in which case the twff is quantifier free.

a genuine data base inconsistency.

Case 2. L_1 is negative, say L_1 is $\sim P(c,t_2,\ldots,t_m)$ for terms $t_2,\ldots,t_m$. Then

$$INT(C) = \sim\tau_P^1(c) \vee \sim\tau_P^2(t_2) \vee \ldots \vee \sim\tau_P^m(t_m) \vee \sim P(c,t_2,\ldots,t_m)$$
$$\vee\ INT(L_2) \vee \ldots \vee INT(L_k)\ .$$

Suppose TDB $\vdash \sim\tau_P^1(c)$. Then TDB $\vdash$ INT(C) i.e. INT(C) is vacuous; it contains no new information. This we treat as an integrity violation.

These observations lead to the following:

Integrity Rule 1

Reject any attempted update of the data base with a twff $(\vec{x}/\vec{\tau})C$ where C is a disjunct of common literals whenever

(i) a constant sign c occurs in C, say as the i-th argument of a common predicate sign P, and

(ii) $c \notin |\tau_P^i|$.

As we shall see, an attempted update which passes Rule 1 may still violate further integrity constraints. However, notice that, in Case 1 above, if $(\vec{x}/\vec{\tau})C$ passes Rule 1 then TDB $\nvdash \sim\tau_P^1(c)$. By the τ-completeness of the TDB, this means TDB $\vdash \tau_P^1(c)$ so that

$$TDB \vdash INT(C) \equiv [\tau_P^2(t_2) \wedge \ldots \wedge \tau_P^m(t_m) \wedge P(c,t_2,\ldots,t_m)]$$
$$\vee\ INT(L_2) \vee \ldots \vee INT(L_k)\ .$$

If $(\vec{x}/\vec{\tau})C$ passes Rule 1 by virtue of Case 2, then we similarly obtain

$$TDB \vdash INT(C) \equiv [\sim\tau_P^2(t_2) \vee \ldots \vee \sim\tau_P^m(t_m) \vee \sim P(c,t_2,\ldots,t_m)]$$
$$\vee\ INT(L_2) \vee \ldots \vee INT(L_k).$$

In either case, INT(C) is equivalent to a formula which is independent of the type literal $\tau_P^1(c)$, so that an update with $(\vec{x}/\vec{\tau})$ INT(C) is equivalent to one in which all literals in INT(C) of the form $\tau_P^1(c)$ have been deleted.

3.3 Typed Normal Form

For subsequent integrity tests, we require the following propositional identity:

$$\sim(U_1 \wedge M_1) \vee \dots \vee \sim(U_r \wedge M_r) \vee (W_1 \wedge L_1) \vee \dots \vee (W_k \wedge L_k)$$

$$\equiv \bigwedge_{(i_1,\dots,i_k)\in\{0,1\}^k} \left\{ \begin{array}{l} U_1 \wedge \dots \wedge U_r \wedge W_1^{i_1} \wedge \dots \wedge W_k^{i_k} \supset [\sim M_1 \vee \dots \\ \vee \sim M_r \vee i_1L_1 \vee \dots \vee i_kL_k] \end{array} \right.$$

where

$$W^i = \begin{cases} W & \text{if } i = 1 \\ \sim W & \text{if } i = 0 \end{cases}$$

and

$$iL = \begin{cases} L & \text{if } i = 1 \\ 0 \text{ (false)} & \text{if } i = 0 \end{cases}$$

For example, when $r = 3$ and $k = 2$ this identity becomes

$$\sim (U_1 \wedge M_1) \vee \sim(U_2 \wedge M_2) \vee \sim(U_3 \wedge M_3) \vee (W_1 \wedge L_1) \vee (W_2 \wedge L_2)$$

$$\equiv \{U_1 \wedge U_2 \wedge U_3 \wedge \sim W_1 \wedge \sim W_2 \supset [\sim M_1 \vee \sim M_2 \vee \sim M_3]$$

$$\wedge \{U_1 \wedge U_2 \wedge U_3 \wedge \sim W_1 \wedge W_2 \supset [\sim M_1 \vee \sim M_2 \vee \sim M_3 \vee L_2]$$

$$\wedge \{U_1 \wedge U_2 \wedge U_3 \wedge W_1 \wedge \sim W_2 \supset [\sim M_1 \vee \sim M_2 \vee \sim M_3 \vee L_1]$$

$$\wedge \{U_1 \wedge U_2 \wedge U_3 \wedge W_1 \wedge W_2 \supset [\sim M_1 \vee \sim M_2 \vee \sim M_3 \vee L_1 \vee L_2]$$

In particular, if $U_1,\dots,U_r$, $W_1,\dots,W_k$ are types in the variable x, then

$$(x/\tau)(\vec{y}/\vec{\theta})[\sim(U_1(x) \wedge M_1) \vee \dots \vee \sim(U_r(x) \wedge M_r) \vee (W_1(x) \wedge L_1) \vee \dots \vee (W_k(x) \wedge L_k)]$$

$$\equiv \bigwedge_{(i_1,\dots,i_k)\in\{0,1\}^k} \left\{ \begin{array}{l} (x/\tau \wedge U_1 \wedge \dots \wedge U_r \wedge W_1^{i_1} \wedge \dots \wedge W_k^{i_k})(\vec{y}/\vec{\theta}) \\ [\sim M_1 \vee \dots \vee \sim M_r \vee i_1L_1 \vee \dots \vee i_kL_k] \;. \end{array} \right. \tag{3.1}$$

Now our concern is with attempted updates with twffs of the form $(x/\tau)(\vec{y}/\vec{\theta})C$ where C is a disjunct of common literals, say

$$C = \sim A_1 \vee \dots \vee \sim A_r \vee B_1 \vee \dots \vee B_k$$

with the A's and B's positive literals. Thus INT(C) has the form

$$\mathrm{INT}(C) = \sim(U_1(x) \wedge M_1) \vee \ldots \vee \sim(U_r(x) \wedge M_r) \vee (W_1(x) \wedge L_1)$$
$$\vee \ldots \vee (W_k(x) \wedge L_k)$$

where U_i is a conjunct of those predicate argument types corresponding to an occurrence of x in A_i (and hence U_i is a type), and M_i is A_i conjoined with type literals corresponding to occurrences of constants or of variables other than x in A_i. Similarly for W_i and L_i respectively. For example, if the formula is $(x/\tau)(y/\theta)C$ where

$$C = \sim P(x,a,y) \vee \sim Q(x,y) \vee P(b,y,y) \vee Q(x,x)$$

then

$$\mathrm{INT}(C) = \sim[\tau_P^1(x) \wedge \tau_P^2(a) \wedge \tau_P^3(y) \wedge P(x,a,y)]$$
$$\vee \sim[\tau_Q^1(x) \wedge \tau_Q^2(y) \wedge Q(x,y)]$$
$$\vee [\tau_P^1(b) \wedge \tau_P^2(y) \wedge \tau_P^3(y) \wedge P(b,y,y)]$$
$$\vee [\tau_Q^1(x) \wedge \tau_Q^2(x) \wedge Q(x,x)]$$

so that

$$U_1 = \tau_P^1 \qquad M_1 = \tau_P^2(a) \wedge \tau_P^3(y) \wedge P(x,a,y)$$
$$U_2 = \tau_Q^1 \qquad M_2 = \tau_Q^2(y) \wedge Q(x,y)$$
$$W_1 = 1 \text{ (true)} \qquad L_1 = \tau_P^1(b) \wedge \tau_P^2(y) \wedge \tau_P^3(y) \wedge P(b,y,y)$$
$$W_2 = \tau_Q^1 \wedge \tau_Q^2 \qquad L_2 = Q(x,x)$$

In general, using (3.1), it follows that $(x/\tau)(\vec{y}/\vec{\theta})C$ can be represented by the right side of (3.1), i.e. as a conjunct of 2^k formulae such that no M or L involves a type literal in x. For the example at hand, we obtain 4 such formulae whose conjunct is equivalent to the original:

$$(x/\tau \wedge \tau_P^1 \wedge \tau_Q^1 \wedge 1 \wedge \tau_Q^1 \quad \tau_Q^2)(y/\theta)[\sim M_1 \vee \sim M_2 \vee L_1 \vee L_2]$$
$$(x/\tau \wedge \tau_P^1 \wedge \tau_Q^1 \wedge 0 \wedge \tau_Q^1 \quad \tau_Q^2)(y/\theta)[\sim M_1 \vee \sim M_2 \vee L_2]$$
$$(x/\tau \wedge \tau_P^1 \wedge \tau_Q^1 \wedge 1 \wedge \sim(\tau_Q^1 \quad \tau_Q^2))(y/\theta)[\sim M_1 \vee \sim M_2 \vee L_1]$$
$$(x/\tau \wedge \tau_P^1 \wedge \tau_Q^1 \wedge 0 \wedge \sim(\tau_Q^1 \wedge \tau_Q^2))(y/\theta)[\sim M_1 \vee \sim M_2]$$

Now for each of the 2^k formulae obtained by applying (3.1) to $(x/\tau)(\vec{y}/\vec{\theta})C$ we can repeat this process with respect to the y's until finally, we obtain a conjunct K of formulae with restricted universal quantifiers, and in which the only occurrences of types are in the restricted quantifier, or as type literals of the form $\tau(a)$ where a is a constant sign. Assuming that the original twff $(x/\tau)(\vec{y}/\vec{\theta})C$ has passed the Integrity Rule 1 of Section 3.1, we can, by the remarks following that rule, delete all occurrences of type literals $\tau(a)$ from K. The resulting set of twffs in this conjunct is called the *typed normal form* of $(x/\tau)(\vec{y}/\vec{\theta})C$.

<u>Example 3.2</u>

1. $(x/\tau)[\sim P(x,x) \vee Q(x,a)]$

   has typed normal form

   $(x/\tau \wedge \tau_P^1 \wedge \tau_P^2 \wedge \tau_Q^1)[\sim P(x,x) \vee Q(x,a)]$

   $(x/\tau \wedge \tau_P^1 \wedge \tau_P^2 \wedge \sim\tau_Q^1)[\sim P(x,x)]$

2. $(x/\tau)[P(x,x) \vee Q(x,a)$

   has typed normal form

   $(x/\tau \wedge \tau_P^1 \wedge \tau_P^2 \wedge \tau_Q^1)[P(x,x) \vee Q(x,a)]$

   $(x/\tau \wedge \tau_P^1 \wedge \tau_P^2 \wedge \sim\tau_Q^1)[P(x,x)]$

   $(x/\tau \wedge \sim(\tau_P^1 \wedge \tau_P^2) \wedge \tau_Q^1)[Q(x,a)]$

   $(x/\tau \wedge \sim(\tau_P^1 \wedge \tau_P^2) \wedge \sim\tau_Q^1)$ FALSE

3. $(x/\tau)[\sim P(x,x) \vee \sim Q(x,a)]$

   has typed normal form

   $(x/\tau \wedge \tau_P^1 \wedge \tau_P^2 \wedge \tau_Q^1)[\sim P(x,x) \vee \sim Q(x,a)]$

4. $(x/\tau)(y/\theta)[\sim P(x,y) \vee Q(x,y)]$

   has typed normal form

   $(x/\tau \wedge \tau_P^1 \wedge \tau_Q^1)(y/\theta \wedge \tau_P^2 \wedge \tau_Q^2)[\sim P(x,y) \vee Q(x,y)]$

   $(x/\tau \wedge \tau_P^1 \wedge \tau_Q^1)(y/\theta \wedge \tau_P^2 \wedge \sim\tau_Q^2)[\sim P(x,y)]$

   $(x/\tau \wedge \tau_P^1 \wedge \sim\tau_Q^1)(y/\theta \wedge \tau_P^2)[\sim P(x,y)]$

5. $(x/\tau)(y/\theta)[\sim P(x,y) \vee \sim Q(x,y)]$

   has the typed normal form

   $(x/\tau \wedge \tau_P^1 \wedge \tau_Q^1)(y/\theta \wedge \tau_P^2 \wedge \tau_Q^2)[\sim P(x,y) \vee \sim Q(x,y)]$

6. $(x/\tau)(y/\theta)[P(x,y) \vee Q(x,y)]$

   has typed normal form

$$(x/\tau \wedge \tau_P^1 \wedge \tau_Q^1)(y/\theta \wedge \tau_P^2 \wedge \tau_Q^2)[P(x,y) \vee Q(x,y)]$$

$$(x/\tau \wedge \tau_P^1 \wedge \tau_Q^1)(y/\theta \wedge \tau_P^2 \wedge \sim\tau_Q^2)[P(x,y)]$$

$$(x/\tau \wedge \tau_P^1 \wedge \tau_Q^1)(y/\theta \wedge \sim\tau_P^2 \wedge \tau_Q^2)[Q(x,y)]$$

$$(x/\tau \wedge \tau_P^1 \wedge \tau_Q^1)(y/\theta \wedge \sim\tau_P^2 \wedge \sim\tau_Q^2)\ \text{FALSE}$$

$$(x/\tau \wedge \tau_P^1 \wedge \sim\tau_Q^1)(y/\theta \wedge \tau_P^2)[P(x,y)]$$

$$(x/\tau \wedge \tau_P^1 \wedge \sim\tau_Q^1)(y/\theta \wedge \sim\tau_P^2)\ \text{FALSE}$$

$$(x/\tau \wedge \sim\tau_P^1 \wedge \tau_Q^1)(y/\theta \wedge \tau_Q^2)[Q(x,y)]$$

$$(x/\tau \wedge \sim\tau_P^1 \wedge \tau_Q^1)(y/\theta \wedge \sim\tau_Q^2)\ \text{FALSE}$$

$$(x/\tau \wedge \sim\tau_P^1 \wedge \sim\tau_Q^1)(y/\theta)\ \text{FALSE}$$

Now notice that if an update is attempted with $(\vec{x}/\vec{\tau})C$ where C is a disjunct of literals, then each twff in its typed normal form is of the form $(\vec{x}/\vec{\theta})\hat{C}$ where $\hat{C}$ is disjunct of some, or all, of the literals of C. Hence, C contains no types so that $(\vec{x}/\vec{\theta})\hat{C}$ is a twff and thus a respectable candidate for inclusion in the data base.

It is natural, therefore, to consider updating the data base with all the twffs in the typed normal form of $(\vec{x}/\vec{\tau})C$. Before doing so, let us consider a typical twff $(\vec{x}/\vec{\theta})\hat{C}$ in this typed normal form. Suppose, for some component θ_i of $\vec{\theta}$, that TDB $\vdash (x)\sim\theta_i(x)$. In that case, the twff $(\vec{x}/\vec{\theta})\hat{C}$ is vacuously true; it contains no new information, and hence is irrelevant to the update. We define a twff $(\vec{x}/\vec{\theta})C$ to be *vacuous* iff for some component θ_i of θ it is the case that TDB $\vdash (x) \sim \theta_i(x)$. Given a typed normal form, its *reduced* form is obtained by deleting all vacuous twffs. Our approach to data base updates, then, is as follows:

Given an attempted update with $(\vec{x}/\vec{\tau})C$, form its reduced typed normal form. Assuming that this reduced form satisfies certain integrity constraints, to be described below, we then update the data base with all of the twffs in this reduced form.

Before we discuss integrity constraints as they apply to reduced reduced type normal forms, it is worth taking a closer look at the notion of a vacuous twff. In particular, notice that TDB $\vdash (x)\sim\theta_i(x)$ is not equivalent to $|\theta_i| = \emptyset$. The former implies the latter (assuming a consistent TDB) but not conversely. For example, suppose the TDB consists of the following facts:

(x)HUMAN(x) ⊃ ANIMATE(x)
ANIMATE (fido)
∼HUMAN (fido)

Then $|HUMAN| = \emptyset$, yet it is not the case that $TDB \vdash (x)\sim HUMAN(x)$. On the other hand, $TDB \vdash (x)\sim(HUMAN(x) \wedge \sim ANIMATE(x))$ and indeed $|HUMAN \wedge \sim ANIMATE| = \emptyset$. Now we were careful, in defining the notion of a vacuous twff, to require the stronger condition $TDB \vdash (x)\sim\theta_i(x)$ rather than the weaker $|\theta_i| = \emptyset$. To see why, consider an attempt to update with "Everyone likes Fido":

$$(x/HUMAN)LIKE(x,fido)$$

Assume $\tau^1_{LIKE} = HUMAN$. Then this has typed normal form:

$$\begin{array}{l}(x/HUMAN)LIKE(x,fido) \\ (x/HUMAN \wedge \sim HUMAN)\ FALSE\end{array} \tag{3.2}$$

The latter is clearly vacuous and is deleted in forming the reduced typed normal form. Under the definition of vacuous twff, the former is not vacuous and hence is retained. However, had we defined the notion of a vacuous twff to require $|\theta_i| = \emptyset$, then (3.2) would also be deleted in forming the reduced form of the original update i.e. the entire update would be rejected. Now it is indeed true that for *this* TDB, the twff (3.2) contains no information. But this is so only because currently the TDB knows of no humans. Should the TDB be subsequently updated with a new fact, say HUMAN (John), (3.2) would no longer be information-free. In other words, $|HUMAN| = \emptyset$ is contingent on the extension of the TDB, and is not a universal fact about the world. Furthermore, any rejection of (3.2) because it is currently information-free would not be immune to subsequent updates of the TDB with facts like HUMAN (John); once the TDB contains such a fact, the rejected formula suddenly becomes relevant. For these reasons, we defined the notion of a vacuous twff as we did. Any such twff is indeed information-free, but only by virtue of general rather than contingent facts about the world.

Now, consider an attempted update with $(\vec{x}/\vec{\tau})C$. As we remarked earlier, each twff in its reduced typed normal form is of the form $(\vec{x}/\vec{\theta})\hat{C}$ where $\hat{C}$ is a disjunct of some, or all, of the common literals of C. Suppose that C contains a common literal L which appears in none of the twffs in this reduced typed normal form. Then L is irrelevant to the attempted update. We interpret this as an integrity violation; at best there is something questionable about the attempted update. Finally, suppose that the reduced typed normal form contains a twff of the form $(\vec{x}/\vec{\theta})FALSE$. By (3.1) this is possible iff C is a disjunct of positive literals. In this case asserting $(\vec{x}/\vec{\theta})FALSE$ is equivalent to updating the TDB with

$$(x_1)\sim\theta_1(x_1) \vee (x_2)\sim\theta_2(x_2) \vee \ldots \vee (x_n)\sim\theta_n(x_n) \tag{3.3}$$

Clearly, we cannot permit the original update if (3.3) is inconsistent with the TDB. On the other hand, if (3.3) is consistent with the TDB, but not provable, then it is a new fact for the TDB and, since this is a subtle consequence of the attempted update, the user should be asked about the relevance of (3.3) for the TDB.

Integrity Rule 2

Suppose the data base is to be updated with $(\vec{x}/\vec{\tau})C$ and that C contains a common literal L which occurs in none of the twffs of the reduced typed normal form of $(\vec{x}/\vec{\tau})C$. Then reject the attempted update. Otherwise, there are two possibilities:

(i) The reduced typed normal form contains no twff of the form $(\vec{x}/\vec{\theta})$FALSE. Then update the data base with all of the twffs in this reduced typed normal form.

(ii) There is a twff of the form $(\vec{x}/\vec{\theta})$FALSE, so that C is a disjunct of positive literals. If (3.3) is inconsistent with the TDB, reject the update. If (3.3) is provable from the TDB, ignore it. Otherwise ask the user whether (3.3) is an appropriate update for the TDB. If so, make that update. If all such TDB updates are acceptable, update the data base with the remaining twffs of the reduced typed normal form.

Example 3.3

Consider an attempted update with example (1.5) of Section 1, namely with:

$$(x/\mathrm{HUMAN})(y/\mathrm{HUMAN})[\mathrm{OFFSPRING}(x,y) \supset \mathrm{MOTHER}(y,x) \vee \mathrm{FATHER}(y,x)] \tag{3.4}$$

Assume

$$\tau^1_{\mathrm{OFFSPRING}} = \tau^2_{\mathrm{OFFSPRING}} = \tau^2_{\mathrm{FATHER}} = \tau^2_{\mathrm{MOTHER}} = \mathrm{HUMAN}$$

$$\tau^1_{\mathrm{MOTHER}} = \mathrm{HUMAN} \wedge \mathrm{FEMALE}$$

$$\tau^1_{\mathrm{FATHER}} = \mathrm{HUMAN} \wedge \mathrm{MALE}$$

and assume further that

$$\mathrm{TDB} \vdash (x) \sim[\mathrm{MALE}(x) \wedge \mathrm{FEMALE}(x)] \tag{3.5}$$

After some simplification, and using (3.5), we obtain the reduced typed normal form of (3.4):

$$(x/\mathrm{HUMAN})(y/\mathrm{HUMAN} \wedge \mathrm{FEMALE})[\mathrm{OFFSPRING}(x,y) \supset \mathrm{MOTHER}(y,x)] \tag{3.6}$$

$$(x/\mathrm{HUMAN})(y/\mathrm{HUMAN} \wedge \mathrm{MALE})[\mathrm{OFFSPRING}(x,y) \supset \mathrm{FATHER}(y,x)] \tag{3.7}$$

These satisfy Integrity Rule 2, so the original twff (3.4) is acceptable, and we update the data base with (3.6) and (3.7).

Notice, incidentally, how the reduced typed normal form decomposes the original twff (3.4) into just the right conceptual "chunks" with respect to the types of the TDB. Thus (3.6) and (3.7) are clearer, and more to the point than the original twff. Notice also that while the original twff is not a Horn formula, the twffs of its reduced typed normal form are Horn. Since there are many representational and computational advantages to Horn representations in data base theory (see e.g. Kowalski [1979]) this Horn decomposition is a fortunate consequence of reduced typed normal forms. Of course, reduced typed normal forms do not always yield Horn formulae, but it is comforting to know that they do on occasion. Moreover, it is easy to see, from (3.1), that Horn formulae never yield non Horn components in their typed normal form, so that reduction to normal form preserves the Horn property.

Example 3.4

Consider an attempted update with

$$(x/\mathrm{HUMAN} \wedge \mathrm{MALE})(y/\mathrm{HUMAN} \wedge \mathrm{MALE})[\mathrm{BROTHER}(x,y) \supset \mathrm{SISTER}(y,x)]$$

Assuming

$$\tau^1_{\mathrm{BROTHER}} = \mathrm{HUMAN} \wedge \mathrm{MALE}$$

$$\tau^1_{\mathrm{SISTER}} = \mathrm{HUMAN} \wedge \mathrm{FEMALE}$$

$$\tau^2_{\mathrm{BROTHER}} = \tau^2_{\mathrm{SISTER}} = \mathrm{HUMAN}$$

the typed normal form is

$$(x/\mathrm{HUMAN} \wedge \mathrm{MALE})(y/\mathrm{HUMAN} \wedge \mathrm{MALE} \wedge \mathrm{FEMALE})[\mathrm{BROTHER}(x,y) \supset \mathrm{SISTER}(y,x)] \quad (3.8)$$

$$(x/\mathrm{HUMAN} \wedge \mathrm{MALE})(y/\mathrm{HUMAN} \wedge \mathrm{MALE} \wedge \sim\mathrm{FEMALE}) \sim\mathrm{BROTHER}(x,y) \quad (3.9)$$

$$(x/\mathrm{HUMAN} \wedge \mathrm{MALE} \wedge \sim\mathrm{HUMAN})(y/\mathrm{HUMAN} \wedge \mathrm{MALE}) \sim\mathrm{BROTHER}(x,y) \quad (3.10)$$

Formula (3.10) is clearly vacuous. (3.8) is vacuous by (3.5). Hence, the reduced typed normal form consists of (3.9) so by Integrity Rule 2, the update is rejected.

Example 3.5

Consider an attempted update with

$$(x/HUMAN)BROTHER(x,John)$$

where the BROTHER relation satisfies the same predicate argument type constraints as in Example 3.4. This has typed normal form

$$(x/HUMAN \wedge MALE)BROTHER(x,John)$$

$$(x/HUMAN \wedge \sim MALE)FALSE$$

This latter formula is equivalent to a TDB update with

$$(x)[\sim HUMAN(x) \vee MALE(x)] \tag{3.11}$$

By Integrity Rule 2, if (3.11) is consistent with the TDB, then the user should be asked whether to update the TDB with (3.11); presumably it will be rejected whence so also will be the original update. On the other hand, if the TDB contains

$$(x)\sim[MALE(x) \wedge FEMALE(x)]$$

$$HUMAN\ (Mary) \quad FEMALE\ (Mary)$$

then (3.11) is inconsistent with the TDB and the system would automatically reject the original update.

4. DISCUSSION AND CONCLUSIONS

We have focused in this paper upon a special class of integrity constraints, namely those which specify, for every data base relation, the allowable arguments to the relation. The primary vehicle for the analysis of these constraints is the notion of a type data base, together with the reduced typed normal form of a universally quantified twff. This normal form enjoys a number of desirable properties:

1. There is an algorithm for obtaining it.
2. There are simple criteria which, when applied to a formula's typed normal form, determine whether that formula violates any argument typing integrity constraints (Integrity Rule 2).
3. The conjunction of the formulae in the reduced typed normal form is logically equivalent to the original formula (modulo the TDB and integrity constraints).
4. As discussed in Example 3.3, the reduced typed normal form often decomposes the original formula into just the right conceptual "chunks". Moreover, non Horn formulae may decompose into Horn "components", while Horn formulae never yield non Horn formulae in their normal forms.

5. In view of 3, a formula may be represented in the data base by its reduced typed normal form. In view of 4, this is a good thing to do.

McSkimin and Minker have independently observed the utility of predicate argument typing in maintaining the integrity of a first order data base (McSkimin [1976], McSkimin and Minker [1977]). Their approach differs significantly from ours, however, and in some respects is less general. Both approaches diverge with respect to what constitutes an acceptable update of the data base. For example, the update of Example 3.3 would be rejected under their approach, whereas we find it acceptable. Moreover, McSkimin and Minker would not detect possible TDB integrity violations arising from twffs of the form $(\vec{x}/\vec{\theta})$FALSE in the reduced typed normal form. For example, they would accept the update of Example 3.5 whereas we find it unacceptable.

There are several directions in which the results of this paper might be extended:

1. Our approach applies only to universally quantified twffs. Is there a normal form for arbitrarily quantified twffs?

2. We have considered only twffs with no function signs. How might the notion of typed functions be incorporated into the theory?

3. The class of predicate argument type constraints considered in this paper, namely those of the form (2.1), is not as general as one might like. Frequently, corresponding to a constraint like (2.1), there is a natural *refinement* of the constraint which does not fit the pattern of (2.1), but which should be enforced. For example, in a personnel world one might define the constraint

$$(x\ y)[\text{EMPLOYED-IN}(x,y) \supset \text{EMPLOYEE}(x) \wedge \text{DEPT}(y)]$$

which is of the form (2.1). This has the natural refinement

$$(x\ y)[\text{EMPLOYED-IN}(x,y) \supset \text{SALES-PERSON}(x) \wedge \text{SALES-DEPT}(y)$$
$$\vee\ \text{CLERICAL-PERSON}(x) \wedge \text{ACCOUNTING-DEPT}(y)]$$

which violates the pattern (2.1) and hence cannot be accommodated by the methods of this paper. The natural approach here is to seek a normal form corresponding to predicate argument type constraints of the form:

$$(x_1,\ldots,x_n)[P(x_1,\ldots,x_n) \supset \tau_1^1(x_1) \wedge \ldots \wedge \tau_n^1(x_n) \vee \ldots \vee \tau_1^k(x_1) \wedge \ldots \wedge \tau_n^k(x_n)]$$

4. Related to the refinement problem is the *specialization* problem. Frequently, a type constraint of the form (2.1) will have various specializations. For example, in an education domain, we might have the relation ELECTIVE(x,y), denoting that course x is an elective for the program y:

$$(x\ y)[\text{ELECTIVE}(x,y) \supset \text{COURSE}(x) \wedge \text{PROGRAM}(y)] \qquad (4.1)$$

The computer science program, however, is more particular:

$$(x)[\text{ELECTIVE}(x,\text{CS}) \supset \text{SECOND-YEAR-COURSE}(x) \wedge \text{MATH}(x)$$

$$\vee\ [\text{THIRD-YEAR-COURSE}(x) \vee \text{FOURTH-YEAR-COURSE}(x)] \wedge \text{ARTS}(x)]$$

Similarly, there will be specialization of (4.1) for all of the other degree programs. How might we simultaneously enforce the general constraint (4.1) together with all of its specializations?

5. Many relations naturally take sets as arguments. For example, in an education domain, the relation PREREQUISITES(x,y) would take a set of courses x as the prerequisites for a course y. This integrity constraint might be denoted by

$$(x\ y)[\text{PREREQUISITES}(x,y) \supset \text{SET-OF(COURSE)}(x) \wedge \text{COURSE}(y)]$$

How might such constraints be enforced?

One can imagine a similar need for the treatment of sequences.

ACKNOWLEDGEMENTS

This work was done with financial assistance from the National Science and Engineering Research Council of Canada, under grant A 7642.

REFERENCES

1. Bishop, C. and Reiter, R. [1980] "On taxonomies," Dept. of Computer Science, Univ. of British Columbia, Technical Report, forthcoming.

2. Date, C. J. [1977] *An Introduction to Data Base Systems*, Second Edition, Addison-Wesley, Reading, Mass., 1977.

3. Hilbert, D. and Ackermann, W. [1950] *Principles of Mathematical Logic*. Chelsea, New York.

4. Kellogg, C., Klahr, P. and Travis, L. [1978] Deductive planning and pathfinding for relational data bases, In *Logic and*

Data Bases (H. Gallaire and J. Minker, Eds.), Plenum Press, New York, 179-200.

5. Kowalski, R. [1979] *Logic for Problem Solving*, North-Holland Publishing Co., New York.

6. McSkimin, J. R. [1976] *The Use of Semantic Information in Deductive Question-Answering Systems*. Ph.D. Thesis, Dept. of Computer Science, Univ. of Maryland, College Park, Md.

7. McSkimin, J. R. and Minker, J. [1977] "The use of a semantic network in a deductive question-answering system", Technical Report TR-506, Dept. of Computer Science, Univ. of Maryland, College Park, Md.

8. Minker, J. [1978]. An experimental relational data base system based on logic, In *Logic and Data Bases* (H. Gallaire and J. Minker, Eds.), Plenum Press, New York, 107-147.

9. Reiter, R. [1977]. An approach to deductive question-answering, Tech. Report 3649, Bolt, Beranek and Newman, Inc., Cambridge, Mass.

10. Reiter, R. [1978] Deductive question-answering on relational data bases, In *Logic and Data Bases* (H. Gallaire and J. Minker, Eds.), Plenum Press, New York, 149-177.

EQUATIONS COMPARED WITH CLAUSES FOR SPECIFICATION OF ABSTRACT DATA TYPES

M. H. van Emden and T. S. E. Maibaum

University of Waterloo

Waterloo, Ontario, Canada

ABSTRACT

Our goal is to obtain a specification of a relational data base as an abstract data type in such a way that a computer program can simulate on a small scale the intended use of the data base by generating formal consequences of the specification (that is, without the existence of any implementation of the data base). There are two candidates for the specification formalism to be used: equations and the Horn clauses of logic.

Apart from a specification of a relational data base, the paper is devoted entirely to a comparison between equations and clauses. We compare three aspects: mathematical semantics, the computational aspect, and expressiveness. We propose to discard equations as a distinct formalism, but will regard them as a special case of clauses. In principle we use as specification a clausal sentence containing literally the equations conventionally used in data type specification, but we find certain slight departures conducive to clarity. As program (to be executed by a PROLOG processor) we use another sentence obtained from the specification by a translation process that guarantees correctness.

INTRODUCTION

It is now widely recognized that data abstraction is an essential tool in the arsenal of structured programming techniques (Hoare [1972], Guttag and Horning [1980], Liskov and Zilles, [1975], Zilles [1974], Lampson et al. [1977], Shaw et al. [1977]). Many languages now provide facilities for the implementation of data types (Euclid, Clu, Alphard, Ada, etc.) and the methodology of program development (and verification) to be used with data types is also receiving considerable attention (Clark and Tärnlund [1977], Guttag [1977], Liskov et al. [1977], Liskov and Zilles [1975], Guttag and Horning [1980]).

Two important and related topics have received less attention. Our paper is concerned with these. The first is based on the notion that the concept of data type can be used fruitfully in a wider context than is done usually. For example, it is advantageous to regard the "data models" of data-base theory as abstract data types, as was argued by Colombetti et al. [1978]. In this paper, we propose a specification of the relational data model, the first, we believe, to be both abstract and functionally complete.

The second topic is concerned with tools which would help programmers develop data types which are suitable for their intended use. Guttag and Horning [1980] state a three stage process for program development which can be summarized as follows:

(i) Develop an intuitive understanding of the problem to be solved.
(ii) Design (specify) a system intended to solve the problem.
(iii) Program an implementation of the design.

Steps (i) and (ii) are considered to be the most difficult by Guttag and Horning [1980]: "Getting the design 'right' is much more difficult than implementing the design."

We intend in this chapter to outline a proposed system which would aid programmers in specifying the right specification. This is done by using the language of first order logic. Logic has already been used as the basis of a very high level programming language PROLOG (Kowalski [1979]) as well as in the specification of data types (Carvalho et al. [1979]), Clark and Tärnlund [1977], Hoare [1972]). We believe that a comparative study of the merits of equations and logic would be useful.

Such a study has a very obvious starting point: equations are a special case of logic, namely, where formulas have to be universally quantified atomic formulas with only a single predicate symbol, in this case the one for equality. The result upon which equational specifications are based is that there exists a unique algebra 'initial' in the class of all algebras satisfying a set of equations. It is this algebra that the equations are taken to define. This is an attractive property which might be believed to be obtainable only at the cost of the extreme parsimony of the equational formalism. However, it is well known (van Emden and Kowalski [1976]) that the Horn clause subset of the first order predicate logic has a property (the model intersection property) which can be regarded as the same, provided that a suitable translation is made. It so happens that equations are not only a special case of full logic, but also of the Horn clause sublanguage of logic.

Another consideration suggesting Horn clauses as an alternative definition formalism is that even within the equational tradition several features of a larger subset of logic have been introduced. One is the introduction of conditional equations, thereby transcending the restriction to atomic formulas. Another example is the introduction of truth values which stems from the desire to define not only functions but also relations.

A final consideration suggesting Horn clauses is our desire to use a computer to confront us with the consequences of proposed data type definitions and the fact that we have a convenient and powerful PROLOG system for logic programming at our disposal. As mentioned before, very little work has been done on providing automated tools to aid the design of a specification. A notable exception to this is the work of Goguen [1978] on OBJ. We hope that the system we outline based on the PROLOG programming language will prove to be as useful.

We proceed in the section ALGEBRAIC PRELIMINARIES to outline the algebraic principles underlying our work. In the section LOGIC — MAINLY PRELIMINARIES we provide a similar treatment for the clausal form of logic. The automatic translation of equations into logic programs is presented in the section LOGIC PROGRAMS FOR REDUCTION TO CANONICAL FORM followed by a discussion of the correctness of the translation method in the section CORRECTNESS OF THE LOGIC PROGRAMS. The section, THE SPECIFICATION OF SETS AS AN ABSTRACT DATA TYPE is devoted to an example (sets) illustrating the use of clausal form for the direct axiomatization of a data type. The section THE DATABASE SPECIFICATION (and Appendix A) then present the remainder of the data base axiomatization while the section CONCLUSIONS consists of some concluding remarks.

ALGEBRAIC PRELIMINARIES

A data type is viewed as a many-sorted algebra. Discussion of data types as many-sorted algebras can be found in Goguen et al. [1978], Guttag [1977], Levy [1978a,b]. An algebra of one sort is roughly speaking a set of objects and a family of operators on the set. The set is called the *carrier* of the algebra. Many-sorted algebras extend this notation by allowing the carrier of the algebra to consist of many disjoint sets. Each of these sets is said to have a *sort*. The operators are sorted and typed, but must be closed with respect to the carrier. For example, if A, B, C, are three sets in the carrier of an algebra, then

$$+ : A \times B \to C$$

could be an operator of *type* <ab,c>, *arity* ab and *sort* c, where a, b and c are distinguished names (the sorts) of A, B and C respectively. A data type is then a many-sorted algebra, while a data structure is an element of the carrier of a data type.

For the formal definitions of sorts, algebras, homomorphisms, congruences, etc. we refer the reader to standard works on the subject (Goguen et al. [1978], Guttag [1977], Levy [1978a,b]). We illustrate our notation by giving the following example.

Example 1

Let $S = \{i\}$ and define Σ by $\Sigma_{\lambda,i} = \{0\}$, $\Sigma_{i,i} = \{'\}$ (a suffix operator), and $\Sigma_{ii,i} = \{+,\cdot\}$. So, for instance, + has *type* <ii,i>, *arity* ii, and *sort* i. Note that λ is the empty string.

We generally give the "syntax" of an algebra in the following form:

$$0 : \to i$$

$$' : i \to i$$

$$+ : i \times i \to i$$

$$\cdot : i \times i \to i$$

Let A_i be the set of natural numbers. With Σ as above, we have 0_A is the zero of the natural numbers, and $'_A$, $+_A$, $\cdot_A$ are the usual successor, addition, and multiplication operations. This then defines the algebra of natural numbers A_i. □

We denote by T_Σ the initial algebra in the class of all Σ-algebras (Alg_Σ). We can include variables in the expressions in the usual way and denote by $T_\Sigma(X)$ the algebra *freely generated* by the variables $X = \{X_s\}$. We then have the result that any *assignment* $\theta: X \to A$ extends in a unique way to a homomorphism $\bar{\theta}: T_\Sigma(X) \to A$. The definition of equations, satisfaction, congruences, and quotient are as usual. We denote by q_ε the congruence on T_Σ *generated* by a set of equations ε and by $T_{\Sigma,\varepsilon}$ the quotient T_Σ/q_ε. We then have the result that $T_{\Sigma,\varepsilon}$ is initial in the class of all algebras satisfying ε ($Alg_{\Sigma,\varepsilon}$).

Example 2

Consider the Σ of example 1 and let ε_N =

$$\{<0+y,y>,\ <x'+y\ ,(x+y)'>$$
$$,<0\cdot y,0>,\ <x'\cdot y,(x\cdot y)+y>$$
$$\}$$

be a set of Σ-equations. It can be shown that the algebra A_i of example 1 satisfies ε_N.

An *equational specification* is a triple $<S,\Sigma,\varepsilon>$ where Σ is an S-sorted operator domain and ε is a set of equations (called the *type axioms*).

Let $<S,\Sigma,\varepsilon_N>$ be a specification with S and Σ as in Example 1 and ε_N as in Example 2. Let q_{ε_N} be the least congruence on T_Σ generated by the equations ε_N. Then $T_\Sigma/q_{\varepsilon_N}$ is initial in $Alg_{\Sigma,\varepsilon_N}$, the class of algebras satisfying ε_N. The objects in $T_\Sigma/q_{\varepsilon_N}$ are of the form $[t] = \{t' | t' \text{ is congruent to } t\}$. These congruence classes can be characterized logically by the axioms:

(i) $x \equiv x$

(ii) $x \equiv y \Rightarrow y \equiv x$

(iii) $x \equiv y \wedge y \equiv z \Rightarrow x \equiv z$

(iv) For each σ in Σ, if $\sigma \in \Sigma_{\omega,s}$ and $\omega = s_1 \ldots s_n$,

$$x_1 \equiv y_1 \wedge \ldots \wedge x_n \equiv y_n \Rightarrow \sigma(x_1,\ldots,x_n) \equiv \sigma(y_1,\ldots,y_n)$$

(v) For each $<L,R> \in \varepsilon_N$, $L \equiv R$. □

We make the common assumption that our axiomatizations always contain implicitly a boolean sort with the usual operations and axiomatization. We also assume the presence of a special value for each sort called the *error* value for the sort. We also assume that the type equations are conditioned in the sense of Goguen et al. [1978], and Goguen [1977].

Reductions

The notation and terminology is from Huet [1977]. See also Huet and Lankford [1978], Courcelle [1979], Rosen [1973], and O'Donnell [1977]. Let $S \subseteq T_\Sigma(X) \times T_\Sigma(X)$. We say t derives t' in S, denoted $t \underset{S}{\rightarrow} t'$, if and only if:

(i) t contains a subexpression r which, if it is replaced by expression r', gives rise to t';

(ii) there is a pair $(s,s') \in S$ so that r is an instantiation of s, r' is an instantiation of s' and the instantiations are obtained by consistently replacing variables in s and s' by the same expressions.

Denote the transitive, reflexive closure of $\underset{S}{\rightarrow}$ by $\overset{*}{\underset{S}{\rightarrow}}$. Denote the transitive, reflexive, symmetric closure of $\underset{S}{\rightarrow}$ by $\overset{*}{\underset{S}{\rightleftarrows}}$. $\underset{S}{\rightarrow}$ is called a *reduction system*. It is confluent (or more commonly said to be Church-Rosser) if for all t_1, t_2, t_3 such that $t_1 \overset{*}{\underset{S}{\rightarrow}} t_2$, $t_1 \overset{*}{\underset{S}{\rightarrow}} t_3$ there exists t_4 so that $t_2 \overset{*}{\underset{S}{\rightarrow}} t_4$, $t_3 \overset{*}{\underset{S}{\rightarrow}} t_4$. It is Noetherian if there is no infinite sequence $t_1, t_2, \ldots$ such that $t_n \underset{S}{\rightarrow} t_{n+1}$ for all $n \geq 0$.

If $\underset{S}{\rightarrow}$ is confluent and Noetherian, then for every t there exists t' so that $t \overset{*}{\underset{S}{\rightarrow}} t'$ and there is no t" so that $t' \underset{S}{\rightarrow} t''$. t' is called the ($S$-)canonical (or normal) form of t. It is obvious that $t \overset{*}{\underset{S}{\Leftrightarrow}} t'$ if and only if t and t' have the same canonical form.

Now, let $\langle S, \Sigma, \sigma \rangle$ be a specification. Then ε gives rise to the reduction S_ε by including in S_ε the relation (L,E) for each L=E in ε. Then it can be shown that the congruence q generated by ε is in fact $\overset{*}{\underset{S_\varepsilon}{\Leftrightarrow}}$.

LOGIC — MAINLY PRELIMINARIES

A *sentence* is a set of clauses.

A *clause* is a pair of sets of atomic formulas written as

$$A_1, \ldots, A_m \leftarrow B_1 \,\&\, \ldots \,\&\, B_n \,, \quad m \geq 0 \,, \quad n \geq 0 \,.$$

The set $\{A_1, \ldots, A_m\}$ is the conclusion of the clause; $\{B_1, \ldots, B_n\}$ is the *premiss* of the clause.

An *atomic formula* is $P(t_1, \ldots, t_k)$, where P is a k-place predicate symbol and where $t_1, \ldots, t_k$ are terms. A *term* is a variable, or is $f(t_1, \ldots, t_j)$ where f is a j-place function symbol and where $t_1, \ldots, t_j$ are terms ($j \geq 0$). The sets of *function symbols*, *predicate symbols*, and *variables* are disjoint sets of symbols. A *constant* is a 0-place function symbol.

<u>Example 3</u>

S_1 =

$\{x \equiv x,\ x \equiv y \leftarrow y \equiv x,\ x \equiv z \leftarrow x \equiv y \,\&\, y \equiv z$ (1)

$,x' \equiv u' \leftarrow x \equiv u$ (2)

$,x+y \equiv u+v \leftarrow x \equiv u \,\&\, y \equiv v$ (3)

$,x \cdot y \equiv u \cdot v \leftarrow x \equiv u \,\&\, y \equiv v$ (4)

$,0+y\equiv y,\ x'+y\equiv(x+y)'$ (5)

$,0\cdot y\equiv 0,\ x'\cdot y\equiv x\cdot y+y$ (6)

}

In this sentence x,y,z,u, and v are variables and 0 is a constant. There are two-place function symbols "+" and "•". Instead of +(x,y) we have used the traditional infix notation x+y. The same has been done with the two-place function symbol "•" and with the two-place predicate symbol "≡". The one-place function symbol "'" has been written in suffix notation: x' instead of '(x).

According to the informal semantics of logic in clausal form, a sentence is to be understood as the conjunction of its clauses. A clause

$$A_1,\ldots,A_m \leftarrow B_1 \ \&\ \ldots\ \&\ B_n$$

is to be understood as:

For all $x_1,\ldots,x_k$, A_1 or ... or A_m if B_1 and ... and B_n

where $x_1,\ldots,x_k$ are the variables in the clause

and where $m > 0$, $n \geq 0$.

A *definite clause* is one where m = 1.
A sentence containing definite clauses only is called a *definite sentence*.
A *negative clause* is a clause where m = 0 and n > 0.
It is to be understood as:

For all $x_1,\ldots,x_k$, it is not the case that B_1 and ... and B_n.

A *Horn clause* is a clause where $m \leq 1$. In the above example S_1 contains Horn clauses only.
An *empty clause* is one where m = 0 and n = 0. Such a clause is to be understood as a contradiction. It is written as □.

The meaning of S_1 should now be clear. The clauses (1) express reflexivity, symmetry, and transitivity of "≡". The additional clauses (2), (3), and (4) invest "≡" with the properties of a congruence. We shall refer to them as the axioms for structural induction; there is one for each function symbol which is not a constant. Finally, the clauses (5) and (6) are a straightforward expression of the equations.

In this example and, in general, we refer to such a sentence as an equational sentence. Such a sentence has to express that "≡"

is a congruence relation, by containing the axioms (1) and the required structural induction axioms (2,3,4). Finally, such a sentence contains each equation as a clause.

We can now proceed with a mathematical treatment of the semantics of the clausal form of logic. The *Herbrand base* H(S) of a sentence *S* is the set of variable-free atomic formulas containing no function or predicate symbols other than those in *S*. Any subset of H(*S*) is an *interpretation* for *S*. We say that an interpretation I *assigns* the relation

$$\{(t_1,\ldots,t_k) \mid P(t_1,\ldots,t_k) \in I\}$$

to the predicate symbol P.

Substitution is an operation, say s, which replaces throughout an expression e (clause, atomic formula, or term) all occurrences of a variable by a term. The result is denoted by es and is called an *instance* of e; e is said to be more *general* than es (even when e = es). If there exists for given expressions $e_1,\ldots,e_n$ a substitution s such that $e = e_1 s = \ldots = e_n s$, then s is said to be a *unifier* of $e_1,\ldots,e_n$.

Let I be an interpretation.

- A sentence is *true in* I iff each of its clauses is true in I.
- A clause is *true in* I iff each of its variable-free instances is true in I.
- A variable-free clause

  $$A_1,\ldots,A_m \leftarrow B_1 \;\&\; \ldots \;\&\; B_n$$

  is *true in* I iff at least one of $A_1,\ldots,A_m$ is true in I or at least one of $B_1,\ldots,B_n$ is not true in I.
- A variable-free atomic formula F in the conclusion of a clause is *true in* I iff $F \in I$.
- A variable-free atomic formula in the premise of a clause is *true in* I iff $F \notin I$.

An interpretation I such that a sentence *S* is true in I is called a *model* of *S*. It may be shown that the set of models of a definite clause (sentence) has a least element: in other words, such sentences have the model-intersection property: the intersection of all models is itself a model (van Emden and Kowalski [1976]).

Each model of an equational sentence associates an algebra with that sentence. The objects of the algebra are congruence classes of the relation assigned by the model to "≡". For each n-place functor f of the sentence, the algebra has an n-place operator. Its function maps an n-tuple $(c_1,\ldots,c_n)$ of congruence classes to a congruence class c. Let $t_1,\ldots,t_n$ be variable-free terms such that $t_1 \in c_1, \ldots, t_n \in c_n$; c is the congruence class containing $f(t_1,\ldots,t_n)$.

Theorem 1

The algebra associated with the least model of an equational sentence E is initial in the class of algebras associated with the models of E.

Proof: The algebra associated with the least model is the quotient algebra $T_{\Sigma,\varepsilon}$ described in the section ALGEBRAIC PRELIMINARIES. □

The existence of a unique initial algebra makes possible the algebraic approach to data type definitions. The above theorem shows that this existence can be regarded as a special case of the model intersection property. It is a special case because this property is not unique to equational sentences but is shared by all Horn clause sentences with any predicate symbols of any arity whatsoever. Independently of the connection with the initial-algebra result, the model-intersection property has been used to justify the definition of relations by definite clauses by van Emden and Kowalski [1976] who showed that the existence of least models in general is itself a simple consequence of the existence of least fixpoints of monotone functions from a partially ordered set to itself.

In logic programming, inference from a clausal sentence is done by refutation. For example, if one wants to show that S_1 implies that (0+0)+0 is congruent to some term one refutes $S_1 \cup \{\leftarrow (0+0)+0 \equiv x\}$. In this example many refutations are possible, giving many different values for x, such as 0+(0+0)+0, to give just one uninteresting example; only some refutations give 0.

Among the many existing refutation systems, SLD resolution has the following advantages: it can be implemented efficiently and its search space is complete for refuting a Horn clause sentence with only one negative clause. The term SLD derives from SL-resolution (Kowalski and Kuehner [1971]) restricted to definite clauses. It is also called LUSH-resolution.

Let P be a definite sentence and N a negative clause. An SLD-refutation of $P \cup \{N\}$ consists of a sequence $N_0,\ldots,N_n$ of negative clauses, a sequence $d_1,\ldots,d_n$ of clauses in P (the input clauses of the refutation), and a sequence $s_1,\ldots,s_n$ of substitutions. For $i = 0,\ldots,n-1$, the N_i are nonempty and contain exactly one atom which is called the *selected atom* of N_i. N_n is the empty clause. For $i = 0,\ldots,n-1$, N_{i+1} is derived by the SLD resolution from N_i and d_i with substitution s_i.

The relationship of being *derived* is defined as follows. Let

$$N_i = \leftarrow A_1 \ \& \ \dots \ \& \ A_k \ \& \ \dots \ \& \ A_m \ , \qquad 0 < i < n, \quad m \geq 1$$

with A_k as selected atom. Let

$$d_i = A \leftarrow B_1 \ \& \ \dots \ \& \ B_q \ , \quad q \geq 0$$

be any clause in P such that A and A_k are unifiable with most general unifier s_i. Then N_{i+1} is

$$\leftarrow (A_1 \ \& \ \dots \ \& \ A_{k-1} \ \& \ B_1 \ \& \ \dots \ \& \ B_q \ \& \ A_{k+1} \ \& \ \dots \ \& \ A_m) \ s_i .$$

Let us illustrate SLD resolution by showing how (0+0)+0 can be reduced to 0 by refuting

$$S_1 \cup \{\leftarrow (0+0)+0 \equiv w\}$$

$$N_0 = \leftarrow (0+0)+0 \equiv w$$

Notice that now none of the clauses (5), (6) can be used as input clause. This points out an important difference with the equational formalism: in resolution logic two entire terms have to unify in order to make a resolution possible and it is not enough to unify a term in one clause with a proper subterm in the other clause.

The following refutation shows that (0+0)+0 is congruent to 0. It can only be found by an intelligent choice of input clause. The underlined atomic formulas are the selected ones.

$N_0 = \leftarrow \underline{(0+0)+0 \equiv w}$

$N_1 = \leftarrow \underline{(0+0)+0 \equiv w_1} \ \& \ w_1 \equiv w$ from N_0 and (1)

$N_2 = \leftarrow \underline{(0+0) \equiv u} \ \& \ 0 \equiv v \ \& \ u+v \equiv w$ from N_1 and (3)

$N_3 = \leftarrow \underline{0 \equiv v} \ \& \ 0+v \equiv w$ from N_2 and (5)

$N_4 = \leftarrow \underline{0+0 \equiv w}$ from N_3 and (1)

$N_5 = \square$ where s_5 assigns 0 to w from N_4 and (5).

An efficient implementation of SLD resolution always tries, when searching for a refutation, to use the textually first possible choice of input clause. For reduction to canonical form SLD-resolution typically requires a fairly sophisticated switch between the choice of the transivity axiom and a structural induction axiom as input clause. Because of this S_1 is not a suitable PROLOG program for reduction to canonical form.

LOGIC PROGRAMS FOR REDUCTION TO CANONICAL FORM

One of our aims is to obtain, as an aid in data type design, a facility for automatic reduction of arbitrary expressions to canonical form. As we observed in the previous section, if the equational sentence is to be used, automatic reduction requires an implementation of SLD-resolution which is more sophisticated than the PROLOG interpreter. The alternative we choose is to translate the equations to a clausal sentence (which we refer to as a *logic program*) in such a way that it controls the PROLOG interpreter to achieve automatic reduction.

This section is devoted to a description of the translation process. In an earlier attempt we tried to describe the translation process in English without achieving a sufficiently precise result. Since then we realized that the process is an easily formalizable exercise in symbol manipulation and as such is eminently suitable for expression in first-order predicate logic.

It turned out to be natural to write the logic definition of the translation process in such a way that the PROLOG interpreter uses it to automatically effect the translation. (In fact, a similar PROLOG program was written in 1974 by David Warren of the University of Edinburgh. A difference is that Warren had no need to distinguish canonical function symbols.) The resulting logic program is then used by the same interpreter to reduce to canonical form. Thus, our definition of the translation process acts as a preprocessor serving to make equational data-type definitions (and other equational programs) palatable to the PROLOG interpreter. We first illustrate the translation process by an example, then we explain its formal definition (and PROLOG program), and finally (in the next section) we discuss its correctness.

The result of translating the equations

$$0+Y \equiv Y \qquad\qquad X'+Y \equiv (X+Y)'$$

$$0 \cdot Y \equiv 0 \qquad\qquad X' \cdot Y \equiv (X \cdot Y)\ Y$$

is the following set of clauses

```
{0≡0
,X'≡Y' <- X≡Y
,X+Y≡Z <- X≡X1 & Y≡Y1 & plus(Z,X1,Y1)
,X•Y≡Z <- X≡X1 & Y≡Y1 & times(Z,X1.Y1)
,plus(Y,0,Y)
,plus(Z',X',Y) <- plus(Z,X,Y)
,times(0,0,Y)
,times(Z,X',Y) <- times(U,X,Y) & plus(Z,U.Y)
}
```

With every n-place function symbol f in the equations the translation process associates an (n+1)-place predicate symbol F. Roughly speaking, the zeroth argument place of F corresponds to $f(x_1,\ldots,x_n)$ and the next n arguments of F correspond to $x_1,\ldots,x_n$.

In the previous section we saw that in order to reduce (0+0)+0 it was necessary to appeal to transitivity and substitutivity before an equation could be used. It is this necessity of choosing between several input clauses unifying with the selected atom that makes PROLOG unsuitable as an implementation of SLD-resolution. However, if subexpressions are known to be canonical already, then the reduction problem is more tractable: PROLOG can handle it using the clauses for *plus* and *times*. The trick which makes the above clauses work with PROLOG is to reduce subexpressions first to canonical form (the first four clauses) and then to reduce expressions where only the top level function symbol is noncanonical (the last four clauses).

We now describe the translation process. The first part (see predicate *reducesubexp*) generates clauses that reduce subexpressions to canonical form; one is generated for each function symbol. Given a function symbol f, an arity n, and a list of canonicals, the following clause generates the clause

$$T_1 \equiv Z \text{ <- Premiss}$$

where T_1 is $f(X_1,\ldots,X_n)$ and Premiss is

$$X_1 \equiv Y_1 \ \& \ \ldots \ \& \ X_n \equiv Y_n \ \& \ f(Z,Y_1,\ldots,Y_n) \ \& \ \text{true}$$

all this under the condition that the f is not a member of the list of canonicals.

```
reducesubexp(F,N,Tl≡Z <- Premiss,Canonicals)
<- not(member(F,Canonicals)) & genlists(N,Xs,Ys,Eqs) &
    Tl = .. [F:Xs] & T2 =.. [F:Z.Ys] &
    append(Premiss,Eqs,T2&true).
```

Throughout this section, those terms beginning with a capital letter are variables. A term such as [F:Xs] is shorthand for F.Xs, which is a list with F as head and Xs as tail. The constant [ ] stands for the empty list. An atomic formula such as

$$T_1 = .. [F:Xs]$$

where =.. is the predicate symbol in infix notation, is true if and only if F is bound to a constant (say, c), Xs is bound to a list of terms, and T_1 is the term having the identifier of c as function symbol and the terms of Xs as arguments.

Given a function symbol f, an arity n and a list of canonicals, the following clause generates the clause

$$T_1 \equiv T_2 \text{ <- Premiss}$$

where T_1 is $f(X_1,\ldots,X_n)$, T_2 is $f(Y_1,\ldots,Y_n)$, and Premiss is

$$X_1 \equiv Y_1 \;\&\; \ldots \;\&\; X_n \equiv Y_n \;\&\; \text{true}$$

provided that f is a member of the list of canonicals.

```
reducesubexp(F,N,T1≡T2 <- Premiss,Canonicals)
<- member(F,Canonicals) & genlists(N,Xs,Ys,Premiss) &
    T1 =.. [F:Xs] & T2 =.. [F:Ys].
```

The main body of the translation process generates a clause for each equation. Each noncanonical function symbol is translated to a predicate with an extra, zeroth, argument place for the result of the function. This is used to obtain a relational expression for a term possibly containing nested noncanonical functions. For example, X•X+Y has as relational expression

U if times(V,X,Y) & plus(U,V,Y) & true

where *times* and *plus* are the predicate symbols for "•" and "+".

For example, (X'•X+Y)' has as relational expression

U' if times(V,X',Y) & plus(U,V,Y) & true

because the canonical function symbol "'" is not affected by the translation process. The relational equivalent of a term is generated by *expandterm*, which is mutually recursive with *expandlist*, which performs the same operation on lists of terms.

In general, the relational equivalent of $f(Arg_1,\ldots,Arg_n)$ is (with noncanonical f)

$$R_0 \text{ if } A_1 \;\&\; \ldots \;\&\; A_m \;\&\; f(R0,F1,\ldots,Rn) \;\&\; \text{true}$$

provided that for i = 1,...,n the relational equivalent of Arg_i is

$$R_i \text{ if } R_{i_1} \;\&\; \ldots \;\&\; A_{i_{m_i}} \;\&\; \text{true}$$

and $A_1 \& \ldots \& A_m \& \text{true}$ is the result of appending all A_{i_j}s. This is expressed in the following clause:

```
expandterm(T,R0 if Conj,Canonicals)
<- T =.. [F:Arglton] /* T is F(Argl,...,Argn) */ &
   not(member(F,Canonicals)) &
   expandlist(Arglton,Rlton if Conjl,Canonicals) &
   Tl =.. [F:R0.Rlton] /* Tl is F(R0,...,Rn) */ &
   append(Conj,Conjl,Tl&true).
```

The relational equivalent of $f(Arg_1,\ldots,Arg_n)$ is (with canonical f)

$$f(R_1,\ldots,R_n) \text{ if } A_1 \ \& \ \ldots \ \& \ A_m \ \& \text{ true}$$

provided that, for i = 1,...,n, the relational equivalent of Argi is

$$R_i \text{ if } A_{i_1} \ \& \ \ldots \ \& \ A_{i_{n_i}} \ \& \text{ true}$$

and A_1 & ... & A_m & true is the result of appending all A_{i_j}s. This is expressed in the following clause:

```
expandterm(T,R if Conj,Canonicals)
<- T =.. [F:Arglton] & member(F,Canonicals) &
   expandlist(Arglton,Rlton if Conj,Canonicals) &
   R =.. [F:Rlton].
```

We are now ready for the translation of the equations. We distinguish three cases. The first is where the equation is $f(X_1,\ldots,X_n) \equiv Tl$; its translation is

$$f(R_0,R_1,\ldots,R_n) \text{ <- } A_1 \ \& \ \ldots \ \& \ A_m \ \& \text{ true}$$

provided that the result of *expandlist* applied to Y,Xl,...,Xn is

$$R_0,R_1,\ldots,R_n \text{ if } A_1 \ \& \ \ldots \ \& \ A_m \ \& \text{ true.}$$

The clause which defines the translation of such equations is:

```
transeq(Fxlton≡Y <- Conds,Fr0ton <- Premiss,Canonicals)
<- var(Y) & Fxlton =.. [F:Xlton] &
   expandlist(Y.Xlton,R0ton if Altom,Canonicals) &
   Fr0ton =.. [F:R0ton] & append(Premiss,Conds,Altom).
```

In the second case the equation is f(Xl,...,Xk)≡g(Yl,...,Yn) with a canonical g; its translation is

$$f(R_0,R_1,\ldots,R_k) \text{ <- } A_1 \ \& \ \ldots \ \& \ A_m \ \& \text{ true}$$

provided that the result of *expandlist* applied to

$$g(Y_1,\ldots,Y_n),X_1,\ldots,X_k$$

is

$$R_0,R_1,\ldots,R_k \text{ if } A_1 \ \& \ \ldots \ \& \ A_m \ \& \text{ true.}$$

The clause which defines the translation of such equations is:

```
transeq(Fxltok≡Gylton <- Conds,Fr0tok <- Premiss,Canonicals)
<- Fxltok =.. [F:Xltok] & Gylton =.. [G:Ylton] &
   member(G,Canonicals) &
   expandlist(Gylton.Xltok,R0tok if Altom,Canonicals) &
   Fr0tok =.. [F:R0tok] & append(Premiss,Conds,Altom).
```

In the third case the equation is

$$f(X_1,\ldots,X_n) \equiv g(Y_1,\ldots,Y_n)$$

with a noncanonical g; its translation is

$$f(R_0,\ldots,R_k) \texttt{ <- } A_1 \,\&\ldots\&\, A_m \,\&\, B_1 \,\&\ldots\&\, B_p \,\&\, g(S_0,\ldots,S_n) \,\&\, \text{true}$$

provided that the result of *expandlist* applied to $U,X_1,\ldots,X_k$ gives

$$R_0,\ldots,R_k \text{ if } A_1 \,\&\ldots\&\, A_m \,\&\, \text{true}$$

and that the result of *expandlist* applied to $U,Y_1,\ldots,Y_n$ gives

$$S_0,\ldots,S_n \text{ if } B_1 \,\&\ldots\&\, B_p \,\&\, \text{true}$$

The clause which defines the translation of such equations is:

```
transeq(Fxltok≡Gylton <- Conds,Fr0tok <- Premiss,Canonicals)
<- Fxltok =.. [F:Xltok] & Gylton =.. [G:Ylton] &
   not(member(G,Canonicals)) &
   expandlist(U.Xltok,R0tok if Altom,Canonicals) &
   expandlist(U.Ylton,S0ton if Bltop,Canonicals) &
   Fr0tok =.. [F:R0tok] & Gs0ton =.. [G:S0ton] &
   append(Bsg,Bltop,Gs0ton&true) &
   append(Asbsg,Altom,Bsg) & append(Premiss,Conds,Asbsg).
```

We give in Appendix B a listing of the complete PROLOG program for translating equations to a logic program.

CORRECTNESS OF THE LOGIC PROGRAMS

As with conventional programs, there are two parts to the correctness problem of logic programs. "Partial correctness" means that a computation can only produce a correct result. Termination means that a result must be produced.

We use the logic program for successor arithmetic as an example of a proof of partial correctness according to the consequence verification method of Clark and Tärnlund [1977]. As mentioned in the previous section, a result produced by a logic program is a logical consequence of the specification if the program is itself a logical consequence of the specification. The consequence verification method proves partial correctness by deriving each of the clauses of a program from the specification, which is in our case the equational sentence.

Our translation method introduces a predicate to be associated with each function symbol. As a result the equational sentence has to be, for the purpose of the correctness proof, augmented with definitions of these predicates. In the example of successor arithmetic these definitions are

$$ZERO(x) \Leftrightarrow x \equiv 0$$

$$SUCC(x,y) \Leftrightarrow x' \equiv y$$

$$PLUS(x,y,z) \Leftrightarrow x+y \equiv z$$

$$TIMES(x,y,z) \Leftrightarrow x \cdot y \equiv z$$

Let us now prove

$$TIMES(x',y,z) \leftarrow TIMES(x,y,u) \;\&\; PLUS(u,y,z)$$

which is a clause of the logic program. From

$$x' \cdot y \equiv x \cdot y + y \quad \text{(an equation)}$$

and

$$x' \cdot y \equiv z \leftarrow x' \cdot y \equiv x \cdot y + y \;\&\; x \cdot y + y \equiv z \quad \text{(an instance of transitivity)}$$

we infer

$$x' \cdot y \equiv z \leftarrow x \cdot y + y \equiv z.$$

From

$$x' \cdot y \equiv z \leftarrow x \cdot y + y \equiv z$$

and

$$x \cdot y + y \equiv z \leftarrow x \cdot y \equiv u \;\&\; u + y \equiv z \quad \text{(from transitivity and structural induction for +)}$$

we infer

$$x' \cdot y \equiv z \leftarrow x \cdot y \equiv u \;\&\; u + y \equiv z \;.$$

Now, making use of the predicate definitions

$$PLUS(x,y,z) \Leftrightarrow x+y \equiv z \text{ and } TIMES(x,y,z) \Leftrightarrow x \cdot y \equiv z$$

we obtain

$$TIMES(x',y,z) \leftarrow TIMES(x,y,u) \;\&\; PLUS(u,y,z)$$

which was to be proved.

For good measure we will also include an example of a proof of one of the first types of clauses produced by our translation method; for example the clause

$$x+y \equiv z \leftarrow x \equiv x_1 \ \& \ y \equiv y_1 \ \& \ \mathrm{PLUS}(x_1,y_1,z).$$

Let us assume the right-hand side

$x \equiv x_1 \ \& \ y \equiv y_1$ & $\mathrm{PLUS}(x_1,y_1,z)$

structural ↓ induction — definition ↓ of PLUS

$x+y \equiv x_1+y_1$ — $x_1+y_1 \equiv z$

↓ transitivity

$x+y \equiv z$

which is the left-hand side.

In the context of an SLD-resolution refutation procedure, such as the PROLOG interpreter, termination means that an attempt at refutation of a negative clause of the form $\leftarrow t \equiv x$ (t a variable-free term, x a variable) always succeeds. Failure can have two causes: (1) an attempt at finding a refutation yields an infinite sequence of negative clauses, and (2) all attempts are finite and fail. The second alternative is eliminated by the completeness of SLD resolution for Horn clauses and by the fact that all variable-free terms are in some congruence class. It remains to consider the first alternative.

In every derivation step an atomic formula is replaced by the premiss of a clause. In an infinite derivation there must be a clause that is used in this way an infinite number of times. It cannot be one of the clauses with "≡" in the conclusion, because every such use decreases the size of the term concerned. Therefore it must be one of the clauses resulting from the translation of an equation. The use of such a clause corresponds to a reduction in the equational sense. If the equations are such that no infinite reduction is possible, then infinite attempts at finding an SLD refutation are also impossible. To summarize, we claim that the PROLOG interpreter is guaranteed to terminate with a correct result for logic programs obtained by translating a Noetherian set of equations.

THE SPECIFICATION OF SETS AS AN ABSTRACT DATA TYPE

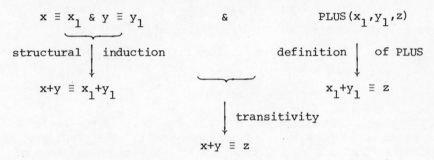

For the specification of a relational data base we need sets. In this section we treat separately the definition of sets. Their operations are listed below.

nil:	→ set	(the empty set)	NULL
• :	element × set → set	(insertion of element into set)	INSERT
mem:	element × set → bool	(membership)	MEMBER
<< :	set × set → bool	(inclusion)	SUBSET
eqv:	set × set → bool	(equivalence)	EQUIV
+ :	set × set → set	(union)	UNION
- :	set × set → set	(difference)	SDIFF
-- :	set × set → set	(intersection)	INT

In the right hand column are the predicate symbols of the logic program which correspond to the function symbols. The predicates are listed as functions of the type "bool". The canonical form of a set $\{a_1, \ldots, a_n\}$ is

$$a_1 \cdot (a_2 \cdot (\ldots \cdot (a_n \quad nil) \ldots)$$

That is, the result of inserting a_1 into the result of inserting a_2 into the result of ... into the result of inserting a_n into nil. The canonical form is made unique by requiring the elements to appear in alphabetic order, as determined by the predicates "<" and ">".

As we contemplate direct execution of specifications to simulate implementations that conform to the specifications, we need to take into account their computational efficiency. For the operations of set union and set difference it is computationally favorable to have their arguments of canonical form, because the operations can then be defined as simple variants of merging. It is advantageous to write the specification directly in the format resulting from the translation process described in the section LOGIC PROGRAMS FOR REDUCTION TO CANONICAL FORM because in this format there is a distinct part of the specification where objects can be assumed to be of canonical form. This part, then, is the place to write definitions of union and difference.

In general we like to be opportunistic in the choice of specification style. In some situations we find equations congenial and then we make use of automatic translation to PROLOG. In other situations we find that the relational style has decisive advantages.

Below we present our specification of sets as an abstract data type.

```
{nil ≡ z ← NULL(z)
,u•s ≡ z ← s ≡ s_1 & INSERT(u,s_1,z)
,s+t ≡ z ← s ≡ s_1 & t ≡ t_1 & UNION(s_1,t_1,z)
,s-t ≡ z ← s ≡ s_1 & t ≡ t_1 & DIFF(s_1,t_1,z)
,s--t ≡ z ← s ≡ s_1 & t ≡ t_1 & INT(s_1,t_1,z)
,s<<t     ← s ≡ s_1 & t ≡ t_1 & SUBSET(s_1,t_1)
,s eqv t  ← s ≡ s_1 & t ≡ t_1 & EQUIV(s_1,t_1)
,u mem s  ← s ≡ s_1 & MEMBER(u,s_1)

,NULL(nil)
,INSERT(u,s,z)       ← UNION(u•nil,s,z)
,UNION(s,nil,s)      , UNION(nil,t,t)
,UNION(u•s,u•t,u•z) ← UNION(s,t,z)
,UNION(u•s,v•t,u•z) ← u<v & UNION(s,v•t,z)
,UNION(u•s,v•t,v•z) ← u>v & UNION(u•s,t,z)

,SDIFF(s,nil,s)      ,SDIFF(nil,t,nil)
,SDIFF(u•s,u•t,z)    ← DIFF(s,t,z)
,SDIFF(u•s,v•t,u•z) ← u<v & SDIFF(s,v•t,z)
,SDIFF(u•s,v•t,z)    ← u>v & SDIFF(u•s,t,z)

,INT(s,t,z)  ← SDIFF(s,t,z_1) & SDIFF(s,z_1,z)
,SUBSET(s,t) ← UNION(s,t,t)
,EQUIV(s,t)  ← SUBSET(s,t) & SUBSET(t,s)
,MEMBER(u,s) ← SUBSET(u•nil,s)
}
```

This logic program is activated by a clause such as

```
← c•((b•a•d•nil -- a•c•a•nil) + e•b•nil) - d•b•b•c•nil ≡ z
```

PROLOG will find a refutation, which substitutes e•nil for z.

THE DATABASE SPECIFICATION

The following equational axiomatization is of a relational data base given as an example in Gotlieb and Gotlieb [1978]. The data base keeps information about courses and instructors. The axiomatization itself is based on three basic data types whose axiomatizations are also given:

(i) *attributes* is a very simple data type which has as constants all the names of attributes used in the data base. The only nonconstant operations are the test for syntactic equivalence between attribute names (denoted ≡) and an order relation (denoted >). The order relation is used in the next data type to define canonical or normal forms for terms.

(ii) *tuple* is a data type used to define all (unordered) tuples defined over values for the attribute names defined by the type *attribute*. (The only operation of this type which might be considered unusual is COMPOSE. This operation is needed in the definition of the type *database*.) Note that "values" stored in a tuple are actually "pairs" consisting of a value and its attribute. This is facilitated by the use of so-called hidden functions — operations which are of auxiliary use and are not considered to be available for users of the type.

(iii) *set of* [*element*] is a so-called parameterized data type. A normal data type is obtained by substituting for *element* some defined data type. Thus we use *set of* [*tuple*], *set of* [*attribute*] in the definition of *database*. We use infix notation for *set of* [*element*] where this conforms to convention.

The definition of type *database* is itself based on a novel idea for modeling data bases, Maibaum [1979]. Although there have been previous attempts at axiomatizing relational data bases using the concept of abstract data types (cf. Lockemann and Wohlleber [1979]) these have either concentrated on the relational algebra (ignoring updates) as in Gotlieb and Gotlieb [1978] or have corrupted the theory of data types (and made its results invalid) by trying to take into account the problem of instances, as in Lockemann and Wohlleber [1979]. We offer here an axiomatization which includes as an integral part the concepts of instance and update to an instance. This is accomplished by distinguishing the basic data base relations (such as COURSE, P-REQ, etc.) from other relations which can be constructed from them using relational algebra operations. This is because the values of COURSE, P-REQ, etc. as relations depend on the instance in which we are interested. Thus if σ is the name of an instance, then COURSE is really a function from instances to the set of all relations definable on the given set of attributes. Thus COURSE (σ) is a relation whereas COURSE is not. So a relational expression involving occurrences of names of basic relations cannot be evaluated unless for each occurrence of a basic relation name we specify the instance in which it is to be evaluated.

Instances are built from the empty instance by using the update operations. Note that the update operations (ADDTUPLE and DELTUPLE) take as arguments a basic relation name, an appropriate tuple, and the current instance and provide as result a new instance. Thus "side-effects" of updates to other relations can be reflected in the axiomatization (although we do not do so here). Note also that a relation is a "pair" consisting of a set of tuples and a set of attributes (over which each of the tuples is defined). Thus the axiomatization proceeds by defining the effect of each operation on these two components of a relation. We do not make any claims as to completeness of this axiomatization — it is provided purely for illustrative purposes.

The form in which the axiomatizations are done is as follows:

<u>type</u> *name* (the name of the type) with

<u>*sorts*</u> $a_1, \ldots, a_n$ (the names of the sorts used in the type)

<u>*syntax*</u> $f_1\colon\ a_{1,1} \times \ldots \times a_{1,n_1} \rightarrow a_{j_1}$

$\vdots$

$f_m\colon\ a_{m,1} \times \ldots \times a_{m,n_m} \rightarrow a_{j_m}$

(the operations of the type together with the sorts of each argument and the sort of the result)

<u>*hidden*</u> $g_1\colon\ b_{1,1} \times \ldots \times b_{1,n_1} \rightarrow b_{j_1}$

$\vdots$

$g_p\colon\ b_{p,1} \times \ldots \times b_{p,n_p} \rightarrow b_{j_p}$

(the hidden [auxiliary] operations of the type)

<u>*semantics*</u> $\ell_1 = r_1$

$\vdots$

$\ell_k = r_k$

(the equations used to axiomatize the type).

CONCLUSIONS

In conclusion we review some of the differences between equations and clauses. Equations have as advantages their simplicity, the power of their rule of inference, and their naturalness in certain applications. Their disadvantages include their lack of naturalness in certain other applications; for example, in the specification of abstract data types certain clausal features seem to be desirable and these have to be obtained at the cost of laborious constructions. Another disadvantage is the complexity of efficient implementations (Hoffmann and O'Donnell [1979]).

The advantages of clauses include their generality: any conjunction can be a premiss and any predicate symbol can be used for a relation which is itself defined in the same set of clauses. In situations where equations are preferred, this generality does not hurt: one can just write equations including, if one wants to, function symbols such as the 3-ary if-then-else and the nullaries TRUE and FALSE used in equations. We advocate consideration of alternative methods of obtaining the if-then-else effect using clauses. One can have the conceptual advantages that equations have to offer by adhering to an equational style in clausal specifications rather than to any specific rigidly defined sublanguage of Horn clauses.

Another advantage of clauses is the greater amount of freedom they allow in the choice of axiomatization method. Take, for example, a specification of stacks using error values (ADJ [1978]). The same treatment is of course available when using clauses, as they include equations as a special case. But, when using clauses, we can also view an error-prone operation (such as popping a stack) as a relation which happens not to be defined for certain arguments. When SLD resolution simulates an evaluation involving an error (such as popping an empty stack), it fails to find a refutation. The failure can be attributed to the attempt to pop an empty stack. In this approach error information is supplied at the level of inference rather than being embedded in the axioms. We do not know which approach is to be preferred. Here we just point out that with clauses such a choice is available.

A disadvantage of clauses is a direct consequence of their generality: because no relation plays any special role, the properties of congruence are only available explicitly in the equational sentence and are not "built-in" the inference mechanism. Equational inference has the transitivity and structural induction of congruence built-in. Our translation method from equational sentences to logic programs mixes the properties of congruence into the equations in such a way that a simple-minded inference system such as SLD resolution produces a result from clauses derived from a Noetherian equational sentence.

ACKNOWLEDGEMENTS

We gratefully acknowledge helpful discussions with Thomas C. Brown. The Natural Sciences and Engineering Research Council of Canada provided partial support. We thank the referees for their helpful suggestions.

REFERENCES

1. ADA: Ichbiah, J.D., Barnes, J.G.P., Heliard, J.C., Krieg-Brueckner, B., Roubine, O., Wichmann, B.A. [1979] *Preliminary ADA Reference Manual and Rationale for the Design of the ADA Programming Language, SIGPLAN Notices 14*, 6 (June 1979),

2. ADJ — Goguen, J.A., Thatcher, J.W., Wagner, E.G., and Wright, J.B. [1978] "An Initital Algebra Approach to the Specification, Correctness, and Implementation of Abstract Data Types," In: *Current Trends in Programming Methodology 4* (R. T. Yeh, Ed.), Prentice-Hall, 1978, 80-149.

3. de Carvalho, R.L., Maibaum, T.S.E., Pequeno, T.H.C., Pereda Borquez, A.A., and Veloso, P.A.S. [1979] "A Model-Theoretic Approach to the Semantics of Data Types and Structures," Technical Report, DI-PUC/RJ, Rio De Janeiro, Brazil, 1979.

4. Clark, K. L., and Tärnlund [1977] "A First-Order Theory of Data and Programs," *Proc. IFIP 1977*, 939-944.

5. Colombetti, M., Paolini, P. , and Pelagatti, G. [1978] "Non-deterministic Languages Used for the Definition of Data Models," In: *Logic and Data Bases* (H. Gallaire and J. Minker, Eds.) Plenum Press, 1978, 237-257.

6. Courcelle, B. [1979] "Infinite Trees in Normal Form and Recursive Equations Having a Unique Solution," Technical Report 7906, U.E.R. de mathematique et informatique U. de Bordeaux I, 1979.

7. van Emden, M.H. and Kowalski, R.A. [1976] "The Semantics of Predicate Logic as a Programming Language," *J. ACM 23* (1976), 733-742.

8. Goguen, J.A. [1977] "Abstract Errors for Abstract Data Types," *Proc. of IFIP Working Conference on Formal Description of*

Programming Concepts, North-Holland, 1977,

9. Goguen, J. A. [1978] "Some Design Principles and Theory for OBJ-O, A Language to Express and Execute Algebraic Specifications of Programs" *Proc. of International Conference on Mathematical Studies of Information Processing*, Kyoto, 1978, 429-475.

10. Gotlieb, C. C. and Gotlieb, L. R. [1978] *Data Types and Structures*, Prentice-Hall, 1978.

11. Guttag, J. V. [1977] "Abstract Data Types and the Development of Data Structures, *CACM 20*, 6 (1977), 396-404.

12. Guttag, J. and Horning, J. J. [1980] "Formal Specification as a Design Tool," In: *7th Annual Symp. on Principles of Programming Languages*, 1980, 251-261

13. Hoare, C.A.R. [1972] "Proof of Correctness of Data Representations", *Acta Informatica 1*, 1 (1972), 271-281.

14. Hoffman, C., and O'Donnell, M. [1979] "Interpreter Generation Using Tree Pattern Matching" *6th Annual Symp. on Principles of Programming Languages* (1979) 169-179.

15. Huet, G. [1977] "Confluent Reductions: Abstract Properties and Applications to Term Rewriting Systems," *Proc. of the 18th IEEE Symp. on Foundations of Computer Science*, Providence (1977) 30-45.

16. Huet, G., and Lankford, D. [1978] "On the Uniform Halting Problem for Term Rewriting Systems," IRIA Laboria Report 283, 1978.

17. Kowalski, R. A. [1979] *Logic for Problem-Solving*, North-Holland, New York (1979).

18. Kowalski, R. A. and Kuehner, D. [1971] "Linear Resolution with Selection Function," *Artificial Intelligence 2*, 227-260.

19. Lampson, B.W. et al. [1977] "Report on the Programming Language Euclid," *SIGPLAN Notices 12*, #2 (Feb. 1977),

20. Levy, M. R. [1978a] "Verification of Programs with Data Referencing", *Proc. of 3me Colloque International sur la Programmation*, Dunod (1978) 411-426.

21. Levy, M. R. [1978b] *Data Types with Sharing and Circularity*, Ph.D. Thesis, Dept. of Comp. Sci., U. of Waterloo, 1978.

(Technical Report CS-78-26)

22. Liskov, B., Snyder, A., Atkinson, R., and Schaffert, C. [1977] "Abstraction Mechanisms in CLU", *CACM 20*, 8 (1977), 564-576.

23. Liskov, B. H., and Zilles, S. N. [1975] "Specification Techniques for Data Abstractions," *IEEE TSE*, SE-1, No. 1, 1975, 7-18.

24. Lockemann, P. C., and Wohlleber, W. H. [1979] "Constraints and Transactions: Extensions to the Algebraic Specification Method," Technical Report, University of Karlsruhe, 1979.

25. Maibaum, T.S.E. [1979b] "Data Base Instances, Abstract Data Types and Data Base Specifications,"

26. Nivat, M. [1973] "On the Interpretation of Recursive Polyadic Program Schemes," *Atti dei Convegno d'Informatica Teorica*, Rome, 1973.

27. O'Donnell, M. J. [1977] "Computing in Systems Described by Equations," *Lecture Notes in Computer Science 58*, Springer-Verlag, 1977.

28. Rosen, B. K. [1973] "Tree-Manipulating Systems and Church-Rosser Theorems," *J. ACM 20* (1973), 160-187.

29. Shaw, M., Wulf, W. A., and London, R. I. [1977] "Abstraction and Verification in ALPHARD: Defining and Specifying Iteration and Generators," *CACM 20*, 8 (1977) 553-564.

30. Zilles, S. N. [1974] "Algebraic Specification of Data Types," *Project MAC Progress Report II*, MIT (1974), 28-52.

APPENDIX A

We present here the details of the types discussed in the section THE DATABASE SPECIFICATION. The presentation is annotated to make the axiomatizations clearer.

type *attribute* with

sorts attribute

syntax

DEPT: → attribute

COURSE#: → attribute

TITLE: → attribute

P-DEPT: → attribute

P-COURSE#: → attribute

SECTION#: → attribute

INSTRUCTOR: → attribute

INST-STATUS: → attribute

DAY: → attribute

TIME: → attribute

BLDG: → attribute

RM: → attribute

≡: attribute × attribute → bool

<: attribute × attribute → bool

semantics with a, a': attribute

{a≡a | a ∈ attribute}

∪

{a<a' | a lexicographically precedes a' and a,a' ∈ attribute}

type *tuple* with

sorts tuple, attribute, set of [attribute], set of [tuple],

value_a for each a ∈ DEPT,COURSE#,TITLE,P-DEPT,P-COURSE#,SECTION#, INSTRUCTOR, INST-STATUS, DAY, TIME, BLDG, RM}, value

(Here each value_a is the set of allowed values for the sort defined by a as obtained from some data type defining the set.)

syntax

NEW: set of [attribute] → tuple
(the empty tuple over the given set of attributes)

STORE: tuple × attribute × value → tuple
(sets the value associated with a given attribute)

COLUMNS: tuple → set of [attribute]
(the attributes over which the tuple is defined)

READ: tuple × attribute → value
(the value associated with a given attribute)

PIECE: tuple × set of [attribute] → tuple
(creates a tuple by restricting the tuple to a smaller set of attributes)

CATENATE: tuple × tuple → tuple
(creates a tuple defined by values associated with attributes in either tuple)

COMPOSE: set of [tuple] × tuple → set of [tuple]
(generalizes CATENATE)

MATCH: tuple × tuple × set of [attribute] → bool
(tests whether two tuples agree over a given set of attributes)

hidden

EQ: value × value → bool
(tests whether two values are equivalent)

IN_a: $value_a$ → value
(creates a value from values of a given attribute)

ATT: value → attribute
(defines the attribute of a given value)

VAL: value → $value_a$ for each a
(defines the value of a particular attribute type)

semantics with t,t': tuple; a,a': attribute; A,A': set of [attribute];

s,s': set of [tuple]; v,v': value; v_a: a for each a ∈ attribute.

[COLUMNS(NEW(A)) ≡ A,

(The empty tuple defined on the attribute set A is just the set A.)

COLUMNS(STORE(t,a,v)) ≡ COLUMNS (t)
← a mem COLUMNS (t) ∧ ATT(v) ≡ a,

(The attribute set over which a tuple is defined after a store operation is unchanged if no "error" has been committed.)

STORE(STORE(t,a,v),a',v') ≡ STORE(STORE(t,a,v),a',v')
← Q ∧ a' < a,

STORE(STORE(t,a,v),a',v') ≡ STORE(STORE(t,a',v'),a,v)
← Q ∧ a <a'

(These axioms guarantee that stores performed on two nonequal attributes of a tuple are equivalent to stores performed in the order defined by the order defined on the attributes involved.)

STORE(STORE(t,a,v),a',v') ≡ STORE(t,a',v')
← Q ∧ ¬(a < a') ∧ ¬(a' < a),

(Consecutive stores defined on the same attribute are equivalent to a single store defining the "last" value for the attribute.)

(Q is (a mem COLUMNS(t) ∧ a' mem COLUMNS(t) ∧ ATT(v) ≡ a ∧ ATT(v') ≡ a'))

READ(STORE(t,a',v),a) ≡ v
← a ≡ a' ∧ ATT(v) ≡ a',

READ(STORE(t,a',v),a) ≡ READ(t,a)
← ¬(a ≡ a'),

(Reading the value associated with a particular attribute is given by the value associated with that attribute by the last store operation.)

PIECE(NEW(A),A') ≡ NEW(A') ← A' << A,

PIECE(STORE(t,a,v),A) ≡ STORE(PIECE(t,A),a,v)
← a mem A,

PIECE(STORE(t,a,v),A) ≡ PIECE(t,A)
← ¬ (a mem A),

(The values associated with the attributes of a tuple resulting from the application of the PIECE operation are the same as those associated with the same attributes in the original tuple.)

CATENATE(NEW(A),NEW(A')) ≡NEW(A + A')
← (A -- A') eqv nil,

(Catenation is defined only if the attribute sets over which the arguments are defined are disjoint.)

CATENATE(NEW(A),STORE(t,a,v)) ≡ STORE(CATENATE(NEW(A),t),a,v),

CATENATE(STORE(t,a,v),
STORE(t',a',v')) ≡ STORE(CATENATE(t,STORE(t',a',
v')),a,v)
← a < a',

CATENATE(STORE(t,a,v,),
STORE(t',a',v')) ≡ STORE(CATENATE(STORE(t,a,v),
t'),a',v')
← (a' < a),

(The values associated with attributes in a catenated tuple are the same as those associated with the same attribute in the appropriate argument to the operation.)

COMPOSE(nil,t) ≡ nil,

COMPOSE(t•s,t') ≡ CATENATE(t,t')•COMPOSE(s,t),

(COMPOSE generalizes catenation by catenating each tuple in a set with a given tuple.)

MATCH(t,t',nil)

(Two tuples always match over the empty set of attributes.)

MATCH(t,t',a•A) ≡ MATCH(t,t',A)
← a•A << COLUMNS(t) ∧ a A << COLUMNS(t') ∧ READ(t,a) EQ READ(t',a),

(Two tuples match over a set of attributes only if they have the same values associated with each element of the attribute set.)

v EQ v' ← ATT(v) ≡ ATT(v') ∧ VAL(v) $=_{\mathrm{ATT}(v)}$ VAL(v')

(Here $=_a$ is equality defined on values of attribute a.)

(Two elements of value are equivalent only if they have the same attribute and they are equivalent within the set defined by that attribute.)

}

∪

{ATT(IN_a(v_a)) ≡ a, VAL(IN_a(v_a)) ≡ v_a | a ∈ attribute}

(ATT and VAL are "inverses" of the IN_a operation.)

type *database* with

sorts relation, tuple, set of [tuple], attribute, set of [attribute], relnames, dbi

syntax

ϕ:	→ dbi (the empty data base instance)
ADDTUPLE:	relnames × tuple × dbi → dbi (an update operation to add a tuple to one of the basic data base relations)
DELTUPLE:	relnames × tuple × dbi → dbi (an update operation to delete a tuple from one of the basic data base relations)
CREATE:	set of [attribute] → relation (creates the empty relation over some set of attributes)
ATTRIBS:	relation → set of [attribute] (ATTRIBS is used to obtain the set of attributes over which a relation is defined)
TUPS:	relation → set of [tuple] (TUPS is used to obtain the set of tuples constituting a relation)
KEYS:	names → set of [attribute]
CARTESIAN:	relation × relation → relation
UNION:	relation × relation → relation
INTERSECT:	relation × relation → relation
DIFFERENCE:	relation × relation → relation
	(The above four operations are the usual operations of cartesian product, union, intersection, and difference).
PROJECT:	relation × set of [attribute] → relation (This is the usual projection operation.)
RESTRICT:	relation × set of [attribute] × restrictor × set of [attribute] → relation (This is the restriction operation.)
JOIN:	relation × set of [attribute] × relation → relation (This is the usual join operation.)
DIVIDE:	relation × set of [attribute] × set of [attribute] × relation → relation
	(This is the usual division operation.)

COURSE: dbi → relation
COURSE: → relnames

P-REQ: dbi → relation
P-REQ: → relnames

SECTION: dbi → relation
SECTION: → relnames

SCHEDULE: dbi → relation
SCHEDULE: → relnames

INSTR-INFO: dbi → relation
INSTR-INFO: → relnames

(Each of the above is the name of one of the basic data base relations and is also a function from data base instances to relations. The relation denoted by, say, COURSE in σ is COURSE(σ).)

hidden

DEL: relation × tuple → relation
(DEL is used to remove a tuple from a relation but is not an update operation. It is just used to facilitate the axiomatization of several operations.)

TUPJOIN: set of [tuple] × set of [attribute] × set of [tuple] → set of [tuple]
(Used in the definition of JOIN.)

semantics with r,r': relation; t,t': tuple; s,s': set of [tuple]; a,a': attribute; A,A': set of [attribute]; R,R': relnames; σ,σ': dbi

{ATTRIBS(CREATE(A)) ≡ A,
(The attributes of an empty relation defined over the attribute set A are A.)

TUPS(CREATE(A)) ≡ nil,
(The set of tuples of the empty relation is empty.)

ATTRIBS(COURSE(σ)) ≡ COURSE#•DEPT•TITLE•nil.

ATTRIBS(P-REQ(σ)) ≡ COURSE#•DEPT•P-COURSE#•P-DEPT•nil,

```
ATTRIBS(SECTION(σ))          ≡ COURSE#•DEPT•INSTRUCTOR
                               •SECTION#•nil,

ATTRIBS(SECHEDULE(σ))        ≡ BLDG•COURSE#•DAY•DEPT•RM SECTION#
                               •SECTION#•TIME•nil,

ATTRIBS(INSTR-INFO(σ))       ≡ INSTR-STATUS•INSTRUCTOR•nil,
```

(The above define the sets of attributes over which the basic relations of the data base are defined.)

```
KEYS(COURSE)                 ≡ COURSE#•DEPT•nil,

KEYS(P-REQ)                  ≡ COURSE#•DEPT•P-COURSE#
                                 •P-DEPT•nil,

KEYS(SECTION)                ≡ COURSE#•DEPT•SECTION#•nil,

KEYS(SCHEDULE)               ≡ COURSE#•DAY•DEPT•SECTION#•nil,

KEYS(INSTR-INFO)             ≡ INSTRUCTOR•nil,
```

(The above define the sets of keys for the basic relations of the data base.)

```
ATTRIBS(CARTESIAN(r,r'))     ≡ ATTRIBS(r) + ATTRIBS(r')
                             ← ATTRIBS(r) -- ATTRIBS(r')
                                                  eqv nil,

TUPS(CARTESIAN(r,r'))        ≡ TUPS(r) × TUPS(r')
                             ← ATTRIBS(r) -- ATTRIBS(r')
                                                  eqv nil,
```

(The cartesian product is defined only if the attribute sets of the two relations are disjoint.)

```
ATTRIBS(UNION(r,r'))         ≡ ATTRIBS(r) + ATTRIBS(r')
                             ← ATTRIBS(r) eqv ATTRIBS(r'),

TUPS(UNION(r,r'))            ≡ TUPS(r) + TUPS(r')
                             ← ATTRIBS(r) eqv ATTRIBS(r'),
```

(UNION is defined in the obvious way providing the relations are defined over the same sets of attributes.)

(We omit axioms analogous to UNION for INTERSECT and DIFFERENCE.)

```
ATTRIBS(PROJECT(r,A))        ≡ ATTRIBS(r) - A
                             ← A << ATTRIBS(r),
```

(PROJECT(r,A) is defined only if A is a subset of the attribute set of r.)

```
TUPS(PROJECT(r,A))          ≡ (PIECE(t,A)•nil)+ TUPS(PROJECT
                                 (DEL(r,t),A))
                            ← A << ATTRIBS(r)  ∧ TUPS(r)
                                 eqv t•s,
```

(This recursive definition works by taking each tuple in the relation and taking the appropriate piece of it.)

```
ATTRIBS(JOIN(r,A,r'))       ≡ ATTRIBS(r) + ATTRIBS(r')
                            ← ((ATTRIBS(r) - (A)) --
                                 ATTRIBS(r') - A)) eqv nil,
```

(JOIN(r,A,r') is defined only if the only attributes r and r' have in common are A.)

```
TUPS(JOIN(r,A,CREATE(A')))  ≡ CREATE(A' + ATTRIBS(r))
                            ← A << A' ∧ A << ATTRIBS(r),

TUPS(JOIN(r,A,r'))          ≡ TUPJOIN (TUPS(r),A,TUPS(r'))
                            ← TUPS(r) eqv t•s,

TUPS(JOIN(r,A,r'))          ≡ TUPS(JOIN(r',A,CREATE
                                 (ATTRIBS(r))))
                            ← ¬(TUPS(r) eqv t•s),
```

(This is a recursive definition of TUPS for JOIN using the auxiliary function TUPJOIN.)

(We omit the axioms for division and restriction.)

```
ATTRIBS(R(ADDTUPLE(R',t,σ)))
                            ≡ ATTRIBS(R(σ))
                            ← COLUMNS(t) eqv ATTRIBS(R'(σ)),

ATTRIBS(R(DELTUPLE(R',t,σ)))
                            ≡ ATTRIBS(R(σ))
                            ← COLUMNS(t) eqv ATTRIBS(R(σ)),
```

(Attributes of the basic relations are defined only if the tuple being added or deleted has the "right" set of attributes.)

```
TUPS(R(ADDTUPLE(R',t,σ)))   ≡ t•nil + TUPS(R(σ))
                            ← COLUMNS(t) eqv ATTRIBS(R(σ))
                              ∧ ¬(PIECE(t,KEYS(R)) mem
                              PROJECT(R(σ),KEYS(R)))
                              ∧ R ≡ R',

TUPS(R(ADDTUPLE(R',t,σ)))   ≡ TUPS(R(σ))
                            ← ¬R ≡ R',
```

(If R is not R' and R' is updated by an insertion, then R is unaffected. Otherwise R has an extra tuple. This axiom also guarantees that the appropriate functional dependencies are met.)

```
TUPS(R(DELTUPLE(R',t,σ)))  ≡ TUPS(R(σ)) - t·nil
                           ← COLUMNS(t) eqv ATTRIBS(R(σ))
                             ∧ R ≡ R',

TUPS(R(DELTUPLE(R',t,σ)))  ≡ TUPS(R(σ))
                           ←  ¬R ≡ R',
```

(Deletion of a tuple is handled analogously to addition of a tuple.)

```
ATTRIBS(DEL(r,t))          ≡ ATTRIBS(r)
                           ← COLUMNS(t) eqv ATTRIBS(r),

TUPS(DEL(r,t))             ≡ TUPS(r) - t·nil
                           ← COLUMNS(t) eqv ATTRIBS(r)
```

(DEL works in the obvious way by deleting the tuple from the tuples of the relation.)

```
TUPJOIN(nil,A,s)           ≡ nil,
TUPJOIN(s,A,nil)           ≡ nil,
TUPJOIN(t·s,A,t'·s')       ≡ TUPJOIN(t·s,A,s')+
                             +TUPJOIN(s,A,t'·s')
                             +CATENATE(t,PIECE(t',
                              COLUMNS(t')-A))
                           ← PIECE(t,A) eqv PIECE(t',A),

TUPJOIN(t·s,A,t'·s')       ≡ TUPJOIN(t·s,A,s')+
                             +TUPJOIN(s,A,t'·s')
}                          ← ¬(PIECE(t,A) eqv PIECE(t',A))
```

APPENDIX B

PROLOG Program for Translating Equations to a Logic Program

```
translate(signature(S).canonicals(C).Equations)
<- procsig(S,C) & proceq(Equations,C).

procsig((Function.Arity).S,Canonicals)
<- reducesubexp(Function,Arity,Clause,Canonicals) &
     write(Clause) & nl & procsig(S,Canonicals).
procsig([ ],Canonicals).

proceq(Equation.Equations,Canonicals)
<- transeq(Equation,Clause,Canonicals) &
     write(Clause) & nl & proceq(Equations,Canonicals).
proceq([],Canonicals).

reducesubexp(F,N,T1=T2 <- Premiss,Canonicals)
<- member(F,Canonicals) & genlists(N,Xs,Ys,Premiss) &
     T1 =.. [F:Xs] & T2 =.. [F:Ys].

reducesubexp(F,N,T1=Z <- Premiss,Canonicals)
<- not(member(F,Canonicals)) & genlists(N,Xs,Ys,Eqs) &
     T1 =.. [F:Xs] & T2 =.. [F:Z.Ys] &
     append(Premiss,Eqs,T2&true).
```

```
genlists(0,[],[],true).
genlists(N,X.Xs,Y.Ys,X=Y&Eqs)
<- N>0 &Nl is N-1 & genlists(Nl,Xs,Ys,Eqs).

append(Y,true,Y).
append(U&Z, U&X, Y) <- append(Z,X,Y).
member(X,X.Y).
member(U,X.Y) <-member(U.Y).

transeq(Fxlton=Y,Clause,Canonicals)
/* For the translation process equations  are assumed to be
     conditional.  An unconditional equation undergoes a
     preliminary conversion to one with the trivial condition.
*/
<- transeq(Fxlton=Y <- true,Clause,Canonicals).

transeq(Fxlton=Y <- Conds,Fr0ton <- Premiss,Canonicals)
<- var(Y) & Fxlton =.. [F:Xlton] &
     expandlist(Y.Xlton,R0ton if Altom,Canonicals) &
     Fr0ton =.. [F:R0ton] & append(Premiss,Conds,Altom).

transeq(Fxltok=Gylton <- Conds,Fr0tok <- Premiss,Canonicals)
<- Fxltok =.. [F:Xltok] & Gylton =.. [G:Ylton] &
     member(G,Canonicals) &
     expandlist(Gylton.Xltok,R0tok if Altom,Canonicals) &
     Fr0tok =.. [F:R0tok] & append(Premiss,Conds,Altom).

transeq(Fxltok=Gylton <- Conds,Fr0tok <- Premiss,Canonicals)
<- Fxltok =.. [F:Xltok] & Gylton =.. [G:Ylton] &
     not(member(G,Canonicals)) &
     expandlist(U.Xltok,R0tok if Altom,Canonicals) &
     expandlist(U.Ylton,S0ton if Bltop,Canonicals) &
     Fr0tok =.. [F:R0tok] & Gs0ton =.. [G:S0ton] &
     append(Bsg,Bltop,Gs0ton&true) &
     append(Asbsg,Altom,Bsg) & append(Premiss,Conds,Asbsg).

expandterm(T,T if true,_)
<- var(T) or atomic(T).

expandterm(T,R if Conj,Canonicals)
<- T =.. [F:Arglton] & member(F,Canonicals) &
     expandlist(Artlton,Rlton if Conj,Canonicals) &
     R =.. [F:Rlton].

expandterm(T,R0 if Conj,Canonicals)
<- T =.. [F:Arglton] & not(member(F,Canonicals)) &
     expandlist(Arglton,Rlton if Conjl,Canonicals) &
     Tl =.. [F:R0.Rlton] & append(Conj,Conjl,Tl&true).

expandlist([ ],[ ] if true,_).
expandlist(Arg.Args,R.Rs if Conj,Canonicals)
<- expandterm(Arg,R if Conjl,Canonicals) &
     expandlist(Args,Rs if Conj2,Canonicals) &
     append(Conj,Conjl,Conj2).
```

OPTIMIZATION IN DEDUCTIVE AND CONVENTIONAL RELATIONAL DATABASE SYSTEMS

John Grant[1] and Jack Minker[2]

Towson State University, Towson, Maryland[1] and

University of Maryland, College Park, Maryland[2]

ABSTRACT

A deductive relational database system is one which permits new relations to be derived from given relations stored in a conventional relational database system, and from axioms. It has been shown that a query in a deductive relational database system can be transformed, using the axioms, into a query that involves searches only over the relational database. The transformed query results in a set of conjuncts which generally share similar if not identical searches that must be made of the indexes and the tables storing the relations. The purpose of this paper is to describe a "global" optimizing algorithm which accounts for similarities between conjuncts.

The algorithm consists of two major parts: the preprocessor and the optimizer. The preprocessor is used once for a given set of axioms and indexes. Its functions are to: transform each atomic query type into a group of formulae, list all possible access methods for single tables and join-supported joins and to calculate costs for the access methods. The optimizer is used to select a method of evaluation of the formulae which answers the query in the shortest possible time. Details concerning the preprocessor and the optimizer are provided. An example is given that shows the effectiveness of "global" optimization in contrast to optimizing the retrieval of individual conjuncts. The changes needed to incorporate semantic knowledge into the algorithm are also given.

INTRODUCTION

In recent years there has been an increasing awareness that such seemingly disparate fields as databases, artificial intelligence, and theorem proving are related in many ways. The existence of relationships among these fields is due to their having an underlying theoretical basis in mathematical logic. We find this common thread particularly useful and illuminating in our study of relational database systems.

If data may be stored explicitly or given implicitly by a set of axioms, then deductive searches become important. This way techniques from the field of theorem proving can be applied to large databases for deductive searches. In conventional databases the implicit data in the form of axioms is left to the user who must essentially define the axioms as part of a query. Hence a major difference in the two approaches is the fact that, in approaches using theorem proving techniques, the axioms are stored as part of an extended database, without the user needing to know whether the required data is explicit or implicit; while in the conventional approach, there are no explicit axioms, and the user must write more complex query statements essentially including the axioms as needed for each query. The theorem proving approaches are described in Chang [1978], Kellogg et al. [1978, 1981], Minker [1975a,1975b, 1978a], and Reiter [1978a, 1978b].

Efforts in artificial intelligence are also related directly to work in databases. The artificial intelligence community refers to work in "knowledge-based" systems. In such systems "knowledge" is encoded about a specific domain in the form of assertions and in many systems as axioms described by productions. An assertion is just an entry in a database, and a production is a restricted form of an axiom in the first order predicate calculus: namely, a Horn axiom that does not contain functions. In a Horn axiom the conjunction of atomic predicates implies a single atomic predicate.

The results, therefore, in artificial intelligence and theorem proving can be used to provide a deductive capability for a database system. One might reasonably wonder if the addition of a deductive capability to a database system can be made practical. After all, relational databases tend to be relatively slow, and the incorporation of a deductive capability to a system might complicate matters further and make it so inefficient that it would be unusable.

We believe that deductive searching should be an integral part of database technology, and that such searches can be performed without the addition of new inefficiencies to relational database technology. In the following sections we provide some background concerning deductive systems, and we show that they are related directly to batched queries that consist of boolean combinations of operations to be applied to databases. In particular, we shall develop an "optimizer" that interfaces between a theorem prover and a run-time executor associated with a relational database that retrieves data stored explicitly in the relational database.

Background on Deductive Systems

A database can be considered to consist of two parts: an explicit part and an implicit part. The explicit part of a database consists of all data (assertions) in the database. Thus, in a relational database, the totality of relational tuples for each relation is the explicit part. The implicit part consists of the general rules which can be used to make implicit data explicit.

For example, consider a university with a single lecture hall. All courses below a certain course number are held in this lecture hall. Assuming that there are a large number of courses below the given course number, one can save space by writing an axiom such as:

"For all courses whose course number is less than 200, the course is held in room 170 of Smith Hall."

This type of situation is common to many database applications. For example, a company may have many plants, each plant manufacturing various parts. However, there is a set of 1000 parts of a certain type which are made in one specific plant. Rather than stating explicitly that each part is made in the specified plant, it suffices to state one axiom.

The axioms that we shall consider here are all of one type: the conjunction of a set of tables implies a single table. If $A_1,\ldots,A_n$ are tables (defined explicitly or implicitly), then we may write

$$B \leftarrow A_1 \;\&\; A_2 \;\&\; \ldots \;\&\; A_n \;.$$

Each A_i is the name of a table whose entries are tuples. The meaning of the statement

$$B(x,w,y) \leftarrow A_1(x,y) \;\&\; A_2(y,w)$$

is that B contains all tuples of the form $\langle x_1,w_1,y_1\rangle$ where $\langle x_1,y_1\rangle$ is in the relation A_1 and $\langle y_1,w_1\rangle$ is in the relation A_2. In other words, the axiom states that B contains the join of two relations and it specifies the order of the elements for the tuples of B.

Now, given a set of axioms such as

$$B_i \leftarrow A_{i_1} \ \& \ A_{i_2} \ \& \ \ldots \ \& \ A_{i_{n_i}}$$

two approaches have been presented to the deduction problem: an interpretive approach and a compiled approach. In the interpretive approach (Minker [1975a, 1978a, 1978b]), a general problem solver is used at the time the query is initiated. Assuming a single table is being searched for, the table is either completely explicit, completely implicit, or partially explicit and implicit. If it is completely explicit, a search is made of the explicit table to answer the query. If it is completely implicit, then for each table defined as a left-hand side of an axiom, the problem of solving for the table is replaced by that of solving for answers that solve the set of conjunctive queries represented by the right-hand side. In the case where the table being searched is partially explicit, and partially implicit, both of the above searches must be performed. A general problem solver (for example a theorem proving system), or an AND/OR problem solver (Nilsson [1971]) may be used to find the solution of each conjunct. Each table specified in a conjunct may itself be defined explicitly or implicitly. If it is defined implicitly, another application of an axiom may be applied. The problem solver interleaves searches in the database with searches of the general axioms to retrieve data. The system described by Minker [1975a,1978a] is of this type.

A second approach, the compiled approach, is accomplished in another manner. The assertions and the axioms are separated. When a query is to be answered, it is entered into the system. In the initial step, only a theorem prover is applied. If the query consists of an implicitly defined single table, all left-hand portions of axioms are matched. If there is a match, the set of right-hand parts consist of conjunctions of tables. The theorem prover replaces each implicitly defined table in the conjunction. This process continues until each conjunct in the set of conjuncts consists only of tables that are explicit. This ends the compilation phase. The set of conjuncts is then given to a relational database system for retrieval. We assume in the above that there are no recursive definitions.

Consider the following example where there are eight relational tables, $A_1, A_2, A_3, A_4, A_5, A_6$, B_1, and B_2. The table B_1 is entirely implicit, B_2 is partially explicit, and $A_1, A_2, A_3, A_4, A_5, A_6$ are entirely explicit. There are four axioms:

$$B_1(x_1, y_1, z_1) \leftarrow A_1(x_1, y_1) \ \& \ A_2(y_1, z_1, b)$$

$$B_1(x_2, y_2, z_2) \leftarrow A_3(x_2, y_2, a) \ \& \ A_4(y_2, z_2)$$

$$B_2(x_3, y_3, z_3) \leftarrow B_1(y_3, x_3, z_3) \ \& \ A_5(x_3, z_3)$$

$$B_2(x_4,y_4,z_4) \leftarrow A_1(z_4,x_4) \ \& \ A_6(a,b,x_4,y_4) \ \& \ B_1(y_4,z_4,x_4)$$

Now suppose the query is $B_2(x,c,z)$, i.e. find all pairs $<x_1,z_1>$ such that the tuple $<x_1,c,z_1>$ is in the relation B_2. Successively applying the above axioms, the following set of queries result, where the variables in each query have been renamed.

(1) $B_2(x,c,z)$ (search the explicit part of the B_2 relation)

(2) $A_1(c,x_1) \ \& \ A_2(x_1,z_1,b) \ \& \ A_5(x_1,z_1)$

(3) $A_3(c,x_2,a) \ \& \ A_4(x_2,z_2) \ \& \ A_5(x_2,z_2)$

(4) $A_1(z_3,x_3) \ \& \ A_6(a,b,x_3,c) \ \& \ A_1(c,z_3) \ \& \ A_2(z_3,x_3,b)$

(5) $A_1(z_4,x_4) \ \& \ A_6(a,b,x_4,c) \ \& \ A_3(c,z_4,a) \ \& \ A_4(z_4,x_4)$.

That is, considering each of these 5 conjunctive formulae as individual queries, where each table in a formula is listed explicitly, we may send each to a relational database system to be answered. The set of values for x and z that satisfy them constitutes the explicit table for $B_2(x,c,z)$.

We may contrast the interpretive and the compiled approaches as follows: the interpretive approach maintains a tree structure to control the search for axioms and explicit facts and dynamically determines the table to be searched for (either to find explicit facts or axioms); while the compiled approach reduces the problem to one in which only explicit tables are accessed. The latter approach permits global decisions to be made concerning which operations are to be performed on which tables and in which sequence, since the entire solution is specified. In the interpretive approach, local decisions have to be made to determine the best step. The compiled approach is described by Chang [1978], Kellogg et al. [1978], and Reiter [1978b].

Having the totality of conjunctive formulae explicit permits one to perform a global optimization to answer the query. The purpose of the remainder of the paper is to describe an optimizer that operates upon the set of queries to interface with a relational database system. The optimizer determines the methods by which each table or conjunction of tables is to be accessed and the sequence in which these should occur. The relational database system performs the actual operations.

Recursion and Indefinite Data

In this paper we treat only the case where we have Horn axioms that are nonrecursive. When recursion exists we do not have a universal method to determine when to stop generating new formulae. Approaches to this problem are described in the chapter by Chang [1981], and in a paper by Reiter [1978b]. Our approach to generating conjuncts could be adapted readily to include the results of Chang and of Reiter. Chang restricts axioms to be "regular". An axiom is "regular" if it is a Horn axiom in which the conjunct of relational tables implies a relational table, where the conjuncts consist of at most a single virtual table, a finite number of tables that are only defined explicitly, and a finite number of relations that are evaluable. Reiter considers axioms that have cycles, and may be recursive. He breaks the cycle by making a relation explicit. Additional work is required to handle recursive axioms.

In the case of a non-Horn axiom database, indefinite data exists. By indefinite data we mean Location(J,CP) V Location(J,B), that is, J is located in CP or J is located in B and we do not know which of the two is correct. One can also transform a query when indefinite data exists so as to interface with a relational database. To do so requires a suitable theorem prover, not discussed in this paper. The inference mechanism underlying the approach described in this paper is generally not sufficiently powerful to handle indefinite data. For a description as to how a theorem prover handles indefinite data, see Reiter [1978b]. Given that an inference mechanism has transformed the non-Horn axioms into an appropriate form to interface with a relational database, one has a set of conjuncts to look up in the database. The techniques described here can be adapted easily to handle indefinite data.

Batched, Compound and Deductive Queries

The formation of the so-called compiled approach leads to a direct relationship among batched, compound, and deductive queries. Consider a batched query system in which individual conjunctive formulae are specified. Thus, formulae (1)-(5) could be specified individually, held for a batch operation, and executed simultaneously. If the batch processor could take advantage of the relationships among the five formulae, it would be optimizing its search time over that of answering each query separately. Similarly, given a compound query consisting of an arbitrary number of boolean conditions, one can put the query into disjunctive normal form. Thus, a compound condition could have been specified which, when placed in disjunctive normal form, yields formulae (1)-(5), above. The use of axioms is, therefore, no different than if compound queries or batched queries arose in a nondeductive system. Hence, our claim is that if relational databases can be developed which efficiently handle queries, then deductive systems of the type we describe here are no more difficult to handle.

One could do optimization by considering each conjunctive form as independent of another. Then, for each conjunct, one can derive an "optimum" order of executing the conjunct. Thus, the approach devised as part of Sytem R would be relevant (Selinger et al. [1979]). We take into account the relationships between formulae and find a global approach to optimization.

Assumptions

There are several assumptions that we make relative to the preprocessor/optimizer to be described in the paper. We expect that some of these restrictions will be removed in subsequent work.

Disjunctive Normal Form. We assume that a query is in disjunctive normal form, that is, a query consists of a disjunction of conjunctions of tables. This is a minor assumption since algorithms exist that can take an arbitrary query and transform it to this form.

Quantifier-Free Form. We assume that a query requires the retrieval of all elements that appear as variables. Also, operations to be performed on the output of a query are not considered. That is, if the number of responses is to be counted, the count is a function applied to the output of the query. If we allowed existential quantifiers in queries we would obtain the class of conjunctive queries (see Ullman [1980]). The existential quantifiers would be evaluated by using projections.

Function-Free Horn Axioms. Our axioms are considered to be function-free. That is, we cannot have an axiom of the form:

$$B_1 \leftarrow A_1 \;\&\; \ldots \;\&\; A_k(f(x,y),\ g(x),\ z) \;\&\; \ldots \;\&\; A_n$$

where f and g are functions. All axioms are assumed to be of the kind

$$B \leftarrow A_1 \;\&\; A_2 \;\&\; \ldots \;\&\; A_n$$

where the A_i are names of tables and can take either variables or constants as arguments. The assumption of function-free axioms is made for two reasons. First, the vast majority of databases with which people deal are of this kind. Second, permitting functions in table arguments raises problems with respect to the handling of equality. We believe that databases, in contrast to theorem proving in mathematical problems, should be defined with axioms that are function-free. For a discussion of this problem see Reiter [1978a].

Equi-Join. The only join operation permitted between tables is the equi-join. That is, we can have the = -join

$$A_1(x,y) \ \& \ A_2(y,z,w)$$

but cannot have the <-join

$$A_1(x,y) \ \& \ A_2(v,z,w) \quad \text{where} \quad y < v \ .$$

If the specification $y < v$ is not given, then the expression is permitted as it is just a conjunction of two tables.

Uniform Distribution. We assume that for each argument in each table the elements are uniformly distributed, and hence are equally likely to occur. So we assume in particular that the number of tuples in A(x,y,a) is the same as the number of tuples in A(x,y,b) (where a and b are in the domain of the third argument of A).

We also assume that when we join two tables the underlying domains for the join variables are identical. So, for example, if $A_1(x,y)$ & $A_2(y,z,a)$ appears in a formula, then it would be assumed that the domain of the second argument of A_1 is identical with the domain of the first argument of A_2, and that entries in the domain are uniformly distributed.

No Intermediate Indices or Intermediate Sorting. Although indexing may exist, intermediate computations do not permit indices to be created dynamically, or entries to be sorted. Thus, given the query

$$A_1(x,a) \ \& \ A_2(y,b) \ \& \ A_3(x,y)$$

one might specify the following method to answer the query where, A_1 is indexed on its second argument, A_2 on its second argument, and A_3 on its first argument. Furthermore all index lists are sorted.

(1) Access A_1 records through the value of a in the index associated with the second argument.

(2) Sort all values of x retrieved.

(3) Access A_2 records through the value of b in the index associated with the second argument.

(4) Sort all values of y retrieved.

(5) For each value of x obtained in (1) access the index through the first argument of A_3, enter the record and test for a value from the set of values of y obtained in (3).

The optimizer defined in this paper could evaluate the query in the same way as above, except for steps (2) and (4). This restriction should be removed in subsequent work, as should the restriction of not permitting intermediate indices to be formed.

Nonclustered Indexing. An index is said to be clustered if the tuples are placed into the pages of the table using the index ordering. Clustered indexing enhances retrieval performance since it limits the reading of any page of the table to one time. If the indexing is nonclustered, a page of the table may be read as many times as there are tuples on it with a specific value. Although we do not consider clustered indexing in the remainder of the paper, it is possible to incorporate it into the work by placing tuples with the same index value near one another. Our optimizer could work equally well with clustered indexing: some of the cost formulae would have to be changed.

Join Support. Join support is a simultaneous indexing on 2 tables that can be used in finding the join of these tables. Suppose for example that the join is

$$A_1(x,y,z) \ \& \ A_2(z,u)$$

and that there is a joint support on the third argument of A_1 and the first argument of A_2. This means that for each element c, that appears as a third argument of A_1 or a first argument of A_2, there are two sets of pointers: one set giving the addresses of all tuples in the A_1 table with c as the value of the third argument, and the other set giving the addresses of all pairs in the A_2 table with c as the value of the first argument.

Notational Conventions

We indicate some of the notational conventions used in the rest of the paper. Additional terminology is defined in later sections as needed. We use A (with subscripts) for explicitly given tables, and B (with subscripts) for tables that are partly or completely implicit. Each table is stored as pages of a file on a secondary storage device, and determines a sequence of domains $<D_i,\ldots,D_n>$ where the ith argument of each tuple in the table is an element of D_i. Variables are denoted by x,y,z,u,v,w; constants by a,b,c,d,e. Work is measured in terms of I/O time: the number of page accesses (both read and written), and CPU time: the number of instructions executed (in terms of searching, sorting and concatenation).

We measure the size of an element in units, typically words of memory. A page consists of p units. An index (address) consists of r units. For a domain D, $|D|$ is the number of elements in D and d is the number of units taken up by an element of D. For a table A with three arguments whose domains are D_1, D_2, D_3 respectively, the length of an element of A is $d_1 + d_2 + d_3$ units, the number of elements and pages are written as n(A) and p(A) respectively. In the calculations we always round a fractional number upward even if the fractional part is < .5 as we deal with units such as pages and numbers of elements.

DISCUSSION OF THE OPTIMIZING ALGORITHM

In this section we give an overview of the optimizing algorithm; we describe the details in subsequent sections. The algorithm consists of two parts: a preprocessor and an optimizer.

Background on the Preprocessor

Knowledge about the Database. In general, the input to the system will be provided by the database administrator. In particular, each table is given as completely explicit, completely implicit, or partially explicit and implicit. For each table A we are given the number of elements of A, n(A), the number of pages of A, p(A), and the domain for each argument. For each domain D, we are given the number of elements in D, $|D|$, and the length of each element of D, d units. Additionally, for each table all the arguments on which the table is indexed are given along with the corresponding indexing hierarchy, h(A,i) for table A and argument i, (h(i) if A is understood). The indexing hierarchy is the number of indexing levels in the multilevel directory structure. We are also given all the join supports on pairs of tables. Finally, to work with the deductive system, we must have all the axioms.

Semantic Knowledge. By semantic knowledge we mean a special kind of counting information. Consider a functional dependency $X \rightarrow Y$ for the table A(x,y). Now suppose that we need to access A(c,y). We can conclude that $n(A(c,y)) \leq 1$. This can be very helpful, since if A(c,y) requires the lookup of a large table, we can stop after the first y is found satisfying A(c,y). More generally, we may have information such as $n(B(x,b)) \leq k$ for some integer k, for all constants b. In particular, if B(x,y) is a table whose meaning is "x is a parent of y", then $n(B(x,a)) \leq 2$. In this type of situation, where the number of solutions is known or we have an upper bound for it, we say that we possess semantic knowledge. We do not include the use of semantic knowledge in the presentation of the algorithm, but indicate how to incorporate it later, under INCORPORATION OF SEMANTIC KNOWLEDGE.

Explanation of the Preprocessor. The preprocessor does preliminary work that is used later by the optimizer. In general, the preprocessor is invoked only once for any system, at the time when the database is loaded into the system and before any queries are submitted. The preprocessor assumes that all tables have been defined, no new axioms are needed, the methods of indexing for each table and join supports between tables are specified, and normal updates to the explicit tables leave the size of the domains and the number of tuples for a table relatively stable. Should these assumptions not hold, then the preprocessor would have to be reinvoked to include the new information. For example, if there is a database reorganization, or new tables are introduced, or a new axiom is added, one might have to revise the input and reinvoke the preprocessor.

Let an atomic query type be the name of a table. Then, an outline of the preprocessor is as follows. First the preprocessor transforms each atomic query type into a group of formulae based on the axioms. Then the preprocessor lists all possible access methods for single tables and for join-supported joins of pairs of tables in each formula. The preprocessor also calculates the cost of each of these access methods.

Background on the Optimizer

The optimizer is given a specific (instantiated) query. During the initialization phase, the formulae obtained for this type of query by the preprocessor are appropriately instantiated. Basically each formula indicates the tables that need to be accessed and the conjunctions that have to be performed over them. But there are many different ways of accessing tables and the conjunctions can be done in different orders by commutativity and associativity. The job of the optimizer is to pick a method of evaluation of the formula which solves the query in the shortest estimated amount of time.

The optimizer uses the costs given by the preprocessor and its own calculations to obtain the best estimated orders for performing the conjunctions. Such an order does not uniquely define a method for evaluating a formula, since there may be many different ways of accessing single tables (via indexings) or performing joins that are join-supported. The optimizer can pick the best estimated method for evaluating each formula to obtain a local solution. But we want the optimizer to yield a global solution, that is, the best estimated method for evaluating the set of all formulae (in the component under consideration). For this purpose, the notion of coalescings between formulae is very important. A coalescing is a common task: for example if table A needs to be looked up for formulae (2) and (4), then there is a coalescing, since the lookup needs to be performed only once. By taking the coalescings into account, the optimizer obtains the best estimated solution for the evaluation of the formulae. Once the optimizer completes its tasks, the formulae can be evaluated to give the answer(s) to the query.

Thus we distinguish three phases in the process of obtaining the answers to a query. The preliminary phase is the preprocessor. The next phase is the optimizer. These two phases together comprise our optimizing algorithm. The final phase is the actual implementation of the solution obtained by the optimizer. The optimizer passes a sequence of commands to the executor which specifies the order and methods by which the tables are to be accessed and intersected. During the processing by the executor, it may be the case that assumptions made by the optimizer do not in fact pertain. For example, the optimizer may have expected an output of, say, two tuples during a particular operation, while the actual output as found by the executor is, say 200 tuples. Because of this knowledge gained at run-time, we may want to go back to the optimizer and revise some of the orders and methods by which subsequent tables are assessed. We discuss aspects of this under INCORPORATION OF SEMANTIC KNOWLEDGE.

THE PREPROCESSOR

We assume throughout this and the next two sections that there is no semantic knowledge of the type presented in the section Background on the Preprocessor. We discuss the incorporation of semantic knowledge into the algorithm later under INCORPORATION OF SEMANTIC KNOWLEDGE.

Outline of Preprocessor Steps

We divide the preprocessor's actions into four steps. In the first step the preprocessor transforms each atomic query type into formulae via the axioms. In the second step the preprocessor groups such a set of formulae, and the tables in the formulae, into components. The idea is that optimization between formulae, because of coalescings, can occur only if the formulae are in the same component (i.e. have common tables). The third step is the listing of all possible access methods and their costs for each table. The fourth step is the listing of all possible join-supported joins for pairs of tables and their costs.

Step PR1: Transform Each Atomic Query Type into a Set of Formulae.

Recall that an atomic query type is formally a table such as B(x,y,z). Assume for now that there are no recursive axioms. We define the level of an atomic query type by recursion as follows:

> If the atomic query type is an explicit table, its level is set to 0.
>
> If the atomic query type is partially or completely implicit

(i.e. is a B-table) its level is set to one more than the largest level of a table on the right-hand side of an axiom solving (i.e. whose left hand side is) B.

Note that if the atomic query types are transformed into formulae in the order of levels, when we reach a table B, all the formulae for solving the tables on the right hand side of each axiom solving B will be known.

So order the atomic query types by levels and do this step in an order of increasing levels. If the level is 0, the atomic query type is an A-table, and there is only one formula containing just the A-table itself. Now assume that the atomic query type is the table B. If B is entirely implicit, obtain one formula B*; otherwise obtain two formulae, B and B*. For the formula B* find all axioms whose left hand side is B (this part can be combined with the calculation of level numbers). For each such axiom construct a new formula by inserting immediately after the * inside brackets the tables on the right hand side of the axioms (with possibly some necessary variable substitutions). Now substitute separately the formulae previously obtained for the newly introduced tables. Note that if one formula contains n tables, and the tables have previously been transformed into $k_1,\ldots,k_n$ formulae respectively, then we obtain $\Pi_{i=1}^{n}\ k_i$ formulae. In these formulae the tables immediately followe by * may be omitted because of the lack of semantic information. We defer a discussion on semantic information until the latter part of the paper (INCORPORATION OF SEMANTIC KNOWLEDGE). Finally we rename variables so that different formulae contain different variables.

We illustrate step PR1 by transforming all the atomic query types of the example given in the Introduction to sets of formulae. First note that

$$\text{level}(A_1) = \text{level}(A_2) = \text{level}(A_3) = \text{level}(A_4) = \text{level}(A_5) =$$

$$\text{level}(A_6) = 0\ ,$$

$$\text{level}(B_1) = 1\ ,$$

$$\text{level}(B_2) = 2.$$

For A_1 there is one formula: $A_1(x,y)$.

For A_2 there is one formula: $A_2(x,y,z)$.

For A_3 there is one formula: $A_3(x,y,z)$.

For A_4 there is one formula: $A_4(x,y)$.

For A_5 there is one formula: $A_5(x,y)$.

For A_6 there is one formula: $A_6(x,y,z,w)$.

For B_1 there are two formulae:

$$B_1(x_1,y_1,z_1) * [A_1(x_1,y_1) \& A_2(y_1,z_1,b)]$$

$$B_1(x_2,y_2,z_2) * [A_3(x_2,y_2,a) \& A_4(y_2,z_2)]$$

Finally, for B_2 we obtain first

1) $B_2(x,y,z)$
2) $B_2(x,y,z) * [B_1(y,x,z) \& A_5(x,z)]$
3) $B_2(x,y,z) * [A_1(z,x) \& A_6(a,b,x,y) \& B_1(y,z,x)]$

and finally

1) $B_2(x_1,y_1,z_1)$
2) $B_2(x_2,y_2,z_2) * [B_1(y_2,x_2,z_2) * [A_1(y_2,x_2) \& A_2(x_2,z_2,b)] \& A_5(x_2,z_2)]$
3) $B_2(x_3,y_3,z_3) * [B_1(y_3,x_3,z_3) * [A_3(y_3,x_3,a) \& A_4(x_3,z_3)] \& A_5(x_3,z_3)]$
4) $B_2(x_4,y_4,z_4) * [A_1(z_4,x_4) \& A_6(a,b,x_4,y_4) \& B_1(y_4,z_4,x_4) * [A_1(y_4,z_4) \& A_2(z_4,x_4,b)]]$
5) $B_2(x_5,y_5,z_5) * [A_1(z_5,x_5) \& A_6(a,b,x_5,y_5) \& B_1(y_5,z_5,x_5) * [A_3(y_5,z_5,a) \& A_4(z_5,x_5)]]$

Since at this point no semantic information is available, we may omit the tables followed by * and remove the brackets to get

1') $B_2(x_1,y_1,z_1)$
2') $A_1(y_2,x_2) \& A_2(x_2,z_2,b) \& A_5(x_2,z_2)$
3') $A_3(y_3,x_3,a) \& A_4(x_3,z_3) \& A_5(x_3,z_3)$
4') $A_1(z_4,x_4) \& A_6(a,b,x_4,y_4) \& A_1(y_4,z_4) \& A_2(z_4,x_4,b)$
5') $A_1(z_5,x_5) \& A_6(a,b,x_5,y_5) \& A_3(y_5,z_5,a) \& A_4(z_5,x_5)$

Until we get to INCORPORATION OF SEMANTIC KNOWLEDGE, when we refer to formulae, we mean the primed formulae.

Step PR2: Group Each Set of Formulae and Corresponding Tables into Components

In this step start with a set of formulae obtained from an atomic query type. Construct an undirected graph with a vertex for each table (that appears in a formula) and the table name the label of the vertex. An edge is drawn between vertices if and only if the two tables which are labels of the vertices appear in the same formula. Now separate the graph into its connected components. The labels of the vertices of each component are the tables which we want to group together. We also group together the formulae in which a (connected) component of tables appears in order to form a (connected) component of formulae. This grouping is used by the optimizer to group the formulae obtained for a query into components. The reason for the grouping is that formulae occurring in different components are independent of one another, so that the methods used for accessing the tables in one formula cannot be used to access tables in another formula. In particular, in the example of Step PR1 there are two components: {1')} and {2'), 3'), 4'), 5')}.

Step PR3: List All Possible Access Methods for Each Table and Compute the Associated Costs.

We measure I/O time by the number of page accesses and calculate CPU time separately by the use of standard operations whose time is assumed to be known. In this step we need the time to compare two elements in memory: γ, the time to construct an n-tuple: δ_n , and the time to intersect k sets of sizes $m_1,\ldots,m_k$: $\beta(m_1,\ldots,m_k)$. In the cost calculation we give separately the I/O time and the CPU time. We write ρ for the time to access a page, so that in our formulae the I/O time portion is multiplied by ρ since it is calculated in terms of page accesses.

By accessing a table we mean the construction of a table which is obtained by selection and projection from an existing table stored as a file. For example, given the table A(x,y,z,u) with 4 arguments, the accessing of A(x,a,z,u) involves the construction of a table consisting of triples <x,z,u> of the original A table which appear as first, third, and fourth arguments respectively of a tuple of A that has a as its second argument.

We allow two ways of accessing a table: do a table lookup or use indexing. But indexing can only be used on those arguments which are already indexed since we do not perform dynamic indexing. Let $\{k_1,\ldots,k_m\}$ be the set of arguments on which A is indexed. Since an access method involves indexing on some subset of $\{k_1,\ldots,k_m\}$, there are 2^m access methods. We write cost (A, $\{k_{i_1},\ldots,k_{i_\ell}\}$) for the estimated cost of accessing A by using indexing on the arguments $i_1,\ldots i_\ell$.

In general when indexing is used by the optimizer on a specific formula, the indexed arguments should be constants. So we assume in our calculation that this is the case. However it is possible to use indexing on a variable argument if this argument occurs elsewhere in the formula yielding a set of constants for the variable. Thus, in the formula

$$A_1(x,y) \;\&\; A_2(x,c) \;\&\; A_3(x,y)$$

if A_3 is indexed on argument 1, this indexing may be usable after the conjunction of A_1 and A_2 yields a set of (constant) elements for x. If the indexing is used for x then the cost formula given below must be appropriately modified by treating x in A_3 as standing for a set of constants rather than a variable.

The estimated cost formula is as follows, where by the symbol $\approx$ we mean that the cost formula is estimated to be equal to what follows.

$$\text{(C1)}\quad \begin{cases} \text{cost}(A,\phi) \approx \begin{cases} 0 \quad \text{if all arguments of } A \text{ are variables} \\ \left[p(A) + \dfrac{n(A)}{\prod_{i\in C}|D_i|}\cdot\dfrac{\sum_{j\in V} d_j}{p}\right]\cdot\rho + n(A)\cdot|C|\cdot\gamma \\ \quad + \dfrac{n(A)}{\prod_{i\in C}|D_i|}\cdot\delta_{|V|} \qquad \text{otherwise} \end{cases} \\[2ex] \text{cost}(A,\{k_{i_1},\ldots,k_{i_\ell}\}) \approx \left[\left(\sum_{j=1}^{\ell} h(k_{i_j})\right) + \dfrac{r\cdot n(A)}{p}\cdot\left(\sum_{j=1}^{\ell}\dfrac{1}{|D_{i_j}|}\right)\right. \\ \quad \left. + \dfrac{n(A)}{\prod_{j=1}^{\ell}|D_{i_j}|} + \dfrac{n(A)}{\prod_{i\in C}|D_i|}\cdot\left(\dfrac{\sum_{j\in V} d_j}{p}\right)\right]\cdot\rho + \beta\left(\dfrac{n(A)}{|D_{i_1}|},\ldots,\dfrac{n(A)}{|D_{i_\ell}|}\right) \\ \quad + \dfrac{n(A)}{\prod_{j=1}^{\ell}|D_{i_j}|}\cdot|\tilde{C}|\gamma + \dfrac{n(A)}{\prod_{i\in C}|D_i|}\cdot\delta_{|V|}, \\[2ex] \text{where} \quad C = \text{the set of constant arguments,} \\ \qquad\qquad V = \text{the set of variable arguments,} \\ \qquad\qquad \tilde{C} = \text{the set of nonindexed constant arguments.} \end{cases}$$

The justification of (C1) is given in the Appendix.

Step PR4: List All Possible Join-Supported Joins for Every Pair of Tables and Compute the Associated Costs

We consider join support on variables only, since join support on constants can be treated as if the respective arguments were indexed. For the join support to be usable, the respective arguments in the two tables must be identical. We use the notation $\vec{x}_i$, $\vec{c}_j$ for a sequence of variables and constants with subscripts i and j respectively. For example, $\vec{x}$ may be $x_i^1, \ldots, x_i^k$. Now write the two tables to be joined as $A_1(x_1, \vec{x}_2, x_3, \vec{c}_5, \vec{c}_7)$ and $A_2(\vec{x}_2, x_3, \vec{x}_4, \vec{c}_6, \vec{c}_8)$ where $\vec{x}_1$ and $\vec{x}_4$ are sequences of all different variables, $\vec{x}_2$ is the sequence of common variables not used with join support, x_3 is the join variable, $\vec{c}_5$ and $\vec{c}_6$ are nonindexed constants, $\vec{c}_7$ and $\vec{c}_8$ are indexed constsants.

If there are k join-supported join variables, ℓ constants with indexing in one table, and m constants with indexing in the other table, then there are $2^{\ell+m} \cdot k$ access methods. The reason is that join support can be used on only one pair of arguments, but indexing can be applied on any set of constant arguments. The provision for indexing on a variable argument, as explained in the previous section, holds in this case too.

In the estimated cost formula we indicate both the join-supported variable, x_3 , and the sequence of constants in both tables which are accessed by indexing, $\vec{c}_7$ and $\vec{c}_8$. We obtain the estimated cost formula:

$$
\text{(C2)} \quad
\begin{aligned}
&\operatorname{cost}(J(A_1, A_2; x_3; \vec{c}_7; \vec{c}_8)) \\
&\approx \Bigg[\frac{|D_3| \cdot (d_3 + 2r)}{p} + \frac{[n(A_1) + n(A_2)] \cdot r}{p} + \Bigg\{ \big(h(7) + h(8)\big) \\
&\quad + \frac{r}{p}\left(\frac{n(A_1)}{\bar{D}_7} + \frac{n(A_2)}{\bar{D}_8} \right) \Bigg\} + \left(\frac{n(A_1)}{|D_7|} + \frac{n(A_2)}{|D_8|} \right) \\
&\quad + \frac{n(A_1) \cdot n(A_2) \cdot \left(\sum (d_1 + d_2 + d_3 + d_4) \right)}{|D_2| \cdot |D_3| \cdot |D_5| \cdot |D_6| \cdot |D_7| \cdot |D_8| \cdot p} \Bigg] \cdot \rho \\
&\quad + \Bigg\{ |D_3| \cdot \Bigg[\beta\left(\frac{n(A_1)}{|D_7^1|}, \ldots, \frac{n(A_1)}{|D_7^{\ell_7}|}, \frac{n(A_1)}{|D_3|} \right) \\
&\quad + \beta\left(\frac{n(A_2)}{|D_8^1|}, \ldots, \frac{n(A_2)}{|D_8^{\ell_8}|}, \frac{n(A_2)}{|D_3|} \right) \Bigg] \Bigg\}
\end{aligned}
$$

$$+\gamma\cdot\left[\frac{n(A_1)}{|D_7|}\cdot|\vec{c}_5| + \frac{n(A_2)}{|D_8|}\cdot|\vec{c}_6| + |\vec{x}_2|\cdot\left\{\frac{n(A_1)\cdot n(A_2)}{|D_3|\cdot|D_5|\cdot|D_6|\cdot|D_7|\cdot|D_8|}\right\}\right] + \frac{n(A_1)\cdot n(A_2)}{|D_2|\cdot|D_3|\cdot|D_5|\cdot|D_6|\cdot|D_7|\cdot|D_8|}$$

$$\cdot\ \delta_{|\vec{x}_1| + |\vec{x}_2| + 1 + |\vec{x}_4|}$$

where

$$\vec{x}_i = \langle x_i^1,\ldots,x_i^{\ell_i}\rangle,$$

$$|D_i| = \prod_{j=1}^{\ell_i} |D_i^j|,$$

$$d_i = \sum_{j=1}^{\ell_i} d_i^j,$$

$$h(i) = \sum_{j=1}^{\ell_i} h(i_j),$$

$$\frac{1}{|\bar{D}_i|} = \sum_{j=1}^{\ell_i} \frac{1}{|D_i^j|},$$

and the terms in braces appear only if the appropriate indexing is used.

The justification of (C2) is given in the Appendix.

Summary of the Preprocessor Steps

The preprocessor obtains groups of formulae for each atomic query type. Additionally, the preprocessor obtains the possible access methods for evaluating single tables and joins of tables with join-support, as well as their costs. We assume that all this information is available to the optimizer without additional cost. While the optimizer is needed in obtaining the optimal table evaluations for each query separately, the preprocessor does its work only once (unless significant changes are made to the database by the database administrator as discussed in the section, Background on the Preprocessor).

THE OPTIMIZER

The optimizer is given the actual query and has available to it all the information prepared by the preprocessor.

Outline of Optimizer Steps

We divide the optimizer's actions into six steps. First, the optimizer obtains the set of (instantiated) formulae (divided into components) which needs to be evaluated. Steps 2-6 are performed separately for each component. In the second step, the optimizer obtains the instances of equivalent conjunctions. Then steps 3-5 are performed separately for each formula. The third step is the generation of the set of table conjunction lists. The fourth step is the generation of the estimated optimal conjunction orders for each table conjunction list. The fifth step is the listing of the preferred methods for evaluating the formula and their costs. In the sixth step, which is done separately for each component, we obtain the estimated optimal evaluation method for the component. In the final step we obtain the estimated optimal evaluation method for the query.

Step OP1: Obtain the Set of Formulae Grouped into Components

The query is given in disjunctive normal form such as

$$(G_{11}\theta_{11} \ \&\ldots\&\ G_{1k}\theta_{1k}) \vee\ldots\vee (G_{\ell 1}\theta_{\ell 1} \ \&\ldots\&\ G_{\ell k_\ell}\theta_{\ell k_\ell})$$

where each G_{ij} is an atomic query type and each θ_{ij} is a substitution. First we obtain a set of formulae for each disjunct, $G_1\theta_1 \ \&\ldots\&\ G_k\theta_k$. Recall that for each G_i the preprocessor has already obtained a set of formulae, $F_{i1},\ldots,F_{im_i}$, divided into components. The corresponding formula for $G_i\theta_i$ are $F_{i1}\theta_i,\ldots,F_{im_i}\theta_i$. But each such formula is just a way to solve an atomic query. So, to solve the conjunction of atomic queries, we need to take all possible conjunctions of these formulae. Thus, if there are m_i formulae for $G_i\theta_i$, then there can be up to $\prod_{i=1}^{k} m_i$ formula for $G_1\theta_1 \ \&\ldots\&\ G_k\theta_k$. The union of the sets of formulae obtained for the disjuncts yields the set of formulae associated with the query.

Next we group the formulae into components. Consider first the case where the query is one disjunct. If the query is just one atomic element, then the preprocessor's grouping is the appropriate one to use. Otherwise the conjunctions of the formulae for the atomic queries collapses the components of the formulae for the single queries into one component. Now suppose that the query is composed of more than one disjunct. Divide the set of formulae for each disjunct into components separately, as indicated above.

Then construct an undirected graph with a vertex for each component of each disjunct. An edge is drawn between two vertices if and only if the two components contain at least one table in common, that is, the same table appears both in a formula of one group and in a formula of the other group. Now separate the graph into its connected components. For each connected component take the union of all the formulae occurring in the groups of formulae representing the vertices of the connected component. Each such set of formulae becomes a component for the query.

The rest of the steps of the optimizer are performed separately for each component.

Step OP2: Obtain the Instances of Equivalent Conjunctions.

We want to take advantage of common subformulae between formulae. In order to do so, we define the notion of equivalent conjunctions. We call two instances of the conjunctions of $A_1,\ldots,A_k$ in two formulae equivalent if one instance can be obtained from the other instance by a renaming of variables (with distinct variables renamed differently).

The following procedure can be used to find the instances of equivalent conjunctions. First, list all conjunctions of two tables for each formula, and if the same conjunction appears in more than one formula, check to see if there is an equivalence. This way we obtain all instances of equivalent conjunctions of two tables. Using these equivalent conjunctions as a starting point, we can check for instances of equivalent conjunctions of three tables. We continue in this manner until we find a k for which no equivalent instance of k conjunctions exist.

Steps OP3, OP4 and OP5 are performed separately for each formula. Basically, these steps are used to optimize the evaluation of one formula at a time, while retaining the possibilities for global (over formulae) optimization later. In Step OP6 the evaluation of each component is separately optimized. Since formulae in different components have no tables in common, there is no chance for global optimization between such formulae.

Step OP3: Generate the Set of Table Conjunction Lists.

A table conjunction list for a formula is a list of tables or table combinations for which either a primitive access method is available or an equivalent instance appears in another formula. The preprocessor obtained primitive access methods for single tables and for join-supported joins between pairs of tables. The optimizer, in Step OP2, has obtained the instances of equivalent conjunctions.

List all the tables, A_i , the pairs of tables $J(A_i,A_j)$ which have an applicable join-supported join, and the k-tuples of tables $E(A_1,\ldots,A_k)$ which have an equivalent instance in some other formula. The table conjunction lists are constructed by first writing out all single tables in the formula, and then performing every possible replacement of A_i, A_j by $J(A_i,A_j)$, and every possible replacement of $A_1,\ldots,A_k$ by $E(A_1,\ldots,A_k)$, in such a way that each separate table of the formula appears in the list once either singly or as part of an E or J entry. If the total number of $E(A_1,\ldots,A_k)$ and $J(A_i,A_j)$ is m, then there are at most 2^m table conjunction lists.

Consider for example some instantiation of formula 5') from Step PR1. Suppose that there are applicable join supports on tables A_1 and A_6 and on tables A_3 and A_4 as well as an equivalent instance of the conjunction of A_1 and A_3 . Then the table conjunction lists are:

$A_1,\ A_6,\ A_3,\ A_4$

$J(A_1,A_6),\ A_3,\ A_4$

$A_1,\ A_6,\ J(A_3,A_4)$

$J(A_1,A_6),\ J(A_3,A_4)$

$A_6,\ E(A_1,A_3),\ A_4.$

Step OP4: Generate the Estimated Optimal Conjunction Orders for Each Table Conjunction List

In a given table conjunction list we consider each element as a primitive element to be accessed separately. The goal is to take conjunctions of these elements in the order of least cost. To do so, we need a formula for the estimated cost of the conjunction of two tables. Because of our convention of projecting on constants, we may assume that the two tables contain variables only. Since these tables may have been obtained from other tables by several conjunctions, we write them as T_1 and T_2. Including the variables we get $T_1(x_1,\ldots,x_k,\ x_{k+1},\ldots,x_\ell)$ and $T_2(x_{k+1},\ldots,x_\ell,x_{\ell+1},\ldots,x_m)$ where the common variables are $x_{k+1},\ldots,x_\ell$. We obtain an estimated cost formula whose justification is given in the Appendix.

$$
(\text{C3})\quad
\begin{cases}
\text{cost}(C(T_1,T_2)) \approx \left[p(T_1)\cdot p(T_2) + \dfrac{n(T_1)\cdot n(T_2)\cdot\left(\sum\limits_{i=1}^{m} d_i\right)}{p\left(\prod\limits_{i=k+1}^{\ell} |D_i|\right)} \right]\cdot \rho \\[2ex]
+ \left\{ n(T_1)\cdot n(T_2)\cdot(\ell-k)\cdot\gamma \right\} + \dfrac{n(T_1)\cdot n(T_2)}{\prod\limits_{i=k+1}^{\ell} |D_i|}\cdot \delta_m .
\end{cases}
$$

In order to use (C3) we need to know for each element T of a table conjunction list both n(T) and p(T). Take the case first where T is an instantiated table, say T = A(x,a,y,b). As shown in the calculation of Step PR3, we use $n(T) = n(A)/\prod_{i\in C}|D_i|$ and $p(T) = n(T)\cdot\sum_{j\in Y} d_j\,/p$. Now suppose that T is the instantiated join of two tables with a join support, say, $T = J(A_1,A_2) = A_1(x,a,y)\ \&\ A_2(y,z,b)$. As shown in the calculation of Step PR4, we use,

$$n(T) = \frac{n(A_1)\cdot n(A_2)}{|D_2|\,|D_3|\,|D_5|\,|D_6|\,|D_7|\,|D_8|}$$

and

$$p(T) = \frac{n(T)\cdot\sum(d_1 + d_2 + d_3 + d_4)}{p}$$

Finally, if T has the form $E(A_1,\ldots,A_k)$, the previous calculations can be performed, possibly several times, to obtain n(T) and p(T).

If a table conjunction list has m elements, there are $\binom{m}{2}$ possible conjunctions. By the calculation above, we can pick a conjunction of two elements in this list whose estimated cost is minimal. Now replace these two elements by their conjunction to obtain a list of m-1 elements, and continue this process until only one element is left. For example, in the table conjunction list

$$J(A_1,A_6),\ A_3,A_4$$

of Step OP3, suppose that the conjunction of $J(A_1,A_6)$ and A_4 has minimal cost. We obtain the list

$$C(J(A_1,A_6),\ A_4),\ A_3$$

and finally

$$C(C(J(A_1,A_6),\ A_4),\ A_3)\ .$$

Also, for every $E(A_1,\ldots,A_k)$ with k > 2, the same process can be applied within the subformula generated by $A_1,\ldots,A_k$, so that the conjunction order within $E(A_1,\ldots,A_k)$ is specified.

We believe that this method is a reasonable way of obtaining a minimal estimated cost for a conjunction list. We do not exclude the possibility that a different conjunction order might yield a lower estimated cost. Otherwise we would have to consider all possible conjunction orders.

Using the method above and assuming that ties are broken arbitrarily, we obtain one conjunction order for each conjunction list. We may obtain several such conjunction orders if we take all conjunctions whose cost is minimal. There is one more case to consider, namely the one mentioned in Step PR3, where indexing is given on a variable argument but the argument occurs elsewhere in the formula yielding a small set of constants for the variable. If this situation exists for a table conjunction list, then we need to generate a conjunction order which is optimal among those that have the delayed accessing of the table in question. This process should be repeated for each table with the property of indexing on such an argument. Finally we note that duplicate conjunction orders should be eliminated from the final list. (Even different table conjunction lists may yield identical conjunction orders.)

Step OP5: List the Preferrred Methods for Evaluating the Formula.

By generating conjunction orders for each formula, via the use of table conjunction lists, we have already selected preferred methods for evaluating it. However, a conjunction order usually does not identify a specific method for evaluating a formula. The reason is that an element in the corresponding table conjunction list might be accessed in many different ways. For example, if A(x,y,a,b) is such an element, then it might possibly be accessed by lookup, or by indexing on argument 3 alone, or by indexing on argument 4 alone, or by indexing on arguments 3 and 4. Thus each conjunction order may actually generate many different methods for evaluating the formula. We call these methods the preferred methods for evaluating the formula. By the actions of the preprocessor in steps PR3 and PR4 and the optimizer in step OP4, all the access methods and their costs have already been or can be calculated.

We indicate here a technique for reducing the number of preferred methods. In most cases indexing is preferable to no indexing, and indexing on k arguments is preferable to indexing on a subset of these arguments. We can therefore eliminate such lack of indexing as follows. For each single table A, consider all possible access methods, $(A,S_1),(A,S_2),\ldots,(A,S_n)$. Suppose that $\mathrm{cost}(A,S_i) \leq \mathrm{cost}(A,S_j)$ whenever $S_i \supseteq S_j$. For each occurrence of A, let $S = \{i \mid$ indexing is possible on argument $i\}$ and set $S_A = \cap S$ over all occurrences of A. Then we can delete any accessing method (A,S_i) if $S_i \subsetneq S_A$. A similar process can be applied to indexing within join-supported joins to delete accessing methods with insufficient indexing.

Since all the costs are either known or can be calculated, we ordinarily obtain the cost of a method to evaluate the formula by adding the sum of the costs of accessing each element and the sum of the costs of the conjunctions. However, if a table appears more than once in a formula, it might suffice to access it only once. We briefly discuss this point now by noting that in any specific evaluation of a formula, a certain number of tasks are performed. For example, a whole table may be read in, or there may be indexing on some argument(s) in a table; in fact, we can identify each atomic task as one for which there is some term in the computation of the cost of the evaluation. It is quite likely that some of these atomic tasks also occur in the evaluation of another formula; although in the case referred to above, an atomic task occurs more than once in the evaluation of a single formula. Since it suffices to do such an atomic task only once, the common tasks allow a further optimization for the evaluation of the formulae for the query. This is the key idea that we exploit in the next and final steps of the optimizer. For now we just mention that when we calculate the cost of a method to evaluate a formula, we should count the cost of an atomic method only once even if it appears more than once. Such a sum of costs we call a coalesced sum. While for a single formula the coalesced sum is in general the same as the actual sum, there may be a substantial difference for a set of formulae.

Step OP6: Obtain the Estimated Optimal Evaluation Method for the Component.

At this point we have the preferred methods for evaluating each formula. Every preferred method is made up of atomic tasks. We use the notation M_{ij} for the jth method to evaluate the ith formula and m_{ij}^k for the kth atomic task in method M_{ij}. Then,

$$\text{cost}(M_{ij}) = \bigoplus_{k=1}^{n_{ij}} \text{cost}(m_{ij}^k)$$

where n_{ij} is the number of atomic tasks in M_{ij} and $\oplus$ is the coalesced sum, that is, each distinct atomic task is counted only once.

Make a list of all atomic tasks, their costs, and for each task list all the methods M_{ij} which contain the performance of this task. (If several tasks always occur together, it may be worthwhile to list them as one task.) Define the coalesced cost of an atomic task as its cost divided by the number of distinct formulae which have an associated method that contains the task. The idea is that we can find a method of evaluating each of n formulae containing the task, and yet the task has to be performed only once. The coalesced cost divides the cost of an atomic task equally between the methods in different formulae that contain it. Define the coalesced cost of a method M_{ij} as the sum of the coalesced costs of the atomic tasks contained in M_{ij}. Order the methods for each formula according to the coalesced cost, so that M_{i1} is the method of least coalesced cost for evaluating the ith formula.

Next we show the procedure for obtaining the optimal method for evaluating the group of formulae by obtaining a set of methods $M_{1j_1}, M_{2j_2}, \ldots, M_{fj_f}$ for the f formulae (in the component) such that

$\left(\bigoplus_{i=1}^{f} \text{cost } M_{ij_i}\right)$ is minimal among all sets of methods $M_{1k_1}, M_{2k_2}, \ldots$ M_{fk_f}. Each "set" of methods is actually a sequence that contains one method for each formula. Start with the methods $M_{11}, M_{21}, \ldots, M_{f1}$. Compute both $\left(\sum_{i=1}^{f} \text{coalesced cost } (M_{i1})\right)$ and $\left(\bigoplus_{i=1}^{f} \text{cost}(M_{i1})\right)$. Now if these two costs are equal, then we are through and obtain the set $M_{11}, M_{21}, \ldots, M_{f1}$ as the answer. Otherwise, let

$$T = \bigoplus_{i=1}^{f} \text{cost}(M_{i1}) ,$$

define the special set of methods to be $M_{11}, M_{21}, \ldots, M_{f1}$, and continue by obtaining another set of methods. We define this process inductively.

Assume that at one point the last set of methods obtained was $M_{1k_1}, \ldots, M_{fk_f}$ and T is the cost of the special set. Note that the special set need not be the same as the last set. Now find the set of methods which has the next higher coalesced cost, say $M_{1k_1}, \ldots,$ $M_{ik_i+1}, \ldots, M_{fk_f}$. (It may turn out that this new set has some second subscripts which are smaller than the corresponding second subscripts in the previous set.) If $\left(\text{coalesced cost}(M_{1k_1}) + \cdots + \text{coalesced cost}(M_{ik_i+1}) + \cdots + \text{coalesced cost}(M_{fk_f})\right) \geq T$, then we obtain the special set which yielded T for its cost as the answer and stop. Otherwise compute

$T' = \left(\text{cost}(M_{1k_1}) \oplus \cdots \oplus \text{cost}(M_{ik_i+1}) \oplus \cdots \oplus \text{cost}(M_{fk_f})\right)$. If $T' < T$

then take $M_{1k_1}, \ldots, M_{ik_i+1}, \ldots, M_{fk_f}$ as the new special set with $T = T'$. Now continue with the process described in this paragraph using $M_{1k_1}, \ldots, M_{ik_i+1}, \ldots, M_{fk_f}$ as the last set. If there are no more sets of methods to consider, then we can stop with the special set as the answer whose cost is T. This technique yields an estimated optimal solution since the time estimate for the special set is smallest among those considered and the solutions not considered must have an associated time which is at least T.

Step OP7: Obtain the Estimated Optimal Evaluation Method for the Query.

In the previous step the optimizer obtained the estimated optimal evaluation method for each component. But the components were obtained in Step OP1 in such a way that no coalescing was possible between formulae in different components. Therefore the estimated optimal evaluation method for the query is obtained by taking the union of the estimated optimal evaluation methods for each component.

If there are many methods for evaluating formulae, the combination of Steps OP6 and OP7 can be very time-consuming. We suggest that in practice the algorithm be set up with several parameters whose values can be given by the database administrator or a user. For example, the optimizer may be given a total cutoff time τ, which can be divided up among the various components. When the cut-off time is reached for a component, the present special set, which is the best estimated solution obtained up to that time for the component, would be taken as the answer. In addition to or instead of τ, there may be a parameter α, so that when the amount of time spent by the optimizer exceeds $\alpha \cdot t$, where $t = T$ is the time estimate for the evaluation of the formulae by the executor, the optimizer would stop and yield the present special set as the answer for that component. The point is that it would not be worthwhile to spend more time optimizing the evaluation of the query than the amount of time saved by this process.

Summary of Optimizer Steps

The optimizer obtains the set of formulae to be evaluated for solving the query. It then optimizes the evaluation of each formula separately, but retains also methods of formula evaluation which may not be best for the formulae separately, but which may be useful for global optimization. In the final step the optimizer obtains the estimated optimal evaluation method for the query. We indicated that depending on some possible user-defined parameters the result may not be optimal if the optimizer would otherwise take too long to get the best solution.

THE PREPROCESSOR AND OPTIMIZER IN ALGORITHMIC FORM

In this section we describe the preprocessor and optimizer as a very high-level algorithm.

The Preprocessor in Algorithmic Form

```
For each atomic query type do
    Transform into a set of formulae
    For each set of formulae do
        Group the formulae and their tables into components
    Endfor
Endfor

For each table do
    List all possible access methods and compute the
    associated costs
Endfor

For each pair of tables do
    List all possible join-supported joins and compute the
    associated costs
Endfor
```

The Optimizer in Algorithmic Form

Transform the query into a set of formulae grouped into components.

```
For each component do
    Obtain all instances of equivalent conjunctions
    For each formula do
        Generate the set of table conjunction lists
        For each table conjunction list do
            Generate the estimated optimal conjunction orders
        Endfor
        List the preferred methods for evaluating the formula
    Endfor
    Obtain the estimated optimal evaluation method
Endfor
Obtain the estimated optimal evaluation method for the query.
```

INCORPORATION OF SEMANTIC KNOWLEDGE

Recall the discussion of semantic knowledge in the section Background on the Preprocessor. In this section we indicate the changes needed to the preprocessor, the optimizer, and the executor in order to incorporate semantic knowledge into the algorithm. We also discuss the changes needed to explain to the user the chain of reasoning used in obtaining the solution to the query. We note that McSkimim and Minker [1977] discuss how to use semantic knowledge such as described in this section in the interpretive approach to developing inferences.

Preprocessor Modifications

As its first step the preprocessor transforms an atomic query type into a set of formulae. In the explanation of Step PR1, we showed how to obtain two sets of formulae (1)-(5) and (1')-(5'), for the example given there. Later we used only the primed formulae. By omitting the '*' 's we lost information which might have been useful in the presence of semantic knowledge. We can see from formulae 2) and 3) that both $A_1(y_2,x_2)$ & $A_2(x_2,z_2,b)$ and $A_3(y_3,x_3,a)$ & $A_4(x_3,z_3)$ are ways of using the axioms to solve for the same table, namely $B_1(y,x,z)$ with renamed variables. This can be very helpful if we know the number of solutions for some instance of B_1: if by performing the conjunction of A_1 and A_2 all the solutions to B_1 are round, then there is no need to perform the conjunction of A_3 and A_4 separately. Therefore we change PR1 by keeping all those tables about which we have semantic knowledge, as well as the immediately following "*" and brackets. Thus we obtain a set of double-primed formulae which can be later used by the optimizer.

In the same example, assume that semantic knowledge is given for B_2 but not for B_1. Then we obtain the following double-primed formulae:

1") $B_2(x_1,y_1,z_1)$

2") $B_2(x_2,y_2,z_2)$ * $[A_1(y_2,x_2)$ & $A_2(x_2,z_2,b)$ & $A_5(x_2,z_2)]$

3") $B_2(x_3,y_3,z_3)$ * $[A_3(y_3,x_3,a)$ & $A_4(x_3,z_3)$ & $A_5(x_3,z_3)]$

4") $B_2(x_4,y_4,z_4)$ * $[A_1(z_4,x_4)$ & $A_6(a,b,x_4,y_4)$ & $A_1(y_4,z_4)$ & $A_2(z_4,x_4,b)]$

5") $B_2(x_5,y_5,z_5)$ * $[A_1(z_5,x_5)$ & $A_6(a,b,x_5,y_5)$ & $A_3(y_5,z_5,a)$ & $A_4(z_5,x_5)]$.

Any change in step PR1 may cause a change to the result obtained in step PR2. The actual procedure of PR2 need not be changed however. So, in the example above, although there are two components for the primed formulae, there is only one component for the double-primed formulae, since B_2 appears in all of them. The availability of semantic knowledge induces no other changes in the preprocessor.

Optimizer Modifications

For its first step, the optimizer obtains the set of instantiated formulae grouped into components. If we retain Step OP1 without any changes and apply them to the double-primed formulae, we may obtain components which are not minimal. This can occur if we have semantic knowledge about a B table that is not usable for a specific instantiation of the B table. For example, we may know that for any constant c, B(x,c,y) has at most 5 elements. However, a specific instantiation of the query yields B(d,u,v) making the semantic information unusable. But the preprocessor sets up the double-primed formulae without being given the query, and therefore in the double-primed formulae B appears with '*' and brackets following it. Therefore, the optimizer in this step should eliminate such B tables along with the corresponding '*' and brackets to obtain the set of triple-primed formulae and group these into components. In particular, continuing with the example of the previous section, if the query is $B_2(x,c,z)$, and semantic knowledge is applicable only when B_2 has a constant in argument 1, we obtain the triple-primed formulae:

1''') $B_2(x_1,c\ ,z_1)$

2''') $A_1(c,x_2)$ & $A_2(x_2,z_2,b)$ & $A_5(x_2,z_2)$

3''') $A_3(c,x_3,a)$ & $A_4(x_3,z_3)$ & $A_5(x_3,z_3)$

4''') $A_1(z_4,x_4)$ & $A_6(a,b,x_4,c)$ & $A_1(c,z_4)$ & $A_2(z_4,x_4,b)$

5''') $A_1(z_5,x_5)$ & $A_6(a,b,x_5,c)$ & $A_3(c,z_5,a)$ & $A_4(z_5,x_5)$

In this case the triple-primed formulae are the primed formulae (with c substituted for y) since no semantic knowledge can be used. There are two components, {1''')} and {2'''), 3'''), 4'''), 5''')}.

We also modify Step OP2 by obtaining, in addition to the instances of equivalent conjunctions, the instances of semantically related conjunctions. For, note that every set of tables inside of brackets represents a solution for some implicitly defined table. If this table also has a solution in another formula, then we should include the set as a unit. We write $S(A_1,\ldots,A_k)$ to denote that the conjunction of tables $A_1,\ldots,A_k$ is a solution of a table and we know the number of solutions. Then in Step OP3 we include all instances of semantically related tables in addition to the single tables, join-supported joins, and instances of equivalent conjunctions to form the set of table conjunction lists. Note also that any table immediately followed by an '*' should not be part of a table conjunction list and that S symbols may be nested.

We give an example. Suppose that there are two formulae (we omit the arguments):

(1''') B_1 * $[A_1\&A_2]$ & A_3 & A_4

(2''') $B_1 * [A_5 \& A_6] \& A_3 \& A_4$.

Now we focus our attention on formula (1'''). The tables A_1 and A_2 are semantically related. Let us suppose that (1''') contains no instance of an equivalent conjunction, and there is one applicable join-supported join, namely on tables A_1 and A_3 . Then the table conjunction lists for (1''') are:

$$A_1,\ A_2,\ A_3,\ A_4$$
$$J(A_1,A_3),\ A_2,\ A_4$$
$$S(A_1,A_2),\ A_3,\ A_4.$$

For Step OP4 we indicate how to handle $S(A_1,\ldots,A_k)$ in a table conjunction list. We note the analogy between $E(A_1,\ldots,A_k)$ and $S(A_1,\ldots,A_k)$: $E(A_1,\ldots,A_k)$ means that the conjunction of tables $A_1,\ldots,A_k$ occurs in another formula also, while $S(A_1,\ldots,A_k)$ means that the conjunction of tables $A_1,\ldots,A_k$ solves a table whose solution is given in another formula also. Thus $S(A_1,\ldots,A_k)$ is handled in the same way as $E(A_1,\ldots,A_k)$. Next, Step OP5 requires no change. However, there may be additional preferred methods for evaluating formulae because of the additional table conjunction lists.

Finally we consider Steps OP6 and OP7. Recall that in these steps the optimal evaluation method is found, first for the components and then for the query. Continuing with the example of formulae (1''') and (2'''), it may be the case that the optimal evaluation method involves not doing the conjunction of A_1 and A_2 or A_5 and A_6. But it is possible that by performing the conjunction of A_1 and A_2, we would obtain all the solutions to B_1, thus eliminating the need to perform the conjunction of A_5 and A_6 in (2''') and thereby reducing the previous minimal time. Therefore, in this step we should also compute the optimal method which includes doing the conjunction of A_1 and A_2 or of A_5 and A_6 . If the new solution is "substantially better" than the otherwise optimal solution in the best case, while it cannot be "much worse" than the otherwise optimal solution in the worst case, then we accept the new solution. A user-defined parameter can be applied here to give meaning to "substantially better" and "much worse".

Executor Modifications

During run-time, as the solution selected by the optimizer is being implemented, the executor needs to possess all the given semantic knowledge involving the sizes of tables. Semantic knowledge about an explicitly given table can be used in a table lookup situation. If the (properly instantiated) table has at most k solutions, and if there are k solutions already, then there is no need to continue the lookup. Next, suppose that semantic knowledge is given about a table that is at least partially implicit. The optimizer has already obtained all instances of semantically related conjunctions, so the executor possesses all subformulae in various formulae which solve for this table. Once again, if all solutions have been found at some point during execution, then there is no need to look further. This way the executor may save time by possibly not having to evaluate some subformulae. At the end of the previous section we indicated changes that might be required of the optimizer in order to take advantage of semantic knowledge.

Algorithmic Form for the Preprocessor and Optimizer

In the section, THE PREPROCESSOR AND OPTIMIZER IN ALGORITHMIC FORM, we described the preprocessor and optimizer in a very high-level algorithmic form. If semantic knowledge is available, some modifications should be made to the implementation of many of these steps as explained in the sections, Preprocessor Modifications, and Optimizer Modifications. Only one change is needed for the algorithm at this high level. Namely replace the statement "Obtain the instances of equivalent conjunctions" by the statement "Obtain the instances of equivalent conjunctions and semantically related conjunctions" in the optimizer.

Explanation to the User of the Chain of Reasoning

By retaining all of the asterisked (*) entries in a conjunct, even those that do not contain semantic counting information, the deductive reasoning chain is embedded within the conjunct. Thus, in formula 3) of Step PR1 we have the following:

$$B_2(x_3,y_3,z_3) * [B_1(y_3,x_3,z_3) * [A_3(y_3,x_3,a) \ \& \ A_4(x_3,z_3)] \ \& \ A_5(x_3,z_3)] .$$

By unravelling the brackets we can state that

$$B_1(y_3,x_3,z_3) \leftarrow A_3(y_3,x_3,a) \ \& \ A_4(x_3,z_3)$$

and

$$B_2(x_3,y_3,z_3) \leftarrow B_1(y_3,x_3,z_3) \ \& \ A_5(x_3,z_3) .$$

See Minker and Powell [1979] for details.

By permitting the optimizer to ignore how tables are related relative to the axioms, it becomes difficult to state to a user how the answer was derived. If it is essential that the user be given the reasoning steps, then this must be transmitted by the user at query entry, and the optimizer must be restrained to actions that will assure that the reasoning steps can be reconstructed.

For example, if it is necessary to have the intermediate table for B_1 as in the above conjunct, then the optimizer cannot be permitted to require the conjunction of A_3 and A_5 for the solution of this formula. The reconstruction of all the reasoning steps can be ensured in the following way. The optimizer starts with the unprimed formulae and considers any two subformulae used to solve for a table as semantically related. Then the optimizer must restrict the set of table conjunction lists to those that contain all possible semantically related entries.

AN EXAMPLE

In this section we trace the steps of the preprocessor/optimizer for a particular (simple) example. The detailed calculations may be found in Grant and Minker [1979]. The example database is the one we used before in the INTRODUCTION with the axioms listed in the section, Background on Deductive Systems. To make our calculations reasonable for easy simulation, we assume that ρ is so much greater than γ, δ_n, and β that we can use $\rho = 1$, $\gamma = \delta_n = \beta = 0$. Recall from Step PR3 that γ, δ_n, and β refer to parameters used in CPU time calculation. So our assumption is reasonable if the work is heavily I/O bound. We also assume that no semantic information is given.

The information needed by the preprocessor is given in the section, Background on the Preprocessor. For completeness we repeat the axioms:

$$B_1(x,y,z) \leftarrow A_1(x,y) \;\&\; A_2(y,z,b)$$
$$B_1(x,y,z) \leftarrow A_3(x,y,a) \;\&\; A_4(y,z)$$
$$B_2(x,y,z) \leftarrow B_1(y,x,z) \;\&\; A_5(x,z)$$
$$B_2(x,y,z) \leftarrow A_1(z,x) \;\&\; A_6(a,b,x,y) \;\&\; B_1(y,z,x).$$

The following size information is also given ($n(A_i)$ is the number of tuples in table A_i; $p(A_i)$ is the number of pages in A_i):

$n(A_1) = 1000$ $\qquad p(A_1) = 40$
$n(A_2) = 10000$ $\qquad p(A_2) = 600$
$n(A_3) = 5000$ $\qquad p(A_3) = 300$
$n(A_4) = 500$ $\qquad p(A_4) = 20$
$n(A_5) = 100$ $\qquad p(A_5) = 4$
$n(A_6) = 50000$ $\qquad p(A_6) = 4000$
$n(B_2) = 200$ $\qquad p(B_2) = 12$

All the domains are the same, D, and $|D| = 100$, $p = 50$ (p is the number of units per page), $r = 1$ (r is the size of an index in units), and $d = 1$ (d is the size of an element of D in units). The following indexings are available:

A_1: argument 1, $h(A_1,1) = 2$

A_2: argument 3, $h(A_2,3) = 3$

A_3: none

A_4: none

A_5: none

A_6: arguments 1,4, $h(A_6,1) = h(A_6,4) = 4$

B_2: none

where h indicates the hierarchy of indexing as explained in the section Bakcground on the Preprocessor. The following join supports are avilable:

A_1 and A_5: arguments 2 and 1 respectively

A_4 and A_5: arguments 2 and 2 respectively

Next we indicate the results of the computation of the preprocessor. Since our query has only one table, B_2, we only list here the set of formulae the preprocessor obtains for $B_2(x,y,z)$. But this is just the set obtained in Step PR1, namely

1') $B_2(x_1,y_1,z_1)$

2') $A_1(y_2,x_2)$ & $A_2(x_2,z_2,b)$ & $A_5(x_2,z_2)$

3') $A_3(y_3,x_3,a)$ & $A_4(x_3,z_3)$ & $A_5(x_3,z_3)$

4') $A_1(z_4,x_4)$ & $A_6(a,b,x_4,y_4)$ & $A_1(y_4,z_4)$ & $A_2(z_4,x_4,b)$

5') $A_1(z_5,x_5)$ & $A_6(a,b,x_5,y_5)$ & $A_3(y_5,z_5,a)$ & $A_4(z_5,x_5)$.

As mentioned in Step PR2, there are two components: {1')} and {2'), 3'), 4'), 5')}. Then the preprocessor computes the costs associated with the various access methods for each table and with the join-supported joins.

The information obtained by the preprocessor is used as input to the optimizer. Suppose that the query is

$$B_2(x,c,z) \ .$$

In Step OP1 the optimizer obtains two sets of formulae corresponding to the two components of formulae:

i. 1 $B_2(x_1,c,z_1)$

and

ii. 1 $A_1(c,x_2)$ & $A_2(x_2,z_2,b)$ & $A_5(x_2,z_2)$

ii. 2 $A_3(c,x_3,a)$ & $A_4(x_3,z_3)$ & $A_5(x_3,z_3)$

ii. 3 $A_1(z_4,x_4)$ & $A_6(a,b,x_4,c)$ & $A_1(c,z_4)$ & $A_2(z_4,x_4,b)$

ii. 4 $A_1(z_5,x_5)$ & $A_6(a,b,x_5,c)$ & $A_3(c,z_5,a)$ & $A_4(z_5,x_5)$

We continue with the second set since no optimization is possible for the first set: $B_2(x_1,c,z_1)$ must be looked up. In Step OP2 the following instances of equivalent conjunctions are generated:

$A_1(c,x)$ & A_2 in formulae 1 and 3 ,

A_3 & A_4 in formulae 2 and 4 ,

$A_1(z,x)$ & A_6 in formulae 3 and 4 .

In Step OP3 the table conjunction lists are generated. In Step OP4 the optimizer obtains the estimated optimal conjunction order for each table conjunction list. The calculations in Step OP5 yield the preferred methods for evaluating each formula. Finally in Step OP6 we obtain the estimated optimal evaluation order.

We find that the cost, in terms of page accesses, of the estimated optimal solution for the second component is 515. Without coalescings, if we optimize formulae individually and compute the sum of the costs for the optimal solution for each formula we would obtain 984. Thus, in this particular case, by optimizing over formulae, we can nearly halve the required time. This is an impressive achievement and suggests that the amount of extra time used in global optimization over just the local optimization is very worthwhile especially in the case of queries whose evaluation is very time-consuming.

COMPARISON WITH OTHER APPROACHES

Considerable work has been done on optimizing queries for relational database systems. However we are not aware of any previous work in optimizing the use of access methods specifically for batched, compound, or "compiled" deductive queries as specified in this paper. Work on optimizing retrieval in an "interpreted" system may be found in Minker [1975b,1978b] and Wilson [1976].

In a recent survey paper, Kim [1979], classifies the literature on the optimization of the relational interface in the following way: relational calculus — translation to algebraic operators; translation to expressions in procedural languages; list processing; iterative decomposition; iterative combination — and relational algebra — algebraic transformation for serial processing, algebraic transformation for parallel processing. Our method would probably fit under the method: relational calculus — iterative combination. In accordance with our statement above concerning batched queries but independently from us, Kim writes "Optimization for a stream of query and data manipulation statements remain to be investigated."

The optimizer for System R, as described in Selinger et al. [1979], is closest to our general approach. The OPTIMIZER component of the algorithm performs access path selection by formulating a cost prediction for various access paths, based on the number of pages fetched and CPU utilization. The system accepts statements in the language SQL, thus it can handle a range of values and various types of joins. Both clustered and nonclustered indexings are covered. Two methods for joining relations are described: the nested loops method and the merging scans methods. The former technique essentially compares the tuples of a table (one at a time) to all the tuples of the other table; the latter technique can be used only if for each join column either indexing is available or the values are sorted. We note here that in our calculations we use a variant of the nested loops method for joins without join support and a variant of the merging scans method for joins with join support. Since their optimizer works on one query at a time, it does not take into account possible coalescings over formulae. We also wish to point out the important fact that the optimizing algorithm for System R has been implemented.

In his text, Ullman [1980], presents several general strategies for optimization at the beginning of the chapter on query optimization. These six strategies, which are not the only ones described in the book are as follows:

1. Perform selections as early as possible.
2. Preprocess files by sorting and creating indices.
3. Look for common subexpressions in an expression.
4. Cascade selections and projections.
5. Combine projections with a binary operation that precedes or follows it.
6. Combine certain selections with a prior Cartesian product to make a join.

Now we briefly discuss Ullman's rules in relation to our optimization algorithm. We conform to the first rule in the way that we access individual relations. Concerning the second rule, we assume given indexings and join support but do not use sorting or dynamic indexing. Use of the third rule is included in our algorithm. We also follow the fourth rule in the way that we derive the formulae and access the tables. The fifth rule is not applicable and the sixth rule is followed. Thus we find that our optimizing algorithm conforms to most of the standard general optimization techniques for query evaluation. In addition, as mentioned previously, we handle the case of optimizing multiple and deductive queries.

In his paper, Yao [1979] presents a general model for database storage and access. He analyzes generalized access cost equations to yield an optimal access algorithm. This is a very careful study that delves into many fine points concerning the evaluation of the various tasks. He measures the cost in terms of page accesses and allows for sorting as well as indexing and various types of links for the storage structures. The paper deals with one and two-variable queries; an n-variable query has to be reduced first by decompositions and substitutions. Again, the problem of optimization for a batch of queries is not investigated.

Additional references concerning query optimization may be found in Demolombe [1978, 1979], Kim [1979], Selinger et al. [1979], Ullman [1980], and Yao [1979]. We do not review work on which their papers are founded.

REFERENCES

1. Chang, C. L. [1978] "DEDUCE — 2: Further Investigations of Deduction in Relational Data Bases," In *Logic and Data Bases* (H. Gallaire and J. Minker, Eds.), Plenum Press, N. Y., 1978, 201-236.

2. Chang, C. L. [1981] "On Evaluation of Queries Containing Derived Relations in a Relational Data Base," In *Advances in Data Base Theory — Vol. 1* (H. Gallaire, J. Minker and J. M. Nicolas, Eds.), Plenum Press, N. Y., 1981, 235-260.

3. Demolombe, R. [1978] "A General Semantic Method for Efficiently Evaluating "AND" Operators", presented at the International Conference on DATABASES: IMPROVING USABILITY AND RESPONSIVENESS, Haifa, Israel, August, 1978.

4. Demolombe, R. [1979] "Estimation of the Number of Tuples Satisfying a Query Expressed in Predicate Calculus Language," Report of the Centre d'Etudes de Recherches, Toulouse, France, December 1979.

5. Grant, J. and Minker, J. [1979] "Optimization in Deductive and Conventional Relational Data Base Systems," TR 828 Department of Computer Science, Univ. of Maryland, College Park, Maryland 20742, 1979.

6. Kellogg, C., Klahr, P. and Travis, L. [1978] "Deductive Planning and Pathfinding for Relational Data Bases," In

Logic and Data Bases (H. Gallaire and J. Minker, Eds.), Plenum Press, N. Y., 1978, 179-200.

7. Kellogg, C. and Travis, L. [1980] "Reasoning with Data in a Deductively Augmented Data Management System," In *Advances in Data Base Theory — Vol. 1* (H. Gallaire, J. Minker and J. M. Nicolas, Eds.), Plenum Press, N. Y., 1981, 261-295.

8. Kim, W. [1979] "Relational Database Systems," *ACM Computing Surveys 11*, 3, September 1979, 185-211.

9. McSkimin, J. and Minker, J. [1977] "The Use of a Semantic Network in a Deductive Question-Answering System," *Proceedings IJCAI - 77*, Cambirdge, Mass., 1977, 50-58.

10. Minker, J. [1975a] "Performing Inferences Over Relational Data Bases," *Proceedings International Workshop on the Management of Data: Description, Access, and Control*, ACM, New York, May 14-16, 1975, 79-87.

11. Minker, J. [1975 b] "Set Operations and Inferences Over Relational Data Bases," Proc. *Fourth Texas Conference on Computing Systems*, Nov. 1975, 5A-1 - 5A-10.

12. Minker, J. [1978a] "An Experimental Relational Data Base System Based on Logic," In *Logic and Data Bases* (H. Gallaire and J. Minker, Eds.), Plenum Press, N. Y., 1978, 107-147.

13. Minker, J. [1978b] "Search Strategy and Selection Function for an Inferential Relational System," *ACM Transactions on Database Systems 3*, 1 (March 1978), 1-31.

14. Minker, J. and Powell, P. B. [1979] "Answer and Reason Extraction, Natural Language and Voice Output for Deductive Relational Data Bases," In *Natural Language Based Computer Systems* (L. Bolc, Ed.), 1980.

15. Nilsson, N. J. [1971] *Problem-Solving Methods in Artificial Intelligence*, McGraw-Hill, New York, 1971.

16. Reiter, R. [1978a] "On Closed World Data Bases," In *Logic and Data Bases* (H. Gallaire and J. Minker, Eds.), Plenum Press, N. Y., 1978, 55-76.

17. Reiter, R. [1978b] "Deductive Question-Answering on Relational Data Bases," In *Logic and Data Bases* (H. Gallaire and J. Minker, Eds.), Plenum Press, N. Y., 1978, 149-177.

18. Selinger, P. G. et al. [1979] "Access Path Selection in a Relational Database Management System," *Proceedings of ACM-SIGMOD Conference*, Boston, Mass. (1979) 23-34.

19. Ullman, J. D. [1980] *Principles of Database Systems*, Computer Science Press, Potomac, Maryland, 1980.

20. Wilson, G. [1976] "A Description and Analysis of the PAR Technique — An Approach for Parallel Inference and Parallel Search in Problem Solving Systems," Ph.D. Thesis, Dept. of Computer Science, Univ. of Maryland, College Park, Md. 20742, 1976 (Also: TR 464 Dept. of Computer Sci., University of Maryland).

21. Yao, S. B. [1979] "Optimization of Query Evaluation Algorithms," *ACM Transactions on Database System 4* (1979) 133-155.

ACKNOWLEDGEMENTS

The authors acknowledge the support given to them by the National Science Foundation under Grant Number NSF MCS 73-034 33002. The second author also acknowledges the support given to him by the National Aeronautics and Space Administration under Grant Number NGR 21-002-270. The authors appreciate the support given to them which made this research possible. The authors wish to particularly thank the referees for very helpful comments and suggestions.

APPENDIX

Here we justify the cost formulae (C1), (C2) and (C3) given in Steps PR3, PR4 and OP4 respectively. The costs we obtain are approximations to the average expected cost of performing the respective operations. We do not repeat the cost formulae here, bur review the terminology:

$p(A)$ = the number of pages of table A,

$n(A)$ = the number of elements of table A,

p = the number of units per page,

D_i = the ith domain (of the table under consideration),

$|D|$ = the number of elements of D,

d_i = the number of units occupied by an element of the ith domain

r = the number of units occupied by an index

ρ = the time to access a page,

γ = the time to compare two elements,

δ_n = the time to construct an n-tuple,

$\beta(m_1,\ldots,m_k)$ = the time to intersect k sets of sizes $m_1,\ldots,m_k$,

h(i) = the indexing hierarchy for argument i (of the table under consideration),

C = the set of constant arguments,

$\tilde{C}$ = the set of nonindexed constant arguments,

V = the set of variable arguments.

First we justify (C1), the estimated cost of accessing a table. If all the arguments are variables, then the table already exists, and the cost is 0. Now suppose that at least one argument is constant, but no indexing is used. The table is read in first; this is p(A) pages. The constant elements in each tuple are compared to the fixed constants giving the term $n(A)\cdot|C|\cdot\gamma$. Then the new tuples are formed in time $[n(A) / \prod_{i\in C} |D_i|]\cdot\delta_{|V|}$. Finally the new tuples are written out on a file taking $[n(A) / \prod_{i\in C}|D_i|]\cdot[\sum_{j\in V} d_j/p]$ page accesses.

Assume next the indexing is used on the arguments $k_{i_1},\ldots,k_{i_\ell}$. It takes $h(k_{i_j})$ page accesses to go through the indexing hierarchy for the i_jth argument. For this argument the number of pages of indices brought into memory is $[r\cdot n(A)]/[p\cdot|D_{ij}|]$. These page accesses are performed for each argument $k_{i_1},\ldots,k_{i_\ell}$. Then the index sets are intersected, giving the term $\beta\left(n(A)/|D_{i_1}|,\ldots,n(A)/|D_{i_\ell}|\right)$. The number of elements in the intersection is estimated as $n(A)/\prod_{j=1}^{\ell} |D_{i_j}|$. In our formula we assume a page fetch for each element in the intersection since the indexing is nonclustered and not sorted. Thus we obtain the term $n(A)/\prod_{j=1}^{\ell} |D_{i_j}|$ for the number of pages brought in. These elements must be compared to the fixed constants, since some constants may not be indexed, in time $[n(A)/\prod_{j=1}^{\ell} |D_{i_j}|]\cdot|\tilde{C}|\cdot\gamma$.

Then the new tuples are formed in time $[n(A)/\prod_{i\in C} |D_i|]\cdot\delta_{|V|}$, and the number of pages written out on a file is $[n(A)/\prod_{i\in C}|D_i|]\cdot[\sum_{j\in V} d_j / p]$.

Now we justify (C2), the estimated cost of accessing a join-supported join of two tables. The number of pages of join index read in depends on the number of elements in the join domain, $|D_3|$, and the length of each element followed by two index pointers, giving $|D_3|\cdot(d_3+2\cdot r)/p$ pages. The total number of pages of indices obtained from the join support is $[n(A_1)+n(A_2)]\cdot r/p$. The number of pages of indexing hierarchy read in for constants is $(h(7)+h(8))$, and the number of pages of indices read in is $(r/p)\cdot(n(A_1)/|\bar{D}_7| + n(A_2)/|\bar{D}_8|)$. Then the index sets are intersected separately for A_1 and A_2 with the join-support indices (once for each element of D_3) giving the term

$$|D_3|\cdot\left[\beta\left(\frac{n(A_1)}{|D_7^1|},\ldots,\frac{n(A_1)}{|D_7^{\ell_7}|},\frac{n(A_1)}{|D_3|}\right)+\beta\left(\frac{n(A_2)}{|D_8^1|},\ldots,\frac{n(A_2)}{|D_8^{\ell_8}|},\frac{n(A_2)}{|D_3|}\right)\right].$$

Now there are two (possibly empty) sets of addresses for each element of D_3. As in the previous case, we assume that all these elements are effectively on different pages. So we take the number of pages read in as $(n(A_1)/|D_7| + n(A_2)/|D_8|)$. These elements are compared to the nonindexed constants in time $\gamma[(n(A_1)/|D_7|)\cdot|\vec{c}_5|+(n(A_2)/|D_8|)\cdot|\vec{c}_6|]$. But now a further join must be performed for the sequence of variables $\vec{x}_2$. This involves a comparison of the tuples of A_1 and A_2 separately for each element of $\vec{x}_2$ giving a time of $\gamma\cdot|\vec{x}_2|\cdot(n(A_1)\cdot n(A_2)/(|D_3|\cdot|D_5|\cdot|D_6|\cdot|D_7|\cdot|D_8|)$.

Therefore there will be a total of $\left(\frac{n(A_1)\cdot n(A_2)}{|D_2|\cdot|D_3|\cdot|D_5|\cdot|D_6|\cdot|D_7|\cdot|D_8|}\right)$ elements in the final join. The time to construct these tuples is $\frac{n(A_1)\cdot n(A_2)}{|D_2|\cdot|D_3|\cdot|D_5|\cdot|D_6|\cdot|D_7|\cdot|D_8|}\cdot\delta_{|\vec{x}_1|+|\vec{x}_2|+1+|\vec{x}_4|}$. At the end, the new tuples are written out on a file of

$$\frac{n(A_1)\cdot n(A_2)\cdot\sum(d_1+d_2+d_3+d_4)}{|D_2|\cdot|D_3|\cdot|D_5|\cdot|D_6|\cdot|D_7|\cdot|D_8|\cdot p}\text{ pages.}$$

Finally we justify (C3), the estimated cost of performing the conjunction of tables $T_1(x_1,\ldots,x_k,x_{k+1},\ldots,x_\ell)$ and $T_2(x_{k+1},\ldots,x_\ell,x_{\ell+1},\ldots,x_m)$. Note first that no indexing or join-support is applied. First, $p(T_1)\cdot p(T_2)$ pages must be read in, since each page of T_1 must be compared with each page of T_2 to find the common elements in the arguments $k+1,\ldots,\ell$ and to concatenate the tuples of T_1 and T_2. The time for the comparision of the tuples is $n(T_1)\cdot n(T_2)\cdot(\ell-k)\cdot\gamma$; the construction of the new m-tuples by concatenation takes time $(n(T_1)\cdot n(T_2)/\prod_{i=k+1}^{\ell}|D_i|)\cdot\delta_m$. At the end, the number of pages of the conjunction written out on a file is $[n(T_1)\cdot n(T_2)\cdot(\sum_{i=1}^{m} d_i)]/[p\cdot(\prod_{i=k+1}^{\ell}|D_i|)]$.

ON EVALUATION OF QUERIES CONTAINING DERIVED RELATIONS IN A RELATIONAL DATA BASE

C. L. Chang

IBM Research Laboratory

San Jose, California

ABSTRACT

A base relation is a relation that is explicitly stored. A derived relation is defined by axioms in terms of base and/or derived relations. A query may contain an arbitrary number of base and derived relations. In this chapter we shall give a method for evaluating a query containing derived relations. The method is to compile the query into a program. Examples are given to illustrate the method.

INTRODUCTION

The relational model defined by Codd [1970] has been shown to be a convenient and powerful tool for describing a data base. Performing deductions over relational data bases has been considered by Chang [1976, 1978], Kellogg et al. [1978], Klahr [1977], Minker [1975, 1978], Nicolas and Gallaire [1978], Reiter [1978], and others. This paper is a follow-up of Chang [1978], where an open problem is posed. The problem is the termination problem. That is, if a derived relation is defined recursively, then a query containing the derived relation is transformed into a sequence of queries. Since the models for base and derived relations are finite, the sequence must terminate. The problem is to find a termination condition. To illustrate the problem by an example, let us consider a base relation, FATHER(x,y), which denotes that x is the father of y. Now, suppose one wants to know who is an ancestor of whom. This type of question can be answered by introducing a new concept ANCESTOR(x,y), which denotes that x is an ancestor of y. The

ANCESTOR relation is a derived relation which is defined by the two axioms,

FATHER(x,y) → ANCESTOR(x,y) ,
FATHER(x,y) & ANCESTOR(y,z) → ANCESTOR(x,z).

Now, suppose we have a query which is to find all ancestors of *a*. The query can be represented formally in the deductive query language DEDUCE [Chang 1976, 1978] for relational data bases as

ANCESTOR(*x, *a*) ,

where the symbol * indicates that every value of x which satisfies the formula, ANCESTOR(x, *a*), will be printed.

Using the axioms, the query can be transformed into the following sequence of queries containing only the base relation: (See Chang [1978].)

FAHTER(*x,*a*) ,
FATHER(*x,y) & FATHER(y,*a*) ,
FATHER(*x,y) & FATHER(y,z) & FATHER(z,*a*) ,
⋮
etc.

Each of these queries in the sequence can be evaluated by a relational data base system such as System R (Astrahan et al. [1976]), and then the answers for all these queries are combined to give the answer to the query, ANCESTOR(*x,*a*). The sequence is terminated when a transformed query Q' is encountered which contains a subcondition contained by all the subsequent transformed queries generated beyond Q' in the sequence such that the subcondition is not satisfied by any values. For example, in the above sequence of the transformed queries, if the answer to the second query,

FATHER(*x,y) & FATHER(y,*a*)

is empty, that is, if there is no value of x that satisfies the second query, then we can terminate the sequence. This is because any subsequent query contains the second query and therefore has no answer. For example, consider the third query,

FATHER(*x,y) & FATHER(y,z) & FATHER(z,*a*) .

This query has a subcondition,

FATHER(y,z) & FATHER(z,*a*) .

This subcondition is exactly the second query. Since we assume the answer of the second query is empty, there is no value of y that satisfies the subcondition, and consequently the answer of the third query is empty. Similarly, the answers of the 4-th query, 5-th query, ..., will be all empty. Therefore, the sequence can be terminated. In general, the termination problem is stated as follows: Given a set of axioms for derived relations and a query, the problem is to synthesize a program to evaluate the query. The program will certainly contain a loop for generating and evaluating a sequence of transformed queries. In this paper, we shall give a method for finding the program.

A SAMPLE DATA BASE

For the purpose of illustration, we shall use the following relational data base taken from Boyce et al. [1975]:

EMP(NAME,SAL,MGR,DEPT)
SALES(DEPT,ITEM,VOL)
SUPPLY(COMP,DEPT,ITEM,VOL)
LOC(DEPT,FLOOR)
CLASS(ITEM,TYPE).

The EMP relation has a row for each store employee, giving his name, salary, manager, and department. The SALES relation gives the volume (yearly count) in which each department sells each item. The SUPPLY relation gives the volume (yearly count) in which each department obtained various items from its various supplier companies. The LOC relation gives the floor on which each department is located, and the CLASS relation classifies the items sold into various types.

EVALUATION OF A QUERY CONTAINING ONLY BASE RELATIONS

In this chapter, we shall consider only conjunctive existential queries. A detailed description of DEDUCE is given in Chang [1976, 1979]. It is based on logic [Chang and Lee 1973, Chang 1979]. Other relational query languages can be found in Astrahan et al. [1976], Boyce et al. [1975], Lacroix and Pirotte [1977], Pirotte [1978], and Zloof [1975]. Briefly, a conjunctive existential DEDUCE query is represented as follows.

Let a *term* be an expression having one of the following forms:

*A ,
ACV,
*ACV,
A=x,
*A=x,

where A is an attribute, V is a value, x is a variable, and C is any of the comparators $=, \neq, <, \leq, >, \geq$. Note that ACV, or *ACV corresponds to a restriction operation of the relational algebra. The symbol * before an attribute A is used to indicate PRINT.

Let a *relational formula* be an expression of the form

R(t1,...,tn) ,

where R is a relation, and each of t1,...,tn is a term.

A conjunctive existential query in DEDUCE has the following form:

$$(\exists x1) \ldots (\exists xm)\ (R1 \,\&\, \ldots \,\&\, Rn \,\&\, F) ,$$

where each of R1,...,Rn is a relational formula, and F is a formula which does not contain the relational formulas. Without any ambiguity, we may drop the quantifiers and represent the query as

R1 &...& Rn & F .

Note that the majority of queries encountered in practice are probably of this type.

Example 1 The query that is to print all companies who supply type A items is represented as

```
SUPPLY(*COMP, ITEM=x) &
CLASS(ITEM=x, TYPE=A) .
```

This DEDUCE query is a conjunction of two relational formulas.

A conjunctive existential DEDUCE query Q can be represented by a graph as follows. Every relational formula of R1,...,Rn is represented by a node, called a *relational node*, F is represented by a box node, and for every two nodes, if there is the same variable occurring in both of them draw an edge between them.

Example 2 The query "Find the names of employees in the toy department who make more than their managers", which is represented in DEDUCE as

```
EMP(*name, sal=x, mgr=y, dept=toy) &
EMP(name=y, sal=z) &
x > z ,
```

can be represented by the following graph:

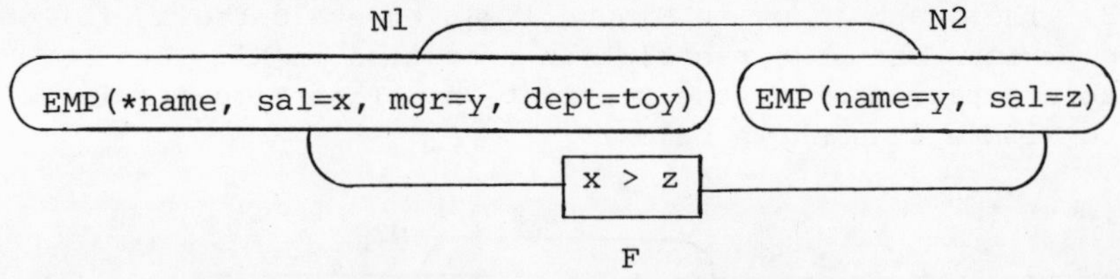

Figure 1. Query Graph

A node N in a query graph is called a *tip node* if and only if N is directly connected to at most one node N'. In Fig. 1, neither N1 nor N2 is a tip node because every node is connected to two nodes.

Given a query which contains only base relations, one way to evaluate it is by using the following sequence:

(1) Graph generation:

First, the query is represented by a graph G.

(2) Node restriction:

For every relational node which has restrictions, perform the restrictions on the node.

(3) Node elimination:

If there is a relational tip node N that contains a variable x and *does not* contain the PRINT symbol '*', find all possible values c1,...,cr for x, eliminate node N and put the formula (x=c1 V...V x=cr) into the box node. Repeat this step for all relational tip nodes. If there is only one relational node in the graph, find all the tuples that satisfy the condition represented in the graph. (Note that this node elimination step is similar to the decomposition method of [Wong and Youssefi 1979].)

(4) Node merging:

After Step (3), if there are still relational nodes left, and if nodes N1 and N2 are connected to each other directly or through the box node, merge nodes N1 and N2 by performing joins between nodes N1 and N2. (Note the joins need not be eq-joins.) If a tip node is generated after merging, perform Step (3). Otherwise, perform Step (4).

Example 3 The graph shown in Figure 1 can be evaluated as follows: First, we perform the node restriction operation on N1. Let TOY-EMP be the table obtained after the restriction. Then Figure 1 is reduced to Figure 2 as shown below:

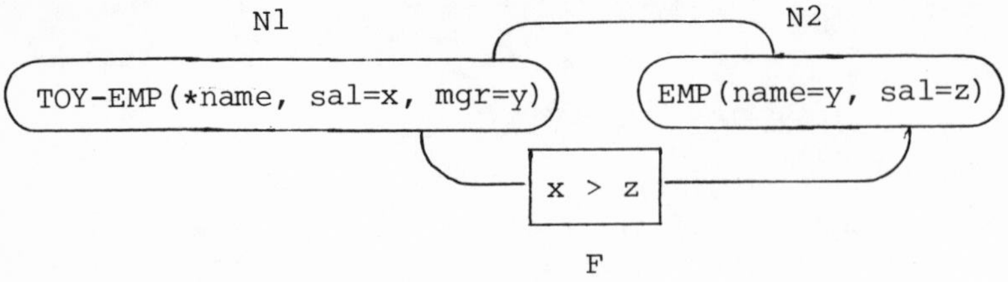

Figure 2. Query Graph after Restriction

Since there is no tip node in Figure 2, we perform the node merging operation on N1 and N2 through the join variable y. Let TEMP be the table obtained after the merging. Then, Figure 2 is reduced to Figure 3 as shown below, where the second "sal" attribute in node N3 represents the salary of the manager:

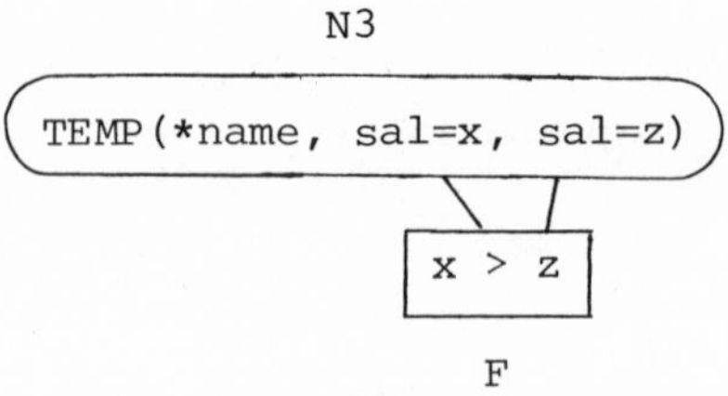

Figure 3. Query Graph after Merging

Now, N3 is the only relational node in the graph. Performing the node elimination operation on N3, we should get the names of the desired employees.

DEFINITIONS OF DERIVED RELATIONS

In DEDUCE, we define new relations through axioms. We shall call a relation that is explicitly stored in a computer a *base relation*, and call a relation defined by axioms a *derived relation (virtual relation, or view)*. We shall use axioms which have the following form:

$$(\forall x_1)\ldots(\forall x_p)\ ((\exists x_{p+1})\ldots(\exists x_p)\ (A_1\ \&\ldots\&\ A_n\ \&\ F) \rightarrow B)\ ,$$

where each of $A_1,\ldots,A_n$ is a relational formula containing a base or derived relation, B is a relational formula containing only variables $x_1,\ldots,x_p$, and F is a formula free of base or derived relations. F may contain user-defined predicates and system-provided predicates such as =, <, $\leq$, >, $\geq$, etc., and it is to be evaluated. (Note that with respect to $A_1,\ldots,A_n$ and B, the axiom of the above form is called a Horn clause.) We restrict ourselves to this form of axioms because it is more efficient to process them than general ones, and for practical purposes, they are quite sufficient to define many useful relations.

Note that the above axiom is equivalent to the following one:

$$(\forall x_1)\ldots(\forall x_p)\ (\forall x_{p+1})\ldots(\forall x_r)\ (\ (A_1\ \&\ldots\&\ A_n\ \&\ F) \rightarrow B)\ ,$$

because, in general, if C and D are formulas, and if variable y does not appear in D, then

$$\begin{aligned} &(\forall x)((\exists y)C \rightarrow D)\\ \equiv\ &(\forall x)((\forall y))\sim C \vee D)\\ \equiv\ &(\forall x)(\forall y)(\sim C \vee D)\\ \equiv\ &(\forall x)(\forall y)(C \rightarrow D)\end{aligned}$$

Example 4 Suppose we want to define a new relation, COMMAND(x,y), which denotes that x commands y. We may associate x and y with the attributes, superior and name, respectively, and define COMMAND by the following two axioms:

(a) $(\forall x)(\forall y)$ (EMP(name=y, mgr=x) $\rightarrow$ COMMAND(superior=x, name=y))

(b) $(\forall x)(\forall z)$ ($(\exists y)$ (EMP(name=z, mgr=y) & COMMAND(superior=x,name=y))

$\rightarrow$ COMMAND(superior=x, name=z)).

The first formula says that if x is the manager of y, then x commands y. The second formula says that if x commands y, and if y is the manager of z, then x commands z. Once the derived relation is defined, a user can make a query against it and the base relations. For example, the query "Find all persons who are commanded by Jones, and who sell guns" will be represented as

EMP(*name=x, dept=y) &
SALES(dept=y, item=gun) &
COMMAND(superior=Jones, name=x).

OBTAINING REWRITING RULES FROM AXIOMS AND QUERIES

As discussed in Chang [1978], given a set of axioms for derived relations, and a DEDUCE query, we can obtain a set of rewriting rules. In this section, we shall briefly describe how to obtain the rewriting rules (Chang and Slagle [1977], Sickel [1977]), because, in the subsequent sections, we shall use them to generate a program to evaluate the query. Essentially, we first find a directed connection graph (Kowalski [1975]) for the set of axioms and the query. (For efficiency, we may prestore a connection graph for the set of axioms, and every time a new query is presented, the connection graph is expanded to include the query.) Then, from the connection graph, we obtain a set of rewriting rules.

Connection Graph

A connection graph for a set of axioms and a query is constructed as follows:

(a) Every axiom, $(A_1 \& \ldots \& A_n \& F) \rightarrow B$, is represented in the graph by the form

A_1	...	A_n	F	B

We call each of $A_1, \ldots, A_n$ a left literal, F a left formula, and B a right literal. A query, $R_1 \& \ldots \& R_m \& G$, is represented in the graph by

R_1	...	R_m	G

Note that in the above, $A_1, \ldots, A_n$, $R_1, \ldots, R_m$ are relational formulas, and F and G are formulas free of base or derived relations.

(b) For every pair of literals L1 and L2 in the graph, if both L1 and L2 contain a virtual relation and are unifiable (see Chang and Lee [1973]), and if L1 is a right literal and L2 is a left literal, draw a directed edge from L1 to L2 and label the edge.

<u>Example 5</u> Figure 4 is a connection graph for the axioms and query given in Example 4, where x, y, u, v, w, s and t are variables. (*We rename the variables so that the clauses (axioms or query) do not share variables in common.*)

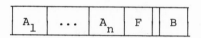

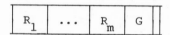

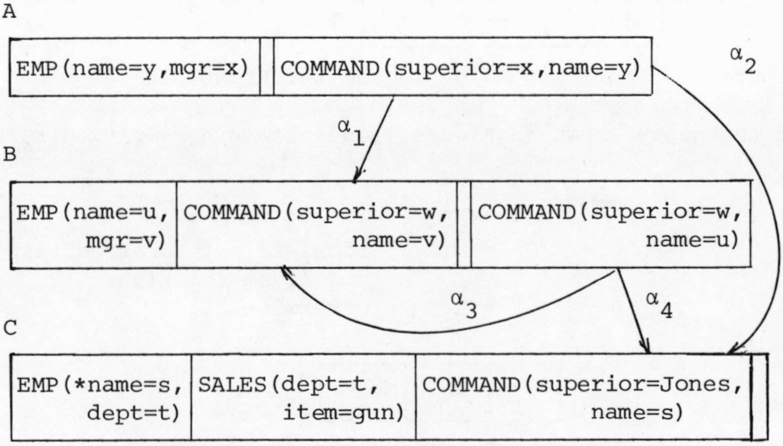

Figure 4. Connection Graph

Obtaining Rewriting Rules

We obtain rewriting rules as follows:

(a) For each left literal n, if $m_1,\ldots,m_r$ are all the right literals having edges pointing to n as shown in Figure 5, we obtain a rewriting rule

$$W(n) = \alpha_1 W(m_1) \cup \ldots \cup \alpha_r W(m_r) \ .$$

Note that "∪" in the rewriting rule means "set union".

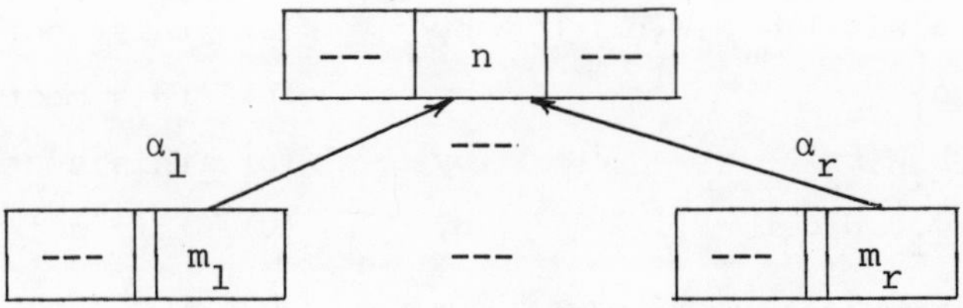

Figure 5. Rewriting Rule Diagram for Left Literals

(b) For each axiom, if there is an edge leaving the right literal n as shown in Figure 6, we obtain a rewriting rule as

$$W(n) = P_1 \ldots P_r$$

where

$P_i = W(m_i)$ if m_i is a literal containing a derived relation;

$\quad = m_i$ otherwise.

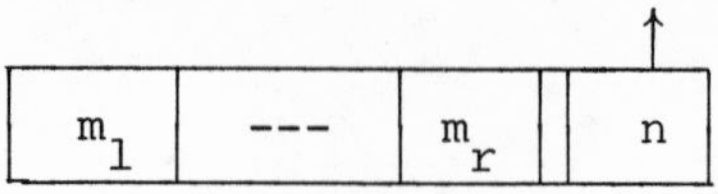

Figure 6. Rewriting Rule Diagram for Right Literals

(c) For the query shown in Figure 7, we obtain a rewriting rule as

$$T = Q_1 \ldots Q_m$$

where

$$Q_i = W(R_i) \quad \text{if } R_i \text{ is a literal containing a derived relation;}$$
$$\quad = R_i \quad \text{otherwise.}$$

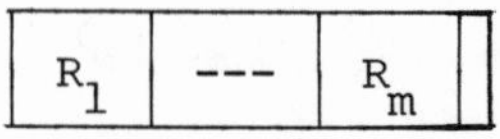

Figure 7. Query Clause

In the above rules, T or W(L) are treated as nonterminal symbols, where L is a literal, and the other symbols as terminal ones as in a context-free grammar. Before we give an example, we use a naming scheme for literals. That is, we label a clause (i.e., an axiom or a query) by a distinct name and then refer to a literal in the clause by its position in the clause. More formally, if C names a clause, then C_n names the n-th literal (counting from the left) of clause C, where n is an integer.

Example 6 For the connection graph shown in Figure 4, using the above naming scheme for literals, we obtain the following rewriting rules:

(1)	$W(b_2) = \alpha_1 W(a_2) \cup \alpha_3 W(b_3)$	by	(a)	this section
(2)	$W(c_3) = \alpha_2 W(a_2) \cup \alpha_4 W(b_3)$	by	(a)	this section
(3)	$W(a_2) = a_1$	by	(b)	this section
(4)	$W(b_3) = b_1 W(b_2)$	by	(b)	this section
(5)	$T = c_1 c_2 W(c_3)$	by	(c)	this section

In the above rules, T, $W(c_3)$, $W(b_2)$, $W(b_3)$ and $W(a_2)$ are nonterminal symbols, and a_1, b_1, c_1, c_2, α_1, α_2, α_3 and α_4 are treated as terminal symbols in a context-free grammar.

These rules can be simplified as follows:

(6) $W(b_2) = \alpha_1 W(a_2) \cup \alpha_3 W(b_3)$ from (1)

$\quad = \alpha_1 a_1 \cup \alpha_3 b_1 W(b_2)$ from (3) and (4)

(7) $T = c_1c_2W(c_3)$ from (5)

$= c_1c_2[\alpha_2W(a_2) \cup \alpha_4W(b_3)]$ from (2)

$= c_1c_2\alpha_2W(a_2) \cup c_1c_2\alpha_4W(b_3)$

$= c_1c_2\alpha_2a_1 \cup c_1c_2\alpha_4b_1W(b_2)$ from (3) and (4)

Note that rules (6) and (7) are regular rules by terminology in automata theory. In the following sections, using these regular rules, we shall first obtain a regular expression for T. Then, based on the regular expression, we can generate a program.

SYNTHESIZING PROGRAMS FOR QUERIES

In this section, given a DEDUCE query containing derived relations defined by axioms, we shall try to find a program to evaluate the query. The approach we take is as follows:

(1) Obtain a connection graph for the query and the axioms.
(2) Obtain rewriting rules from the connection graph.
(3) Obtain a regular expression, using the rewriting rules.
(4) Obtain a program from the regular expression.

We have discussed Steps (1) and (2) in the previous sections. In this section, we shall describe Steps (3) and (4).

The problem of finding a regular expression is well described in finite automata theory. Briefly, in the terminology of finite automata theory, a finite string of symbols is called a *word*. A string of no symbols is called the *empty word*, and is denoted by λ. The *concatenation* of words w_1 and w_2 is w_1w_2. If S_1 and S_2 are sets of words, the concatenation of S_1 and S_2 is defined as

$$S_1S_2 = \{w_1w_2 \mid w_1 \in S_1 \text{ and } w_2 \in S_2\} .$$

For simplicity, if w is a word, the set {w} is also denoted by w. Let S be a set of words. Then, S^* is defined as

$$S^* = \lambda \cup S \cup S^2 \cup S^3 \cup \ldots$$

The empty set is denoted by Φ.

Definition 1 Regular expressions over alphabet $A = \{a_1,\ldots,a_k\}$ are defined inductively as follows:

(a) $a_1,\ldots,a_k$, λ and Φ are regular expressions.

(b) If P and Q are regular expressions, so are $P \cup Q$, PQ and P^* .

(c) All regular expressions are generated by finite applications of the above rules.

Definition 2 The function δ from a regular expression to $\{1,0\}$, is defined inductively as follows:

(a) $\delta(a_i) = 0;$

(b) $\delta(\Phi) = 0;$

(c) $\delta(\lambda) = 1;$

(d) $\delta(P \cup Q) = 0$ if both $\delta(P)$ and $\delta(Q)$ are 0,
$= 1$ otherwise;

(e) $\delta(PQ) = 1$ if both $\delta(P)$ and $\delta(Q)$ are 1,
$= 0$ otherwise ;

(f) $\delta(P^*) = 1$.

Theorem 1 An equation of the form $D=a \cup bD$, where a and b are regular expressions, and $\delta(a) = 0$, has the solution $D=b^*a$.

The above material on automata theory, including Theorem 1, can be found in Brzozowski [1966].

Example 7 From Example 6, we have the two regular rules

$$W(b_2) = \alpha_1 a_1 \cup \alpha_3 b_1 W(b_2)$$

$$T = c_1 c_2 \alpha_2 a_1 \cup c_1 c_2 \alpha_4 b_1 W(b_2) \ .$$

Using Theorem 1, from the first rule we obtain a regular expression for $W(b_2)$ as

$$W(b_2) = (\alpha_3 b_1)^* \alpha_1 a_1 \ .$$

Replacing $W(b_2)$ in T by the regular expression, we obtain a regular expression for T as

$$T = c_1 c_2 \alpha_2 a_1 \cup c_1 c_2 \alpha_4 b_1 \ (\alpha_3 b_1)^* \alpha_1 a_1 \ ,$$

where *the ordering of the symbols is to be preserved.* In the regular expression for T, we shall replace edges $\alpha_1, \alpha_2, \alpha_3$ and α_4 by the corresponding pairs of literals that link the edges. That is, from Figure 4, since α_1 is the edge linking from the second literal of clause A (i.e., a_2) to the second literal of clause B (i.e. b_2), α_1 will be replaced by $(b_2\ a_2)$. Similarly, α_2 will be replaced by $(c_3\ a_2)$, α_3 by $(b_2\ b_3)$, α_4 by $(c_3\ b_3)$. Note that the first literal in each pair of the literals is a right literal, while the second one is a left literal. Therefore, replacing $\alpha_1, \alpha_2, \alpha_3$ and α_4 by the pairs of the literals, the regular expression for T is expressed as

$$T = c_1 c_2 (c_3\ a_2) a_1 \cup c_1 c_2 (c_3\ b_3) b_1 \{(b_2\ b_3) b_1\}^* \ (b_2\ a_2) a_1 \ .$$

Later, we shall unify the literals within each pair of parentheses. If (L(t1,...,tn),L(x1,...,xn)) is a pair of literals, where ti is either a constant or a variable, and xi is a variable, then, when we unify the first literal L(t1,...,tn) with the second literal L(x1,...,xn), *we shall always substitute* ti for xi, i = 1,...,n.

We now describe a method to obtain a program from a regular expression. We note that the regular expression conveys much information. For example, a star * operator in the regular expression indicates a loop. We shall illustrate the method by using the regular expression in Example 7. Since the regular expression for T in Example 7 is the union of two regular expressions, the program will consist of two parts --- one corresponding to the first regular expression, while the other to the second regular expression. Since the first part is done in Chang [1978], we shall not repeat it here. Therefore, we only consider the second regular expression of T in Example 7,

$$c_1 c_2 (c_3\ b_3)\ b_1\ \{(b_2\ b_3)\ b_1\}^*\ (b_2\ a_2)\ a_1\ .$$

We write the regular expression as

$$\begin{array}{c} c_1 \\ c_2 \\ \begin{pmatrix} c_3 \\ b_3 \end{pmatrix} \\ b_1 \\ \left\{ \begin{array}{c} \begin{pmatrix} b_2 \\ b_3 \end{pmatrix} \\ b_1 \end{array} \right\}^* \\ \begin{pmatrix} b_2 \\ a_2 \end{pmatrix} \\ a_1 \end{array}$$

Note that the first $b_3\ b_1\ b_2$ belongs to a copy of clause B, and the second $b_3\ b_1\ b_2$ belongs to the second copy of clause B. From Figure 4 substituting actual literals for a_1 , a_2 , b_1 , b_2 , b_3 , c_1 , c_2 and c_3 , we obtain

```
       EMP(*name=s,dept=t)
       SALES(dept=t, item=gun)
     ( COMMAND(superior=Jones, name=s) )
     ( COMMAND(superior=w, name=u)     )
       EMP(name=u, mgr=v)
  {  ( COMMAND(superior=w,  name=v)    )  }*
  {  ( COMMAND(superior=ww, name=uu)   )  }
  {    EMP(name=uu, mgr=vv)               }
     ( COMMAND(superior=ww, name=vv)   )
     ( COMMAND(superior=x, name=y)     )
       EMP(name=y, mgr=x)
```

Note that *the variables for the first copy of clause B are u, v, and w, while the variables for the second copy of clause B are uu, vv, and ww.* Unifying the literals within each pair of parentheses, we obtain the following substitution ,

{Jones/w, s/u, w/ww, v/uu, ww/x, vv/y}.

This substitution is equivalent to

{Jones/w, s/u, Jones/ww, v/uu, Jones/x, vv/y}.

Using this substitution for the variables and deleting all the pairs of literals in the above expression, we obtain

```
    EMP(*name=s, dept=t)
    SALES(dept=t, item=gun)
    EMP(name=s, mgr=v)
  { EMP(name=v, mgr=vv) }*
    EMP(name=vv, mgr=Jones)
```

Let us denote the above expression by Q. The regular star * operation in Q indicates that Q represents a sequence of queries. To generate the sequence, we can apply the star * operation on the expression EMP(name=v, mgr=vv) as follows:

{EMP(name=v, mgr=vv)}^{0} is λ

{EMP(name=v, mgr=vv)}^{1} is EMP(name=v, mgr=vv)

{EMP(name=v, mgr=vv)}^{2} is EMP(name=v, mgr=vv)
EMP(name=vv, mgr=vvv)

{EMP(name=v, mgr=vv)}^{3} is EMP(name=v, mgr=vv)
EMP(name=vv, mgr=vvv)
EMP(name=vvv, mgr=vvvv)

⋮

etc.

Therefore, Q corresponds to the following sequence of queries:

```
EMP(*name=s, dept=t)
SALES(dept=t, item=gun)          corresponds to
EMP(name=s, mgr=v)               {EMP(name=v, mgr=vv)}^0
EMP(name=v, mgr=Jones)

EMP(*name=s, dept=t)
SALES(dept=t, item=gun)
EMP(name=s, mgr=v)               corresponds to
EMP(name=v, mgr=vv)              {EMP(name=v, mgr=vv)}^1
EMP(name=vv, mgr=Jones)

EMP(*name=s, dept=t)
SALES(dept=t, item=gun)
EMP(name=s, mgr=v)               corresponds to
EMP(name=v, mgr=vv)              {EMP(name=v, mgr=vv)}^2
EMP(name=vv, mgr=vvv)
EMP(name=vvv, mgr=Jones)

.
.
.
etc.
```

(Note that the above sequence does not account for the case where the individual to be found reports directly to his supervisor Jones without intermediary. This case, which is considered in Chang [1978], corresponds to the first regular expression, namely, $c_1c_2\alpha_2a_1$, for T.)

Treating the expression Q as a query, as discussed previously, it can be represented by the graph shown in Figure 8.

```
E:                   SALES(dept=t, item=gun)
                                 |
D:          EMP(*name=s, dept=t)
                    |
C:           EMP(name=s, mgr=v)
                           |
B:                  {EMP(name=v, mgr=vv)}*
                                    |
A:                          EMP(name=vv, mgr=Jones)
```

Figure 8. Recursive Query Graph

The program P corresponding to Figure 8 is as follows:

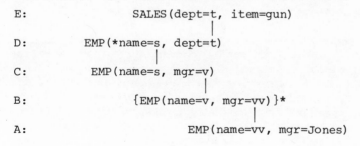

```
(al )  EVALUATE EMP(*name=vv, mgr=Jones);
(a2 )  *V ← *VV;
(bl )  DO WHILE *V≠empty;
(cde)    EVALUATE( EMP(name=s, mgr=v) &
                   EMP(*name=s, dept=t) &
                   SALES(dept=t, item=gun) ) for each v ∈ *V;
         PRINT *S;
(b2 )    EVALUATE EMP(*name=v, mgr=vv) for each  vv ∈ *VV;
(b3 )    *VV ← *V;
       END;
```

We now explain how program P is obtained.

In Figure 8, node B is the node we should concentrate on, because it involves the "*" operation. There are two subgraphs, namely, A and CDE, connected to node B. (Note that the subgraph CDE can be considered as a generalized tip node of node B.) Since the subgraph CDE contains the PRINT symbol '*', we cannot apply the node elimination step given in the section EVALUATION OF A QUERY CONTAINING ONLY BASE RELATIONS. However, node A does not contain the PRINT symbol '*', we can use the node elimination step. This essentially corresponds to Statement (al). The EVALUATE command takes a DEDUCE query, evaluates it and returns a set of values which are indicated by the symbol *. The set returned is denoted by * followed by the variable name in the upper case. For example, in Statement (al), the returned set for the query, EMP(*name=vv,mgr= Jones), is denoted by *VV because the variable is vv. In general, the syntax for EVALUATE is

EVALUATE <DEDUCE-query> [for each <variable> ∈ <set>] .

Statement (a2) is to initialize *V. It corresponds to the case where the expression {EMP(name=v, mgr=vv)}* at node B is $\{EMP(name=v, mgr=vv)\}^0$. In this case, v is the same as vv.

Statements (bl), (b2) and (b3) correspond to node B. Since node B has the regular * operation, a loop is needed. At the iteration where {EMP(name=v, mgr=vv)}* is $\{EMP(name=v, mgr=vv)\}^0$, after the partial query represented by node A is evaluated as shown by Statement (al), the next partial query to be evaluated is the one represented by the subgraph CDE. To do this, we have to make sure that the set of values for v is not empty. Therefore, we have Statement (bl). If *V is not empty, then we have Statement (cde) that corresponds to subgraph CDE. The set *S returned from Statement (cde) and printed eventually is the set of names of the desired employees. After the initial iteration, we have to consider the next iteration where {EMP(name=v, mgr=vv)}* is $\{EMP(name=v, mgr=vv)\}^1$. This means that we need to find new values of v. Therefore, we have Statement (b2). To prepare the next iteration again, we have Statement (b3).

The above technique can be used to handle YES/NO queries also. For example, consider the query 'Is Martin in a department in which guns are sold and Martin's superior is Jones ?' This query can be represented in DEDUCE as

```
EMP(name-Martin, dept=y) &
SALES(dept=y, item=gun) &
COMMAND(superior=Jones, name=Martin) .
```

Using the above method, we can obtain the following expression:

```
 EMP(name=Martin, dept=t)
 SALES(dept=t, item=gun)
 EMP(name=Martin, mgr=v)
{EMP(name=v, mgr=vv)}*
 EMP(name=vv, mgr=Jones) .
```

The graph for this expression is shown in Figure 9.

```
E:                       SALES(dept=t, item=gun)
                                      |
D:          EMP(name=Martin, dept=t)
                          |
C:          EMP(name=Martin, mgr=v)
                                  |
B:                        {EMP(name=v, mgr=vv)}*
                                         |
A:                                 EMP(name=vv, mgr=Jones)
```

Figure 9. Another Recursive Query Graph

The program corresponding to Figure 9 is as follows:

```
(a1 )   EVALUATE EMP(*name=vv, mgr=Jones);
(a2 )   *V ← *VV;
(b1 )   DO WHILE *V≠empty;
(cde)     VERIFY (EMP(name=Martin, mgr=v) &
                  EMP(name=Martin, dept=t) &
                  SALES(dept=t, item=gun) ) for each v ∈ *V;
          IF RETURN=YES,  PRINT YES and LEAVE;
(b2 )     EVALUATE EMP(*name=v, mgr=vv) for each vv ∈ *VV;
(b3 )     *VV ← *V;
        END;
```

The VERIFY command takes a YES/NO DEDUCE query and returns YES or NO, depending upon whether there are values satisfying the query. Of course, the above program can terminate as soon as a YES is generated.

Before we leave the discussion of this section, let us consider another more complicated query 'Find all employees who earn more than one of their superiors.' This query can be represented in DEDUCE as

```
COMMAND(superior=p, *name=q) &
EMP(name=p, sal=s) &
EMP(name=q, sal=t) &
t > s .
```

Using the above rewriting rule method, we can obtain the following expression: (Again, we skip the nonrecursive regular expression which is treated in Chang [1978].)

```
 EMP(*name=q, mgr=v)
{EMP(name=v, mgr=vv)}*
 EMP(name=vv, mgr=p)
 EMP(name=p,  sal=s)
 EMP(name=q,  sal=t)
 t > s
```

The graph for this expression is shown in Figure 10.

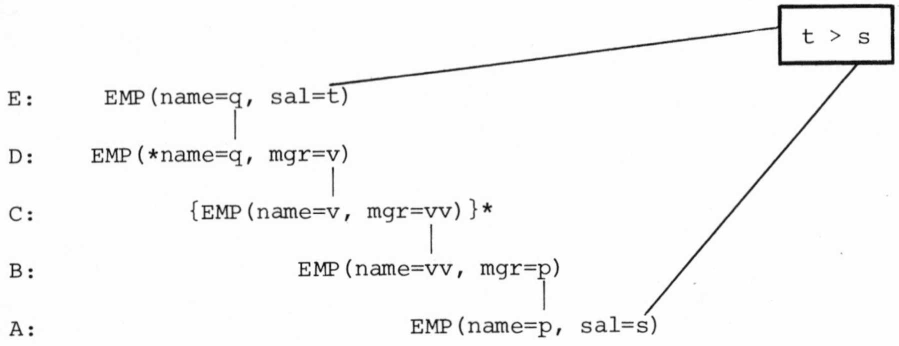

Figure 10. Recursive Query Graph Without Tip Nodes

Since 'name' is the key of the EMP relation, nodes D and E represent one tuple. Therefore Figure 10 can be simplified to Figure 11.

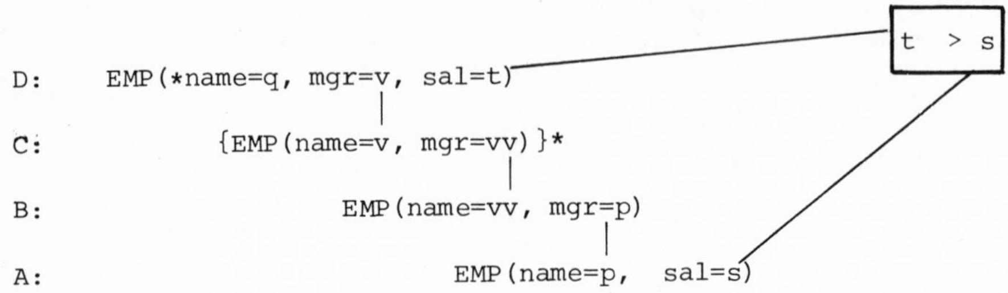

Figure 11. Simplified Recursive Query Graph

The *recursive* query structure represented by the graph shown in Figure 11 is different from the one shown in Figures 8 or 9. Since Figure 11 does not have a tip node, we cannot use the node elimination step. One solution to this problem is to use a different program schemata to generate the following program for Figure 11.

```
(d1)  DO for each tuple (q,v,t) from EMP(name=q, mgr=v, sal=t);
(d2)    *V ← {v};
(d3)    *VV ← *V;
(c1)    DO WHILE *VV≠empty;
(ab)      VERIFY ( EMP(name=vv, mgr=p) &
                   EMP(name=p,  sal=s) &
                   t > s )      for each  vv ∈ *VV;
          IF RETURN=YES, PRINT q and LEAVE;
(c2)      EVALUATE EMP(name=v, *mgr=vv) for each v ∈ *V;
(c3)      *VV ← *V;
        END;
      END;
```

The above program is obtained by trying to make node D of Figure 11 a tip node. To do this, we take a tuple one at a time from EMP(name=q, mgr=v, sal=t). Once we have a tuple (q,v,t), Figure 11 becomes Figure 12, where v and t are treated as constants. Clearly, Figure 12 is similar to Figure 9. Therefore the DO WHILE loop in the above program is similar to the DO WHILE loop of the program corresponding to Figure 9.

```
                                    v
                                    |
C:                      {EMP(name=v, mgr=vv)}*
                                          |
B:                              EMP(name=vv, mgr=p)
                                                 |
A:                                      EMP(name=p, sal=s)
                                                        |
                                                    t > s
```

Figure 12. Recursive Query Graph Obtained from Query Decomposition

We note that other different program schemata are possible for Figure 11. For example, we can have a different program for Figure 11 by trying to make the subgraph AB a (generalized) tip node. We shall leave this to the reader.

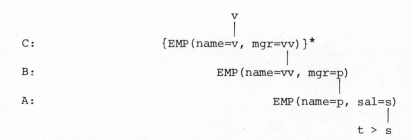

In general, finding a "good" program from a recursive query graph is a fruitful area for research. A good program will depend upon many factors. For example, what are the access paths (indexing, hashing, linking, sorting, etc.) available in the data base management system? If they are not available, which ones should be created? (See Chang [1978].) What control structures are allowed in the generated program? In this chapter, we use some of the control structures in PL/1. Also, one of the important factors is the way the recursive query graph is decomposed into simple query graphs. As we have seen in the previous example, a program schemata for a complicated query graph can be obtained by first breaking the query graph into simple query graphs, and then using their program schemata.

DESIGN ISSUES FOR DERIVED RELATIONS

The method described in the previous sections works for the case where there is a regular expression for T. This means that each axiom has at most one derived relation on the left hand side of $\rightarrow$. Let us call such axioms *regular axioms*. If a derived relation can be defined in many ways, we should choose the one whose axioms are regular. For example, consider the ANCESTOR relation described in the INTRODUCTION. The ANCESTOR relation can be defined by any of the following representations: (Note that in the left hand side of $\rightarrow$, *without loss of generality the base relation always appears before the derived relation.)*

Representation 1

FATHER(x,y) $\rightarrow$ ANCESTOR(x,y),
FATHER(u,v) & ANCESTOR(v,w) $\rightarrow$ ANCESTOR(u,w).

Representation 2

FATHER(x,y) $\rightarrow$ ANCESTOR(x,y),
FATHER(v,w) & ANCESTOR(u,v) $\rightarrow$ ANCESTOR(u,w).

Representation 3

FATHER(x,y) $\rightarrow$ ANCESTOR(x,y),
ANCESTOR(u,v) & ANCESTOR(v,w) $\rightarrow$ ANCESTOR(u,w).

Since Representation 3 contains a nonregular axiom, we will not be able to obtain a regular expression for T. Therefore, we should choose either Representation 1 or Representation 2 for the ANCESTOR relation. For the query, ANCESTOR(*z,a), if we use Representation 1, using the method described in the previous sections, we shall obtain the following expression E1: (As in Example 7, the regular expression for the query has two parts — one does not have the "*" operator, and the other has the "*" operator. Here, we consider only the latter part.)

FATHER(*z,v)
{FATHER(v,vv)}*
FATHER(vv,a) .

The program corresponding to expression E1 is as follows:

```
EVALUATE FATHER(*vv,a);
*V ← *VV;
DO WHILE *V≠empty;
  EVALUATE FATHER(*z,v) for each  v ∈ *V;
  PRINT *Z;
  EVALUATE FATHER(*v,vv) for each vv ∈ *VV;
  *VV ← *V;
END;
```

If we choose Representation 2, for the same query, ANCESTOR(*z,a), we shall obtain the following expression E2: (Note that the variables v and vv in E1 are at the symmetrical positions of the ones occupied by the variables v and vv in E2.)

```
 FATHER(v,a)
{FATHER(vv,v)}*
 FATHER(*z,vv)
```

The program corresponding to expression E2 is as follows:

```
EVALUATE FATHER (*v,a);
*VV ← *V;
DO WHILE *VV≠empty;
  EVALUATE FATHER(*z,vv) for each vv ∈ *VV;
  PRINT *Z;
  EVALUATE FATHER(*vv,v) for each  v ∈ *V;
  *V ← *VV;
END;
```

Another example is the inheritance property problem which is well known in artificial intelligence and data modeling (Codd [1979], Smith and Smith [1977]). This problem says that a descendant in a hierarchical tree (need not be a family tree) will inherit all the properties of his ancestors. To represent this problem, we choose FATHER and HAS as two base relations, and ANCESTOR and INHERIT as two derived relations, where

```
FATHER(x,y)   means that x is the father of y;
ANCESTOR(x,y) means that x is an ancestor of y;
HAS(x,y)      means that x has y;
INHERIT(x,y)  means that x inherits y.
```

The derived relations ANCESTOR and INHERIT can be defined by the following axioms:

```
FATHER(x,y)  →  ANCESTOR(x,y)
FATHER(u,v)  &  ANCESTOR(v,w)  →  ANCESTOR(u,w)
HAS(s,t)     →  INHERIT(s,t)
INHERIT(p,q) &  ANCESTOR(p,r)  →  INHERIT(r,q)
```

However, the fourth axiom is not regular. Therefore, it is not a good representation, because the axiom does not tell which derived relation should be computed (fixed) first. A better representation for the inheritance property problem is given as follows:

```
FATHER(x,y)  →  ANCESTOR(x,y)
FATHER(u,v)  &  ANCESTOR(v,w)  →  ANCESTOR(u,w)
HAS(p,q)     &  ANCESTOR(p,r)  →  INHERIT(r,q)
```

We note that all these axioms are regular.

Now, if a query is to find all the properties inherited by John, we can represent it as INHERT(John, *z). Using the method described in the previous sections, we can obtain the following expression:

```
 HAS(p,*z)
 FATHER(p,v)
{FATHER(v,vv)}*
 FATHER(vv,John)
```

The program corresponding to this expression is as follows:

```
EVALUATE FATHER(*vv,John);
*V ← *VV;
DO WHILE *V≠empty;
  EVALUATE ( HAS(p,*z) & FATHER(p,v) ) for each v ∈ *V;
  PRINT *z;
  EVALUATE FATHER(*v,vv) for each vv ∈ *VV;
  *VV ← *V;
END;
```

Finally, we comment on programs containing nested loops. For example, suppose the derived relations A and B are defined by the following regular axioms,

```
P → A
Q & A → A
R & A → T
S & B → B,
```

where P, Q, R and S are base relations. (For simplicity, parameters in the axioms are not shown.) If we have a query consisting of the derived relation B, then a program obtained by our method for the query will contain two loops shown in Figure 13.

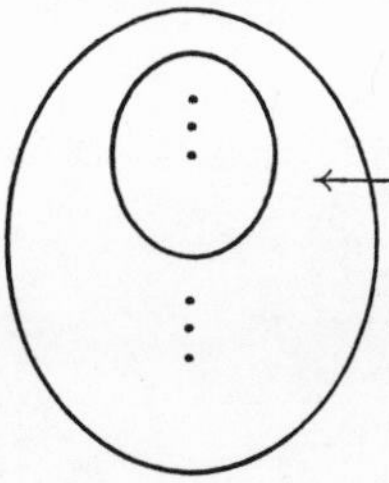

Figure 13. Nested Loops

The inner loop is obtained from the first and second axioms, while the outer loop from the third and fourth axioms. This is because to compute B we have to first compute A.

CONCLUDING REMARKS

We have given a method for compiling a nonprocedural DEDUCE query into a program. Since the program involves only base relations, it can then be considered as a transaction, and executed by using relational data base systems such as System R (Astrahan et al. [1976]). The program may not be optimal. However, the optimizer of System R presumably will figure out a best access path to execute the program efficiently.

Our method applies to the case where derived relations are defined by regular axioms. If the derived relations cannot be defined by regular axioms, we may have to explicitly create some derived relations to make them base relations. By doing so, we may change the nonregular axioms into regular ones.

Our approach for evaluating a query containing derived relations is to generate a program. The approach has a very clean interface with a relational data base management system. That is, axioms defining the derived relations are used to generate the program, while facts stored in base relations are used to execute the program. Other approaches such as PROLOG do not have such a clean interface. In PROLOG (Warren and Pereira [1977]), clauses are executed directly as programs, and control may jump around back and forth among axioms and facts. As we discussed in Chang [1978], their approach may be very hard to handle "for all" type queries, because it may be very hard for a system to know whether "all possible" deduction paths have been considered. Also, in [Reiter, 1978], Reiter has obtained some interesting results with respect to recursive axioms.

ACKNOWLEDGMENTS

The author would like to thank the referees for their comments.

REFERENCES

1. Astrahan, M. M., Blasgen, M. W., Chamberlin, D. D., Eswaran, K. P., Gray, J. N., Griffiths, P. P., King, W. F., Lorie, R. A., McJones, P. R., Mehl, J. W., Putzolu, G. R., Traiger, I. L., Wade, B. W., and Watson, V. [1976] System R: Relational Approach to Database Management, *ACM Trans. on Database Systems*, 1, 2, (June 1976), 97-137.

2. Boyce, R. F., Chamberlin, D. D., King, W. F., III, and Hammer. M. M. [1975] Specifying queries as relational expressions: SQUARE, *Comm. of the ACM 18*, 11 (November 1975), 621-628.

3. Brzozowski, J. A. [1966] Class Notes of Switching and Automata Theory, Spring 1966, Dept. of Electrical Engineering and Computer Science, University of California, Berkeley, Calif.

4. Chang, C. L. [1976] DEDUCE — A Deductive Query Language for Relational Data Bases, In: *Pattern Recognition and Artificial Intelligence* (C. H. Chen, Ed.), Academic Press, Inc., New York, 1976, 108-134.

5. Chang, C. L. [1978] DEDUCE 2: Further Investigations of Deduction in Relational Data Bases, In: *Logic and Data Bases* (H. Gallaire and J. Minker, Eds.), Plenum Publishing Corp., New York, N. Y., 1978, 201-236.

6. Chang, C. L. [1978] An optimization problem in relational data bases, *IBM Research Report RJ2287*, San Jose, Calif., 1978.

7. Chang, C. L. [1979] Resolution plans in theorem proving, *Proc. of the 6th International Joint Conference on Artificial Intelligence*, 1979, Tokyo, Japan, 143-148.

8. Chang, C. L., and Lee, R. C. T. [1973] *Symbolic Logic and Mechanical Theorem Proving*, Academic Press, New York, 1973.

9. Chang, C. L., and Slagle, J. R. [1977] Using Rewriting Rules for Connection Graphs to Prove Theorems, *IBM Research Report RJ 2117*, San Jose, California, 1977. Also appears in *Artificial Intelligence 12* (1979), 159-180.

10. Codd, E. F. [1970] A Relational Model for Large Shared Data Banks, *Comm. of the ACM 13*, 6 (June 1970) 377-387.

11. Codd, E. F. [1979] Extending the data base relational model to capture more meaning, *IBM Research Report No. RJ-2472*, IBM Research Laboratory, San Jose, Ca 95193, Jan. 1979.

12. Kellogg, C., Klahr, P., and Travis, L. [1978] Deductive planning and pathfinding for relational data bases, In: *Logic and Data Bases* (H. Gallaire and J. Minker, Eds.), Plenum Press, New York, N. Y., 1978, 179-200.

13. Klahr, P. [1977] Planning techniques for rule selection in deductive question-answering, In: *Pattern-Directed Inference Systems* (D. Waterman and F. Hayes-Roth, Eds.), Academic Press, New York, 1977.

14. Kowalski, R. [1975] A proof procedure using connection graphs, *JACM 22, 4* (October 1975), 572-595.

15. Lacroix, M., and Pirotte, A. [1977] Domain-oriented relational languages, *Proc. of Third International Conference on Very Large Data Bases*, Tokyo, Japan, October 6-8, 1977, 370-378.

16. Minker, J. [1975] Performing inferences over relational data bases, *Proc. of 1975 ACM-SIGMOD International Conference on Management of Data*, 1975, 79-91.

17. Minker, J. [1978] An experimental relational data base system based on logic, In *Logic and Data Bases* (H. Gallaire and J. Minker, Eds.), Plenum Press, New York, N. Y., 1978, 107-147.

18. Nicolas, J. M., and Gallaire, H. [1978] Data bases: Theory vs. interpretation, In: *Logic and Data Bases* H. Gallaire and J. Minker, Eds.), Plenum Press, New York, N. Y., 1978.

19. Pirotte, A. [1978] High level data base query languages, In: *Logic and Data Bases* (H. Gallaire and J. Minker, Eds.), Plenum Press, New York, N. Y., 1978, 409-436.

20. Reiter, R. [1978] On structuring a first order data base, *Proc. of the Canadian Society for Computational Studies of Intelligence, Second National Conference* (R. Penault, Ed.), Toronto, July 19-21, 1978.

21. Reiter, R. [1978] Deductive question-answering on relational data bases, In: *Logic and Data Bases* (H. Gallaire and J. Minker, Eds.), Plenum Press, New York, N. Y., 1978, 149-177.

22. Sickel, S. [1977] Formal grammars as models of logic derivations, *Proc. of IJCAI-77*, 544-551.

23. Smith, J. M., and Smith, D. C. P. [1977] Data abstractions: Aggregation and generalization, *ACM TODS 2,2* (June 1977), 105-133.

24. Warren, D. H., and Pereira, L. M. [1977] PROLOG: The language and its implementation compared with LISP, *Proc. ACM Symp. on*

Artificial Intelligence and Programming, University of Rochester, Rochester, N. Y., August 15-17, 1977, 109-115.

25. Wong, E., and Youssefi, K. [1979] Decomposition — a strategy for query processing, *ACM Trans. on Database Systems, 1, 3*, September 1979, 223-241.

26. Zloof, M. M. [1975] Query by Example, *Proc. National Computer Conference*, Anaheim, Calif., May 1975, 431-438.

REASONING WITH DATA IN A DEDUCTIVELY AUGMENTED DATA MANAGEMENT SYSTEM

Charles Kellogg[1] and Larry Travis[2]

System Development Corporation, Santa Monica, Calif.[1]

University of Wisconsin, Madison, Wisconsin [2]

ABSTRACT

A system for applying the theory of logical deduction and proof procedures to the accessing of data stored in conventional data management systems is described and illustrated with several examples. The DADM (Deductively Augmented Data Management) system has been developed along several dimensions of utility and performance to provide a vehicle for research on interactive techniques for reasoning with data, answering questions, and supporting on-line decision making. After illustrating present system operation by means of several examples, new performance-enhancing features of the system are described. These features include improved user interfaces, improved visibility of processes and data structures, structure sharing, improvements in inference-planning mechanisms, methods for dealing with incomplete information, utilization of semantic advice, and means for controlling recursive premises.

INTRODUCTION

The DADM (Deductively Augmented Data Management) project is concerned with the development of a deductive processor specifically designed to utilize an intensional store of general assertions (for example, meaning postulates) in mediating between a language processor and one or more conventional data management systems (DMS's) controlling stores of extensional data (for example, *n*-tuples of individuals, as in a relational DMS). See Figure 1.

Our research on DADM serves as an environment within which to bring to bear, upon the improvement of data access and data management, a large body of theory — in particular, the theory of logical

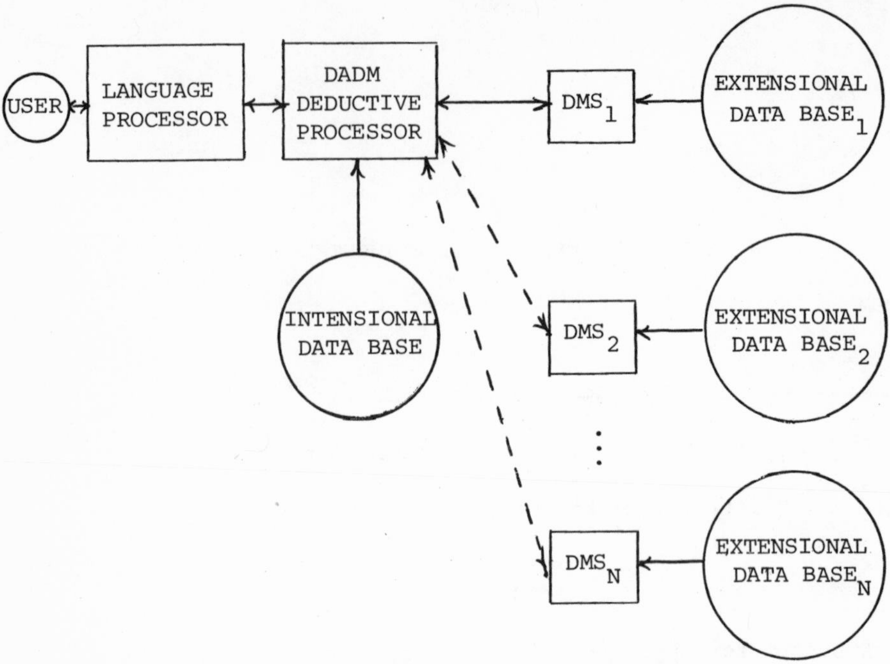

Figure 1. The Deductively Augmented Data Management (DADM) Environment

deduction and proof procedures. One goal is to discover how that theory may best be adapted and extended to support mechanized inference over the content of large data bases. This application area is quite different from the source of the theory which was primarily the modeling and justification of mathematics.

A deductive processor can provide data base users and administrators with a precise formalism and mechanism for representing and applying *abstractions*. The general assertions utilized by the deductive processor correspond to theorems developed by mathematicians as they articulate new concepts — that is, abstractions. Abstractions may be used to define further abstractions, providing the potential for very high level, very powerful concepts quite far removed from the primitive concepts of a data base system. The useful properties of these concepts are summed up in theorems (what we call premises), general rules which allow a concept to be directly applied but which abstract from the mass of details upon which the concept is definitionally based. By abstracting from definitional details the mathematician is able to keep complexity within manageable bounds. The data base users and administrators of the future, faced with ever larger and more complex data bases and database-dependent applications, will have a comparable need to abstract from the details of system implementation and low-level data representation in order to interact with a data base system in terms of high-level, problem specific concepts.

The DADM deductive processor prototype is being used to develop, refine, and apply inferential mechanisms designed to support such abstractions. DADM has recently been converted to INTERLISP and now runs on a DEC-10 computer. The current version requires input from the user expressed in a logic-based formalism, and it sends search requests to a relational data management system also realized in INTERLISP. In the future we plan to apply DADM to real world applications through an interface with the INGRES (Stonebraker et al. [1976]) data management system. A relational algebra-based intermediate-language formalism will be used for sending DADM-created data base access strategies to INGRES (and eventually other data management systems). DADM will also be interfaced with a language processor that translates user inputs formulated in a subset of ordinary English into the logic-based formalism currently used for posing problems to the system.

In this chapter we report on how DADM has been extended along two principal dimensions since our previous paper (Kellogg, Klahr, Travis [1978]) by improving its user interface and by increasing its inference-making effectiveness, and we report on preliminary empirical explorations of large premise files (files of general knowledge) and their control by DADM mechanisms. Briefly, user control of all aspects of DADM operation (such as the insertion, deletion, modification, and interrogation of intensional and extensional data) is now supported by an easy-to-use menu mechanism; forward, backward, and bidirectional reasoning is displayed in a uniform, perspicuous format; and techniques that permit reasoning with incomplete information in queries, in the intensional data base, and in the extensional data base have been realized. Performance enhancements include the use of structure-sharing techniques to eliminate duplicate deductive subproblems; an ability to utilize high-level, application-specific semantic advice for determining deductive strategy; the ordering of deductive, search, and computational subproblems for efficient evaluation; and a greatly improved method of controlling recursive premises.

In order to emphasize new aspects of the user interface and to provide readers with a better experimental feel for the point of a system like DADM, we present some examples before turning to a description of the design of the system and its recent improvements. The later description will explicate some of the system-specific jargon (e.g., inference "plans", etc.) that may not be clear on first reading.

DADM-USER INTERACTION: EXAMPLES

DADM treats user requests as problems to be solved. In general, a request (problem) will be decomposed into a set of *deduce, search,* and/or *compute* subproblems. A query may have extensional support, intensional support, or both. In the first case, DADM scans the query, determines that no deductive processing is required, and transforms the query into the form required for processing by the DMS. DADM's deductive apparatus is thus invisible to the user if it is not required. In the second case, DADM attempts to generate a general response to the query by constructing a proof from the premises in its intensional data base. In the third (and most interesting) case DADM constructs from its intensional file one or more proof skeletons or *inference plans*, which when instantiated with appropriate extensional data, yield *answers* and *evidence chains* (proofs).

Answering Questions with General and Specific Knowledge

In our first example we illustrate how a "classic" deduction can be formalized and related to conventional data base search. The source of the following deduction is the Sherlock Holmes "Adventure of the Dancing Men":

> "So, Watson, ... You do not propose to invest in South African securities?"
> "... It was not really difficult, by an inspection of the groove between your left forefinger and thumb, to feel sure that you did not propose to invest your small capital in the goldfields."
> "Here are the missing links of the very simple chain:
>
> 1. You had chalk between your left finger and thumb when you returned from the club last night.
> 2. You put chalk there when you play billiards to steady the cue.
> 3. You never play billiards except with Thurston.
> 4. You told me four weeks ago that Thurston had an option on some South African property which would expire in a month, and which he desired you to share with him.
> 5. Your cheque-book is locked in my drawer, and you have not asked for the key.
> 6. You do not propose to invest your money in this manner."
>
> "How absurdly simple!" I cried.
> "Quite so!" said he.

We can attribute Holmes' successful deduction to his ability to selectively retrieve concrete facts from a large data base of specific world knowledge and his ability to construct plausible (though relatively shallow) inferences from this information. In this example, Holmes needs only two concrete facts as a base for his involved ratiocination, (1) that Thurston wanted Watson to share his South African securities and (2) that Watson did not have his cheque book.

The gist of this deduction can be formulated in terms of a *query* expressing the desired conclusion, an *Inference Plan*, composed of three premises, and two *Find* statements that must be satisfiable in an extensional data base of concrete facts.

Query: If chalk in groove then
Watson did not buy securities.

Inference Plan:

Premise: If Watson played billiards with Thurston and Thurston wanted Watson to share securities and Watson did not have cheque book, then Watson did not buy securities.

Premise: If chalk in groove
then Watson played billiards.

Premise: If Watson played billiards
then Watson played billiards with Thurston.

Find: Thurston wanted Watson to share securities.

Find: Watson did not have cheque book.

To relate this deduction more closely to data base searching, we define two one-place *base* (*search*) relations (relations extensionally represented in the data base of concrete facts), one two-place *procedural* (*compute*) relation, and four one- and zero-place *virtual* (*deduce*) relations (relations intensionally represented by means of general assertions that link the relations to other relations)[1]:

BASE (SEARCH) RELATIONS:
B1: THURSTON-WANTED-WATSON-TO-SHARE-SECURITIES (DATE)
B2: WATSON-DID-NOT-HAVE-CHEQUE-BOOK (DATE)
PROCEDURAL (COMPUTE) RELATION:
C1: DIFFERENCE-BETWEEN ($DATE_1$ $DATE_2$ TIME-INTERVAL)
VIRTUAL (DEDUCE) RELATIONS:
V1: CHALK-IN-GROOVE (DATE)
V2: WATSON-PLAYED-BILLIARDS-(DATE)
V3: WATSON-PLAYED-BILLIARDS-WITH-THURSTON (DATE)
V4: WATSON-DID-NOT-BUY-SECURITIES

1 At the present time a relation must be one of *base*, *virtual*, or *procedural*. However, the extensions needed to allow a relation to be partially given in extension (*base*) and also defined by premises (*virtual*) are relatively straightforward.

Upon entering the three premises into DADM along with appropriate tuples in the data base and a LISP function to compute DIFFERENCE-BETWEEN, the HOLMES query was typed in and inference and search/compute plans were generated as shown in Figure 2. DADM responds to queries by treating them as problems to be solved. In this case there is one top level (Watson-Did-Not-Buy-Securities) problem and three subproblems (one *compute*, two *search*). One deductive path (chain of middle-term relations) suffices to link together the three relevant premises into a single inference plan. (In the formalism used for communicating with DADM, read IF α THEN β for α IMP β used for specifying premises, and read GIVEN α FIND β for α IMP β used for queries.)

The inference plan indicates that in order to conclude that Watson didn't buy the securities (step **Ø), it is sufficient to conclude that Watson played billiards with Thurston (step **1) and in order to reach that conclusion it is sufficient to conclude that Watson played billiards (step **2). These conclusions are forthcoming if the derived search/compute plan shown can be satisfied.

That it is satisfied is indicated by the answer (YES) and the resultant evidence chain. An evidence chain has the same overall structure as an inference plan. Each evidence chain is an instantiation of an inference plan where the inference plan's variables (e.g., DATE-1) are replaced by found or computed values (e.g., JUNE 27, 1898) and SEARCH and COMPUTE are replaced by FACT and COMPUTED, respectively.

Explicating an "Invisible College" Microtheory: Augmenting a Bibliographic Data Base

In our second example we illustrate DADM's ability to produce, for a single high-level conjecture, multiple inference plans, search strategies, and evidence chains. Because of space limitations we can illustrate in detail only one of the inference plans and its articulation, but one of the important practical uses of a deductively augmented data base system will be its ability to generate alternative paths through the data and to generate alternative chains of evidence supporting a user's conjecture or working hypothesis. These alternative chains will frequently have a mutually reinforcing effect that can increase a user's confidence in the plausibility of derived results.

Consider a bibliographic data base that contains the usual author, title, subject, citation, institutional-affiliation, and source information. Suppose that a user familiar with this data base wants to find out if a certain scientific result achieved in 1978 but not yet published in the general scientific literature may also be known by research workers at British laboratories.

```
MODE:
Query:
.((CHALK-IN-GROOVE (JULY 27, 1898))
IMP
(WATSON-DID-NOT-BUY-SECURITIES))

1 PATHS  4 PROBLEMS  1 PLANS

NEXT? Full plans

<<INFERENCE PLAN 1 PLAUSIBILITY:  99
====================

   **2
   ASSUME CHALK-IN-GROOVE (JULY27,1898)
   CONCLUDE WATSON-PLAYED-BILLIARDS (JULY27,1898)

  **1
  CONCLUDE WATSON-PLAYED-BILLIARDS-WITH-THURSTON (JULY27,1898)

 **Ø
 COMPUTE DIFFERENCE-BETWEEN (JULY27,1898 DATE-1 ONE-MONTH)
 SEARCH WATSON-DID-NOT-HAVE-CHEQUE-BOOK (JULY27,1898)
 SEARCH THURSTON-WANTED-WATSON-TO-SHARE-SECURITIES (DATE-1)
 CONCLUDE WATSON-DID-NOT-BUY-SECURITIES
 ====================

 SEARCH/COMPUTE PLAN:
     SEARCH    *THURSTON-WANTED-WATSON-TO-SHARE-SECURITIES DATE-1
     SEARCH    *WATSON-DID-NOT-HAVE-CHEQUE-BOOK JULY27,1898
     COMPUTE   *DIFFERENCE-BETWEEN JULY27,1898 DATE-1 ONE-MONTH

 ENTERING DATA BASE

 DATA-BASE SEARCH SUCCESSFUL
 ***************
 ANSWER SUMMARY --
 YES
 ***************
 EVIDENCE CHAIN 1 FROM PLAN 1 PLAUSIBILITY:  99
 ====================

   **2
   ASSUME CHALK-IN-GROOVE (JULY27,1898)
   CONCLUDE WATSON-PLAYED-BILLIARDS (JULY27,1898)

  **1
  CONCLUDE WATSON-PLAYED-BILLIARDS-WITH-THURSTON (JULY27,1898)

 **Ø
 COMPUTED DIFFERENCE-BETWEEN (JULY27,1898 JUNE27,1898 ONE-MONTH)
 FACT WATSON-DID-NOT-HAVE-CHEQUE-BOOK (JULY27,1898)
 FACT THURSTON-WANTED-WATSON-TO-SHARE-SECURITIES (JUNE27,1898)
 CONCLUDE WATSON-DID-NOT-BUY-SECURITIES
 ====================                               >>
```

Figure 2. Given chalk in groove—Find Watson did not buy securities

Notice the use of "may" in the last sentence. It is unlikely that the user can, from the available data, establish with certainty that a British laboratory knew about the particular result. However, through the use of inference, it may be possible to build a body of evidence to support a conjecture to that effect.

One formalizes the conceptual abstraction *invisible college*[1] with premises such as:

SCIENTISTS WHO COAUTHOR A PUBLICATION MAY BE MEMBERS OF THE SAME INVISIBLE COLLEGE.

SCIENTISTS WHOSE PAPERS CITE EACH OTHER MAY BE MEMBERS OF THE SAME INVISIBLE COLLEGE.

.
.
.
etc.

and:

A SCIENTIST WHO ORIGINATES A NEW RESULT DURING A YEAR IS LIKELY TO TRANSMIT KNOWLEDGE OF THAT RESULT TO OTHER MEMBERS OF THE INVISIBLE COLLEGE DURING THAT YEAR.

Assume that premises of this form along with plausibility weights ranging from 0 to 99 (near certainty) are entered into the system and the user asks the question: "Which UK laboratories might have known of Barker's result in magnetic-bubble technology in 1978?" Figures 3, 4 and 5 illustrate a partial result for this kind of query.

In Figure 3 the query is symbolized using a variable type (LAB L), an assumption predicate (ORIGINATES) and two goal predicates. Two plans are found before the limits (CHAINS LIMIT REACHED) on the deductive search space stop further progress. One of the many possible responses to NEXT? is T(ry harder) which increases the size of the deductive search space and causes more work[2] to be carried out on subproblems marked "deduction-required", yielding 2 additional paths, 6 additional subproblems, and 4 additional

1 The concept *invisible college* is used by sociologists of science to connote a group of scholars who regularly keep in touch with, and communicate new results to, each other through informal channels more efficient and quicker than the channels of formal publication.

2 Means are available by which the user can view an abstracted version of the subproblem graph and then select particular subproblems on which further effort is to be expended. Also the user can specify which of several limits are to be relaxed and by how much. Providing the user with means of precisely controlling the system's travels through the deductive search space is an important DADM design goal, not illustrated or further discussed in this paper.

```
MODE:
Query:
.((LAB  L) (ORIGINATES (BARKER) (MAG-BUBBLE) (1978))
IMP
(AND (KNOWS L (MAG-BUBBLE) (1978))
(LOCATED-IN  L (UK))))

CHAINS LIMIT REACHED

4 PATHS  15 PROBLEMS  2 PLANS

NEXT?  Try harder
TRYING HARDER:

CHAINS LIMIT REACHED

6 PATHS  21 PROBLEMS  6 PLANS

NEXT?  Usage flow. Enter plan number or list of plan numbers:
(1 to 6)

PLAN 1
WT   PREMISES
95   (11 12 14)

PLAN 2
WT   PREMISES
8Ø   (1Ø 12 14)

PLAN 3
WT   PREMISES
7Ø   (9  12 14)

PLAN 4
WT   PREMISES
95   (11 12 13 14 15)

PLAN 5
WT   PREMISES
8Ø   (1Ø 12 13 14 15)

PLAN 6
WT   PREMISES
7Ø   (9  12 13 14 15)

Next?  Plan display.  Enter plan number or list of plan numbers:
4
```

Figure 3. Which UK laboratories might know about Barker's result?

```
<<INFERENCE PLAN 4 PLAUSIBILITY:  95

2 SUBPLANS:
====================
  **3
  SEARCH CONFERENCE-ON (MEETING-1 SUBJECT-1 1978)
  SEARCH ATTEND (SCIENTIST-1 MEETING-1 1978)
  SEARCH ATTEND (SCIENTIST-2 MEETING-1 1978)
  CONCLUDE SCIENTIFIC-INFORMATION-FLOW (SCIENTIST-2 SCIENTIST-1
SUBJECT-1 1978)

  **4
  SEARCH CITES  (PUBLICATION-2 PUBLICATION-1)
  SEARCH CITES  (PUBLICATION-1 PUBLICATION-2)
  SEARCH AUTHOR (SCIENTIST-2 PUBLICATION-2)
  SEARCH AUTHOR (BARKER PUBLICATION-1)
  CONCLUDE MEMBER-SAME-IC (BARKER SCIENTIST-2)

  **2
  ASSUME ORIGINATES (BARKER MAG-BUBBLE 1978)
  CONCLUDE KNOWS (SCIENTIST-2 MAG-BUBBLE 1978)

 **1
 SEARCH ABOUT (MAG-BUBBLE SUBJECT-1)
 CONCLUDE KNOWS (SCIENTIST-1 MAG-BUBBLE 1978)

**Ø
SEARCH CONDUCTS-RESEARCH-AT (SCIENTIST-1 LAB-L 1978)
CONCLUDE KNOWS (LAB-L MAG-BUBBLE 1978)

====================
SEARCH LOCATED-IN (LAB-L UK)
====================

SEARCH/COMPUTE PLAN:
    SEARCH      *AUTHOR BARKER PUBLICATION-1
    SEARCH      *AUTHOR SCIENTIST-2 PUBLICATION-2
    SEARCH      *CITES  PUBLICATION-1 PUBLICATION-2
    SEARCH      *CITES  PUBLICATION-2 PUBLICATION-1
    SEARCH      *ABOUT MAG-BUBBLE SUBJECT-1
    SEARCH      *ATTEND SCIENTIST-2 MEETING-1 1978
    SEARCH      *ATTEND SCIENTIST-1 MEETING-1 1978
    SEARCH      *CONFERENCE-ON MEETING-1 SUBJECT-1 1978
    SEARCH      *CONDUCTS-RESEARCH-AT SCIENTIST-1 LAB-L 1978
    SEARCH      *LOCATED-IN LAB-L UK
```

```
EXECUTE?Yes
put[retrieve[AUTHOR.SCIENTIST,AUTHOR.TITLE]]into __ØØ76;
put[retrieve[CITES.TITLE,CITES.CITEDBY]]into __ØØ77;
put[retrieve[ATTEND.SCIENTIST,ATTEND.CONFERENCE,ATTEND.DATE]]into
                                                         __ØØ78;
:
:
retrieve]AUTHOR.TITLE,__ØØ76.Ø,__ØØ76.1,ABOUT.MAJOR-AREA,ATTEND.
CONFERENCE,__ØØ78.Ø,CONDUCTS-RESEARCH-AT.LOCATION]
  where(AUTHOR.SCIENTIST="BARKER")
  and (CITES.TITLE=AUTHOR.TITLE)
  and(CITES.CITEDBY=__ØØ76.1)
  and(__ØØ77.Ø=__ØØ76.1)
  and(__ØØ77.1=AUTHOR.TITLE)
  and(ABOUT.TOPIC="MAG-BUBBLE")
  and(ATTEND.SCIENTIST=__ØØ76.Ø)
  and(ATTEND.DATE=1978)
  and(__ØØ78.1=ATTEND.CONFERENCE)
  and(__ØØ78.2=1978)
  and(CONFERENCE-ON.CONFERENCE=ATTEND.CONFERENCE)
  and(CONFERENCE-ON.TOPIC=ABOUT.MAJOR-AREA)
  and(CONFERENCE-ON.YEAR=1978)
  and(CONDUCTS-RESEARCH-AT.SCIENTIST=__ØØ78.Ø)
  and(CONDUCTS-RESEARCH-AT.YEAR=1978)
  and(LOCATED-IN.PLACE1=CONDUCTS-RESEARCH-AT.LOCATION)
  and(LOCATED-IN.PLACE2="UK")
```

Figure 4. An inference plan, search/compute plan, and data base access strategy for the query shown in Figure 3.

```
DATA-BASE SEARCH SUCCESSFUL
***************
ANSWER SUMMARY --
VARIABLES:
(L)
ANSWERS:
(CAMBRIDGE)
***************
EVIDENCE CHAIN 1 FROM PLAN 4 PLAUSIBILITY:  95
2 CONCLUSIONS:
====================
     **3
     FACT CONFERENCE-ON (APS BUBBLE-MEMORIES 1978)
     FACT ATTEND (SOUTHWOOD APS 1978)
     FACT ATTEND (BOYCE APS 1978)
     CONCLUDE SCIENTIFIC-INFORMATION-FLOW (BOYCE SOUTHWOOD BUBBLE-
       MEMORIES 1978)
     **4
     FACT CITES  (HIGH-SPEED-BUBBLE-MEMORIES VISCOUS-FLOW-IN-BUBBLE-
       MEMORIES)
     FACT CITES  (VISCOUS-FLOW-IN-BUBBLE-MEMORIES HIGH-SPEED-BUBBLE-
       MEMORIES)
     FACT AUTHOR (BOYCE HIGH-SPEED-BUBBLE-MEMORIES)
     FACT AUTHOR (BARKER VISCOUS-FLOW-IN-BUBBLE-MEMORIES)
     CONCLUDE MEMBER-SAME-IC (BARKER BOYCE)
    **2
    ASSUME ORIGINATES (BARKER MAG-BUBBLE 1978)
    CONCLUDE KNOWS (BOYCE MAG-BUBBLE 1978)
  **1
  FACT ABOUT (MAG-BUBBLE BUBBLE-MEMORIES)
  CONCLUDE KNOWS (SOUTHWOOD MAG-BUBBLE 1978)
**Ø
FACT CONDUCTS-RESEARCH-AT (SOUTHWOOD CAMBRIDGE 1978)
CONCLUDE KNOWS (CAMBRIDGE MAG-BUBBLE 1978)
====================
FACT LOCATED-IN (CAMBRIDGE UK)
====================                >>
NEXT?Usage flow. Enter plan number or list of plan numbers:
4
PLAN 4
STEP WT  USES
**3  99  PREMISE 13
**4  95  PREMISE 11
**2  99  **4 PREMISE 12
**1  99  **2 **3 PREMISE 15
**Ø  99  **1 PREMISE 14
```

Figure 5. An answer summary, evidence chain, and proof structure display for the Figure 3 query.

inference plans. A U(sage flow) response results in a synopsis of the six plans — generated in order of shorter first, ties decided by plausibility.[1] The fourth inference plan is displayed in the next figure (4). It has a plausibility of 95 and consists of two subplans: one comprising five steps, each step resulting from a Horn clause (a clause consisting of a conjunction of atomic expressions implying a single atomic expression) synthesized from a premise and the other requiring data base search for UK laboratories. Given the assumption in step **2, we are led to find scientists who are members of Barker's invisible college SCIENTIST-2 (step **4) and therefore may know about his result. From information transfer between SCIENTIST-2 and SCIENTIST-1 (step **3), we can conclude that SCIENTIST-1 (step **1) and SCIENTIST-1's laboratory, which must be located in the United Kingdom (step **0), also know the result.

Below the inference plan we display the search/compute plan, respond affirmatively to EXECUTE? and receive (since we have turned on a "generate intermediate language" mode) a relational-algebra representation of the search plan. Search plans of this type can be directed to an external DMS. Notice that field (relation domain) names have been supplied, and temporary relations have been created. The answer summary and one of the evidence chains stemming from the successful data base search is shown in Figure 5. At the bottom of Figure 5 we again evoke the Usage flow mode. This time, since the inference plan has been instantiated, we obtain a display of the skeletal structure of the proof showing the plausibilities of the individual premises used and, for each proof step, the premise and the previous steps from which the step is directly derived.

The above examples illustrate the DADM system's ability to carry out bidirectional chaining that deductively links assumptions and goals of a query. One-directional chaining is also possible, forward chaining to discover implicational consequences of a given expression and backward chaining to enable assumptionless queries. The display control options available to the user permit display of only as much information as is desired. Display of inference plan detail, search/compute plan detail, and evidence chain detail, as exemplified in the figures, is all optional. If the user desires to see only the answer to his question, all other information can be suppressed.

The examples in Figure 6 illustrate the use of forward and backward reasoning to support generalized navigation through the

---

1 Plausibility of an inference plan or a proof at present is computed by finding the fuzzy intersection (Zadeh [1965]) of the plausibility of the participating premises.

premises into the explicit-fact data base. The first query requests forward chaining from instances of *knows* through the premises into the data base and a display of the first evidence chain is shown. This chain shows that if it can be assumed that Yoshida knows a certain (mag-bubble) result in 1978, then it follows that Cambridge knows that result during the same time period (here secondary derivations are displayed as *supportive chains*). Missing arguments and variable type constraints are automatically supplied by the system.

The ability to browse through the premises by backward chaining from a goal relation towards supporting information is illustrated in the second example of Figure 6. Here a *deadend subproblem* — an instance of the relation *originates* that has no deductive, search, or compute support — prohibits generation of a complete inference plan. Instantiation of the partial plan leads to a *conditional* chain *viz.* a chain conditional on some form of support (SUPP-REQ) for *originates* and further deduction (which presumably could be achieved via *Try Harder*) on *Member-Same-IC*.

The illustrated navigational and partial plan generation features are proving to be very helpful in the exploration and exploitation of large premise sets. In order to move from toy knowledge bases to a realistic knowledge base that, with respect to size, complexity, and semantic structure, is more representative of expected eventual applications, we have created a freight-shipping data base and premise set. We deliberately avoided picking a domain (like the traditionally well-worked one of family trees) where it is immediately obvious that there is a high payoff in being able to express requests against the domain in terms of inference-invoking virtual relations. The application is grounded on an extensional data base containing information about a series of companies (Excello, Emperor, Ambassador, ...) located in territories or areas (Valley-Acres, Lakeland, ---). Within a specified time period, company X ships a specified quantity of freight (of type light, heavy, ---) to company Y by various routes involving a series of warehouses (VA1,LA2 ...) each of which is used by many companies. Companies are of a few basic kinds (wholesaler, processor, extractor, trucker, ...). This extensional data is stored in 11 base relations.

Interesting results appear. For deductive augmentation of a domain even as simple as this one, a large number of abstractions (i.e., virtual relations) quickly prove to be useful (a total of 41 so far). One hundred twenty three premises have been created to provide definitional specification of these abstractions, and these premises deductively link relations in quite complex ways that require the expressive power of the full predicate calculus. For a domain with no obvious mathematical ordering, there are a

```
MODE:  Query:
.((KNOWS) IMP( ))
(KNOWS HAS MISSING ARGUMENTS.  3  HAVE BEEN SUPPLIED.)
4 PATHS  11 PROBLEMS  2 PLANS
EVIDENCE CHAIN 1 FROM PLAN 1 PLAUSIBILITY:  99
====================
MAIN FORWARD CHAINS:
--------------------
**1
ASSUME KNOWS (YOSHIDA MAG-BUBBLE 1978)
FACT ABOUT (MAG-BUBBLE BUBBLE-MEMORIES)
CONCLUDE KNOWS (MACKENZIE MAG-BUBBLE 1978)
 **2
 FACT CONDUCTS-RESEARCH-AT (MACKENZIE CAMBRIDGE 1978)
 CONCLUDE KNOWS (CAMBRIDGE MAG-BUBBLE 1978)
SUPPORTIVE CHAINS:
------------------
 **3
 FACT CONFERENCE-ON (IEEE BUBBLE-MEMORIES 1978)
 FACT ATTEND (MACKENZIE IEEE 1978)
 FACT ATTEND (YOSHIDA IEEE 1978)
 CONCLUDE SCIENTIFIC-INFORMATION-FLOW (YOSHIDA MACKENZIE BUBBLE-
====================                                  MEMORIES 1978)
                                        >>
MODE:  Query:
.(( ) IMP (KNOWS))
(KNOWS HAS MISSING ARGUMENTS.  3  HAVE BEEN SUPPLIED.)
CHAINS LIMIT REACHED
DEADEND SUBPROBLEMS THAT REQUIRE NEW PREMISE/TUPLE/PROCEDURE:
(ORIGINATES.4.1)
PARTIAL PLANS?Yes
6 PATHS  16 PROBLEMS  3 PLANS
EVIDENCE CHAIN 1 FROM PLAN 2 PLAUSIBILITY:  99
====================
 **3
 FACT CONFERENCE-ON (APS BUBBLE-MEMORIES 1978)
 FACT ATTEND (SOUTHWOOD APS 1978)
 FACT ATTEND (BOYCE APS 1978)
 CONCLUDE SCIENTIFIC-INFORMATION-FLOW (BOYCE SOUTHWOOD BUBBLE-
                                                      MEMORIES 1978)
 **2
 DED-REQ MEMBER-SAME-IC (SCIENTIST-2 BOYCE)
 SUPP-RED ORIGINATES (SCIENTIST-2 MAG-BUBBLE 1978)
 CONCLUDE KNOWS (BOYCE MAG-BUBBLE 1978)
 **1
 FACT ABOUT (MAG-BUBBLE BUBBLE-MEMORIES)
 CONCLUDE KNOWS (SOUTHWOOD MAG-BUBBLE 1978)
**Ø
FACT CONDUCTS-RESEARCH-AT (SOUTHWOOD CAMBRIDGE 1978)
CONCLUDE KNOWS (CAMBRIDGE MAG-BUBBLE 1978)
====================
                                        >>
```

Figure 6. Forward and backward reasoning from the relation *knows*.

surprising number of recursive links of relation occurrences to other occurrences of the same relation, both direct recursive links within single premises and indirect recursive links across several premises. These results have reinforced our belief that a system capable of providing nontrivial deductive augmentation of data base access must be able to find its way through a large search space, and that various powerful heuristics are required to contain deductive search within manageable bounds (heuristics like construction of deductive plans on the basis of middle-term chains, use of semantic advice, etc.).

Additional particular characteristics of the freight-shipping domain of discourse are presented in the section below on DADM performance features, where the domain is used to illustrate some of the DADM features that enable users and data base administrators to discover various characteristics of a premise base.

DADM SYSTEM OVERVIEW

The DADM deductive processor (DP) has been designed to interface with existing and emerging DMS's rather than to work with an embedded data base. Given this orientation, we make a sharp distinction between specific facts that reside in a DMS data base and the general premises that are directly accessible to the DP. Since the number of premises that may be required for a practical application is likely to be large, particular attention has been paid to the development of effective techniques for selecting the small set of premises relevant to answering a user's specific request.

These premise-selection techniques place heavy emphasis on planning. Inference plans are constructed and then used to guide the generation of full deductions. Such planning appears essential for cutting through the massive number of dead ends and irrelevant inferences that can result from brute-force application of theorem proving techniques to large premise collections. The DP first builds derivation skeletons that represent possible inference plans and then attempts to verify and instantiate them. The premise-selection process is thus separated from the process of verifying the consistency of variable substitutions.

The generation of inference plans makes use, when possible, of an efficient technique for middle-term chaining (Klahr [1978]). This process finds deductive chains from assumptions to goals through premises. Middle-term chaining combines forward chaining from assumptions of a given problem or subproblem with backward chaining from goals. As forward and backward "waves" are generated, their intersections are regularly tested. When a nonempty intersection occurs, the system has found a deductive chain from an assumption to a goal. The resulting chain is passed to the inference plan generator, which extracts the premises whose occurrences are involved in the chain. Subproblems typically result, requiring new chaining steps, data base search, or evaluation of relations that are computable. The system may return at a later time to produce additional chains for the same problem or subproblem, either because the first one doesn't successfully develop into a valid proof or because, even though it does, alternative proofs are useful.

The chaining (pathfinding) process does not operate on the premises themselves but on a net structure called the *connection graph* (CG), a graph abstracted from the premises. When a premise is introduced into the system, the truth-dependency connections (links) existing among the separate predicate (relation) occurrences in the premise are encoded into the CG. Further, deductive interactions (unifications) between predicate occurrences in the new premise and occurrences from premises already represented in the graph are pre-computed and also encoded into the CG. The variable substitutions required to effect the unifications are stored elsewhere, for later use by the verifier. The CG thus represents in a single graph the dependencies within premises and the deductive interactions among premises. During the generation of middle-term chains and plans, the system builds paths across unifications among the premises, but it does not generate the unificiations nor does it merge the variable substitutions associated with different unifications. The former is done during premise input, while the latter is done by the verifier after plans have been generated.[1]

There exist at present two major approaches to the deductive question answering problem: the interpreter approach exemplified by MRPPS (Minker [1978]) and the compiler approach realized in the DADM prototype and also described by Reiter [1978] and Chang [1978, 1981]. In the former, deductive queries are interpreted with respect to a combined intensional and extensional data file while the latter approach "compiles" deductive queries into extensional data base access strategies by use of intensional (i.e., premise or axiom) information. DADM compiles deductive queries into relational data base search requests using the indicated pathfinding and planning techniques for fast selection of relevant premises from large files of (mostly irrelevant) premises. DADM also supports the dynamic modification of the premise file (and associated connection graph) by a data base administrator. In Grant and Minker [1981], a compiler approach that converts deductive queries into optimized relational data base searches is described.

---

1 The CG somewhat resembles Sickel's clause interconnectivity graph (Sickel [1976]) in that both graphs represent the initial deductive search space and are not changed in the course of constructing particular deductions.

DADM Deductive Processor Comments

The major DADM components are illustrated in Figure 7. At present users communicate directly with the controller. This module accepts premises, procedural knowledge (as LISP functions), advice rules, queries, and commands. For the present it accesses and coordinates the use of a relational data management system as well as the seven major processing components of DADM:

(1) Array maintenance: This module inserts, deletes, retrieves, and compacts (i.e., garbage-collects) the large amount of information kept by the system in the form of LISP arrays. For example, information abstracted from the premises is segmented into seven separate arrays. The segmentation contributes to comprehensible system structuring and to processing efficiency. Each predicate (relation) occurrence is assigned a unique integer index. Information about a particular predicate occurrence is obtained from the array containing the kind of information needed by indexing into the array with the integer assigned to the occurrence.

(2) Pathfinder: This module uses the connection graph to find the deductive paths necessary to support forward, backward, and middle-term chaining processes.

(3) Planner: This module uses middle-term paths, premises, and the concept graph to construct plans. Where the Pathfinder produces simple linear structures, the Planner must combine these chains into the much more complex structures that can be assumed by complete derivations.

(4) Verifier: This module merges the different variable substitutions required by the unifications in an inference plan. Plans that do not verify (i.e., that contain inconsistent variable substitutions) are rejected (or marked for salvage).

(5) Plan, Evidence Display: This module supports the wide variety of display options that are available for monitoring the operation of the deductive system, enabling a user to examine deductive paths, plans, answers, evidence chains, etc.

(6) Answer Construction: This module extracts answers from the data values returned by *search* and *compute* operations.

(7) Assistant: This module incorporates the INTERLISP Programmer's Assistant into DADM. The assistant keeps a history list of user inputs and supports the modification and reuse of those inputs.

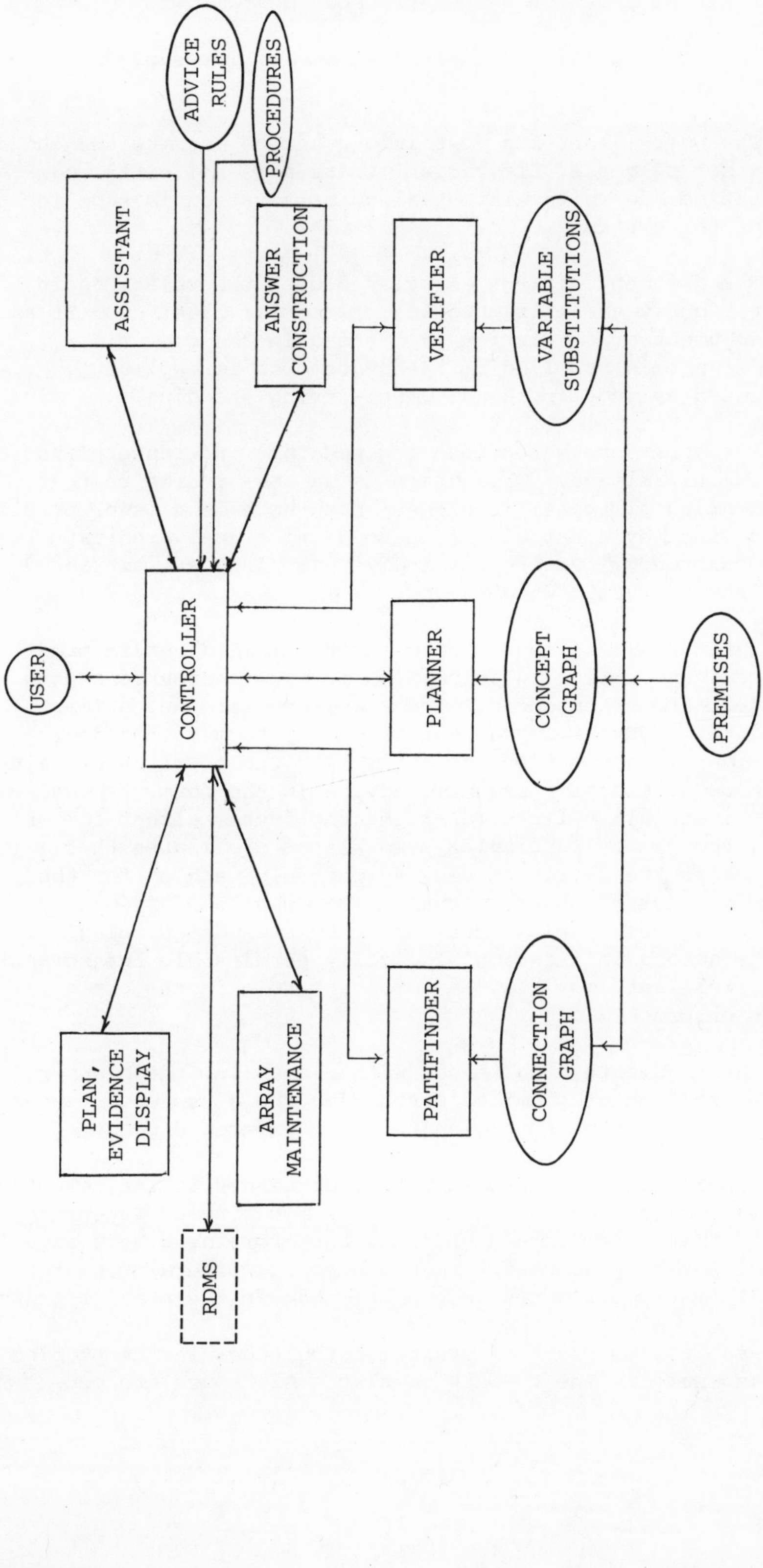

Figure 7. DADM Deductive Processor Components

When a query is entered, the system proceeds as follows:

(1) The query is sent to the Planner which initiates plan generation:

a. The query is broken down into a set of assumptions and a set of goals. If variables are not explicitly quantified, default existential quantification is supplied by the system.

b. The argument strings associated with the relations in the query are extracted and stored for later use. If an argument of a relation is missing in the query, a default is supplied by the system but is explicitly noted as such in the argument-string encoding.

c. A *problem graph* representing possible inference plans is initialized. This graph is an *and-or* tree representing all possible plans. Each node is a (sub) problem defined by a set of assumptions and a goal predicate occurrence. Particular individual plans are extracted from the graph when needed.

(2) The Pathfinder is called to find chains of middle-term predicate occurrences linking assumption predicate occurrences to goal predicate occurrences. These chains represent attempts to find key predicate occurrences (middle terms) that deductively connect assumptions to goals (via the premises containing the occurrences). Semantic advice in the form of premise and predicate alert lists (alerting the system either for or against the use of particular premises or predicates that arise during the search process as possibly usable for the construction of middle-term chains), and in the form of relation-argument typing that serves to exclude chaining attempts across unifications logically permissible but semantically irrelevant, may play an important role in the chain generation process.

(3) Using the predicate occurrences within a chain, the Planner isolates the set of premises containing the given occurrences. This set represents the beginning of an inference plan.

(4) The Planner examines the predicate occurrences in the selected premises but not part of the middle-term chain and determines which of these are "unresolved" and therefore need deductive or other forms of support. Each unresolved literal results in the formation of a new subproblem node in the problem graph.

(5) A next-subproblem function evaluates the nodes in the problem graph and selects one to work on next. All nodes are con-

sidered for selection, those that are completely unprocessed as well as those on which some processing has already been done. (A part of our current work on improving performance of the system is an attempt to incorporate strategic intelligence into this node evaluation.)

(6) When plan generation is completed or temporarily suspended, the Verifier merges the variable-flow classes of chains comprising each plan to check for clashes. A clash is a variable involved in more than one unification being replaced by two different constant values. A decision confirming presence or absence of a clash may have to be deferred until some data base search has occurred, if the variable substitutions being merged involve functions that can be evaluated (i.e., functions other than Skolem functions, which are not computable).

(7) The Data Management System is called for each inference plan not rejected by the Verifier. The DMS searches over the data base of specific facts to resolve subproblems involving *base* relations, i.e., relations about which information is contained explicitly in the extensional data base. If data base search is successful, values for the variables occurring in the search requests are returned and answers are formulated.

Representation of Premises and Queries

The basic representation used for premises and queries is the *primitive conditional*. Internally, such conditionals are represented in Skolemized, quantifier-free form. Primitive conditionals have the following possible forms:

(1) $\&(\ldots) \supset \vee(\ldots)$

(2) $\&(\ldots) \supset \&(\ldots)$

(3) $\vee(\ldots) \supset \vee(\ldots)$

(4) $\vee(\ldots) \supset \&(\ldots)$

Within the parentheses are literals (negated or affirmed predicates and their arguments). The primitive-conditional format has the full expressibility of the first-order preaicate calculus, i.e., every first-order predicate calculus expression can be represented by one or more primtiive conditionals.

DADM PERFORMANCE FEATURES

DADM's main performance-oriented features until recently have been its use of the connection graph to support planning based on the construction of middle-term chains and its use of semantic advice. In this section we briefly discuss additional performance-enhancing features of DADM, some of them just recently implemented.

The Concept Graph

The Concept Graph's function is to aid the user, the data base administrator, and the system in maintaining a large collection of virtual relations. Part of its content is generated automatically, as new premises are entered into the system, while the rest is the responsibility of the data base administrator. The Concept Graph is also used to represent set relationships between argument types. Class inclusion paths within the graph are used, for example, to permit unification of relation arguments of type SCIENTIST with arguments of type HUMAN.

Part of the Concept Graph for the freight-shipping application is shown in Figure 8. The 62 relations were entered automatically during generation of the intensional data base, while the partitioning of these relations into various subgroupings (BR-Base relations, VR-Virtual relations, CR-Compute relations, and DATA-Original INGRES-type relations from which the relations marked "BR" were formed by projection) was accomplished by the data base administrator. In effect the relations were classified by domain type (C-BR: company (unary) base relations, RC-VR: Route-Company (binary) virtual relations, etc.). Also entered into the concept graph automatically are the names of all domains, functions, premises (if named by the user during premise input), and advice rules. All of these entities are cross referenced in the Concept Graph so users, administrators or the system can ask questions such as: which premises use relation R in their antecedent?, which functions used as relation *R* arguments range over domain *D*?, etc. The system uses this cross-reference information for, among other purposes, maintenance. For example, when asked to delete a series of premises, it not only deletes the premises but maintains the integrity of the concept graph by deleting all references to virtual relations, functions, and domains that were used *only* in those premises. An illustration of this process is shown in Figure 9 where the *invisible college* premises and an integrity-constraint premise are deleted from the system.

Transitive Closure of Concept, Connection Graphs

Warshall's algorithm (Warshall [1962]) provides an efficient means of computing the transitive closure of Boolean matrices. We have implemented several different versions of the algorithm that can be applied to the concept and connection graphs to produce matrices such as the one shown in Figure 10. This matrix, computed from the 62 relations in the concept graph of Figure 8, represents the transitive closure of these relations under implication where

```
(CONCEPTS (RELATIONS (C-BR (RETAILER)
                           (PROCESSOR)
                           (EXTRACTOR)
                           (SPECULATOR)
                           (WHOLESALER)
                           (TRUCKER)
                     (CA-BR (DOMESTIC-TO))
                     (CW-BR (TRANSACTIONS)
                            (SPACE-RENTED))
                     (CCW-BR (SHIPS-TO))
                     (WA-BR (SITUATED-IN))
                     (VR (RRN-VR (HANDLING-COST-COMPARE)
                                 (DISTANCE-COST-COMPARE)
                                 (EFFICIENCY-COMPARE))
                         (RR-VR (CONCAT)
                                (ROUTE-PART))
                         (RN-VR (SPAN)
                                (EFFICIENCY-RATING)
                                (EFFICIENCY)
                                (HANDLING-COST)
                                (DISTANCE-COST))
                         (RL-VR (COMPANY-TRACK)
                                (WAREHOUSE-TRACK)
                                (RESOURCE-TYPE))
                         (RC-VR (CONTAINS)
                                (AN-INTERMEDIATE-COMPANY)
                                (THE-PIVOT-COMPANY)
                                (THE-DESTINATION-COMPANY)
                                (THE-ORIGINATOR-COMPANY)
                         (RA-VR (GOES-THROUGH)
                         (R-VR  (AVERAGE-EFFICIENCY)
                                (LOW-EFFICIENCY)
                                (HIGH-EFFICIENCY)
                                (VIABLE)
                                (MIDDLEMAN-ROUTE)
                                (RESOURCE-ROUTE))
                         (CCARR-VR (HANDLING-EQUIV)
                                   (HANDLING-ADVANTAGE)
                                   (DISTANCE-EQUIV)
                                   (DISTANCE-ADVANTAGE)
                                   (EFFICIENCY-EQUIV)
                                   (EFFICIENCY-ADVANTAGE)
                                   (COMPETITORS))
                         (CCA-VR   (ALL-ROUTES-LESS-HANDLING)
                                   (ALL-ROUTES-LESS-DISTANT)
                                   (ALL-ROUTES-MORE-EFFICIENT))
                         (CA-VR    (FOREIGN-TO))
```

[continued]

```
          (C-VR       (PRODUCER)
                      (MIDDLEMAN))
          (AC*AR-VR  (FACILITIES-DEPENDENT)
                     (TRANSPORTATION-DEPENDENT)
                     (RESOURCE-DEPENDENT)))
      (CR (GREATERP)
          (MEMBER)
          (EQUAL)
      (DATA (ROW)
            (RO)
            (WSU)
            (WH)
            (CWT)
            (CCT)
            (CO)))
```

Figure 8. Part of the Shipping Application Concept Graph

```
PREMISE:  9:
(If (author scientist-1 publication-1) and (author scientist-2
                                                publication-1)
then (member-same-ic scientist-1 scientist-2)
AUTHOR-MBR)
  DELETED.
PREMISE:  10:
(If (author scientist-1 publication-1) and (author scientist-2
                                                publication-2)
  and (cites publication-1 scientist-2) and (cites publication-2)
                                                scientist-1)
then (member-same-ic scientist-1 scientist-2)
CITE-AUTHOR-MBR)
  DELETED.
PREMISE:  11:
(If (author scientist-1 publication-1) and (author scientist-2
                                                publication-2)
  and (cites publication-1 publication-2) and (cites publication-2
                                                  publication-1)
then (member-same-ic scientist-1 scientist-2)
CITE-PUB-MBR)
  DELETED.
PREMISE:  12:
(If (originates scientist-1 result-1 year-1) and (member-same-ic
                                                     scientist-1
                                                     scientist-2)
then(knows scientist-2 result-1 year-1)
ORIG-IC)
  DELETED.
PREMISE:  13:
(If (attend scientist-1 meeting-1 year-1) and (attend scientist-2
                                             meeting-1 year-1)
  and (conference-on meeting-1 subject-1 year-1)
then (scientific-information-flow scientist-1 scientist-2 subject-1
                                    year-1)
CONF-IC)
  DELETED.
PREMISE:  14:
(If _conducts-research-at scientist-1 lab-1 year-1)
  and (knows scientist-1 result-1 year-1)
then (knows lab-1 result-1 year-1)
IC-LAB)
  DELETED.
PREMISE:  15:
(If (knows scientist-1 result-1 year-1) and (about result-1
  subject-1) and (scientific-information-flow scientist-1
  scientist-2 subject-1 year-1)
then (knows scientist-2 result-1 year-1)
IC-IC)
  DELETED    [continued]
```

```
PREMISE:  16:
(If (new-salary employee-1 amount-1) and (greaterp amount-1
                                               (salary
                                                 (manager
                                                     employee-1)))
then  (integrity-failure-employee-salary)
  SALARY-INTEG)
  DELETED.
RELATION:  INTEGRITY-FAILURE-EMPLOYEE-SALARY   DELETED.
RELATION:  GREATERP  DELETED.
RELATION:  NEW-SALARY   DELETED.
RELATION:  SCIENTIFIC-INFORMATION-FLOW   DELETED.
RELATION:  KNOWS   DELETED.
RELATION:  ORIGINATES   DELETED.
RELATION:  MEMBER-SAME-IC   DELETED.
 CONCEPT:  IC-VIRTUAL-RELATIONS   DELETED.
 CONCEPT:  INTEGRITY-RELATIONS    DELETED.
  DOMAIN:  AMOUNT   DELETED.
  DOMAIN:  EMPLOYEE DELETED.
FUNCTION:  MANAGER  DELETED.
FUNCTION:  SALARY   DELETED.
  DELETE:  end delete.
```

Figure 9. Premise deletion and resultant deletion of concepts from the Concept Graph.

```
                            11111111112222222222333333333344444444445555555555666
                   12345678901234567890123456789012345678901234567890123456789012
                   †
CO                 1 :..............................................................
RO                 2 :..............................................................
WH                 3 :..............................................................
ROW                4 :..............................................................
CWT                5 :..............................................................
CCT                6 :..............................................................
WSU                7 :..............................................................
TRUCKER            8 :.......12221566...42222..232.3333324543.12.3343343334333433444
WHOLESALER         9 :.......22221566...42222..232.3333324543.34.3343343334333433444
SPECULATOR         1Ø:.......22221566...42222..232.3333324543.34.3343343334333433444
RETAILER           11:.......22211566...42222..232.3333324541.22.2333343334333433444
MIDDLEMAN          12:.......11111455...31111..121.2222213432.23.2232232223222322333
PRODUCER           13:.......55554111...11111..121.2222233431.22.2232232223222322333
PROCESSOR          14:.......66665122...22222..232.3333344542.33.3343343334333433444
EXTRACTOR          15:.......66665122...22222..232.3333344542.33.3343343334333433444
FOREIGN-TO         16:..............................................................
DOMESTIC-TO        17:.......88887788...67247..434.1555566761.11.2533348334533445444
SHIPS-TO           18:.......33332233...11111..122.2222213432.33.2232232223322322333
RESOURCE-ROUTE     19:.......44443122...12222..231.3132222321.22.2333343334233423444
RESOURCE-TYPE      2Ø:...................1.......1...............1.2112.11221121.333
WAREHOUSE-TRACK    21:.......66665566...45125..212.1333344544.23.5344456566344533444
COMPANY-TRACK      22:.......44443344...23213..211.2111122322.22.3334454445233423444
DISTANCE-COST      23:......................1....................4.23541223.3543.333
SPACE-RENTED       24:.......33332233...11111..122.2222213432.33.2232232223322322333
TRANSACTIONS       25:.......33332233...11111..122.2222213432.33.2232232223322322333
EFFICIENCY         26:.........................1.................412223.354.35431222
SPAN               27:.......55554455...34114..111.2222233433.33.4233345455233422333
HANDLING-COST      28:...........................................4.2354.35412231.333
MEMBER             29:.......44443344...23223..333.1111122322.22.3444454445444544555
GOES-THROUGH       3Ø:.......77776677...56136..323.1444455655.12.6455567677455644555
THE-ORIGINATOR-CO  31:.......33332233...12212..222.2121111211.22.2333343334333433444
THE-DESTINATION-CO 32:.......44443344...22212..222.2211121211.22.2333343334333433444
AN-INTERMEDIATE-CO 33:.......55554455...34334..444.2221133431.11.2533345334533445444
CONTAINS           34:.......44443344...23223..333.1111122322.22.3444454445444544555
MIDDLEMAN-ROUTE    35:.......22221344...22222..231.3132212322.33.3333343334233423444
CONCAT             36:.......33332233...11111..111.2221211112.22.2232232223222322333
ROUTE-PART         37:.......55554455...34234..434.1221133132.22.3544455445544555555
THE-PIVOT-COMPANY  38:...........................1.........1.....5.3465.46523342.444
RESOURCE-DEPENDENT 39:......................................1.11.1.2223.223.2233.333
SITUATED-IN        40:.......88887788...67247..434.1555566766.12.7566678788566755666
TRANSPORTATION-DEP 41:........................................11....................
FACILITIES-DEPENDE 42:.........................................1....................
EQUAL              43:...........................................1.2112.112.1123.333
COMPETITORS        44:...........................................1.1112.112.1122.222
EFFICIENCY-COMPARE 45:...........................................311112.243.2432.222
GREATERP           46:...........................................3.1142.142.1421.111
EFFICIENCY-ADVANTAGE 47:.........................................2.3131.334.3344.444
EFFICIENCY-EQUIV   48:...............................................1..............
ALL-ROUTES-MORE-EFFI 49:.........................................1.2122.223.2233.333
DISTANCE-COST-COMPAR 5Ø:.........................................3.12431112.2432.222
DISTANCE-ADVANTAGE 51:...........................................2.3334.131.3344.444
DISTANCE-EQUIV     52:...................................................1..........
ALL-ROUTES-LESS-DIST 53:.........................................1.2223.122.2233.333
HANDLING-COST-COMPAR 54:.........................................3.1243.24311122.222
HANDLING-ADVANTAGE 55:...........................................2.3334.334.1314.444
HANDLING-EQUIV     56:.......................................................1......
ALL-ROUTES-LESS-HAND 57:.........................................1.2223.223.1223.333
VIABLE             58:..............................................................
EFFICIENCY-RATING  59:..........................................................1111
HIGH-EFFICIENCY    60:..............................................................
LOW-EFFICIENCY     61:..............................................................
AVERAGE-EFFICIENCY 62:..............................................................
```

Figure 10. Transitive closure matrix for the Shipping application relations

a dot indicates no implication connection for a row-column intersection, and a digit indicates the number of premises in the minimum implicational path between the row predicate and the column predicate. We are currently in the process of using this information to create a hierarchy of base relations (level Ø), virtual relations defined only in terms of base relations (level 1), virtual relations whose definitions make no nonrecursive reference to relations higher than level 1, etc. This hierarchy will be of use to data base administrators but also to the DADM system in more intelligently controlling and guiding the inference planning process. Other useful information available from the application of the transitive-closure algorithm includes: disjoint groupings of relations, identification of relations involved in indirect recursion (recursion across more than one premise), groupings of goal (consequent) relations supported by the same assumptions, and groupings of assumptions (antecedents) leading to the same goals. We have relaxed the condition that row vectors and column vectors be identical for the last two groupings, and are experimenting with using "similar" vectors to determine a concept "similarity" space. Such a space should be useable for a quite sophisticated kind of deductive planning.

Structure Sharing in the Problem Graph

Structure sharing in the form of automatic collapsing of duplicate subproblems is now an important component of problem graph generation. Figure 11 illustrates the problem graph created by the system for the *invisible college* query shown in Figures 3 through 6. Here one top level problem (for the relation KNOWS) and 22 subproblems result to create the structure from which the 8 inference plans may be generated. The dashed line indicates that G4 has the same truth-functional structure as G3, and therefore G4 and G3 can share a single subtree. Without this single occurrence of structure sharing the problem graph would consist of 36 subproblems (23 plus counterparts of the descendants of G3 repeated under G4), and processing time and space would grow proportionately. Cycles that can result from this structure sharing are found by a cycle detector that checks for cycles on the creation of each new duplicate subproblem. Among other things, cycles indicate that work on certain subproblems (in particular, AND-mates of subproblems involved in a cycle) should be aborted.

Recursive Premises

A recursive premise is a premise containing multiple occurrences of a predicate that unify with each other. Consider, for example, an assertion of hereditariness of a property across a relation. If they are not controlled, recursive premises may invoke themselves an indefinite number of times in many parts of an inference plan.

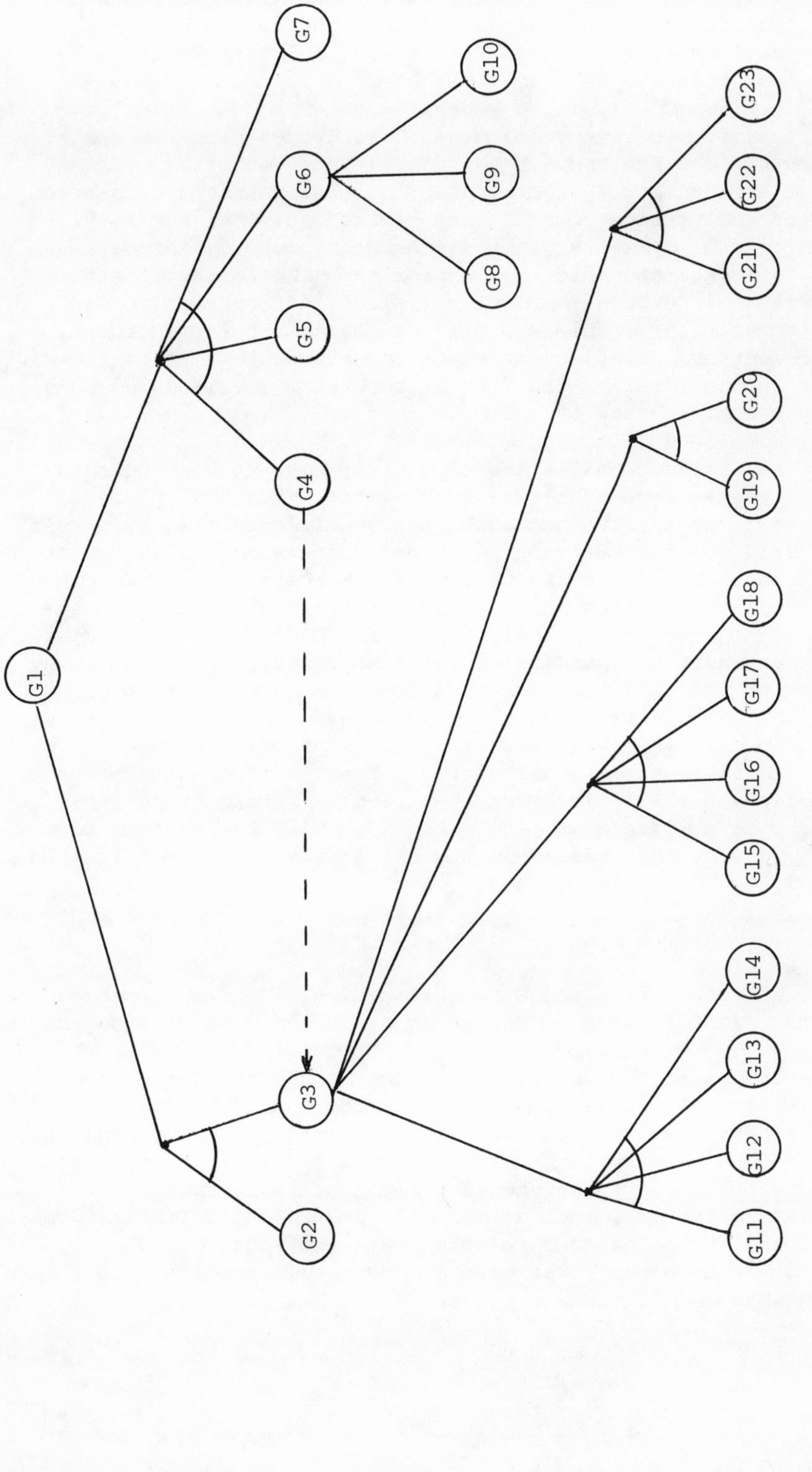

Figure 11. Structure Sharing in the Problem Graph.

The problem is how to apply intelligence to this invocation: How can the deductive planning central to DADM apply to a recursive premise when it serves a purpose but avoid doing so when the result is only to proliferate useless subproblems?

Our approach to this problem was briefly described in Kellogg et al. [1978], but has since been significantly modified and enhanced. We identify the patterns of recursion that are asserted in premises and premise combinations — transitivity, symmetry, transitivity plus symmetry, inheritance of a property across a relation, unloopedness, etc. — and for each recursion pattern create a special purpose subroutine (called a "recursion module") that takes a partial or blocked plan utilizing a relation for which this pattern holds and attempts to articulate a logical structure that is justified by the kind of recursion involved and that will complete or unblock the plan.

When recursive premises are input they have to be processed quite differently from nonrecursive premises. For one thing, *all* the premises that involve recursion for a particular relation must be considered together because of interaction among the different ways a relation may be recursive.[1] (Recall the significance of transitivity and symmetry being present simultaneously as opposed to either being present in isolation.) The premises asserting recursiveness must be transformed into two parts, a part involving the recurring relation[2] and a part involving other relations, with logical dependency between the parts made explicit. The first part is then used mainly to determine the kind of data base search required (if any), as a result of the pattern of recursion present and to determine allowable argument-string transformations; the second part determines what plan extensions will be required to logically justify the search and the transformations. For example, a schema like

$$A(\ldots) \;\&\; B(\ldots) \rightarrow (R(\ldots) \rightarrow R(\ldots))$$

might result from this premise transformation. Whenever the recursion on the right is used to determine a kind of data base search

1 This construction of a single recursion module to represent the recursiveness of a relation, no matter how many different premises assert aspects of the recursiveness, is a major way our handling of recursiveness differs from that of Chang [1981]. Another comparison with his approach occurs on the following page.

2 Complicating factors, such as multiple recursion (interdependent recursion of more than one relation) and indirect recursion (recursion that occurs over more than a single premise) are discussed briefly below.

or to justify an argument-string transformation, the literals on the left must be added to the plan involved as conditions that justify an application of the recursion and that thus must be established to complete the deduction. At the present, this translation of premises into recursion modules is performed manually.

Most recursive premises transformed as just described are such that the part restricted to the recurring relation does conform to one of a relatively small set of patterns of recursion, a fact that was anticipated in the research of Elliott [1965] some years ago. Thus a large volume of *ad hoc* recursion modules is not needed to handle *most* recursive premises. We are designing a compiler that can take recursive premises and compile them into the data-base-searching, argument-transforming, and plan-extending recursion modules required. The possibility of such a compiler is suggested in Chang [1981] though his ideas have to be extended to more general rewrite rules and to compilation of a program that serves a different function than does the object of his compilation. Our compiler must produce a component of our deduction plan generation and verification system whereas his produces a program for supplying an answer to a particular query from an extensional data base. The rewrite rules are more general in that they may reference any number of occurrences of any number of virtual relations, and it is not necessary that every rewrite rule reference at least one occurrence of a base relation. This latter restriction imposed by Chang puts a severe limit on the degree of abstraction that can be achieved, i.e., on the conceptual distance possible between virtual and base relations.

Within the plan generation and verification process, a recursion module is activated for two different kinds of need. The first is during middle-term chaining when two occurrences of a relation do not unify. If the relation has an associated recursion module, a subproblem can be created that requires for its solution connecting the forward-wave occurrence of the relation with the backward-wave occurrence not by unification but by applying the recursion module. The second is during a plan salvaging state. A plan may fail to verify because, even though two occurrences of a relation could be unified in the plan generation, the result of the unification is the merger of variable-substitution classes that for a successful deduction must remain distinct. If the relation has an associated recursion module, it may be possible to salvage the plan by undoing the unification and connecting the two relation occurrences with a logical structure to be built by the recursion module rather than connecting them directly by unification. The translation from recursion to iteration effected by a recursion module is realized in a deductive plan as a substructure that may be repeated an indefinite number of times. The actual number of times needed for proof realization is determined when the plan is subjected to verification and to instantiation through data base search. These processes operate by successively increasing the number of repetitions of the substructure until some heuristically determined upper limit is reached (for example, the plausible length of a transitivity chain) that will be an automatically determined, well defined stop condition.

Indirect recursion across several premises can be handled with the same kinds of mechanisms, but implementation of this approach awaits enhancement of DADM to enable it to plan with macro-premises, i.e., deductive-plan building blocks incorporating several different premises, as well as with single premises.

Partially Specified Information

An argument need not be specified if its value does not contribute to what is being asserted or requested. In DADM a "*" is employed for missing "don't care" arguments in premises and queries. Each "*" in a premise functions as a variable existentially bound at minimum scope; correspondingly a "*" in a query acts as a variable of which there are no other occurrences in the query and which is existentially bound at maximum scope. Interpreted this way the "*" blocks inappropriate unifications, but allows desired ones. For example, a "*" in a premise assumption always unifies with a "*", a particular variable, or a constant in a query assumption, but a "*" in a premise goal does not unify with a constant in a query goal. Note that this is indeed what should happen, if logical soundness is to be maintained.

We have found this approach to the handling of missing arguments of great usefulness. A logical system which does not require full specification of arguments is unusual, but our interpretation of missing arguments allows the user to leave arguments out when they are irrelevant to his purposes — and yet not forego logical correctness. This corresponds to the use of optional cases in natural language and allows the same word to stand for different relations, related in meaning but of different dimensionality.

Semantic Advice

The system now accepts advice on the use or avoidance of particular premises or predicates for application at four different levels of selectivity. Advised premises and predicates are placed on alert lists that are used in two ways. During the chain construction process, the Pathfinder considers several possible predicate occurrences in its search for dependency links and unification arcs. Those occurrences that represent instances of advised predicates or that occur within advised premises are given preferential status in chain generation. In addition, completed chains are examined and only those chains passing advice tests are passed on to the Planner. Advice is thus used both for pruning during chain generation and for filtering completed chains. Premises and predicates may be advised during the entry of a query, to apply just to inference planning done for that query, or they may be permanently advised by the specification of advice rules.

Advice rules have the form:

condition ⇒ recommendation

where the condition part specifies groupings of predicates that must appear as assumptions or goals of problems to which the recommendation part is to apply.

With advice the user or data base administrator can, for example, direct the system to use a particular proof strategy by entering and advising use of a temporary premise such as:

( ) IMP(OR P Q)

for a proof-by-cases strategy. The four different advice selectivity levels are as follows:

(1) Use advice on top-level problems, selecting only chains that contain at least one advised premise or predicate.

(2) Same as (1) but apply to subproblems as well.

(3) Use advice on top-level problems, selecting chains that contain only advised premises or predicates.

(4) Same as (3) but apply to subproblems as well.

On first glance (3) and (4) may appear as too restrictive, but note that, if a set of premises or predicates sufficient to achieve a derivation has been advised, then operating at levels (3) or (4) serves to limit deductive processing just to that set. Among other things, this allows a user to test whether a particular set is sufficient for some desired derivation.

SUMMARY

The DADM prototype is being used to explore the utility of adding deductive inference mechanisms and an intensional data base to conventional data management systems. The intensional data base consists of general rules (premises), from which information is automatically abstracted and stored in connection-graph, variable-substitution and concept-graph structures. To control and guide the system's use of these structures, the user may enter second-order rules (advice rules).

The deductive mechanisms are built around an interactive pathfinding and inference-plan generation procedure. Forward, backward and bidirectional chaining are utilized. The system can build partial plans, answers, and evidence chains when complete information is not available. Structure sharing is used to eliminate duplicate subproblems, and the project is currently involved in increasing the intelligence with which the system is able to use recursive premises effectively.

ACKNOWLEDGEMENTS

The research reported here has been supported by the Advanced Research Projects Agency of the Department of Defense and monitored by the Office of Naval Research under Contract N00014-76-C-0885. Darrel Van Buer has played a central and expert role in the conversion to INTERLISP, implementation of the transitive closure algorithms, and maintenance of DADM code. Philip Klahr was a major contributor to earlier versions of the DADM system. John Olney has provided many useful insights concerning methods and representations useful for solution of the recursive-premise problem.

REFERENCES

1. Chang, C. L. [1978] "Deduce 2: Further Investigation of Deduction in Relational Data Bases", In *Logic and Data Bases* (H. Gallaire and J. Minker, Eds.), Plenum Press, 1978, 201-236.

2. Chang, C. L. [1981] "On Evaluation of Queries Containing Derived Relations in a Relational Data Base", (this volume).

3. Elliott, R. W. [1965] "A Model for a Fact Retrieval System", *TNN-42*, Computation Center, University of Texas, Austin, 1965.

4. Grant, J. and Minker, J. [1981] "Optimization in a Deductive Relational System", (this volume).

5. Kellogg, C., P. Klahr, and L. Travis [1978] "Deductive Planning and Pathfinding for Relational Data Bases". In *Logic and Data Bases* (H. Gallaire and J. Minker, Eds.), Plenum Press, 1978, 179-200.

6. Klahr, P. [1978] "Planning Techniques for Rule Selection in Deductive Question-Answering", In *Pattern-Directed Inference Systems* (D. Waterman and F. Hayes-Roth, Eds.), Academic Press, 1978, 223-239.

7. Minker, J. [1978] "An Experimental Relational Data Base System Based on Logic", In *Logic and Data Bases* (H. Gallaire and J. Minker, Eds.), Plenum Press, 1978, 107-147.

8. Reiter, R. [1978] "Deductive Question-Answering in Relational Data Bases", in *Logic and Data Bases* (H. Gallaire and J. Minker, Eds.), Plenum Press, 1978, 149-177.

9. Sickel, S. [1976] "A Search Technique for Clause Interconnectivity Graphs", *IEEE Trans. Computers C-25*, 8 (August 1976), 823-835.

10. Stonebraker, M. et al. [1976] "The Design and Implementation of INGRES", *ACM Trans. on Data Base Systems 1*, 3 (September 1976), 189-222.

11. Warshall, S. [1962] A Theorem on Boolean Matrices, *JACM 9* (January 1962), 11-12.

12. Zadeh, L. A. [1965] Fuzzy Sets, *Information and Control 8*, (1965), 338-353.

INFORMATIVE CAPABILITIES FOR USERS

A FORMAL APPROACH TO NULL VALUES IN DATABASE RELATIONS

Joachim Biskup

Technische Hochschule Aachen

Aachen, Germany

ABSTRACT

We study the problem of null values. By this we mean that an attribute is applicable but its value at present is unknown and also that an attribute is applicable but its value is arbitrary. We adopt the view that tuples denote statements of predicate logic about database relations. Then, a null value of the first kind, respectively second kind, corresponds to an existentially quantified variable, respectively universally quantified variable. For instance if r is a database relation without null values and $\mathcal{X}$ is a range declaration for r then the tuple $(a,\forall,b,\exists) \in R$ is intended to mean "there exists an $x \in \mathcal{X}$ such that for all $y \in \mathcal{X}$: $(a,y,b,x) \in r$". We extend basic operations of the well-known relational algebra to relations with null values. Using formal notions of correctness and completeness (adapted from predicate logic) we show that our extensions are meaningful and natural. Furthermore we reexamine the generalized join within our framework. Finally we investigate the algebraic structure of the class of relations with null values under a partial ordering which can be interpreted as a kind of logical implication.

INTRODUCTION

A missing value — or a null value — in a database relation can occur in many different situations. In ANSI [1975], p. IV-28/29, there is a list of 13 "manifestations of null" in stored database relations (the 14th manifestation results from processing nulls). Often, a much simpler classification is given (e.g. Language Structure Group [1962] or Codd [1975,1979]): a missing value means:

1. attribute (property) is inapplicable
(ANSI [1975]: manifestations 1, 2), or
2. attribute is applicable but its value at present is unknown
(ANSI [1975]: manifestations 3-13).

We believe that, at least from a theoretical point of view, one further meaning should be investigated, namely:

3. attribute is applicable but its value is arbitrary.

In the following we shall discuss typical situations for these three types of missing values.

1. *The explicitly defined meaning of database relations does not reflect all relevant aspects of reality.* For instance consider relation r_1 defined by

$(e,t) \in r_1 :\Leftrightarrow$ e is (the name of an) employee, and
t is his telephone number.

If an employee does not possess a telephone connection we either cannot store his name or we must use some "null value" in order to indicate this fact. However the latter means more precisely that we agree to use a new value, say Λ, and to define a new relation r_2 by

$(e,t) \in r_2 :\Leftrightarrow$ e is (the name of an) employee, and
(either e has a telephone connection and
t is his telephone number, or e does not
have a telephone connection and $t = \Lambda$).

Sometimes special values like Λ are called attribute-dependent null values. In this paper we do *not* adopt this view. On the contrary we consider Λ as a regular value. And, in general, we require that all relations are to be defined in such a way that all events of reality (which are of interest) can be expressed by means of regular values. In particular we should use relation r_2 instead of relation r_1. In practice, it may appear to be rather hard always to achieve this requirement. However, we can use the following simple rule: if we need a special value for an unforeseen event then we just *define* this value to be regular. The reader is referred to Grant [1977] for a different view of our example.

2. *The actual value of a tuple component corresponding to some attribute* A *is unknown, respectively not available.* For example, because we have forgotten to ask for it, or it has been lost of destroyed in the course of data processing, respectively, because of security constraints, the actual value is unknown. Then, by the requirement above, we definitely know that there exists a value (from a value set declared for the attribute A). Thus we can

make an existential statement. For instance assume that for an employee e we neither know whether he has a telephone connection nor his telephone number. Then we can state: "there exists an x such that $(e,x) \in r_2$". Using the special symbol $\exists$ we abbreviate this statement by "$(e,\exists) \in R_2$".

3. *The value of a tuple component corresponding to some attribute is arbitrary.* For instance define a relation r by

$(t,s,c) \in r$: t is a toy (in stock)
s is its size, and
c is its color.

Suppose we want to store the fact that marbles of size 2 are available *in all colors*. In particular we wish to ensure that we retrieve the tuple (marble, 2) if we ask for all toys having a certain color, say green. One way to achieve our goal is to generate a long list of tuples, namely for each color c the tuple (marble,2,c).

However, there are two obvious difficulties. First, we must explicitly know all possible colors, and second, we would waste space in storing nearly identical tuples which differ only in an attribute for which we are allowed to choose essentially arbitrarily any value.

We propose an alternate solution, namely to store a statement of the form "for all c: $(\text{marble},2,c) \in r$". Using the special symbol $\forall$ we abbreviate this statement by "$(\text{marble},2,\forall) \in R$".

There is another situation where the value of some tuple component can be chosen arbitrarily. Suppose that we have stored a relation r on attributes {A,B} and a relation s on attributes {B,C}. Consider the following query:

"get all tuples (a,b,c) such that
$(a,b) \in r$ *or* $(b,c) \in s$".

(This query is the *disjunctive* counterpart to the conjunctive query which is obtained by substituting "and" for "or" and which can be answered by computing the natural join of r and s.)

If (a_0,b_0) is an element of r then for any element c_0 (from a value set declared for the attribute C) we must put the tuple (a_0,b_0,c_0) into the answer relation t. Once again we are faced with the two difficulties mentioned above: we must know all possible values for C and we must waste space for redundant information. Hence, we propose to replace the listing of all tuples of the form (a_0,b_0,c) by a statement of the form "for all c:

$(a_0,b_0,c) \in t$", which can be abbreviated by "$(a_0,b_0,\forall) \in T$".

As intended by the disjunctive query the special symbol $\forall$ indicates that we *do not care* (in the sense of switching theory) about the value of attribute C: if we further process the tuple $(a\ ,b\ ,\forall)$ then we are allowed to substitute any regular value for $\forall$.

Let us summarize the discussion of the three types of missing values. We introduced $\exists$ and $\forall$ as special symbols which may occur in tuples. We call $\exists$ and $\forall$ *null values*. A generalized tuple, each component of which is either a regular value or a null value, is considered as a *statement*. Then a conventional database relation (without null values) r is described by a set R of such statements as follows.

Let $\mu = (a_1,\ldots,a_n) \in R$, and $I := \{i_1,\ldots,i_k\} := \{i \mid a_i = \exists\}$, and $J := \{j_1,\ldots,j_l\} := \{j \mid a_j = \forall\}$, then μ asserts the following: "there exist $x_{i_1},\ldots,x_{i_k}$ such that for all $y_{j_1},\ldots,y_{j_l}$:

$$(b_1,\ldots,b_n) \in r\text{"}, \quad \text{where } b_i := \begin{cases} x_i & \text{if } i \in I, \\ y_i & \text{if } i \in J, \\ a_i, & \text{otherwise.} \end{cases}$$

Note the rule of quantifier alternation: all existential quantifiers precede all universal quantifiers. If μ has no null values then μ asserts, as usual, that $\mu = (a_1,\ldots,a_n) \in r$.

Hence, we adopt the view that a conventional relation is an interpretation or model (in the sense of formal logic) of a set of statements. For a discussion of this view the reader is referred to Gallaire and Minker [1978], see also Lipski [1979]. In particular our treatment of null values will be in the spirit of some brief remarks made by Nicolas and Gallaire [1978] on this topic.

In order to make precise our idea that (generalized) tuples denote statements of the form given above, we have to modify the notion of a database relation. For if we want to interpret quantified variables we need some definition of ranges for the variables (in formal logic: a universe).

We propose that a 'database relation' is given by a conventional relation r (without null values) together with a *range declaration* X, where X is a set of regular values such that all values occurring in r are elements of X. In practice, we obviously should use separate declarations for each attribute, however, for simplicity we assume that all attributes have the same declaration without loss of generality. Of course, range declarations are not new; in database literature they are well-known as *domains*, see Date [1977] or Ullman [1980] (in this paper we do not use this term in order to avoid confusion with another concept). However, formerly they were used mainly to support the database system whereas we need them at a theoretical level in order to define precisely the meaning of statements and operations on statements.

Next we have to decide which kind of range $\mathcal{X}$ we want to allow. Since we are dealing with universal quantifiers and, on the other hand, database relations are finite objects, we require that $\mathcal{X}$ is always a *finite* set. However, our investigations will show that we should *not* take a *fixed* finite set. Roughly speaking, the range declaration strictly increases the information given to us by the set of tuples. The reader can find a similar observation on the combinatorial consequences of fixed finite ranges in a recent paper on relational normal forms by Fagin [1979]. Thus, we assume that we have an *infinite* set $\mathcal{V}$ of regular values and each range declaration has to be a *finite subset of* $\mathcal{V}$.

Intuitively null values represent some kind of "ignorance". For the null value $\exists$ this point should be clear. For the null value $\forall$ the ignorance is just that we do not specify a range. Hence in processing sets of statements (generalized tuples with occurrences of $\exists$ and $\forall$) we try to infer information without using the actual range. This means in particular that our results have to be correct with respect to all possible ranges.

BASIC CONCEPTS

Tuples, Relations and Value-Relations

Let $\mathcal{A}$ be a set of *attributes*. $\mathcal{A}$ may be finite or infinite. Throughout the paper A, B, C, D, and E will denote attributes and U, V, W, X, Y, and Z will denote *finite* sets of attributes. In practice each attribute is associated with some set of values which can be declared by the user. For simplicity of notation however we assume that all atrributes are associated with the *same* set of *regular values* $\mathcal{V}$. We suppose that $\mathcal{V}$ is (countably) infinite. Let $\exists$ and $\forall$ be two new symbols which we call *null values*. $\mathcal{V}^* := \mathcal{V} \cup \{\exists,\forall\}$ is the *set of values*.

A (generalized) *tuple* is a finite sequence of values (regular or null) where the positions are identified by attributes. In order to have a precise notation we shall use the functional representation of tuples as follows (cf. Ullman [1980]). Let $(x_1,\ldots,x_n)$ be a tuple with $x_i \in \mathcal{V}^*$ and assume that position i is identified by attribute $A_i \in \mathcal{A}$ where $A_i \neq A_j$ for $i \neq j$. Then we denote this tuple by the function μ: $\{A_1,\ldots,A_n\} \rightarrow \mathcal{V}^*$ that maps attribute A_i on value x. For example, the tuple $(\forall, a, \exists, \forall, b)$, where we assume that positions are identified by attributes A,B,C,D,E in this order, is denoted by the function μ: $\{A,B,C,D,E\} \rightarrow \mathcal{V}^*$ with $\mu(A) = \mu(D) = \forall$, $\mu(B) = a$, $\mu(C) = \exists$, $\mu(E) = b$. Sometimes we also write $\mu = \left\{ \binom{A}{\forall}, \binom{B}{a}, \binom{C}{\exists}, \binom{D}{\forall}, \binom{E}{b} \right\}$. We shall use small Greek letters for tuples.

If μ: $X \rightarrow \mathcal{V}^*$ is a tuple then dom μ := X is called the *domain* of μ, and we partition the domain according to the types of associated values as follows:

$$d\mathcal{V}\mu \;:= \{A \mid A \in X \text{ and } \mu(A) \in \mathcal{V}\},$$

$$d\exists\mu \;:= \{A \mid A \in X \text{ and } \mu(A) = \exists\},$$

$$d\forall\mu \;:= \{A \mid A \in X \text{ and } \mu(A) = \forall\}.$$

Furthermore, let $\mathcal{V}$ range $\mu := \mathcal{V} \cap \{\mu(A) \mid A \in X\}$ be the set of all regular values occurring in the tuple μ.

In our example above we have

$$\text{dom } \mu = \{A,B,C,D,E\},\quad d\mathcal{V}\mu = \{B,E\},\quad d\exists\mu = \{C\},\quad d\forall\mu = \{A,D\},$$

and

$$\mathcal{V} \text{ range } \mu = \{a,b\}.$$

There is exactly one tuple μ with dom $\mu = \emptyset$, namely just $\mu = \emptyset$. The set of all tuples is denoted by $\mathcal{T}$.

A finite set of tuples each of which has the *same* domain X is called a (generalized) *relation*. Relations (which possibly contain null values) are denoted by R, S, and T, but whenever we want to emphasize that we are concerned with a relation *without* null values we use the letters r, s, and t.

The *domain* of a relation R is defined by

$$\text{dom } R := \begin{cases} \emptyset & \text{if } R = \emptyset\,, \\ X & \text{if } R \neq \emptyset \text{ and all tuples of R have domain X.} \end{cases}$$

We say that R is a *relation on* dom R. The *$\mathcal{V}$-range* of R is defined by $\mathcal{V}$ range R := $\bigcup_{\xi \in R} \mathcal{V}$ range ξ. We can think of the domain of R as the heading of columns in the tabular representation of R. For instance, let

$$R = \{((\begin{smallmatrix}\text{EMPLOYEE}\\ \text{smith}\end{smallmatrix}), (\begin{smallmatrix}\text{PHONE}\\ 111\end{smallmatrix})),$$
$$((\begin{smallmatrix}\text{EMPLOYEE}\\ \text{meyer}\end{smallmatrix}), (\begin{smallmatrix}\text{PHONE}\\ 112\end{smallmatrix})),$$
$$((\begin{smallmatrix}\text{EMPLOYEE}\\ \text{young}\end{smallmatrix}), (\begin{smallmatrix}\text{PHONE}\\ \exists\end{smallmatrix}))\},$$

then dom $R = \{\text{EMPLOYEE}, \text{PHONE}\}$,
$\mathcal{V}$ range $R = \{\text{smith}, \text{meyer}, \text{young}, 111, 112\}$,
and the tabular representation of R looks as follows:

EMPLOYEE	PHONE
smith	111
meyer	112
young	∃

There are exactly two relations on $\emptyset$, namely $\emptyset$ and $\{\emptyset\} = \{\mu \mid \mu: \emptyset \to \mathcal{V}^*\}$. The set of all relations is denoted by $\mathcal{R}$.

It has been suggested (see Gallaire and Minker [1978], in particular Gallaire, Minker and Nicolas [1978] and Nicolas and Gallaire [1978]) that a tuple μ that has regular values be considered as a quantifier free ground statement in predicate logic. We want to extend this interpretation to arbitrary generalized tuples. Assume that we have a usual database relation r such that all values occurring in r are regular values. If $R \in \mathcal{R}$ with dom R = dom r then, for instance,

(1) $\mu = ((\begin{smallmatrix}A\\ \forall\end{smallmatrix}), (\begin{smallmatrix}B\\ a\end{smallmatrix}), (\begin{smallmatrix}C\\ \exists\end{smallmatrix}), (\begin{smallmatrix}D\\ \forall\end{smallmatrix}), (\begin{smallmatrix}E\\ b\end{smallmatrix})) \in R$

is intended to assert the following statement:

(2) "there exists x_3 such that for all x_1, for all x_4:
$(x_1, a, x_3, x_4, b) \in r$".

Note the rule of quantifier alternation: all existential quantifiers precede all universal quantifiers.

Up to now statement (2) is still ambiguous since we have not specified over which sets the variables x_3, x_1, and x_4 should range. As we require that a usual database relation has only regular values these sets should be subsets of $\mathcal{V}$. However, since database relations are finite sets, we can take only *finite* subsets of $\mathcal{V}$. Therefore we shall associate such a finite subset of $\mathcal{V}$ as a *range declaration* with every relation r. More precisely we call $\langle r,\mathcal{X}\rangle$ a *value-relation*, abbreviated v-relation, if $\mathcal{X}$ is a nonempty finite set of regular values and r is a relation (without null values) such that all values appearing in r are elements of $\mathcal{X}$. We say that $\langle r,\mathcal{X}\rangle$ is a v-relation *on* dom r.

For example, consider the relation

r =

EMPLOYEE	PHONE
smith	111
meyer	112
young	119

As a range declaration we may choose $\mathcal{X} = \mathcal{X}_{EMP} \cup \mathcal{X}_{PH}$, where $\mathcal{X}_{EMP}$ is the set of all words over the usual alphabet with length at most 20, and $\mathcal{X}_{PH}$ is the set of all words over the set of decimal digits of length at most 8. Then $\langle r,\mathcal{X}\rangle$ is a v-relation on {EMPLOYEE,PHONE}. Now we can interpret (1) as a statement with respect to a value-relation $\langle r,\mathcal{X}\rangle$ as follows:

(3) "there exists $x_3 \in \mathcal{X}$ such that for all $x_1 \in \mathcal{X}$, $x_4 \in \mathcal{X}$: $(x_1,a,x_3,x_4,b) \in r$"

Using the notions of predicate logic (cf. for instance Chang and Lee [1978] or Yasuhara [1971]) this means that the *relational system* or *structure* $\langle r,\mathcal{X}\rangle$ (in logic usually denoted by $\langle \mathcal{X},r\rangle$) is a *model* of the *formula*

(4) $F_\mu := (\exists x_3)\ (\forall x_1)\ (\forall x_4)\ R(x_1,a,x_3,x_4,b)$,

or stated otherwise, the formula (4) is *true* in $\langle r,\mathcal{X}\rangle$.
We shall adopt the classical definition of truth within predicate logic as explained below.

Let, for instance R :=

A	B	C
$\exists$	a_2	a_3
a_1	$\exists$	$\forall$
a_2	a_1	a_2

be a relation on {A,B,C}.

$\mathcal{X} := \{a_1,a_2,a_3,a_4\} \subset \mathcal{V}$ a range declaration, and r := a relation on {A,B,C} without null values.

A	B	C
a_2	a_2	a_3
a_3	a_2	a_3
a_1	a_1	a_1
a_1	a_1	a_2
a_1	a_1	a_3
a_1	a_1	a_4
a_2	a_1	a_2

We say that the tuple $(\exists, a_2, a_3) \in R$ *is true* in the v-relation $\langle r, X \rangle$, because we can find a regular value from the range declaration X, namely a_2 or a_3, such that if we substitute this value for the null value $\exists$ then the resulting tuple is an element of the relation r. Analogously, the tuple $(a_1, \exists, \forall)$ is true in $\langle r, X \rangle$ because if we substitute $a_1 \in X$ for $\exists$ then *all* tuples that can be obtained by replacing the null value $\forall$ by any element from X are elements of r. The tuple $(a_2, a_1, a_2) \in R$ is true in $\langle r, X \rangle$ because this tuple itself is an element of r. Furthermore we say that relation R is true in the v-relation $\langle r, X \rangle$ because all tuples of R are true in $\langle r, X \rangle$. Given a tuple μ and a v-relation $\langle r, X \rangle$ we shall describe an 'appropriate' substitution of the occurrences of $\exists$ in μ by a function (or tuple) η that is defined on $d\exists\mu$ (the set of attributes for which we must find the right values) and that has values in X. By 'appropriate' we mean that the substitution shows that μ is true in $\langle r, X \rangle$. For example the functional representation of the tuple $(a_1, \exists, \forall)$ is

$$\mu: \{A,B,C\} \to V^* \quad \text{with} \quad \mu(A) = a_1, \quad \mu(B) = \exists, \quad \mu(C) = \forall.$$

We have $d\exists\mu = \{B\}$ and $d\forall\mu = \{C\}$.
The tuple $\eta: \{B\} \to \{a_1, a_2, a_3, a_4\}$ defined by $\eta(B) := a_1$ is an appropriate substitution. This substitution shows that μ is true in $\langle r, X \rangle$ because all tuples α that are obtained from μ by replacing $\exists$ (the value of attribute B) by $\eta(B) = a_1$ and $\forall$ (the value of attribute C) by any value from X are elements of r.
More precisely we have the following definitions.

<u>Definition 1</u>

Let $\mu: X \to V^*$ be a tuple and $\langle r, X \rangle$ be a v-relation on X.

1. $\eta \in T$ *is* $\langle r, X \rangle$*-substitution for* μ: iff

$\eta: d\exists\mu \to \mathcal{X}$ and

$\{\alpha \mid \alpha: X \to \mathcal{X} \wedge (\forall A \in d\mathcal{V}\mu)[\alpha(A) = \mu(A)]$

$\wedge (\forall A \in d\exists\mu)[\alpha(A) = \eta(A)]\} \subset r.$

2. μ *is true in* $<r,\mathcal{X}>$, μ true $<r,\mathcal{X}>$, : iff

there exists a $<r,\mathcal{X}>$-substitution η for μ.

<u>Definition 2</u>

Let R be a relation and $<r,\mathcal{X}>$ be a v-relation.

R *is true in* $<r,\mathcal{X}>$, R true $<r,\mathcal{X}>$, : iff

for all $\mu \in R$: μ true $<r,\mathcal{X}>$.

The notions introduced by Definitions 1 and 2 are ambiguous for the case $\mu = \emptyset$, respectively $R = \emptyset$:

for $\emptyset =: \mu \in \mathcal{T}$ we have by Definition 1:

(5) μ true $<r,\mathcal{X}> \Leftrightarrow r = \{\emptyset\}$;

for $\emptyset =: R \in \mathcal{R}$ we have by Definition 2:

(6) R true $<r,\mathcal{X}>$ for all v-relations $<r,\mathcal{X}>$.

Furthermore we note that for all $R \in \mathcal{R}$:

(7) for all v-relations $<r,\mathcal{X}>$: R true $<r,\mathcal{X}> \Rightarrow \mathcal{V}$ range $R \subset \mathcal{X}$;

there exists a v-relation $<r,\mathcal{X}>$ such that R true $<r,\mathcal{X}>$

(8) and $\begin{cases} \mathcal{V} \text{ range } R = \mathcal{X} & \text{if } \mathcal{V} \text{ range } R \neq \emptyset \\ \text{card } \mathcal{X} = 1 & \text{if } \mathcal{V} \text{ range } R = \emptyset \end{cases}$.

We have seen that we can *represent* statements of the form $(\exists x)(\forall y)\ R\ (x,y,b)$ where each variable occurs exactly once in the list (x,y,b) as easily as quantifier free ground statements of the form $R(b)$, namely just by tuples, where quantified variables are denoted by the null values $\exists$ and $\forall$. In this chapter we shall investigate the question whether and how we can *manipulate* statements of the first form as easily as statements of the second form. In the following section we introduce a formalism for comparing tuples (respectively relations). Then, in the section Partial Orderings and Logical Implication, this formalism will be interpreted as some kind of logical implication.

Partial Orderings on V^*, T, and R

We define the following 'relation' [1]$\preccurlyeq$ on V^* which obviously is a *partial ordering*, that means is reflexive, transitive, and antisymmetric:

$$a \preccurlyeq b \ :\text{iff} \quad a = \exists \quad \text{or} \quad b = \forall \quad \text{or} \quad a = b \ .$$

Thus extends the equality 'relation' on V, the set of *regular* values, by considering $\forall$ as top element and $\exists$ as bottom element:

V :

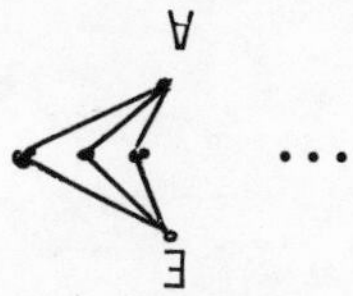

Some of the well-known operations on database relations require some "matching procedures" which test for equality of regular values (e.g. join, selection, difference). We shall see in the section OPERATIONS ON RELATIONS that $\preccurlyeq$ is the natural extension of = for these matching procedures. (Note that the intended meaning of $\forall$ is essentially different from the use of *top* in Vassiliou [1979] though we have the same partial ordering.)

The 'relation' $\preccurlyeq$ on V^* canonically induces a 'relation' $\preccurlyeq$ on the set τ of all (generalized) tuples:

$$\mu \preccurlyeq \nu \ :\text{iff} \quad \begin{array}{ll} 1. & \text{dom}\ \mu \subset \text{dom}\ \nu \quad \text{and} \\ 2. & \mu(A) \preccurlyeq \nu(A) \quad \text{for all} \quad A \in \text{dom}\ \mu . \end{array}$$

For example, we have

$$(\binom{\text{EMPLOYEE}}{\text{young}}, \binom{\text{PHONE}}{\exists}) \preccurlyeq (\binom{\text{EMPLOYEE}}{\text{young}}, \binom{\text{PHONE}}{113}, \binom{\text{ADDRESS}}{\text{boston}}) .$$

<u>Theorem 1</u>

1. $\preccurlyeq$ is a partial ordering on T.
2. $\emptyset \preccurlyeq \mu$ for all $\mu \in T$.
3. If A is finite, say $A = \{A_1, \ldots, A_n\}$, then

$$\mu \preccurlyeq (\binom{A_1}{\forall}, \ldots, \binom{A_n}{\forall}) \quad \text{for all } \mu \in T \ .$$

Proof: Direct consequences of the definitions. □

[1] Here 'relation' has the usual mathematical meaning, namely to be a subset of the Cartesian product $V^* \times V^*$.

Finally, we define a 'relation' $\precsim$ on the set $\mathcal{R}$ of all (generalized) relations:

$$R \precsim S \text{ : iff for all } \mu \in R \text{ there exists } \nu \in S \text{ such that } \mu \precsim \nu.$$

Theorem 2

1. $\precsim$ is reflexive and transitive on $\mathcal{R}$.
2. $\precsim$ is *not* antisymmetric on $\mathcal{R}$.
3. $\emptyset \precsim R$ for all $R \in \mathcal{R}$.
4. $\{\emptyset\} \precsim R$ for all $R \in \mathcal{R}$ such that $R \neq \emptyset$.
5. If $\mathcal{A}$ is finite, say $\mathcal{A} = \{A_1,\ldots,A_n\}$, then

$$R \precsim \{((\begin{smallmatrix} A_1 \\ \forall \end{smallmatrix}),\ldots,(\begin{smallmatrix} A_n \\ \forall \end{smallmatrix}))\} \quad \text{for all} \quad R \in \mathcal{R}.$$

Proof: Direct consequences of the definitions and of Theorem 1. □

The 'relation' $\precsim$ canonically induces an equivalence relation $\sim$ on $\mathcal{R}$, namely $R \sim S$: iff $R \precsim S$ and $S \precsim R$. Then we define

$$[R] := \{S \mid S \sim R\} \quad \text{for all} \quad R \in \mathcal{R},$$

$$[\mathcal{R}] := \mathcal{R}/\sim \; = \{[R] \mid R \in \mathcal{R}\}$$

$$[R] \precsim [S] \text{ : iff } R \quad S .$$

Theorem 3

The 'relation' $\precsim$ is a partial ordering on $[\mathcal{R}]$.

Proof: Immediate consequence of the definitions. □

Each equivalence class $\mathcal{C} \in [\mathcal{R}]$ has a natural representative. Given any element R of the class $\mathcal{C}$ we can compute this representative by eliminating those tuples that are 'redundant' in R (with respect to the relation $\sim$). More precisely we define:

$$R^0 := \{\mu \mid \mu \in R \text{ and } (\forall \nu \in R)[\mu \precsim \nu \Rightarrow \mu = \nu]\}.$$

Theorem 4

For all $R,S \in \mathcal{R}$:

1. $R \sim R^0$.
2. $R \sim S \Leftrightarrow R^0 = S^0$.

Proof: Omitted for the sake of brevity. □

By Theorem 4 we can identify $[\mathcal{R}]$ with $\mathcal{R}^0 := \{R^0 \mid R \in \mathcal{R}\}$. In particular $\lesssim$ is a partial ordering on $\mathcal{R}^0$. In Section 2.4 we shall even prove that $\lesssim$ is a lattice on $[\mathcal{R}]$ respectively $\mathcal{R}^0$.

Partial Orderings and Logical Implication

For $R \in \mathcal{R}$, R true $<r,\mathcal{X}>$ means that the v-relation $<r,\mathcal{X}>$ is a model of the set of formulas $\mathcal{F}_R := \{\mathcal{F}_\mu \mid \mu \in R\}$ where $\mathcal{F}_\mu$ is the formula denoted by the tuple μ as indicated in the section Tuples, Relations and Value-Relations. Another formula $\mathcal{G}$ is said to be a *logical implication* of $\mathcal{F}_R$ if $<r,\mathcal{X}>$ is a model of $\mathcal{G}$ whenever $<r,\mathcal{X}>$ is a model of $\mathcal{F}_R$ and all constants (regular values) occurring in $\mathcal{G}$ are elements of $\mathcal{X}$. In this section we are interested in those logical implications which can be denoted by tuples. Thus we shall consider those tuples $\tau \in \mathcal{T}$ such that for all v-relations $<r,\mathcal{X}>$ with $\mathcal{V}$ range $\tau \subset \mathcal{X}$:

$$R \text{ true } <r,\mathcal{X}> \Rightarrow \tau \text{ true } <r,\mathcal{X}> \quad .$$

More generally we shall also investigate logical implications with respect to projections. In order to define the operation of projection we introduce the following notion.

For a tuple $\mu: X \to \mathcal{V}^*$ and $Y \subset \mathcal{A}$, $\mu \nearrow Y$ is the subtuple of μ that has only those components that are named in Y. More precisely,

if $\quad \text{dom } \mu \cap Y = \emptyset$ then $\mu \nearrow Y := \emptyset$,

otherwise $\quad \mu \nearrow Y(A) := \mu(A)$ for all $A \in \text{dom } \mu \cap Y$.

For example, $(\binom{A}{\forall}, \binom{B}{a}, \binom{C}{\exists}, \binom{D}{\forall}, \binom{E}{b}) \nearrow \{A,C,E\} = (\binom{A}{\forall}, \binom{C}{\exists}, \binom{E}{b})$.

<u>Definition 3</u>

Let $Y \subset \mathcal{A}$ and $<r,\mathcal{X}>$ be a v-relation.

$\pi_Y(<r,\mathcal{X}>) := <\{\mu \nearrow Y \mid \mu \in r\},\mathcal{X}>$ is called the *Y-projection* of $<r,\mathcal{X}>$.

Thus we take the usual projection of the relation r and maintain the range declaration $\mathcal{X}$.

We consider three special cases:

(a) $\pi_Y(<\emptyset,\mathcal{X}>) = <\emptyset,\mathcal{X}>$;

(b) for $r \neq \emptyset$ and dom $r \cap Y = \emptyset$:

$\pi_Y(<r,\mathcal{X}>) = <\{\mu \nearrow Y \mid \mu \in r\},\mathcal{X}> = <\{\emptyset\},\mathcal{X}>$;

(c) the identity on v-relations can be represented as $\text{id}(<r,\mathcal{X}>) := <r,\mathcal{X}> = \pi_{\text{dom } r}(<r,\mathcal{X}>)$.

We have introduced the partial orderings $\lesssim$ by purely *syntactic* means. The following theorem will provide the precise *semantic* meaning of these partial orderings. The theorem essentially states that $\tau \lesssim \mu$ if and only if F_τ is a logical implication of F_μ, and that any logical implication F_τ of a *set* of formulas F_R, where $R \in \mathcal{R}$, is already a logical implication of a *single* formula F_μ with $\mu \in R$. The second assertion of the theorem shows that the class of formulas that can be denoted by tuples is very easily manageable. For, in order to make inferences from a given set F_R, where $R \in \mathcal{R}$, we never need to consider combinations of formulas of F_R as we generally must do in predicate logic (with the disastrous effect of the so-called 'combinatorial explosion').

Theorem 5

1. If $\tau \lesssim \mu$ and μ true $\langle r,X\rangle$ and V range $\tau \subset X$ then τ true $\pi_{\mathrm{dom}\ \tau}(\langle r,X\rangle)$.
2. Let Y be a finite set of regular values such that V range $\tau \subset Y$. If for all v-relations $\langle r,X\rangle$ with $Y \subset X$ R true $\langle r,X\rangle$ implies τ true $\pi_{\mathrm{dom}\ \tau}(\langle r,X\rangle)$ then there exists $\mu \in R$ such that $\tau \lesssim \mu$.

Proof:

1. Suppose $\tau \lesssim \mu$, μ true $\langle r,X\rangle$, and V range $\tau \subset X$. By Definition 1 there exists a $\langle r,X\rangle$-substitution η for μ. Then define $\lambda\colon d\exists\tau \to X$ by

$$\lambda(A) := \begin{cases} \eta(A) & \text{if } A \in d\exists\tau \cap d\exists\mu, \\ \mu(A) & \text{if } A \in d\exists\tau \cap dV\mu, \\ a & \text{if } A \in d\exists\tau \cap d\forall\mu, \end{cases}$$

where a is any element of X.
Then one can verify that λ is a $\pi_{\mathrm{dom}\ \tau}(\langle r,X\rangle)$-substitution for τ.

2. (Proof by contraposition): Suppose that

$$\text{for all } \mu \in R : \neg(\tau \lesssim \mu) \tag{1}$$

We shall construct a v-relation $\langle r,X\rangle$ with $Y \subset X$ such that
(i) R is true in $\langle r,X\rangle$, and
(ii) τ is not true in $\pi_{\mathrm{dom}\ \tau}(\langle r,X\rangle)$.

Define

$$X_0 := V \text{ range } R \cup Y .$$
$$X := X_0 \cup \{a,b\} \text{ where } a \neq b,\ \{a,b\} \subset V \setminus X_0 .$$

Note that V is supposed to be an infinite set and that X_0 is finite. Therefore we can always find a and b as desired.

$$r := \bigcup_{\xi\in R} r_\xi \quad \text{with}$$

$$r_\xi := \{\alpha \mid \alpha : \text{dom } R \to X \ \wedge (A \in dV\xi)[\alpha(A) = \xi(A)] \ \wedge (A \in d\exists\xi)[\alpha(A) = b]\}$$

Property (i) obviously holds from the definitions.

We prove property (ii) indirectly: assume that

τ is true in $\pi_{\text{dom }\tau}(\langle r,X\rangle)$.

Then there exists a $\pi_{\text{dom }\tau}(\langle r,X\rangle)$-substitution η for τ. Consider σ: dom $\tau \to X$ defined by

$$\sigma(A) := \begin{cases} \tau(A) \text{ if } A \in dV\tau , \\ \eta(A) \text{ if } A \in d\exists\tau , \\ a \quad \text{if } A \in d\forall\tau . \end{cases} \tag{2}$$

Then,

$$\sigma \in \pi_{\text{dom }\tau}(\langle r,X\rangle) = \pi_{\text{dom }\tau}(\bigcup_{\xi\in R} r_\xi, X\rangle) = \bigcup_{\xi\in R} \pi_{\text{dom }\tau}(\langle r_\xi,X\rangle)$$

Let $\xi \in R$ such that $\sigma \in \pi_{\text{dom }\tau}(\langle r_\xi,X\rangle)$. By definition of r_ξ this implies that

$$\begin{aligned} \sigma(A) &= \xi(A) \text{ if } A \in \text{dom } \tau \cap dV\xi , \\ \sigma(A) &= b \quad \text{if } A \in \text{dom } \tau \cap d\exists\xi . \end{aligned} \tag{3}$$

Since $(\tau \not\leq \xi)$ by supposition (1) and dom $\tau \subset$ dom ξ there exists an attribute $A \in$ dom τ such that $\neg(\tau(A) \not\leq \xi(A))$. According to the definition of $\leq$ on V^* we have to consider four cases for such an A. All cases will produce an obvious contradiction:

<u>Case 1</u>: $\tau(A) \in V$ and $\xi(A) \in V$ and $\tau(A) \neq \xi(A)$.

Then, by (2), the case assumption, and (3),

$$\sigma(A) = \tau(A) \neq \xi(A) = \sigma(A).$$

Case 2: $\tau(A) \in V$ and $\xi(A) = \exists$.

Then, by (2), the choice of b and (3),

$\sigma(A) = \tau(A) \neq b = \sigma(A)$.

Case 3: $\tau(A) = \forall$ and $\xi(A) \in V$.

Then, by (2), the choice of a, and (3),

$\sigma(A) = a \neq \xi(A) = \sigma(A)$.

Case 4: $\tau(A) = \forall$ and $\xi(A) = \exists$.

Then, by (2), the choice of a and b, and (3),

$\sigma(A) = a \neq b = \sigma(A)$.

Hence, our indirect assumption is false. That means that $\langle r,X\rangle$ has property (ii) as desired. □

Corollary 6

The following assertions are equivalent:

(a) $\tau \lesssim \mu$.

(b) For all v-relations $\langle r,X\rangle$ with V range $\tau \subset X$:
μ true $\langle r,X\rangle \Rightarrow \tau$ true $\pi_{\mathrm{dom}\ \tau}(\langle r,X\rangle)$.

Proof: (a) ⇒ (b) Follows from 1 of Theorem 5.
(b) ⇒ (a) Take $Y := V$ range τ and $R := \{\mu\}$ in 2 of Theorem 5.

Corollary 7

The following assertions are equivalent:

(a) $R \lesssim S$.

(b) For all v-relations $\langle r,X\rangle$ with V range $R \cup V$ range $S \subset X$:
S true $\langle r,X\rangle \Rightarrow R$ true $\langle r,X\rangle$.

Proof: (a) ⇒ (b): Follows from 1 of Theorem 5.
(b) ⇒ (a): Follows from 2 of Theorem 5.

We know that $R \sim R^0$. From Corollary 7 we see that the operation of computing the representative of a relation corresponds to the well-known operation of "removing duplicate rows" in a usual database relation. However, one should note that we possibly lose some *information about ranges* when using R^0 instead of R. For it may happen that V range $R^0 \subsetneq V$ range R. Consider for instance

$\mu := \binom{A}{\forall}$, $\nu := \binom{A}{a}$ where $a \in V$, and

$R := \{\mu,\nu\}$; then $R^0 = \{u\}$.

We end this section with a short discussion of our requirement that there are *infinitely* many regular values. This fact was used in the proof of 2 of Theorem 5 when we defined the v-relation $\langle r, \mathcal{X}\rangle$. The following two examples show that 2 of Theorem 5 is *not* valid if $\mathcal{V}$ is finite, respectively $\mathcal{X}$ is assumed to be a fixed finite set.

Example 1

Let $\mathcal{X} := \{a,b\}$. Define

$$\mu_1 := \left(\binom{A_1}{a}, \binom{A_2}{a} \right)$$

$$\mu_2 := \left(\binom{A_1}{a}, \binom{A_2}{b} \right)$$

$$\tau := \left(\binom{A_1}{a}, \binom{A_2}{\forall} \right),$$

and consider $R := \{\mu_1,\mu_2\}$. Then, having $\mathcal{X}$ fixed, for all r: R true $\langle r,\mathcal{X}\rangle \Rightarrow \tau$ true $\langle r,\mathcal{X}\rangle$. However, neither $\tau \precsim \mu_1$ nor $\tau \precsim \mu_2$ hold.

Example 2

Let $\mathcal{X} := \{a\}$, $\mu := (\binom{A_1}{a},\binom{A_2}{\exists})$, $\tau := (\binom{A_1}{a}, \binom{A_2}{a})$.

Then for all r: $\{\mu\}$ true $\langle r,\mathcal{X}\rangle \Rightarrow \tau$ true $\langle r,\mathcal{X}\rangle$. However, $\tau \precsim \mu$ does not hold.

In the section OPERATIONS ON RELATIONS we shall discuss the influence of a fixed finite set $\mathcal{X}$ on inferences with respect to the null value $\exists$.

The Partial Ordering $\precsim$ on $[\mathcal{R}]$ is a Distributive Lattice

Recall from the section Partial Orderings on $\mathcal{V}^*$, $\mathcal{T}$, and $\mathcal{R}$, that $[\mathcal{R}]$ is the set of equivalence classes on $\mathcal{R}$ with respect to $\sim$ and that $[\mathcal{R}]$ can be identified with $\mathcal{R}^0$. By Theorem 3, the 'relation' $\precsim$ is a partial ordering on $[\mathcal{R}]$ respectively $\mathcal{R}^0$. In order to show that the 'relation' $\precsim$ is even a lattice we have to show that any pair of elements has a least upper bound, $\precsim$-sup, and a greatest lower bound, $\precsim$-inf (cf. Hermes [1967]).

Definition 4

Let $R,S \in \mathcal{R}$.

1. $E_Z(R) := \{\mu \mid \mu\colon \text{dom } R \cup Z \to \mathcal{V}^* \wedge \mu \upharpoonright \text{dom } R \in R$
$\wedge\ (\forall A \in Z \setminus \text{dom } R)[\mu(A) = \exists]\}$
is called the *Z-expansion* of R.

2. $R + S := E_{\text{dom } R \cup \text{dom } S}(R) \cup E_{\text{dom } R \cup \text{dom } S}(S)$
is called the *outer union* of R and S.

3. $R \times S := \{\mu \mid \mu\colon \mathrm{dom}\, R \cap \mathrm{dom}\, S \to V^* \wedge (\exists \xi \in R)(\exists \zeta \in S)\ [$
$(\forall A \in \mathrm{dom}\, R \cap \mathrm{dom}\, S)[\mu(A) = \lesssim\text{-inf}\ (\xi(A), \zeta(A))]\}$

is called the *product* of R and S.

The *Z-expansion* enlarges the domain of a relation R by those attributes of Z which were not in dom R before. Each tuple is enlarged by assigning the null value $\exists$ to every new attribute $A \in Z \setminus \mathrm{dom}\, R$.

The *outer union* of R and S is obtained by first making R and S "union-compatible" by means of $\mathrm{dom}\, R \cup \mathrm{dom}\, S$ -expansions and then taking the usual (set theoretical) union. The name "outer union" has been proposed by Codd [1979].

Example

Let $R :=$

A	B
a_1	b_1
a_2	b_2

and $S :=$

B	C
b_3	c_3

. Then

$E_{\{A,B,C\}}(R) =$

A	B	C
a_1	b_1	$\exists$
a_2	b_2	$\exists$

, $E_{\{A,B,C\}}(S) =$

A	B	C
$\exists$	b_3	c_3

,

$R + S =$

A	B	C
a_1	b_1	$\exists$
a_2	b_2	$\exists$
$\exists$	b_3	c_3

, $R \times S =$

B
$\exists$

, where we assume that $b_1 \neq b_3$ and $b_2 \neq b_3$.

We note that Z-expansion, outer union, and product are compatible with the 'relation' $\sim$:

Theorem 8

For all R_1, R_2, S, Z:

1. $R_1 \sim R_2 \Rightarrow E_Z(R_1) \sim E_Z(R_2)$.
2. $R_1 \sim R_2 \Rightarrow R_1 + S \sim R_2 + S$.
3. $R_1 \sim R_2 \Rightarrow R_1 \times S \sim R_2 \times S$.

Proof: The result follows by use of the definitions.

Hence we can define

$$[R] \oplus [S] := [R + S] \quad ,$$
$$[R] \otimes [S] := [R \times S] \quad .$$

Theorem 9

For all $R, S \in \mathcal{R}$:

1. $[R] \oplus [S] = \precsim\text{-sup}([R],[S])$.
2. $[R] \otimes [S] = \precsim\text{-inf}([R],[S])$.

(This means that the 'relation' $\precsim$ on $[\mathcal{R}]$ is a lattice.)

Proof:

1: We have to prove that for all $R, S, T \in \mathcal{R}$:

i) $R \precsim R + S$ and $S \precsim R + S$,

ii) $R \precsim T \wedge S \precsim T \Rightarrow R + S \precsim T$.

Property i) follows directly from the definitions. In order to prove property ii) suppose $R \precsim T$ and $S \precsim T$. It follows that $\text{dom}\,(R + S) = \text{dom}\,R \cup \text{dom}\,S \subset \text{dom}\,T$. Let $\mu \in R + S$. Assume $\mu \in E_{\text{dom}\,R \cup \text{dom}\,S}(R)$. Then $\mu_1 := \mu \restriction \text{dom}\,R \in R$, and since $R \precsim T$ there exists $\nu \in T$ such that $\mu_1 \precsim \nu$. Hence

$$\mu(A) = \begin{cases} \mu_1(A) \precsim \nu(A) & \text{if } A \in \text{dom}\,R \subset \text{dom}\,T\,, \\ \exists \precsim \nu(A) & \text{if } A \in \text{dom}\,S \setminus \text{dom}\,R \subset \text{dom}\,T\,. \end{cases}$$

This means $\mu \precsim \nu$. The case $\mu \in E_{\text{dom}\,R \cup \text{dom}\,S}(S)$ is quite similar.

2: We have to prove that for all $R, S, T \in \mathcal{R}$:

i) $R \times S \precsim R$ and $R \times S \precsim S$,

ii) $T \precsim R \wedge T \precsim S \Rightarrow T \precsim R \times S$.

Property i) follows directly from the definitions. In order to prove property ii) suppose $T \precsim R$ and $T \precsim S$. It follows that $\text{dom}\,T \subset \text{dom}\,R \cap \text{dom}\,S = \text{dom}\,R \times S$.

Let $\mu \in T$. By supposition there exist $\xi \in R$, $\zeta \in S$ such that $\mu \precsim \xi$ and $\mu \precsim \zeta$. Consider $\nu\colon \text{dom}\,R \times S \to \mathcal{V}^*$,

$$\nu(A) := \precsim\text{-inf}(\xi(A), \zeta(A)) \quad \text{for all } A \in \text{dom}\,R \times S.$$

Then $\nu \in R \times S$ and $\mu \precsim \nu$. □

Theorem 10

The lattice $\precsim$ on $[\mathcal{R}]$ is *distributive*, this means that for all $\mathcal{e}, \mathcal{f}, \mathcal{g} \in [\mathcal{R}]$:

$$\mathcal{e} \otimes (\mathcal{f} \oplus \mathcal{g}) = (\mathcal{e} \otimes \mathcal{f}) \oplus (\mathcal{e} \otimes \mathcal{g}),$$
$$\mathcal{e} \oplus (\mathcal{f} \otimes \mathcal{g}) = (\mathcal{e} \oplus \mathcal{f}) \otimes (\mathcal{e} \oplus \mathcal{g}).$$

Proof: It suffices to show (cf. Hermes [1967], chapter 8) that for all $R,S,T \in \mathcal{R}$: $(R + S) \times (R + T) \lesssim R + (S \times T)$. We first observe that both sides have the same domain, namely

$$Z := (\text{dom } R \cup \text{dom } S) \cap (\text{dom } R \cup \text{dom } T) = \text{dom } R \cup (\text{dom } S \cap \text{dom } T).$$

Let $\mu \in (R + S) \times (R + T)$. By definition of the product there exist ξ and ζ such that

$$\xi \in R + S = E_{\text{dom } R \cup \text{dom } S}(R) \cup E_{\text{dom } R \cup \text{dom } S}(S) ,$$

$$\zeta \in R + T = E_{\text{dom } R \cup \text{dom } T}(R) \cup E_{\text{dom } R \cup \text{dom } T}(T) ,$$

$$\mu(A) = \lesssim\text{-inf}(\xi(A),\zeta(A)) \quad \text{for all} \quad A \in Z.$$

We consider three cases:

Case 1: $\xi \in E_{\text{dom } R \cup \text{dom } S}(R)$.

Consider ν: $Z \to \mathcal{V}^*$ defined by $\nu := \xi \upharpoonright Z$.

Observe that $Z = \text{dom } R \cup (\text{dom } S \cap \text{dom } T) \subset \text{dom } \xi$. Then

$\nu \in E_{\text{dom } R \cup \text{dom } S \times T}(R) \subset R + (S \times T)$ and

$$\mu(A) \lesssim \xi(A) = \nu(A) \quad \text{for all} \quad A \in Z, \quad \text{hence } \mu \lesssim \nu .$$

Case 2: $\zeta \in E_{\text{dom } R \cup \text{dom } T}(R)$.

Analogous to Case 1.

Case 3: $\xi \in E_{\text{dom } R \cup \text{dom } S}(S)$ and $\zeta \in E_{\text{dom } R \cup \text{dom } T}(T)$.

We claim that $\mu \in E_{\text{dom } R \cup \text{dom } S \times T}(S \times T)$.

For, let $\xi_1 := \xi \upharpoonright \text{dom } S \in S$ and $\zeta_1 := \zeta \upharpoonright \text{dom } T \in T$.

If $A \in \text{dom } S \times T$ then $\mu(A) = \lesssim\text{-inf}(\xi(A),\zeta(A)) = \lesssim\text{-inf}(\xi_1(A),\zeta_1(A))$.

If $A \in \text{dom } R \setminus \text{dom } S \times T = (\text{dom } R \setminus \text{dom } S) \cup (\text{dom } R \setminus \text{dom } T)$ then

$\mu(A) = \lesssim\text{-inf}(\xi(A),\zeta(A)) = \exists$. □

The results of this section show that the null value $\exists$ allows the definition of a nice algebraic structure, the 'relation' $\lesssim$ on the class of all relations (resp. its equivalence classes). By means of $\lesssim$ we can compare relations with respect to their information content. Hopefully these investigations will be helpful in discussing such topics as "normalization" and "goodness" of data base schemes (cf. Beeri, Bernstein and Goodman [1978]). Our research on this topic was stimulated by some (partially erroneous) remarks in Hall, Hitchcock and Todd [1975] where intentionally a similar concept of a partial ordering on database relations was discussed.

OPERATIONS ON RELATIONS

Let $\{<r_1,X>,\ldots,<r_n,X>\}$ be a database consisting of v-relations. Suppose, however, that we have not stored the relations $r_1,\ldots,r_n$ inside the computer but only relations $R_1,\ldots,R_n$ which represent our possibly incomplete knowledge on the database. Thus we have stored relations $R_1,\ldots,R_n$ and we know that R_1 true $<r_i,X>$, but we do *not* know X and $r_1,\ldots,r_n$. If we intend to perform an operation $o(<r_1,X>,\ldots,<r_k,X>)$ on some of the (unknown) v-relations, for instance a join or a projection (see, for instance, Codd [1970, 1972]), then we must perform a corresponding operation $o(R_1,\ldots,R_k)$ on the representing relations. The result of $o(R_1,\ldots,R_k)$ should give as much correct information about $o(<r_1,X>,\ldots,<r_k,X>)$ as possible.

Stated otherwise, assume that we have stored relations $R_1,\ldots,R_n$. Then the actual database may be any set $\{<r_1,X>,\ldots,<r_n,X>\}$ such that R_i true $<r_i,X>$, however, we do not know which is the right one. Any operation on the stored relations should produce information which is correct with respect to any possible database, and it should give us all such information.

How can we precisely specify the second requirement? As we shall see below, our formalism, together with Theorem 5, will allow us to find a precise definition for this requirement which we call *completeness* (as in logic). Further explanations will be given afterwards. We are faced now with the problem of finding an appropriate definition of the operation O on relations given the operation o on v-relations.

More formally we pose the following problem:

Representation problem for database operations:

Let o be an n-ary operation on v-relations. Find a corresponding operation O on relations such that the following properties hold:

1. O is correct with respect to o. By this we mean that for all relations $R_1,\ldots,R_n$, for all v-relations $<r_1,X>,\ldots,<r_n,X>$: if R_i true $<r_i,X>$ for $i = 1,\ldots,n$ then $O(R_1,\ldots,R_n)$ true $o(<r_1,X>,\ldots,<r_n,X>)$.

2. O is complete with respect to o. By this we mean that for all relations $R_1,\ldots,R_n$, for all tuples τ: if for all v-relations $<r_1,X>,\ldots,<r_n,X>$ R_i true $<r_i,X_i>$ for $i = 1,\ldots,n$ implies τ true $o(<r_1,X>,\ldots,<r_n,X>)$ then there exists $\mu \in O(R_1,\ldots,R_n)$ such that $\tau \lessapprox \mu$.

3. O is "easy to compute". Informally this means that the complexity of computing O should be essentially the same as the complexity of computing o.

Requirements 1 and 3 should be intuitively clear. The intuitive idea behind requirement 2 is as follows. Given $R_1,\ldots,R_n$ it seems to be a natural starting point to produce the relation $T := T(R_1,\ldots,R_n)$ of *all* tuples τ that are correct with respect to o as described by requirement 1, that means τ is true for all possible results $o(<r_1,X>,\ldots,<r_n,X>)$. However, in general the relation T will be unnecessarily large because it contains much 'redundant information'. For instance, if $\tau = (a_1,a_2)$ is an element of T then also $(\exists,a_2)$, $(a_1,\exists)$, $(\exists,\exists)$ are elements of T, but there is no need to store these three tuples additionally. Hence we do not require that $O(R_1,\ldots,R_n)$ be equal to T but only that "$O(R_1,\ldots,R_n)$ contains all information expressed in T".

This concept is made precise by requiring that the information expressed in T be a logical implication of the information expressed in $O(R_1,\ldots,R_n)$. Now, by Theorem 5 and its corollaries, this means that $T \lessapprox O(R_1,\ldots,R_n)$, or equivalently, that for all $\tau \in T$ there exists $\mu \in O(R_1,\ldots,R_n)$ such that $\tau \preccurlyeq \mu$. Thus we are led to our requirement 2. of completeness stated above. Completeness can be rephrased by saying that any formula F_τ which is true for every structure $o(<r_1,X>,\ldots,<r_n,X>)$ provided R_i is true for $<r_i,X>$ is a logical implication of the set of formulas $F_{O(R_1,\ldots,R_n)}$ which is produced by the operation O on relations.

Requirement 1 of correctness shows that in this paper we are *not* concerned with maybe operations as defined by Codd [1975,1979] For, by Codd's "null substitution principle", a tuple μ has to be added to the result of a corresponding "maybe operation" θ if there are possible databases $\{<r_1,X>,\ldots,<r_n,X>\}$ and $\{<\bar{r}_1,X>,\ldots,<\bar{r}_n,X>\}$ (with both R_i true $<r_i,X>$ and R_i true $<\bar{r}_i,X>$) such that μ is true in $o(<r_1,X>,\ldots,<r_n,X>)$ but μ is *not true* in $o(<\bar{r}_1,X>,\ldots,<\bar{r}_n,X>)$.

PROJECTION

Definition 5

Let $Y \subset A$. The Y-*projection* is defined as follows:

1. (cf. Definition 3 in the section Partial Orderings and Logical Implication). For all v-relations $<r,X>$:

   $\pi_Y(<r,X>) := <t,X>$ where $t := \{\mu \upharpoonright Y \mid \mu \in r\}$.

2. For all relations $R \in \mathcal{R}$: $\Pi_Y(R) := \{\mu \upharpoonright Y \mid \mu \in R\}$.

Theorem 11

The Y-projection Π_Y on $\mathcal{R}$ is correct and complete with respect to the Y-projection π_Y on v-relations.

Proof: This is essentially a corollary to Theorem 5. For, if R true $\langle r,\mathcal{X}\rangle$ and $\tau \in \Pi_Y(R)$ then $\mathcal{V}$ range $\tau \subset \mathcal{V}$ range $R \subset \mathcal{X}$ and there exists $\mu \in R$ such that $\tau \lesssim \mu$; hence statement 1 of Theorem 5 states the *correctness* of Π_Y.

On the other hand if $\tau \lesssim \mu$ and $\mu \in R$ then $\tau \lesssim \mu / \text{dom}\ \tau \in \Pi_{\text{dom}\ \tau}(R)$; hence statement 2 of Theorem 5 specifies the *completeness* of Π_Y. □

Natural Join

The usual natural join of two relations r and s (without null values) is computed by considering each pair of tuples $\xi \in r$, $\zeta \in s$: we first check the *matching condition* (that on common attributes ξ and ζ have identical (regular) values), and if it holds, then ξ and ζ are *combined to a new tuple* μ which is put into the result relation.

We shall define in a similar manner the natural join of two relations R and S that possibly contain null values. Again, we consider each pair of tuples $\xi \in R$, $\zeta \in S$: we first check a new *matching condition* (that on common attributes ξ and ζ either have identical *regular* values or ξ or ζ has the null value $\forall$), and if it holds then we use a new *combination rule* (that the combined tuple μ gets the $\lesssim$-minimum of the ξ-value and the ζ-value) to produce a tuple μ which is put into the result relation.

The following definitions are intended to point out their similarities in a formal fashion.

Definition 6

The (*natural*) *join* is defined as follows:

1. For all v-relations $\langle r,\mathcal{X}\rangle$, $\langle s,\mathcal{X}\rangle$:

$$\langle r,\mathcal{X}\rangle \bowtie \langle s,\mathcal{X}\rangle := \langle t,\mathcal{X}\rangle$$

where
$$t := \{\mu \mid \mu\colon \text{dom}\ r \cup \text{dom}\ s \to \mathcal{X} \wedge (\exists \xi \in r)(\exists \zeta \in s)[\\ (\forall A \in \text{dom}\ r \cap \text{dom}\ s)[\mu(A) = \xi(A) = \zeta(A)]\\ \wedge (\forall A \in \text{dom}\ r \setminus \text{dom}\ s)[\mu(A) = \xi(A)]\\ \wedge (\forall A \in \text{dom}\ s \setminus \text{dom}\ r)[\mu(A) = \zeta(A)]]\ .$$

2. For all relations $R,S \in \mathcal{R}$:

$$\begin{aligned} R \boxtimes S := \{\mu \mid \mu: \text{dom } R \cup \text{dom } S \to V^* \wedge (\exists\xi \in R)(\exists\zeta \in S) \\ [(\forall A \in \text{dom } R \cap \text{dom } S)[\mu(A) = \xi(A) = \zeta(A) \neq \exists \\ \vee\ (\mu(A) = \xi(A) \wedge \zeta(A) = \forall) \\ \vee\ (\mu(A) = \zeta(A) \wedge \xi(A) = \forall)] \\ \wedge\ (\forall A \in \text{dom } R \setminus \text{dom } S)[\mu(A) = \xi(A)] \\ \wedge\ (\forall A \in \text{dom } S \setminus \text{dom } R)[\mu(A) = \zeta(A)]\ ]\ \}. \end{aligned}$$

Example

relation	tuples	A	B	C	D	E
R	ξ	a	a	∀	∃	
S	ζ_1		a	a	∀	a
	ζ_2		a	∀	∀	a
	ζ_3		b	a	∀	a
	ζ_4		a	a	∃	a
$R \boxtimes S$	$\xi - \zeta_1$	a	a	a	∃	a
	$\xi - \zeta_2$	a	a	∀	∃	a

Let Z be the set of attributes A which are in the domain of both operands R and S. The matching condition of $\boxtimes$ can be expressed as *unifiability* of the subtuples $\mu \upharpoonright Z$ and $\zeta \upharpoonright Z$, where we refer to the unification of expressions as defined in logic in particular for resolution based theorem proving (cf. for instance Robinson [1965], Sec. 5.3 - 5.4 of Chang and Lee [1973], or Sec. 13.6 of Yasuhara [1971]).

For, denote the subtuples by sequences:

$$\xi \upharpoonright Z = (k_1, \ldots, k_n) ,$$

$$\xi \upharpoonright Z = (l_1, \ldots, l_n) .$$

Replace each occurrence of ∃ by a *distinct Skolem constant* (which is, in particular, distinct from each regular value) and each occurrence of ∀ by a *distinct variable*. Then it is easy to see that the matching condition given in Definition 5.2 is equivalent to unifiability of the modified sequences.

We further note that the *matching condition* for $\boxtimes$ is nearly as easy to check as the matching condition for $\bowtie$. Hence requirement 3 of the representation problem is achieved for $\boxtimes$.

Theorem 12

The join $\boxtimes$ on $\mathcal{R}$ is correct and complete with respect to the join $\bowtie$ on v-relations.

Proof:

1. Correctness:

Suppose that R is true in $<r,\mathcal{X}>$ and S is true in $<s,\mathcal{X}>$. Let $\mu \in R \boxtimes S$. We must prove that μ is true in $<t,\mathcal{X}> := <r,\mathcal{X}> \bowtie <s,\mathcal{X}>$. Let μ be the result of combining $\xi \in R$ and $\zeta \in S$. Then

$$d\exists\mu = d\exists\xi \cup d\exists\zeta \qquad \text{and} \qquad d\exists\xi \cap d\exists\zeta = \emptyset .$$

By supposition there exist η_1, η_2 such that

$\eta_1 : d\exists\xi \to \mathcal{X}$ is an $<r,\mathcal{X}>$-substitution for ξ.

$\eta_2 : d\exists\zeta \to \mathcal{X}$ is an $<s,\mathcal{X}>$-substitution for ζ.

Then $\mu: d\exists\mu \to \mathcal{X}$, $\eta := \eta_1 \cup \eta_2$ is well-defined, and one can verify that η actually is a $<t,\mathcal{X}>$-substitution for μ.

2. Completeness: (proof by contraposition):

Suppose that for all $\mu \in \mathbf{R} \boxtimes S : \neg(\tau \preccurlyeq \mu)$.

We shall construct v-relations $<r,\mathcal{X}>$ and $<s,\mathcal{X}>$ such that

i) R is true in $<r,\mathcal{X}>$, and S is true in $<s,\mathcal{X}>$, and
ii) τ is not true in $<r,\mathcal{X}> \bowtie <s,\mathcal{X}>$.

Define

$$\mathcal{X}_0 := \mathcal{V} \text{ range } R \cup \mathcal{V} \text{ range } S \cup \mathcal{V} \text{ range } \tau,$$

$$\mathcal{X} := \mathcal{X}_0 \cup \{a,b,c\} \text{ where } a,b,c \text{ are pairwise distinct and } \{a,b,c\} \subset \mathcal{V} \setminus \mathcal{X}_0 ,$$

(since $\mathcal{V}$ is infinite and $\mathcal{X}_0$ finite such a,b,c actually exist),

$$r := \bigcup_{\xi \in R} r_\xi \quad \text{with}$$

$$r_\xi := \{\alpha \mid \alpha: \text{dom } R \to \mathcal{X} \wedge (\forall A \in d\mathcal{V}\xi)[\alpha(A) = \xi(A)] \wedge (\forall A \in d\exists\xi)[\alpha(A) = b]\} ,$$

$$s := \bigcup_{\zeta \in S} s_\zeta \quad \text{with}$$

$$s_\zeta := \{\beta \mid \beta: \text{dom } S \to \mathcal{X} \wedge (\forall A \in d\mathcal{V}\zeta)[\beta(A) = \zeta(A)] \wedge (\forall A \in d\exists\zeta)[\beta(A) = c]\} .$$

We defined r and s in such a way that no pair of tuples $\alpha \in r$ and $\beta \in s$ satisfies the matching condition because of an appropriate assignment of regular values to occurrences of the null value $\exists$ in R respectively S. The role of the new regular value a will be the same as in the proof of statement 2 of Theorem 5.

Property i) obviously holds by the definitions.

We prove property ii) indirectly: let $\langle t,\mathcal{X}\rangle := \langle r,\mathcal{X}\rangle \quad \langle s,\mathcal{X}\rangle$

and assume that τ is true in $\langle t,\mathcal{X}\rangle$.
Then there exists a $\langle t,\mathcal{X}\rangle$-substitution η for τ.

Consider σ: dom R $\cup$ dom S $\rightarrow \mathcal{X}$ defined by

$$\sigma(A) := \begin{cases} \tau(A) & \text{if } A \in d\mathcal{V}\tau \;, \\ \eta(A) & \text{if } A \in d\exists\tau \;, \\ a & \text{if } A \in d\forall\tau \;. \end{cases} \tag{2}$$

Then $\sigma \quad \in t$. Let σ be the result of combining $\alpha \in r$ and $\beta \in s$. By definition of $\bowtie$ we have

$$\sigma(A) := \begin{cases} \alpha(A) & \text{if } A \in \text{dom } R \setminus \text{dom } S \;, \\ \alpha(A) = \beta(A) & \text{if } A \in \text{dom } R \cap \text{dom } S \;, \\ \beta(A) & \text{if } A \in \text{dom } S \setminus \text{dom } R \;. \end{cases} \tag{3}$$

By definition of r and s there exist $\xi \in R$, $\zeta \in S$ such that $\alpha \in r_\xi$ and $\beta \in s_\zeta$, hence we have:

$$\begin{aligned} \alpha(A) &= \xi(A) && \text{if } A \in d\mathcal{V}\xi \;, \\ \alpha(A) &= b && \text{if } A \in d\exists\xi \;, \\ \beta(A) &= \zeta(A) && \text{if } A \in d\mathcal{V}\zeta \;, \\ \beta(A) &= c && \text{if } A \in d\exists\zeta \;. \end{aligned} \tag{4}$$

We claim that

$$\begin{aligned} \tau_R &:= \tau \restriction \text{dom } R \precsim \xi \;, \\ \tau_S &:= \tau \restriction \text{dom } S \precsim \zeta \;. \end{aligned} \tag{5}$$

For otherwise assume $\neg(\tau_R \precsim \xi)$ (for τ_S similarly). Then there exists an attribute $A \in$ dom R such that $\neg(\tau_R(A) \precsim \xi(A))$, hence $\neg(\tau(A) \precsim \xi(A))$. According to the definiton of $\precsim$ on $\mathcal{V}^*$ we have to consider four cases for such an A. All cases will produce an obvious contradiction:

Case 1: $\tau(A) \in \mathcal{V}$ and $\xi(A) \in \mathcal{V}$ and $\tau(A) \neq \xi(A)$.

Then, by (2), case assumption, (4), and (3),

$$\sigma(A) = \tau(A) \neq \xi(A) = \alpha(A) = \sigma(A) \ .$$

Case 2: $\tau(A) \in \mathcal{V}$ and $\xi(A) = \exists$.

Then, by (2), choice of b, (4), and (3),

$$\sigma(A) = \tau(A) \neq b = \alpha(A) = \sigma(A) \ .$$

Case 3: $\tau(A) = \forall$ and $\xi(A) \in \mathcal{V}$.

Then, by (2), choice of a, (4), and (3),

$$\sigma(A) = a \neq \xi(A) = \alpha(A) = \sigma(A) \ .$$

Case 4: $\tau(A) = \forall$ and $\xi(A) = \exists$.

Then, by (2), choice of a and b, (4), and (3),

$$\sigma(A) = a \neq b = \alpha(A) = \sigma(A) \ .$$

From (5) we conclude that

$$\xi \text{ and } \zeta \text{ do not satisfy the matching condition.} \qquad (6)$$

For otherwise, let μ be the result of combining ξ and ζ according to Definition 5, statement 2. Then, by (5) and the definition of $\boxtimes$, $\mu \in R \boxtimes S$ and

$$\begin{aligned}
&\tau(A) \lesssim \xi(A) = \mu(A) && \text{if } A \in \text{dom } R \setminus \text{dom } S,\\
&\tau(A) \lesssim \lesssim\text{-inf}(\xi(A),\zeta(A)) = \mu(A) && \text{if } A \in \text{dom } R \cap \text{dom } S,\\
&\tau(A) \lesssim \zeta(A) = \mu(A) && \text{if } A \in \text{dom } S \setminus \text{dom } R;
\end{aligned}$$

hence $\tau \lesssim \mu$. But this is a contradiction to our supposition (1). This proves (6).

Assertion (6) implies that there exists an attribute $A \in \text{dom } R \cap \text{dom } S$ such that ξ and ζ do not match at A. According to the definition of $\boxtimes$ we have to consider three cases for such an A. All cases will produce an obvious contradiction. This will falsify our indirect assumption that τ is true in $\langle t,\mathcal{X}\rangle$ thus proving property ii) of $\langle r,\mathcal{X}\rangle$ and $\langle s,\mathcal{X}\rangle$, and the completeness of $\boxtimes$ will be proved.

Consider now the three cases:

Case 1: $\xi(A) \in \mathcal{V}$ and $\zeta(A) \in \mathcal{V}$ and $\xi(A) \neq \zeta(A)$.

Then, by (3), (4), case assumption, (4), and (3),

$$\sigma(A) = \alpha(A) = \xi(A) \neq \zeta(A) = \beta(A) = \sigma(A) \ .$$

<u>Case 2</u>: $\xi(A) = \exists$ and $\zeta(A) \neq \forall$.

Then, by (3), (4), choice of b and c, (4), and (3),

$$\sigma(A) = \alpha(A) = b \neq \begin{cases} \zeta(A) \\ \\ c \end{cases} = \beta(A) = \sigma(A) .$$

<u>Case 3</u>: $\zeta(A) = \exists$ and $\xi(A) \neq \forall$.

Then, by (3), (4), choice of b and c, (4), and (3),

$$\sigma(A) = \beta(A) = c \neq \begin{cases} \xi(A) \\ \\ b \end{cases} = \alpha(A) = \sigma(A) .$$

□

As statement 2 of Theorem 5, the completeness part of Theorem 12, is *not* valid if V is finite respectively X is assumed to be a fixed finite set.

<u>Example</u> Let $X := \{v_1, \ldots, v_k\}$. Define

$$\xi := \binom{A}{\exists}, \quad \zeta_i := \binom{A}{v_i} \quad \text{for } i = 1, \ldots, k,$$

$$R := \{\xi\} \quad \text{and} \quad S := \{\zeta_i \mid i = 1, \ldots, k\}.$$

Then, having X fixed, for all r and s:

R true $<r,X> \wedge$ S true $<s,X> \Rightarrow \xi$ true $<r,X> \bowtie <s,X>$.

However $R \boxtimes S = \emptyset$, hence there does not exist $\mu \in R \boxtimes S$ such that $\xi \lessapprox \mu$.

Selection

<u>Definition 7</u>

Let $C \in A$ and $w \in V$. The *C=w-selection* is defined as follows:

1. For all v-relations $<r,X>$: $\sigma_{C=w}(<r,X> := <t,X>$

   where

$$t := \begin{cases} \{\mu \mid \mu \in r \wedge \mu(C) = w\} & \text{if } C \in \text{dom } r \\ \\ \emptyset & \text{otherwise} . \end{cases}$$

2. For all relations $R \in \mathcal{R}$:

$$\Sigma_{C=w}(R) := \begin{cases} \{\mu \mid \mu: \text{dom } R \to V^* \wedge (\exists \nu \in R)[(\forall A \in \text{dom } R \setminus \{C\}) \\ \quad [\mu(A) = \nu(A)] \wedge \mu(C) = w \lesssim \nu(C)] \\ \qquad\qquad \text{if } C \in \text{dom } R \text{ and } w \in V \text{ range } R, \\ \emptyset \qquad\qquad \text{otherwise.} \end{cases}$$

$\Sigma_{C=w}(R)$ can be computed easily as follows:

1. If $C \notin \text{dom } R$ return $\emptyset$.
2. Otherwise, scanning the relation R tuplewise
   — test whether the value w occurs and
   — if $\mu \in R$ such that $\mu(C) \in \{w, \forall\}$ then change the value of $\mu(C)$ into w (if necessary) and add the (possibly modified) tuple to a new relation S (which has been initialized as the empty set).
3. If, in step 2, we did not find any occurrence of w in R then return $\emptyset$; otherwise return the final value of S.

This shows that both the complexity of computing $\Sigma_{C=w}$ and the complexity of $\sigma_{C=w}$ are essentially determined by the complexity of scanning the input relation.

Theorem 13

The C=w-selection $\Sigma_{C=w}$ on R is correct and complete with respect to the C=w-selection $\sigma_{C=w}$ on v-relations.

Proof: Define $\rho: \{C\} \to V$ by $\rho(C) := w$. It is well known that

(1) $\qquad \sigma_{C=w}(\langle r, X\rangle) = \langle r, X\rangle \bowtie \langle\{\rho\}, X\rangle$ if $C \in \text{dom } r$.

Comparing the definitions of ⊠ and $\Sigma_{C=w}$ we can verify that also

(2) $\qquad \Sigma_{C=w}(R) = R \boxtimes \{\rho\}$ if $C \in \text{dom } R$ and $w \in V$ range R.

Hence the C=w-selection is essentially a special kind of join. Then we can use Theorem 12, the correctness and completeness of ⊠, to verify that $\Sigma_{C=w}$ is correct and complete. For the sake of brevity we omit all details.

Union

Definition 8

The *union* is defined as follows:

1. For all v-relations $\langle r, X\rangle$ and $\langle s, X\rangle$: $\langle r, X\rangle \cup \langle s, X\rangle := \langle t, X\rangle$ where $t := \{\mu \mid \mu: \text{dom } r \cup \text{dom } s \to X \wedge [\mu \upharpoonright \text{dom } r \in r \vee \mu \upharpoonright \text{dom } s \in s]\}$.

2. For all relations $R,S \in \mathcal{R}$: $R \uplus S := \{\mu \mid \mu: \text{dom } R \cup \text{dom } S \to \mathcal{V}^* \wedge$

$$[(\mu / \text{dom } R \in R \wedge (\forall A \in \text{dom } S \setminus \text{dom } R)[\mu(A) = \forall])$$

$$\vee (\mu / \text{dom } S \in S \wedge (\forall A \wedge \text{dom } R \setminus \text{dom } S)[\mu(A) = \forall])]\}.$$

<u>Example</u> Let $X := \{a,b,c\}$.

relation	A	B	C
r	b	c	
s		a	a
t	b	c	a
	b	c	b
	b	c	c
	a	a	a
	b	a	a
	c	a	a
R	∃	c	
S		a	a
$R \uplus S$	∃	c	∀
	∀	a	a

If dom r = dom s then the relation t such that $\langle r,X\rangle \cup \langle s,X\rangle = \langle t,X\rangle$ is the usual set theoretical union of r and s whatever X is. However, if dom r $\neq$ dom s then the result of $\langle r,X\rangle \cup \langle s,X\rangle$ actually *depends on the range declaration* X.
Note that if we take r and s without range declaration, thus omitting the requirement that all values are elements of a fixed *finite* set, we would get the set

$$\tilde{t} := \{\mu \mid \mu: \text{dom } r \cup \text{dom } s \to \mathcal{V} \wedge [(\mu / \text{dom } r \in r \vee \mu / \text{dom } s \in s)]\}.$$

Since the set of all regular values $\mathcal{V}$ is assumed to be infinite $\tilde{t}$ would be infinite too (if $r \neq \emptyset$ or $s \neq \emptyset$) and thus $\tilde{t}$ could not be a database relation. Our definition 8.1 of union is essentially the same as that given by Hall, Hitchcock and Todd [1975], however, these authors did not use v-relations (as defined in the section Tuples, Relations and Value-Relations of this paper).

Observe that statement 1 of Definition 6 of the join is equivalent to $\langle r,X\rangle \bowtie \langle s,X\rangle = \langle t,X\rangle$ where $t := \{\mu \mid \mu: \text{dom } r \cup \text{dom } s \to X \wedge [\mu / \text{dom } r \in r \wedge \mu / \text{dom } s \in s]\}$. Comparing this definition of $\bowtie$ with the definition of $\cup$ we see that the join corresponds to a *conjunctive* query whereas the union corresponds to a *disjunctive* query.

Finally we note that the *outer union* of $\mathcal{R}$, statement 2 of Definition 4, is very similar to the *union* on $\mathcal{R}$, statement 2 of Definition 8. In both cases we enlarge the tuples of the operand relations by assigning a null value to every new attribute: for the outer union we take $\exists$ and for the union we take $\forall$. The following theorem shows that we could not use the outer union as an operation corresponding to the union on v-relations.

<u>Theorem 14</u>

The union $\uplus$ on $\mathcal{R}$ is correct and complete with respect to the union $\cup$ on v-relations.

Proof: This theorem can be proven by the same method used in the proofs of Theorems 5 and 12. For the sake of brevity we omit the proof. □

Comparison

The operation of comparison selects those tuples of a (usual) database relation that have identical values for two fixed attributes C and D (see below for the formal definition). Here we are faced with some problems which are caused by the use of the null value $\forall$. For instance, let

$$\mu := (\binom{A}{a}, \binom{B}{b}, \binom{C}{\forall}, \binom{D}{\forall}) \quad \text{and} \quad \mu \text{ true } \langle r, X\rangle .$$

As discussed in the section Tuples, Relations and Value-Relations the intended interpretation is

"for all $x \in X$, for all $y \in X$: $(\binom{A}{a}, \binom{B}{b}, \binom{C}{x}, \binom{D}{y}) \in r$".

Then we can make the following statement on the comparison of r:

"for all $x \in X$: $(\binom{A}{a}, \binom{B}{b}, \binom{C}{x}, \binom{D}{x}) \in \text{comparison}(r)$ ".

However, this statement can *not* be represented by a (generalized) tuple.

<u>Definition 9</u>

Let $C \in \mathcal{A}$, $D \in \mathcal{A}$, and $C \neq D$. The C=D-*comparison* is defined as follows:

1. For all v-relations $\langle r,X\rangle$: $\sigma_{C=D}(\langle r,X\rangle) := \langle t,X\rangle$

$$\text{where } t := \begin{cases} \{\mu \mid \mu \in r \wedge \mu(C) \stackrel{C=D}{=} \mu(D)\} & \text{if } (C,D) \subset \text{dom } r, \\ \emptyset & \text{otherwise} \end{cases}$$

2. For all relations $R \in \mathcal{R}$: if $C \notin \text{dom } R$ or $D \notin \text{dom } R$ then $\Sigma_{C=D}(R) := \emptyset$, otherwise, if $\{C,D\} \subset \text{dom } R$ then

$$
\begin{aligned}
\Sigma_{C=D}(R) := \{\mu \mid \mu: \text{dom } R \to \mathcal{V}^{*} \wedge (\exists \nu \in R) & \\
[(\forall A \in \text{dom } R \setminus \{C,D\})[\mu(A) = \nu(A)] & \\
① \quad \wedge [(\mu(C) = \mu(D) = \nu(C) = \nu(D) \in \mathcal{V}) & \\
② \quad \vee (\mu(C) = \mu(D) = \nu(C) \in \mathcal{V} \wedge \nu(D) = \forall) & \\
③ \quad \vee (\mu(C) = \mu(D) = \nu(D) \in \mathcal{V} \wedge \nu(C) = \forall) & \\
④ \quad \vee (\mu(C) = \mu(D) = \exists \wedge \nu(C) = \forall \wedge \nu(D) = \forall) & \\
⑤ \quad \vee (\mu(C) = \mu(D) = \exists \wedge \nu(C) = \exists \wedge \nu(D) = \exists) & \\
⑥ \quad \vee (\mu(C) = \mu(D) \in \mathcal{V} \text{ range } R \wedge \nu(C) = \nu(D) = \forall) & \\
\vee (\mathcal{V} \text{ range } R = \emptyset \wedge \mu(C) = \mu(D) = \exists \wedge \nu(C) = \nu(D) = & \\
= \forall)]]\}. &
\end{aligned}
$$

The C=D-comparision on $\mathcal{R}$ can be computed by scanning the input relation R, tuplewise. For each tuple $\nu \in R$ we use the following "output-modification-table" in order to determine

- whether ν gives a contribution to the result $\Sigma_{C=D}(R)$ (no contribution is indicated by "-"),
- how to modify a contributing tuple (contribution is indicated by "+" followed by new assignments):

$\nu(C)$ \ $\nu(D)$	$\exists$	$\in \mathcal{V}$	$\forall$
$\exists$	-	-	$+ \nu(D) := \exists$ ④
$\in \mathcal{V}$	-	if $\nu(C) \neq \nu(D)$: - if $\nu(C) = \nu(D)$: + ①	$+ \nu(D) := \nu(C)$ ②
$\forall$	$+\nu(C) := \exists$ ⑤	$+ \nu(C) := \nu(D)$ ③	⑥ if $\mathcal{V}$ range $R = \emptyset$: $+ \nu(C) := \nu(D) := \exists$; if $\mathcal{V}$ range $R \neq \emptyset$: + for all $x \in \mathcal{V}$ range R $\nu(C) := \nu(D) := x$

If $\nu(C) \neq \forall$ or $\nu(D) \neq \forall$ then at most one tuple is added to the result relation. However, if $\nu(C) = \nu(D) = \forall$ then a (possibly) long list of tuples is produced, namely one tuple for each element in V range R. In this case the complexity of computing $\Sigma_{C=D}$ can be substantially higher than the complexity of computing $\sigma_{C=D}$. Furthermore the production of a long list of nearly identical tuples, as required by case ⑥, is not in the spirit of the motivation for introducing the null value $\forall$.

We suggest that the long list be replaced just by one tuple, namely by ν with new assignments $\nu(C) := \nu(D) := \exists$ (as in the case V range R = $\emptyset$). Then, however, we cannot further expect that the modified comparison on $\mathcal{R}$ is complete.

Theorem 15

The C=D-comparision $\Sigma_{C=D}$ on $\mathcal{R}$ is *correct* and *complete* with respect to the C=D-comparison $\sigma_{C=D}$ on v-relations.

Proof: Omitted since it is similar to previous proofs. □

We finally note that the *modified* comparison is of course complete for those relations R that do not contain any element ν with $\nu(C) = \nu(D) = \forall$.

Other Operations

Up to now we have discussed the most basic operations on database relations. Our method of defining operations on $\mathcal{R}$ and showing their properties could also be used for other operations. However, we encountered two types of difficulties. The first one is caused by the use of the null value $\forall$ and has been exhibited by considering the operation of comparison. The second difficulty is related to the problem of "negative information" (cf. Gallaire and Minker [1978], in particular Gallaire, Minker and Nicolas [1978] and Reiter [1978]) which is, for instance, needed for the operations of difference and division. We defer a rigorous treatment of this topic to another context whereas in the present paper we shall only sketch some rough ideas.

Suppose that R is true in $\langle r,X\rangle$ and S is true in $\langle s,X\rangle$ and, for simplicity, dom R = dom S. What do we know about $\langle r,X\rangle - \langle s,X\rangle := \langle r \setminus s,X\rangle$?

The disappointing answer is that actually there is not a single tuple which is known to be definitely an element of $r \setminus s$. For it is always possible that $r \subset s$ and hence $r \setminus s = \emptyset$. We only have some some knowledge about tuples which are definitely *not* elements of $r \setminus s$, for instance a tuple without null values which is an element of both R and S. Hence the assumptions on our knowledge about

$<r,X>$ and $<s,X>$ are too weak for handling negative information. We propose to strengthen the notion of truth (Definition 2) to the following strong concept of representation:

R *is an image of* $<r,X>$: iff

i) R true $<r,X>$, and

ii) for all $\nu \in r$ there exist $\mu \in R$ and a $<r,X>$-substitution η for μ such that

$$\nu \in \{\alpha \mid \alpha\colon \text{dom } R \to X \wedge (A \in d\mathcal{V}\mu)[\alpha(A) = \mu(A)] \wedge (A \in d\exists\mu)[\alpha(A) = \eta(A)]\} \subset r.$$

Informally speaking property ii) requires that every tuple of the model $<r,X>$ can be reconstructed by taking an appropriate tuple of R and assigning correct regular values to its null values.

If R does not contain null values at all, then for all X with $\mathcal{V}$ range $R \subset X$:

$$R \text{ is an image of } <r,X> \Leftrightarrow R = r$$

(whereas R is true in $<r,X> \Leftrightarrow R \subset r$) .

If we use the concept of image (instead of truth) the absence of null values means that we assume a *closed world* (instead of an open world) in the sense of Reiter [1978]. Then the presence of null values "partially opens the world". For instance if $\eta := ((\begin{smallmatrix}A\\a\end{smallmatrix}), (\begin{smallmatrix}B\\\exists\end{smallmatrix})) \in S = S^0$ then we *do not know* whether a particular tuple $\eta_x := ((\begin{smallmatrix}A\\a\end{smallmatrix}), (\begin{smallmatrix}B\\x\end{smallmatrix})) \in r$ is (not) an element of the intended model $<s,X>$ of S and hence we cannot claim that $\eta_x \in r \setminus s$. Thus we can use null values for dynamically presenting or eliminating "partial open world assumptions" to the database system. In particular after adding the tuple $(\exists,\ldots,\exists)$ to a relation R all inferences based on (the updated) R must be in accordance with the open world assumption. This example also shows that under the image convention R and R^0 possibly give essentially different information to the database system.

Finally we note that many operations on relations do not *preserve images*. For instance there are R, S, $<r,X>$ and $<s,X>$ such that R is an image of $<r,X>$ and S is an image of $<s,X>$, but $R \boxtimes S$ is *not* an image of $<r,X> \bowtie <s,X>$. Therefore corrections and image preserving can be conflicting requirements.

GENERALIZED JOIN AND A WEAKENED UNIVERSAL RELATION ASSUMPTION

For the usual (natural) join the following inclusion is always true:

$$\pi_{\text{dom } r}(r \bowtie s) \subset r \ .$$

But in general there is no equality, because r can contain an element α such that for any $\beta \in s$ the *matching condition* does not hold. Sometimes it seems to be desirable to use a kind of join operation that ensures equality in all cases. Several authors, LaCroix and Pirotte [1976], Zaniolo [1976], Navathe and Lemke [1979], suggest that a so-called generalized join be defined as follows:

> compute $r \bowtie s$ (the usual join), and for each tuple $\xi \in r \setminus \pi_{\text{dom } r}(r \bowtie s)$ [resp. $\zeta \in s \setminus \pi_{\text{dom } s}(r \bowtie s)$] create "null values" for the attributes $A \in \text{dom } s \setminus \text{dom } r$ [resp. $A \in \text{dom } r \setminus \text{dom } s$] and add the new tuple to $r \bowtie s$.

We adopt this definition by using the *null value* $\exists$ as follows.

<u>Definition 10</u>

For all relations $R, S \in \mathcal{R}$:

$$R \underset{g}{\boxtimes} S := R \boxtimes S \cup E_{\text{dom } R \cup \text{dom } S}(R \setminus \ _{\text{dom } R}(R \boxtimes S))$$
$$\cup\ E_{\text{dom } R \cup \text{dom } S}(S \setminus \ _{\text{dom } S}(R \boxtimes S)) \ .$$

$R \underset{g}{\boxtimes} S$ is called the *generalized join* of R and S (cf. statement 1 of Definitions 4 and 6 for E and $\boxtimes$).

We shall describe a situation where the generalized join produces correct information and actually gives us all such information. Informally speaking this situation is essentially characterized by the following *weakened universal relation assumption:*

each (stored) relation represents a *subset* of a projection of a universal relation.

More formally suppose that we have stored relations $R \in \mathcal{R}$ and $S \in \mathcal{R}$. Then we assume that there is a so-called universal v-relation $\langle u, \mathcal{X} \rangle$ on $U \supset \text{dom } R \cup \text{dom } S$ such that

$$R \text{ is true in } \pi_{\text{dom } R}(\langle u, \mathcal{X} \rangle) \text{ and } S \text{ is true in } \pi_{\text{dom } S}(\langle u, \mathcal{X} \rangle).$$

We ask the following question: given R and S, what can we assert about $\pi_{\text{dom } R \cup \text{dom } S}(\langle u, \mathcal{X} \rangle)$? Theorem 16 below states that the generalized join $R \boxtimes_g S$ gives us precisely the desired knowledge provided u has a lossless join with respect to dom R and dom S (cf. Aho, Beeri and Ullman [1979]).

Theorem 16 *

Let $R,S \in \mathcal{R}$ and define $X :=$ dom R, $Y :=$ dom S.

1. If the v-relation $\langle u,\mathcal{X}\rangle$ satisfies

   a. [weakened universal relation assumption]

   R true $\pi_X(\langle u,\mathcal{X}\rangle$,

   S true $\pi_Y(\langle u,\mathcal{X}\rangle)$ and

   b. [lossless join with respect to X and Y]

   $\pi_{X\cup Y}(\langle u,\mathcal{X}\rangle) = \pi_X(\langle u,\mathcal{X}\rangle) \bowtie \pi_Y(\langle u,\mathcal{X}\rangle)$,

   then $R \boxtimes_g S$ is true in $\pi_{X\cup Y}(\langle u,\mathcal{X}\rangle)$.

2. If for all v-relations $\langle u,\mathcal{X}\rangle$ satisfying properties a and b above τ true $\pi_{X\cup Y}(\langle u,\mathcal{X}\rangle)$, then there exists $\mu \in R \boxtimes_g S$ such that $\tau \lesssim \mu$.

Part 1 states an appropriate version of "correctness", and part 2 states the corresponding version of "completeness" (compare the representation problem at the beginning of the section OPERATIONS ON RELATIONS).

Proof: Since the proofs use the same method that we developed earlier we give only short sketches.

1. "correctness":

By the correctness of $\boxtimes$ (Theorem 12) and property a:

$$R \boxtimes S \text{ true } \pi_X(\langle u,\mathcal{X}\rangle) \bowtie \pi_Y(\langle u,\mathcal{X}\rangle) .$$

Then property b implies

$$R \boxtimes S \text{ true } \pi_{X\cup Y}(\langle u,\mathcal{X}\rangle) .$$

Now let $\mu \in R \boxtimes_g S \setminus R \boxtimes S$, say $\mu \in E_{X\cup Y}(R \setminus \pi_X(R \boxtimes S))$. Then by property a

$$\mu \curlywedge X \text{ true } \pi_X(\langle u,\mathcal{X}\rangle)$$

and hence, since dom $\mu = X \cup Y \subset$ dom ,

$$\mu \text{ true } \pi_{X\cup Y}(\langle u,\mathcal{X}\rangle).$$

---

* Correction added in proof: Attempting to prove Theorem 16 I claimed that for $\mu \in E_{X\cup Y}(R)$, if $\mu \curlywedge X$ true $\pi_X(\langle u,\mathcal{X}\rangle)$ then μ true $\pi_{X\cup Y}(\langle u,\mathcal{X}\rangle)$. However, obviously this is true only if $d_{\forall}\mu=\emptyset$ because we decided to consider tuples as statements with a quantifier alternation of the form $(\exists x)(\forall y)$. Thus Theorem 16 holds only if we suppose that the null value $\forall$ does not occur in $R \boxtimes_g S \setminus R \boxtimes S$.

2. "*completeness*": (proof by contraposition):

Suppose that for all $\mu \in R \underset{g}{\boxtimes} S : \neg(\tau \lessapprox \mu)$.

We shall construct a v-relation $<u,\mathcal{X}>$ such that

i) $<u,\mathcal{X}>$ satisfies properties a and b, and

ii) τ is not true in $\Pi_{X \cup Y}(<u,\mathcal{X}>)$.

Define $\mathcal{X}_0$, $\mathcal{X}$, r and s as in part 2 of the proof of Theorem 12. Furthermore let

$$\mu_j := r \boxtimes s ,$$

$$u_r := \{\mu \mid \mu: X \cup Y \to \mathcal{X} \wedge \mu \upharpoonright X \in r \setminus \Pi_X(u_j) \wedge (\forall A \in Y \setminus X)[\mu(A)=b]\},$$

$$u_s := \{\mu \mid \mu: X \cup Y \to \mathcal{X} \wedge \mu \upharpoonright Y \in s \setminus \Pi_Y(u_j) \wedge (\forall A \in X \setminus Y)[\mu(A)=c]\},$$

$$u := u_j \cup u_r \cup u_s .$$

Since $r \subset \Pi_X(u)$ and $s \subset \Pi_Y(u)$ we can show that R is true in $\Pi_X(<u,\mathcal{X}>)$ and S is true in $\Pi_Y(<u,\mathcal{X}>)$, that is property a. In order to show the lossless join property b we have to verify the following identities:

$$\begin{aligned}\Pi_X(u) \boxtimes \Pi_Y(u) &= \bigcup_{e,f \in \{j,r,s\}} \Pi_X(u_e) \boxtimes \Pi_Y(u_f) \\ &= \bigcup_{e \in \{j,r,s\}} \Pi_X(u_e) \boxtimes \Pi_Y(u_e) \\ &= u_j \cup u_r \cup u_s = u = \Pi_{X \cup Y}(u) .\end{aligned}$$

Note that

$\Pi_X(u_j) \boxtimes \Pi_Y(u_j) = u_j$ by definition of $u_j = r \boxtimes s$;

$\Pi_X(u_r) \boxtimes \Pi_Y(u_r) = u_r$ since u_r satisfies the functional dependency $X \cap Y \to Y$ (cf. Aho, Beeri and Ullman [1979]);

$\Pi_X(u_s) \boxtimes \Pi_Y(u_s) = u_s$ since u_s satisfies the functional dependency $X \cap Y \to X$.

Finally, we prove property ii) of $<u,\mathcal{X}>$ indirectly: assume that τ is true in $<u,\mathcal{X}>$. Let η be a $<u,\mathcal{X}>$-substitution for τ and define

$$\sigma(A) := \begin{cases} \tau(A) \text{ if } A \in d\mathcal{V}\tau , \\ \eta(A) \text{ if } A \in d\exists\tau , \\ a \text{ if } A \in d\forall\tau . \end{cases}$$

Then $\sigma \in u = u_j \cup u_r \cup u_s$.

Case J: $\sigma \in u_j = r \boxtimes s$.

In proving the completeness of $\boxtimes$, Theorem 12, we already showed that we can derive a contradiction.

Case R: $\sigma \in u_r$.

Choose ξ such that $\xi \in R$ and $\sigma / X \in r_\xi$ and such that ξ is *maximal* (with respect to $\lesssim$). Using the case assumption that $\sigma \quad X \notin \Pi_X(r \boxtimes s)$ we can show that also $\xi \notin \Pi_X(R \boxtimes S)$. Then $\mu : X \cup Y \to V^*$ defined by

$$\mu(A) := \begin{cases} \xi(A) \text{ if } A \in X , \\ \exists \text{ if } A \in Y \setminus X , \end{cases}$$

is an element of $R \underset{g}{\boxtimes} S$.

It follows from the supposition (1) that $\neg(\tau \lesssim \mu)$. Hence there exists $A \in X \cup Y$ such that $\neg(\tau(A) \lesssim \mu(A))$. Similarly as in previous proofs all possible cases will produce a contradiction.

Case S: $\sigma \in u_s$.

Proven in a manner analogous to case R. □

A DIFFERENT VIEW OF EXISTENTIAL NULL VALUES

In the section Natural Join, we already mentioned that our null value $\exists$ is related to the notion of a Skolem constant (cf. Section 4.2 of Chang and Lee [1978] or Section 13.3 of Yasuhara [1971]). Usually each existentially quantified variable is replaced by a *distinct* Skolem constant. This ensures that we cannot unify (match) two Skolem constants which originate from two different situations. On the other hand any particular Skolem constant matches itself.

In the context of our approach to the existential null value $\exists$ this means the following. If, instead of using just one existential null value $\exists$, we introduce indexed existential null values $\exists_1, \exists_2, \exists_3, \ldots$ which are intended to denote distinct missing values of the type "attribute at present is unknown", then we can always decide whether two indexed nulls $\exists_i$ and $\exists_j$ originate from the same source of ignorance, namely just by looking to see whether $i=j$. This modified approach to the missing value "attribute at present is unknown" will sometimes allow us to *infer* more information than before. This is indicated by the following example of a join:

	one null value ∃			indexed null values $\exists_1, \exists_2, \exists_3, \ldots$		
relation	A	B	C	A	B	C
U	a	∃	b	a	$\exists_1$	b
	b	∃	b	b	$\exists_2$	b
$\Pi_{\{A,B\}}(U) =: R$	a	∃		a	$\exists_1$	
	b	∃		b	$\exists_2$	
$\Pi_{\{B,C\}}(U) =: S$		∃	b		$\exists_1$	b
					$\exists_2$	b
join of R and S		∅		a	$\exists_1$	b
				b	$\exists_2$	b

Furthermore the modified approach would allow us to *represent* some more statements of interest by tuples. For instance, consider the statement

(1) "there exists $x \in X$ such that $(a,b,x,x) \in r$ ".

Whatever the right value of x may be, the resulting tuple will qualify for the condition tested by the operation of C=D-comparison.

If we use indexed existential null values, then statement (1) could be represented by a tuple of the form $\mu = (a,b,\exists_i,\exists_i)$, and of course, we should define the C=D-comparison on R in such a way that μ also qualifies for the C=D-comparision. On the other hand, using just one existential null value, statement (1) can *not* be represented by a tuple, because the statement denoted by the tuple (a,b,∃,∃) is apparently weaker than statement (1). However, the use of indexed existential nulls causes some trouble at the theoretical, practical, and semantic level of consideration. With respect to the theoretical level we now need a notion of truth which always takes care of the whole database instead of considering each database tuple separately. This must be done in order to ensure that *each occurrence of a particular indexed null value* $\exists_i$ is interpreted by the *same* regular value within the whole database. At a practical level this means that the database management system must carefully *support the global view* of indexed existential nulls in order to avoid inappropriate identifications. Possible difficulties can arise for instance from distributed processing, missing values caused by system errors, or small field sizes for ranges of low cardinality.

With regard to the semantic level of consideration we make the following observations. Indexed existential null values are appropriate for extending the usual database operations to relations with null values as discussed in the section OPERATIONS ON RELATIONS. Indexed existential null values are *not* appropriate when we consider the *product operation* described in the section The Partial Ordering $\lesssim$ on $[\mathcal{R}]$ is a Distributive Lattice. For instance let R := $\{(\begin{smallmatrix}A\\a\end{smallmatrix})\}$ and S := $\{(\begin{smallmatrix}A\\b\end{smallmatrix})\}$ where $a \neq b$. Using indexed null values the product of R and S would be equal to $\{(\begin{smallmatrix}A\\\exists_i\end{smallmatrix})\}$ where i is any new index. Then the global view of existential null values would give the impression that the occurrence of $\exists_i$ refers to *one* regular value. But obviously this is not true here. This semantic difficulty is also reflected at the theoretical level: for the purpose of the section BASIC CONCEPTS, in particular for the study of the lattice structure of $[\mathcal{R}]$, we must reidentify all indexed existential nulls. At a practical level this means that the database management system must be able to distinguish two kinds of relations, namely on the one hand the basic relations together with those generated by the operations of the section OPERATIONS ON RELATIONS, and on the other hand defined relations as for instance a product as discussed above. Another semantic difficulty is that indexed existential nulls (which actually are special instances of more general Skolem functions) could suggest the existence of functionalities which might not be true. This becomes a crucial point when we want to handle "negative information" (cf. the section Other Operations).

SUMMARY

We studied two types of null values which have the meaning "attribute is applicable but its value at present is unknown" and "attribute is applicable but its value is arbitrary". Adopting notions of predicate logic we gave precise definitions of these meanings. Within this framework tuples with null values are considered as first order predicate calculus statements of the form $\exists x \, \forall y \, R(x, y, b)$ where the existentially quantified variables x correspond to null values of the first type, the universally quantified variables y correspond to null values of the second type, b denotes regular values (constants) and R denotes a database relation.

We introduced partial orderings on tuples (with null values) and relations (with null values). It turned out that the partial ordering for (some equivalence classes) of relations actually is a distributive lattice. Intuitively the partial orderings compare tuples, respectively relations, with respect to their "information content", more formally the partial orderings can be interpreted as a kind of logical implication.

We extended well-known relational operations which need no "negative information" to relations with null values. Using notions and proof methods of predicate logic we showed that these extensions are natural and meaningful under our supposition that relations with null values denote statements about partially unknown database relations without null values. Finally the generalized join is reexamined within our framework. For relational operations requiring "negative information" we sketched some remarks as to how our approach might be modified.

ACKNOWLEDGEMENTS

I gratefully acknowledge that the section A DIFFERENT VIEW OF EXISTENTIAL NULL VALUES of the present version of this paper originates from valuable discussions during the Workshop on Formal Databases, Toulouse, December 1979, and from critical remarks of one of the reviewers. Furthermore I would like to particularly thank all reviewers and the editors of this volume for their combined effort to assist me to make the paper (hopefully) clearer than before and to improve my English.

REFERENCES

1. ANSI/X3/SPARC Study Group on Data Base Management Systems [1975] "Interim Report", *FDT (ACM SIGMOD Records) 7*, 2 (1975),

2. Aho, A. V., Beeri, C. and Ullman, J. D. [1979] "The Theory of Joins in Relational Data Bases," *ACM Trans. on Database Systems 3*, 3 (1979), 297-314.

3. Beeri, C., Bernstein, P. A. and Goodman, N. [1978] "A Sophisticate's Introduction to Database Normalization Theory," *Proc. 4th Int. Conf. on Very Large Data Bases*, Berlin (Sept. 1978), 113-124.

4. Chang, C. L. and Lee, R.C.T. [1973] *Symbolic Logic and Mechanical Theorem Proving*, Academic Press, New York-London, 1973.

5. Codd, E. F. [1970] "A Relational Model for Large Shared Data Bases," *Comm. ACM 13*, 6 (June 1970), 377-387.

6. Codd, E. F. [1972] "Relational Completeness of Data Base Sublanguages." In: *Data Base Systems, Courant Computer Science Symposia Series 6* (R. Rustin, Ed.), Prentice-Hall, Englewood Cliffs, N.J. (1972) 65-98.

7. Codd, E. F. [1975] "Understanding Relations." *FDT (ACM SIGMOD Records) 7*, 3-4 (1975), 23-28.

8. Codd, E. F. [1979] "Extending the Database Relational Model to Capture More Meaning," *ACM Trans. on Database Systems 4*, 4 (1979), 397-434.

9. Date, C. J. [1977] *An Introduction to Database Systems (Second Edition)*, Addison-Wesley, Reading, Mass., 1977.

10. Fagin, R. [1979] "A Normal Form for Relational Databases that is Based on Domains and Keys." *IBM Research Report RJ 2520*, San Josè, California, May 1979.

11. Gallaire, H. and Minker, J. (Eds.) [1978] *Logic and Data Bases*. Plenum, New York, 1978.

12. Gallaire, H., Minker, J. and Nicolas, J. M. [1978] "An Overview and Introduction to Logic and Data Bases." In: *Logic and Data Bases* (H. Gallaire and J. Minker, Eds.), Plenum Press, New York, 1978, 3-30.

13. Grant, J. [1977] "Null Values in a Relational Data Base." *Information Processing Letters 6*, 5 (1977), 156-157.

14. Hall, P.A.V., Hitchcock, P., and Todd, S.J.P. [1975] "An Algebra of Relations for Machine Computation." *IBM UKSC 0066* (Jan. 1975), Peterlee, Great Britain.

15. Hermes, H. [1967] *Einführung in die Verbandstheorie*, Springer-Verlag, Berlin-Heidelberg-New York, 1967.

16. Lacroix, M. and Pirotte, A. [1976] "Generalized Joins," *ACM SIGMOD Records 8*, 3 (Sept. 1976), 14-15.

17. Lipski, W., Jr. [1979] "On Semantic Issues Connected with Incomplete Information Data Bases," *ACM Trans. on Database Systems 4*, 3 (1979), 262-296.

18. Language Structure Group of the CODASYL Development Committee [1962] "An Information Algebra," *Comm. ACM 5* (1962), 190-204.

19. Navathe, S. B. and Lemke, J. [1979] "On the Implementation of a Conceptual Schema Model within a Three Level DBMS Architecture," *Prod. National Computer Conf. '79*, AFIPS Press, 1979,

697-708.

20. Nicolas, J. M., and Gallaire, H. [1978] "Data Base: Theory vs. Interpretation." In: *Logic and Data Bases* (H. Gallaire and J. Minker, Eds.), Plenum, New York, 1978, 33-54.

21. Reiter, R. [1978] "On Closed World Databases." In: *Logic and Data Bases* (H. Gallaire and J. Minker, Eds.), Plenum, New York, 1978, 55-76.

22. Robinson, J. A. [1965] "A Machine Oriented Logic Based on the Resolution Principle," *Journal ACM 12*, 1 (1965) 23-41.

23. Ullman, J. D. [1980] *Principles of Database Systems*. Computer Science Press, Potomac, Maryland, 1980.

24. Vassiliou, Y. [1979] "Null Values in Data Base Management — A Denotational Semantics Approach," *Proc. ACM SIGMOD 1979 Conference*, Boston, 162-169.

25. Yasuhara, A. [1971] *Recursive Function Theory and Logic*. Academic Press, New York-London, 1971.

26. Zaniolo, C. [1976] "Analysis and Design of Relational Schemata for Database Systems," Ph.D. Dissertation, UCLA, 1976 (Technical Report UCLA-ENG-7669, July 1976).

ABOUT NATURAL LOGIC

A. Colmerauer and J. F. Pique

Université d'Aix-Marseille II

Marseille, France

ABSTRACT

The use of first-order logic in data bases raises problems about representing relations that are not defined everywhere. The solution to this problem is to use a 3-valued logic with the truth value "undefined". This paper is concerned with the naturalness of such a logic, its power and its connection with classical logic.

INTRODUCTION

Many problems which arise in knowledge representation with classical 2-valued logic come from the absence of the notion of presupposition. As Keenan [1972] has shown, at the least, a 3-valued logic must be introduced to deal with presuppositions in natural languages. We present here a 3-valued extension of classical logic which, from our point of view, is convenient and natural. After an informal introduction to the basis of our system, we study in detail the boolean algebra which underlines it; this algebra is an extension of the one developed by D. A. Bochvar as described in Rescher [1969]. Then we define precisely the whole system with its quantifiers. It turns out that every deduction can be transformed into a deduction in classical 2-valued logic. This is a very interesting result. We conclude by describing very briefly the question-answering (QA) system which originated this paper and was implemented by J. F. Pique [1978]. This system, which deals with natural language, was influenced deeply by the work described in A. Colmerauer [1979] and in R. Pasero [1980]. Readers who are interested by the treatment of presupposition in linguistics may consult L. Karttunen [1963] and R. Zuber [1972].

PRESUPPOSITION AND 3-VALUED LOGIC

Natural Language and Presupposition

Any assertion in natural language carries a certain number of presuppositions: if we assert

(1) toc saw mary

without knowing anything about toc, anyone will conclude that toc is a being capable of seeing *and* that mary was in his field of vision. But if we say

(2) toc did not see mary

in this case we conclude that toc is a being capable of seeing *and* that mary was *not* in his field of vision. Thus it appears that an assertion in natural language links two types of properties. A property which cannot be denied, which we shall call a presupposition, and which can be seen as the semantic field of the assertion, and a description property which is asserted as true or false (in the case of a negation). To represent such a behavior we shall introduce the presupposition operator "if" with the fundamental properties:

(3) if(p,q) = true ⇔ and(p,q) = true

(4) not(if(p,q)) = true ⇔ if(p,not(q)) = true

where p is a presupposition and q a description property. We notice that the operator "if" enables us to introduce quite naturally the domains used in question answering systems for limiting the scope of negative questions: to the questions

(5) who does not distribute the product Ul ?

(6) who distributes the product Ul ?

we are only interested in the answers for which certain properties (domains) are true (for example bolt 49, table 66... will not be considered as valid answers). The domains of the relationship "x distributes the product y" are respectively the persons for x and the products for y. These domains appear in fact as presuppositions on the arguments of the relationship. If we represent this by something like:

(7) distribute (x,y) = if(and(person(x),product(y)),
isdistributorof(x,y))

we can see that, using (3) and (4), the questions

(8) x ? not(distribute(x,Ul) = true

(9) x ? distribute(x,Ul) = true

will give respectively the correct answers to the questions (5) and (6).

What happens when a presupposition is not true? If we find out for example that toc is a second name for the object bolt 49, the assertion (1) cannot be true, but its negation (2) seems hardly any more acceptable. This is still clearer if we consider the property "work with"; the assertion:

(10) john works with himself

is not true, but its negation

(11) john does not work with himself

is not true either. It appears then that two values of truth are not sufficient to account for the properties of natural language. We shall therefore introduce the truth value "undefined" to represent the idea of "absurd" or "meaningless". Thus the presupposition operator "if" is such that:

(12) $p \neq \text{true} \Rightarrow \text{if}(p,q) = \text{undefined}$.

If we consider that the relation "x works with y" presupposes that x and y are persons and that x is different from y, from (12) we deduce immediately that (10) and (11) are undefined. If we ask questions like

(13) who works with john ?

(14) who does not work with john ?

with

x works with y = if(and(person(x),differentfrom(x,y)),
isworkmate(x,y))

we shall never obtain abnormal answers such as (10) or (11). One notices that a QA system provided simply with domains does not enable us to avoid such anomalies. From the above we define the connector "if" and extend the connector "not" thus:

if(p,q) =
undefined if p is not true
q otherwise

not(p) =
 undefined if and only if p is undefined.

If we remember that "undefined" stands for "meaningless", it seems quite natural to say that the conjunction or the disjunction of a proposition with something meaningless yields a sentence which can neither be true nor false as for example:

john sells or eats cars

So we extend "and" and "or" to three values by stating:

and(p,q) = or(p,q) =
 undefined as soon as one of the propositions is undefined

One can notice that these extensions preserve De Morgan laws.

Quantifiers and Presupposition

Sentences in natural language contain articles. The latter may be considered as quantifiers joining a statement around a common noun introduced by the article, to a statement built around the verb of the sentence (Colmerauer [1979]). We shall represent them by quantifiers with three arguments: the first is the quantified variable, the second, the statement around the common noun, the third the statement around the verb. Let us consider the assertion:

(15) each salesman distributes Ul.

which we shall represent by

each(x,pl,p2)
 pl = salesman(x)
 p2 = distribute(x,Ul).

What shall we say about this assertion if there is no salesman? If we say that it is true, then to the question

(16) which products does each salesman distribute?,

we shall obtain the answer Ul (in fact all the products) since (15) is true, which is unacceptable. If we say it is false, then the assertion

(17) a salesman does not distribute Ul

ought to be true since it is the negation of (15). As it is obviously not true, it appears that the assertion (15) is undefined in this case. So the article "each" in (15) introduces the presupposition that an entity satisfies the property "to be a salesman". The presupposition is even stronger because:

(18) each bolt distributes Ul

will also be undefined because, even if entities satisfying the statement pl exist, the statement p2 will not be defined for any of these. Moreover, one cannot impose that p2 is defined for all entities satisfying pl, since the sentence

(19) each person works with john

would be undefined because, for the person john, the property "works with" is undefined. So it appears that "each(x,pl,p2)" presupposes that there exists at least one entity for which pl is true and p2 is defined. The value of a proposition "each(x,pl,p2)" will then be

- undefined if there exists no entity such that pl is true and p2 is defined
- false if there exists an entity such that pl is true and p2 is false,
- true if there exists an entity such that pl and p2 are true and, for all entities, pl true implies p2 true or undefined.

We notice that to a question like

(20) who distributes each product?,

represented by,

(21) x? each(y,product(y),distribute(x,y)) = true,

we can only obtain the answer "nil" if the products and persons likely to distribute them actually exist. If not, the question will be undefined and we can reply "there is a false presupposition in your question".

N.B. In a question like (20) where the question deals with an argument of the proposition, and not with its truth value, the role of "each" can be used to introduce a multiple question (see Pique [1978] for a discussion on this subject). In order to remain clear we shall restrict ourselves to sentences outside these cases, which does not alter in any way the validity of our system.

The quantifier "a(x,pl,p2)" will enable us in the same way to express assertions like

(22) "a car is blue"
pl = car(x)
p2 = isblue(x)

we shall define the value of "a(x,pl,p2)" as

- undefined if there exists no entity such that pl is true and p2 is defined,
- true if there exists an entity such that pl and p2 are true,
- false if there exists an entity such that pl is true and p2 is false and, for each entity, when pl is true p2 is false or undefined.

The value of the proposition "no(x,pl,p2)" is deduced immediately by observing that it is the negation of "a(x,pl,p2)":

no(x,pl,p2) = not(a(x,pl,p2)).

One can notice moreover that

each(x,pl,p2) = no(x,pl,not(p2)).

Let us now see if it is possible, with some extensions, to express the natural quantifiers "a", "each", "no" by the quantifiers "exist" and "all" of classical logic. If we look at the definition of the value of the proposition "each(x,pl,p2)" for example, one can note that this definition can be formulated solely in relation to the value of "if(pl,p2)", instead of those of pl and p2 separately (for example "each(x,pl,p2)" will be undefined when "if(pl,p2)" is undefined for any x). This leads us to generalize the quantifier "all(x,p)" to three values as follows:

all(x,p) will be

- undefined iff for all x, p is undefined,
- false iff there exists x such that p is false,
- true iff whatever x is, p is true or undefined, and there exists x such that p is true.

We have, therefore:

each(x,pl,p2) = all(x,if(pl,p2)),

no(x,pl,p2) = all(x,if(pl,not(p2))).

We shall also generalize the existential quantifier by:

exist(x,p) will be

— undefined iff for all x, p is undefined,

— true iff there exists x such that p is true,

— false iff whatever x is, p is false or undefined, and there exists x such that p is false.

This leads us to the relationship,

a(x,p1,p2) = exist(x,if(p1,p2)).

Note that the relations of classical logic are maintained:

not(exist (x,p)) = all(x,not(p)) , and

not(all(x,p)) = exist(x,not(p)),

but that the quantifiers "exist" and "all" cannot be seen as a generalization of "and" and "or". Various types of quantifiers have been defined and studied in A. Mostowski [1957].

THE ADEQUATE 3-VALUED BOOLEAN ALGEBRA

Before formalizing a complete logical system with quantification, we will first define and study the 3-valued boolean algebra which we have introduced informally.

Basic Functions

Let us take the three truth-values:

1 to represent "true"

0 to represent "false"

ω to represent "undefined" or "meaningless"

The classical boolean functions are extended to three values by considering that it is sufficient that one operand is undefined to produce an undefined result:

not[*1*] = *0*, *not*[*0*] = *1*, *not*[ω] = ω,

and[p,q] = min{p,q} with $\omega < 0 < 1$,

or[p,q] = max{p,q} with $0 < 1 < \omega$.

It follows that the usual equalities still hold:

not[*not*[p]] = p ,

not[*and*[p,q]] = *or*[*not*[p], *not*[q]],

not[*or*[p,q]] = *and*[*not*[p], *not*[q]].

To deal with presuppositions we introduce:

if[p,q] =

q if p = *1*

ω if p $\neq$ *1*.

The behavior of this function with regard to negation is characteristic:

not[*if*[p,q]] = *if*[p, *not*[q]] .

It is convenient to be able to go back to a two-valued logic. The two simplest functions allowing this to be done are:

true[p] =	*defined*[p] =
1 if p = *1*	*1* if p $\neq$ ω
0 if p $\neq$ *1*	*0* if p = ω

Completeness

It is interesting to show that it is possible to express any n-ary 3-valued Boolean function by the means of composition of our previous defined functions and constants: *not, true, defined, and, or, if, 1, 0,* ω.

First we prove that it is possible to express the function:

case[ω,p,q,r] = p

case[*0*,p,q,r] = q

case[*1*,p,q,r] = r.

We have:

case[k,p,q,r] =

or[*pick*[*undef*[k],p], *or*[*pick*[*false*[k],q], *pick*[*true*[k],r]]]

with:

pick[l,p] =	*undef*[k] =	*false*[k] =
p if l = *1*	*1* if k = ω	*1* if k = *0*
1 if l $\neq$ *1*	*0* if k $\neq$ ω	*0* if k $\neq$ *0*

We can now represent these three functions by:

$$pick[l,p] = if[or[not[l],\ defined[p]],\ and[l,true[p]]]\ ,$$
$$undef[k] = not[defined[k]],$$
$$false[k] = true[not[k]].$$

To express any n-ary function $f[p_1,\ldots,p_n]$, we note that in the special case where n = 0 it is reduced to *1*, *0*, or ω and that in the other cases it is possible to decrease n as much as one wants by decomposing the function according to the scheme:

$$f[p_1,\ldots,p_n] = case[p_n, f[p_1,\ldots,p_{n-1},\omega],\ f[p_1,\ldots,p_{n-1},0],\ f[p_1,\ldots,p_{n-1},1]].$$

A stronger result can be obtained by considering the equalities:

$$1 = not[0]$$
$$0 = true[if[not[p],\ p]]$$
$$\omega = if[not[p],\ if[p,p]]$$
$$or[p,q] = not[and[not[p],\ not[q]]]$$
$$and[p,q] = if[defined[p],\ if[defined[q],\ true[if[p,q]]]]$$
$$true[p] = defined[if[p,p]]$$
$$defined[p] = not[true[if[not[true[not[p]]],\ not[true[p]]]].$$

This result is:

> Any n-ary 3-valued Boolean function (n > 0) can be expressed using only functions from the set {*if*,*not*,*true*} or using only functions from the set {*if*,*not*,*defined*}

Moreover the sets {*if*,*not*,*true*} and {*if*,*not*,*defined*}are minimal, which means that they contain no strict subset which allows one to express every function. To prove this last point let f be a unary function. It has the properties:

$f[\omega] = \omega$ if f is constructed only from {*if*,*not*}

$f[1] = 1$ if f is constructed only from {*if*,*true*,*defined*}

$f[0] \neq \omega$ if f is constructed only from {*if*,*true*,*defined*}.

The function

$$f[p] = \begin{cases} 0 \text{ if } p = \omega \\ \omega \text{ if } p \neq \omega \end{cases}$$

has none of the three properties and so it cannot be constructed only from one of the three last sets and a fortiori not from a strict subset of {*if*,*not*,*true*} or {*if*,*not*,*defined*}.

We conclude by noting that if we had taken as primitive the function:

$$undef[p] = \begin{cases} 1 \text{ if } p = \omega \\ 0 \text{ if } p \neq \omega \end{cases}$$

the equalities

$$defined[p] = not[undef[p]]$$

$$not[p] = if[undef[if[undef[p], undef[p]]], undef[if[p,p]]]$$

would have allowed us to reduce the minimal subset {*if*,*not*,*defined*} to {*if*,*undef*}

DEFINITION OF OUR LOGICAL SYSTEM

We now have all the elements to define, in a very precise way, the logic with quantification introduced at the beginning of the chapter. As usual, we distinguish two aspects: syntax, which deals with the way formulae look, and semantics, which deals with what they mean.

Syntax

Let F be a set of functional symbols, R a set of relational symbols and V an infinite enumerable set of variables. F_n and R_n represent respectively the set of n-ary functional and n-ary relational symbols. We define two types of formulae: terms, which are related to individuals, and propositions, which are related to truth-values.

Definition 1

The *set* T *of terms* is the smallest set of words over the alphabet $V \cup F \cup \{(\ , \ ), \text{comma}\}$, which are of one of the 3 forms:

(1) x with $x \in V$

(2) f_0 with $f_0 \in F_0$

(3) $f_n(t_1,\ldots,t_n)$ with $t_1,\ldots,t_n \in T$ and $f_n \in F_n$.

Definition 2

The *set* P *of propositions* is the smallest set of words over the alphabet $V \cup F \cup R \cup \{1,0,\Omega$,not,true,defined,and,or,if,exist,all,(,), comma}, which are of one of the 13 forms:

(1)	1		
(2)	0		
(3)	Ω		
(4)	r_0 with $r_0 \in R_0$		
(5)	$r_n(t_1,\ldots,t_n)$	with	$r_n \in R_n$ and $t_1,\ldots,t_n \in T$
(6)	not(p)	with	$P^n \in P^n$
(7)	true(p)	with	$p \in P$
(8)	defined(p)	with	$p \in P$
(9)	and(p,q)	with	$p,q \in P$
(10)	or(p,q)	with	$p,q \in P$
(11)	if(p,q)	with	$p,q \in P$
(12)	exist(x,p)	with	$x \in V$, $p \in P$
(13)	all(x,p)	with	$x \in V$, $p \in P$.

Semantics

The meaning of a formula will be the values it takes in different interpretations of the variables, the functional symbols and the relational symbols.

To define an interpretation we need:

- the set of truth-values: $\{1,0,\omega\}$
- a *nonempty* set D: the domain of interpretation.

Definition 3

An *interpretation* I is a mapping from $V \cup F \cup R$ to a set constructed from $\{\omega,0,1\}$ and D, which is such that:

$Ix \in D$ if $x \in V$

$If_0 \in D$ if $f_0 \in F_0$

If_n is a mapping from D^n to D if $f_n \in F_n$

$Ir_0 \in 0,1$ if $r_0 \in R_0$

Ir_n is a mapping from D^n to $\{0,1\}$ if $r_n \in R_n$.

It should be noted that the truth value ω is not really used here, which means that relational symbols are interpreted as classical 2-valued relations. We will come back to this subject later. As done by Lyndon [1964] in his nice little book, *Notes on Logic*, we introduce the notion of interpretations which differs from one another just on one variable. This helps to define the meaning of quantification:

Definition 4

The *set* S[I,x] is the set of all interpretations that agree with I on $V \cup F \cup R$ except possibly on x.

For every formula f we can now define its value $\phi_I[f]$ in a given interpretation I.

Definition 5

The *value* $\phi_I[t] \in D$ *of a term* t *in an interpretation* I is defined recursively on the 3 possible forms of t:

(1) $\phi_I[x] = Ix$

(2) $\phi_I[f_0] = If_0$

(3) $\phi_I[f_n(t_1,\ldots,t_n)] = [If_n][\phi_I[t_1],\ldots,\phi_I[t_n]]$.

Definition 6

The *value* $\phi_I[p] \in \{\omega,0,1\}$ *of a proposition* p *in an interpretation* I is defined recursively on the 13 possible forms of p:

(1) $\phi_I[1] = 1$

(2) $\phi_I[0] = 0$

(3) $\phi_I[\Omega] = \omega$

(4) $\phi_I[r_0] = Ir_0$

(5) $\phi_I[r_n(t_1,\ldots,t_n)] = [Ir_n][\phi_I[t_1],\ldots,\phi_I[t_n]]$

(6) $\phi_I[\text{not}(p)] = \textit{not}[\phi_I[p]]$

(7) $\phi_I[\text{true}(p)] = \textit{true}[\phi_I[p]]$

(8) $\phi_I[\text{defined}(p)]] = \textit{defined}[\phi_I[p]]$

(9) $\phi_I[\text{and}(p,q)] = \textit{and}[\phi_I[p],\ \phi_I[q]]$

(10) $\phi_I[\text{or}(p,q)] = \textit{or}[\phi_I[p],\ \phi_I[q]]$

(11) $\phi_I[\text{if}(p,q)] = \textit{if}[\phi_I[p],\ \phi_I[q]]$

(12) $\phi_I[\text{exist}(x,p)] =$

1 if there exists $J \in S[I,x]$ with $\phi_J[p] = 1$

0 if there does not exist $J \in S[I,x]$ with $\phi_J[p] = 1$ but there exists $K \in S[I,x]$ with $\phi_K[p] = 0$

ω if for all $J \in S[I,x]$ we have $\phi_J[p] = \omega$

(13) $\phi_I[\text{all}(x,p)] =$

1 if there does not exist $J \in S[I,x]$ with $\phi_J[p] = 0$ but there exists $K \in S[I,x]$ with $\phi_K[p] = 1$

0 if there exists $J \in S[I,x]$ with $\phi_J[p] = 0$

ω if for all $J \in S[I,x]$ we have $\phi_J[p] = \omega$.

Of course, *not, true, defined, and, or, if* are defined by

$\textit{not}[1] = 0$ $\qquad$ $\textit{true}[p] =$ $\qquad$ $\textit{defined}[p] =$

$\textit{not}[0] = 1$ $\qquad$ 1 if $p = 1$ $\qquad$ 1 if $p \neq \omega$

$\textit{not}[\omega] = \omega$ $\qquad$ 0 if $p \neq 1$ $\qquad$ 0 if $p = \omega$

$\textit{and}[p,q] = \min\{p,q\}$ with $\omega < 0 < 1$

$\textit{or}[p,q] = \max\{p,q\}$ with $0 < 1 < \omega$

$\textit{if}[p,q] =$

q if $p = 1$

ω if $p \neq 1$.

Two remarks are necessary before ending this section.

It is obvious that the value of a proposition, in general, depends on the interpretation of free-occurring variables, but not on the interpretation of bound-occurring variables.
(The notion of free and bounded occurrences of variables is assumed to be familiar to the reader.)

We interpret relational symbols by 2-valued relations instead of 3-valued relations for the following reasons:

— for the sake of simplicity and to be able, later on, to switch back smoothly to 2-valued logic,

— because it is not a restriction: any 3-valued relation r can be expressed by two 2-valued relations r' and r" using the fact that if

$$r'[t_1,\ldots,t_n] = \textit{defined}[r[t_1,\ldots,t_n]]$$
$$r''[t_1,\ldots,t_n] = \textit{true}[r[t_1,\ldots,t_n]]$$

then

$$r[t_1,\ldots,t_n] = \textit{if}[r'[t_1,\ldots,t_n],\ r''[t_1,\ldots,t_n]].$$

PROPERTIES OF OUR LOGICAL SYSTEM

Some Equivalences

It is natural to introduce the following equivalence relation between propositions:

$$p \equiv q \quad \text{iff} \quad \text{in every interpretation I}$$
$$\phi_I[p] = \phi_I[q]$$

It must be noted that this equivalence relation has the same property as equality with respect to substitution, that is:

> if in a proposition p one replaces a subproposition q by a proposition equivalent to q, one obtains a new proposition equivalent to p.

The following equivalence rules concern the three unary connectors: "not", "true" and "defined". They are directly deducible from the definition of ϕ_I. The ntoations are those of the syntactic definition of a proposition.

not(1) ≡ 0
not(0) ≡ 1
not(Ω) ≡ Ω
not(not(p)) ≡ p
not(and(p,q)) ≡ or(not(p),not(q))
not(or(p,q)) ≡ and(not(p),not(q))
not(if(p,q)) ≡ if(p,not(q))
not(exit(x,p)) ≡ all(x,not(p))
not(all(x,p)) ≡ exist(x,not(p))

true(1) ≡ 1
true(0) ≡ 0
true(Ω) ≡ 0
true(r_0) ≡ r_0
true($r_n(t_1,\ldots,t_n)$) ≡ $r_n(t_1,\ldots,t_n)$
true(not(true(p))) ≡ not(true(p))
true(true(p)) ≡ true(p)
true(defined(p)) ≡ defined(p)
true(and(p,q)) ≡ and(true(p),true(q))
true(or(p,q)) ≡ and(and(defined(p),defined(q)),or(true(p),
true(q)))

true(if(p,q))≡ and(true(p),true(q))
true(exist(x,p)) ≡ exist(x,true(p))
true(all(x,p))≡and(exist(x,true(p)),not(exist(x,true(not(p)))))

defined(1) ≡ 1
defined(0) ≡ 1
defined(Ω) ≡ 0
defined(r_0) ≡ 1
defined($r_n(t_1,\ldots,t_n)$) ≡ 1
defined(not(p)) ≡ defined(p)
defined(true(p)) ≡ 1
defined(defined(p)) ≡ 1
defined(and(p,q)) ≡ and(defined(p),defined(q))
defined(or(p,q)) ≡ and(defined(p),defined(q))
defined(if(p,q)) ≡ and(true(p),defined(q))
defined(exist(x,p)) ≡ exist(x,defined(p))
defined(all(x,p)) ≡ exist(x,defined(p)).

Back to Two Truth-Values

Let us look at the syntactic definition of the set P of propositions described in the section DEFINITION OF OUR LOGICAL SYSTEM, Syntax, Consider the subset P' of propositions obtained by suppressing the forms (3), (7), (8) and (11). There are therefore only 9 forms left:

(1)	1	
(2)	0	
(4)	r_0 with $r_0 \in R_0$	
(5)	$r_n(t_1,\ldots,t_n)$	with $r_n \in R_n$ and $t_1,\ldots,t_n \in T$
(6)	not(p)	with $p \in P'$
(9)	and(p,q)	with $p,q \in P'$
(10)	or(p,q)	with $p,q \in P'$
(12)	exist(x,p)	with $x \in V$ and $p \in P'$
(13)	all(x,p)	with $x \in V$ and $p \in P'$.

We see now that the value of a proposition $p \in P'$ is never "undefined". This results on the one hand, from the fact that the relational symbols are interpreted as 2-valued relations and on the other hand, from the absence of the proposition "Ω" and the connector "if". Thus the definition of ϕ_I is simplified into:

(1a) $\phi_I[1] = \mathit{1}$

(2a) $\phi_I[0] = \mathit{0}$

(4a) $\phi_I[r_0] = Ir_0$

(5a) $\phi_I[r_n(t_1,\ldots,t_n)] = [Ir_n][\phi_I[t_1],\ldots,\phi_I[t_n]]$

(6a) $\phi_I[\text{not}[p]] =$

1 if $\phi_I[p] = 0$

0 if $\phi_I[p] = 1$

(9a) $\phi_I[\text{and}(p,q)] = \min\{\phi_I[p], \phi_I[q]\}$ with $0 < 1$

(10a) $\phi_I[\text{or}(p,q)] = \max\{\phi_I[p], \phi_I[q]\}$ with $0 < 1$

(12a) $\phi_I[\text{exist}(x,p)] =$

1 if there exists $J \in S[I,x]$ with $\phi_J[p] = 1$

0 if for all $J \in S[I,x]$ we have $\phi_J[p] = 0$

(13a) $\phi_I[\text{all}(x,p)] =$

1 if for all $J \in S[I,x]$ we have $\phi_J[p] = 1$

0 if there exists $J \in S[I,x]$ with $\phi_J[p] = 0$.

It is pleasant to see then that things are settled back to classical two-valued first order logic, the signs $\neg, \wedge, \vee, \exists, \forall$ being respectively "not", "and", "or", "exist", and "all". We will now consider three interesting mappings from P to P'.

Definition 7

The *mappings* T, F, D *from* P *to* P' are defined recursively on the 13 possible forms of a proposition:

(01a) T[1] = 1
(02a) T[0] = 0
(03a) T[Ω] = 0
(04a) $T[r_0] = r_0$
(05a) $T[r_n(t_1,\ldots,t_n)] = r_n(t_1,\ldots,t_n)$
(06a) T[not(p)] = F[p]
(07a) T[true(p)] = T[p]
(08a) T[defined(p)] = D[p]
(09a) T[and(p,q)] = and(T[p],T[q])
(10a) T[or(p,q)] = and(and(D[p],D[q]),or(T[p],T[q]))
(11a) T[if(p,q)] = and(T[p],T[q])
(12a) T[exist(x,p)] = exist(x,T[p])
(13a) T[all(x,p)] = and(exist(x,T[p]),not(exist(x,F[p])))
(01b) F[1] = 0
(02b) F[0] = 1
(03b) F[Ω] = 0
(04b) $F[r_0] = \text{not}(r_0)$
(05b) $F[r_n(t_1,\ldots,t_n)] = \text{not}(r_n(t_1,\ldots,t_n))$
(06b) F[not(p)] = T[p]
(07b) F[true(p)] = not(T[p])

(08b) F[defined(p)] = not(D[p])
(09b) F[and(p,q)] = and(and(D[p],D[q]),or(F[p],F[q]))
(10b) F[or(p,q)] = and(F[p],F[q])
(11b) F[if(p,q)] = and(T[p],F[q])
(12b) F[exist(x,p)] = and(exist(x,F[p]),not(exist(x,T[p])))
(13b) F[all(x,p)] = exist(x,F[p])
(01c) D[1] = 1
(02c) D[0] = 1
[03c) D[Ω] = 0
(04c) $D[r_0] = 1$
(05c) $D[r_n(t_1,\ldots,t_n)] = 1$
(06c) D[not(p)] = D[p]
(07c) D[true(p)] = 1
(08c) D[defined(p)] = 1
(09c) D[and(p,q)] = and(D[p],D[q])
(10c) D[or(p,q)] =and(D[p],D[q])
(11c) D[if(p,q)] = and(T[p],D[q])
(12c) D[exist(x,p)] = exist(x,D[p])
(13c) D[all(x,p)] = exist(x,D[p]).

We notice that if "T[ ]", "F[ ]", "D[ ]", "=" are respectively replaced by "true( )", "true(not( ))", "defined", "≡" these definitions are transformed in equivalences directly deducible from those described in the section PROPERTIES OF OUR LOGICAL SYSTEM, Some Equivalences. It follows that:

T[p] ≡ true(p)
F[p] ≡ true(not(p))
D[p] ≡ defined(p)

and of course T[p], F[p] and D[p], contrariwise to p, are necessarily propositions of classical 2-valued logic.

Consider now a set of propositions $p_1,\ldots,p_n$. Let W be the set of all the interpretations in which each p_i has the value "true", that is, *1*. We may consider that W represents a partially known "world". It is interesting to be able to deduce all the statements q which have the value "true" in this "world". We write them $\{p_1,\ldots,p_n\} \models q$. More precisely, we have the following

Definition 8

The *deduction relation* $\models$ is defined by:

$\{p_1,\ldots,p_n\} \models q$ iff for every interpretation I

$\phi_I[p_1] = 1,\ldots$ and $\phi_I[p_n] = 1$
imply $\phi_I[q] = 1$.

Definition 8 is the classical definition of semantic deduction. We have:

$$\{p_1,\ldots,p_n\} \models q \quad \text{iff}$$
$$\{true(p_1),\ldots,true(p_n)\} \models true(q) \quad \text{iff}$$
$$\{T[p_1],\ldots,T[p_n]\} \models T[q].$$

This proves that every deduction in our 3-valued logic can be reduced easily to a deduction in classical 2-valued first order logic.

Let us take an example. Consider the assertions

P_1 : A is a table
P_2 : B is a person
P_3 : nobody is laughing
P_4 : A is not laughing
P_5 : B is not laughing.

We suppose that only persons can laugh. So we take:

x is a table ⇔ table(x)
x is a person ⇔ person(x)
x is laughing ⇔ if(person(x),laugh(x)).

We obtain:

P_1 = table(A)
P_2 = person(B)
P_3 = all(x,not(if(person(x),laugh(x)))
P_4 = not(if(person(A),laugh(A))
P_5 = not(if(person(B),laugh(B)).

And so:

$$T[P_1] = table(A)$$
$$T[P_2] = person(B)$$
$$T[P_3] = \exists x(person(x) \land \neg laugh(x)) \land \forall y(\neg person(y) \lor \neg laugh(y))$$
$$T[P_4] = person(A) \land \neg laugh(A)$$
$$T[P_5] = person(B) \land \neg laugh(B).$$

We want to prove that:

$$\{P_1, P_2, P_3\} \models P_5.$$

That is,

$$T[P_1], T[P_2], T[P_3] \models T[P_5].$$

We can do a proof by inconsistency (that is, deny the conclusion and show that a contradiction arises):

$$\{T[P_1], T[P_2], T[P_3], \neg T[P_5]\} \models 0$$

We transform the propositions into clauses:

(1)	table(A)
(2)	person(B)
(3a)	person(K)
(3b)	$\neg$laugh(K)
(3c)	$\neg$person(x) V $\neg$laugh(x)
(5)	$\neg$person(B) V laugh(B)

The proof by resolution (see the chapter by Gallaire, Minker, and Nicolas for a discussion of resolution) gives:

(2) and (3c) $\Rightarrow$ (6) $\neg$laugh(B)

(6) and (5) $\Rightarrow$ (7) $\neg$person(B)

(7) and (2) $\Rightarrow \Box$.

By the same technique it would not have been possible to prove:

$$\{P_1, P_2, P_3\} \models P_4$$

This is reasonable since it is hard to assert that a table is not laughing, at least in data bases.

AN EXAMPLE APPLICATION

In this section we illustrate the application of our system to querying a data base. The example used represents a specific interpretation (closed world assumption as in Reiter [1978]) and describes in a 2-valued system the relationships existing between teachers, students, language courses and residence. The true facts are represented explicitly, the false ones implicitly. The queries are made in natural language and translated by a metamorphosis grammar (Colmerauer [1978]), into a formula p of the 3-valued system. As we have a finite world and only one interpretation, we can evaluate p to obtain the answer by following recursively the definition of $\phi_I[p]$. The value of a formula can also be obtained from the evaluation of several formulas: the value of p can be deduced from the values of the three formulas "true(p)", "true(not(p))", "not(defined(p))" (which are respectively true if and only if $\phi_I[p] = 1$, $\phi_I[p] = 0$, $\phi_I[p] = \omega$). We notice that, for each value of p, one and only one of the three formulas can be true. For example we can deduce the value of p from the value of the first and the second one. This is interesting because, as stated in the section Back to Two Truth-Values, values of the formulas "true(p)" and "true(not(p))", are respectively equal to those of the formulas $p_1' = T[p]$ and $p_2' = F[p]$ of the 2-valued logic. Thus we can restrict ourselves to the simpler and more classical evaluations of $\phi_I[p_1']$ and $\phi_I[p_2']$ of 2-valued logic.

We obtain the formulas p_1' and p_2' with the mapping defined also in the section Back to Two Truth-Values. Moreover, if the value of $p_1' = T[p]$ turns out to be true, it is unnecessary to evaluate F[p]. Thus in most cases only one evaluation is needed since queries are true propositions in general.

The entire system is written in PROLOG (Roussel [1975]), a very high level programming language based on first order logic, and runs with virtual memory on a MOTOROLA 6800 micro computer with two floppy disks. In the trace below, the querying session is in bold capitals, English translation in italic and commentary in this font.

computer: J'ECOUTE
I listen
The system waits for a query to be entered.

user: OU HABITE YAN?
Where does Yan live?

computer: NICE
This is the answer, Nice.

computer: J'ECOUTE
I listen

user: OU N'HABITE PAS YAN?
Where doesn't Yan live?

computer: AIX
ARLES
NIMES
The answers are solely those for which the relationship "live" has a meaning (the only residences known from the system are Aix, Arles, Nice, Nimes).

J'ECOUTE

user: EST-CE QUE CHAQUE ETUDIANT DE GREC HABITE A NIMES?
Does each student of Greek live in Nimes?

computer: NON
no

The system is not successful in the evaluation of the transposed formula T[p], but is in F[p]: it concludes that some student of Greek doesn't live in Nimes.

J'ECOUTE

user: QUELS SONT LES ETUDIANTS DE GREC QUI N'HABITENT PAS NIMES?
Who are the students of Greek who do not live in Nimes?

computer: LUC
LEON

J'ECOUTE

user: QUELS SONT LES ETUDIANTS D'ALLEMAND QUI HABITENT A AIX?
Who are the students of German who live in Aix?

computer: VOTRE QUESTION N'A PAS DE SENS: IL DOIT Y AVOIR UNE PRESUPPOSITION FAUSSE.
Your question is meaningless: there must be a false presupposition.

The system evaluates to false both T[p] and F[p] since there are no students of German in the data base; thus p has the value "undefined". We would have obtained the same answer to the query "does a student of German live in Aix?".

computer: J'ECOUTE:

user: EST-CE QU'UN ETUDIANT APPREND L'ALLEMAND?
Does a student learn German?

computer: NON
no

As the presupposition is now only related to student existence, we obtain a defined answer.

computer: J'ECOUTE:

user: BONSOIR
Good evening.

The end of the session.

SUMMARY

We have shown how presuppositions introduce problems in data base systems. To handle these problems in a clean manner, we defined a complete three valued logic. We then proved that it is possible to transpose any deduction in the three-valued logical system into a deduction in classical first-order logic. This made it possible for us to use techniques, devised for first order logic, for deduction based on a three-valued logic. Finally, a natural language question-answering system was implemented in the language PROLOG using the techniques described in this chapter.

REFERENCES

1. Colmerauer, A. [1978] "Metamorphosis Grammars." In *Natural Language Communication with Computers* (L. Bolc Ed.) Lecture Notes in Computer Science 63, Springer-Verlag, 1978, 133-189.

2. Colmerauer, A. [1979] "Un Sous Ensemble Intéressant du Francais" *R.A.I.R.O. 13,* 4 (Oct. 1979), 309-336. In English as: "A Useful Subset of French," *Proceedings of the Workshop on Logic and Data Bases,* Toulouse, 1977, xxiv-1.

3. Karttunen, L. [1963] "Implicative Verbs." *Language 47*, 2 (1963).

4. Keenan, E. L. [1972] "On Semantically Based Grammar ", *Linguistic Inquiry 3,* 4 (Fall 1972), 413-459.

5. Lyndon, R. C. [1964] *Notes on Logic*, Van Nostrand Mathematical Studies #6, Van Nostrand Co., London, 1964.

6. Mostowski, A. [1957] "On a Generalization of Quantifiers", *Fundamenta Mathematicae* 44, 1 (Jan. 1957), 12-36.

7. Pasero, R. [1980] Thèse d'etat, On a Logical Model for Natural Languages, Groupe d'Intelligence Artificielle, Université d'Aix-Marseille II (to appear in 1980).

8. Pique, J. F. [1978] *Interrogation en Francais d'une Base de Donnée Relationnelle, memoire de DEA*, Groupe d'Intelligence Artificielle, Universite d'Aix-Marseille II, 1978.

9. Reiter, R. [1978] "On Closed World Data Bases." In *Logic and Data Bases* (H. Gallaire and J. Minker, Eds.), Plenum Press, New York, 55-76.

10. Rescher, N. [1969] *Many-Valued Logic,* McGraw-Hill, New York, 1969.

11. Roussel, Ph. [1975] *PROLOG, Manuel de Référence et d'Utilisation,* Groupe d'Intelligence Artificielle, Universite d'Aix-Marseille II, 1975.

12. Zuber, R. [1972] *Structure Presuppositionnelle du Language,* Dunod, Paris, 1972.

ASSIGNING MEANING TO ILL-DEFINED QUERIES EXPRESSED IN PREDICATE CALCULUS LANGUAGE [1]

Robert Demolombe

ONERA-CERT, Toulouse, France

ABSTRACT

When First Order Predicate Calculus (FOPC) is used as a query language without restriction, it may happen that the meaning of some queries is ill-defined. We syntactically characterize a subset of well formed formulas (WFFs) of FOPC which are "well defined", and we investigate different kinds of transformations which transform an ill-defined query into one that is "well defined". In one transformation we consider the range of unrestricted variables from the domains associated with the arguments of predicates. The root of the tree representing the query is then modified to restrict the variables to that range. We study the cases where the range is the union or the intersection of the domains associated with each occurrence of a variable. In a second transformation we modify the leaves of the tree in order to obtain a "well defined" query. Examples are used to compare the advantages and disadvantages of each method.

INTRODUCTION

In the relational model defined by Codd, a domain is assigned to each attribute of each relation. The values of the tuple arguments of the relations have to belong to these domains. The domains could be used to reject queries in which a variable has several occurrences, in the arguments of the relations, which are not associated with the same domain (as in languages defined from

1 This study was sponsored by IRIA project SIRIUS under contract No. 76-159.

many-sorted logic as described by Reiter [1981] in his chapter and by McSkimin and Minker [1978]). This is not actually done in implemented relational systems such as INGRES, System R and QBE. This constraint may be too strong. Indeed, if the user defines domains which are too wide (for example the domain Person), they will be useless (if in a query a variable occurs in two arguments of relations which are associated with the domains Man and Woman, for example). On the other hand, if the defined domains are too limited, some interesting queries may be rejected (if, for example, we have a query the answer to which contains men and women in the same set).

In more sophisticated systems, which allow queries in natural language or which use deductive procedures (MRPPs (Minker [1978]), DEDUCE (Chang [1978]), SYNTEX (Artaud and Nicolas [1972]), the query languages are, in many cases, based on the First Order Predicate Calculus. In these systems, the concept of domain is not introduced into the syntax of the languages, but as a special kind of information. This allows more facilities in the definition and use of the domains.

However, if we use First Order Predicate Calculus (FOPC) as a query language without any restriction, the meaning of some queries may be ill-defined. Some investigators (Kuhns [1970], DiPaola [1971], Artaud and Nicolas [1974], Pirotte [1976]) have studied, in depth, ways of characterizing ill defined queries. In Demolombe [1979a], we gave a syntactic characterization of a class of queries which are "well defined". This class is larger than the previous one. These queries are called "evaluable queries". Broadly, in these queries the range of each variable is explicitly defined. For example, instead of $\neg Q(a,x)$ we must have $P(x) \wedge \neg Q(a,x)$, where $P(x)$ makes the range of the variable x precise. In this chapter, we will use the same concept, slightly extended, in order to explain the various modules which can be defined on an evaluator of queries expressed in FOPC.

An overview of our approach is shown in Figure 1, Architecture of the Modules. An outline is presented here of the first three modules, and details are provided in the chapter.

Module 1 (see Figure 1) is used to determine if the query is evaluable. This module does not need any information related to the semantics of the relations; the criteria used are purely syntactic and do not use the concept of domain. If the query is evaluable, its meaning is well defined.

The role of Module 2 is to carry out a semantic check, using information concerning the domains of the relations and their structure. If, from the query and the semantic information, it is possible to deduce that no element in the data base can satisfy the query, then it can be rejected.

In Demolombe [1979a] we defined two transformations which associates, to each query, a condition which has to be satisfied by the domains in order to obtain an answer which is not an empty set.

When a query is not evaluable, it may be because the user made a mistake in writing the query or because the range of a variable was not defined. In the latter case we believe it to be too severe to reject the query and that it is preferable to try to modify it (function of module 3) so as to obtain an evaluable query and, at the same time, to change the meaning of the query as little as possible.

When we assign a precise meaning to an ill defined query, it is sometimes necessary to make subjective choices, hence the user must be notified and the transformed query printed for the user.

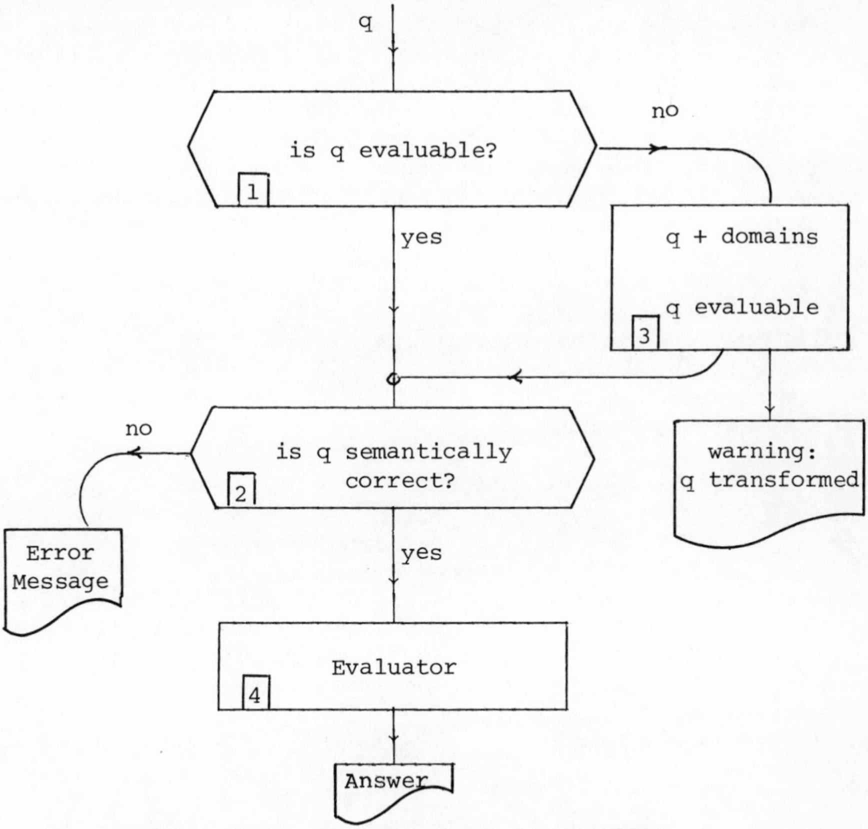

Figure 1. Architecture of the Modules

The aim of this paper is to present the various ways by which unevaluable queries can be transformed into evaluable queries (function of module 3). Clearly it is impossible to go from an ill-defined FOPC query back to the query the user had in mind. This chapter investigates what we believe are the transformations that give definite queries closest to the FOPC query given by the user.

In the section DEFINED QUERIES AND EVALUABLE QUERIES we summarize the concepts of defined and evaluable queries. In the section TRANSFORMATION OF QUERY ROOT we will study a first type of transformation which modifies the root of the tree representing the query. A second type of transformation which mainly modifies the leaves of the tree will be examined in the section TRANSFORMATION OF QUERY LEAVES.

DEFINED QUERIES AND EVALUABLE QUERIES

Defined Queries

We will first outline the definition of defined queries; a more precise definition can be found in Di Paola [1971]. If we consider the extensions of the relations of a data base as an interpretation of a First Order Theory in which the only true information is that corresponding to the extensions of the relations, then a defined query is a query the answer to which does not change when we add a new element to the domain of the interpretation without changing the true information.

Let us consider, for example, the relation:

live(x,y), with the following extensions:
live(a, Paris)
live(b, London)
live(c, London)

The domain of the interpretation is:

$$D = \{a, b, c, \text{Paris}, \text{London}\}$$

The answers to the queries q_1 and q_2, which will follow, will be, respectively a_1 and a_2, where the closed world assumption has been made (Reiter [1978]), that is, if we cannot find the data listed positively, we assume the negation to be true.

$q_1 = \neg \text{live}(x,\text{London})$

$a_1 = \{a, \text{Paris}, \text{London}\}$

$q_2 = \text{Live}(x,\text{Paris}) \vee \text{Live}(y,\text{London})$

$$a_2 = \{\langle a,a\rangle,\langle a,b\rangle,\langle a,c\rangle,\langle b,b\rangle,\langle c,b\rangle,\langle b,c\rangle,\langle c,c\rangle,\langle a,\text{Paris}\rangle,$$
$$\langle a,\text{London}\rangle,\langle \text{Paris},b\rangle,\langle \text{London},b\rangle,\langle \text{Paris},c\rangle,\langle \text{London},c\rangle\}$$

Now we add a new element, d, to the domain of the interpretation D, and we do not modify the extensions of the relations. Therefore, the true information is the same.

The new domain is:

$$D' = \{a,b,c,d, \text{ Paris, London}\}$$

It is easy to verify that the answers to queries q_1 and q_2 are not the same. We now have:

$$a_1' = a_1 \cup \{d\}$$

$$a_2' = a_2 \cup \{\langle a,d\rangle,\langle d,b\rangle,\langle d,c\rangle\}$$

The queries q_1 and q_2 are not defined queries. From this example, we can see intuitively that this kind of query cannot be accepted. It is obvious that it would be necessary to define the range of the variable x in q_1 and the range of the variables x and y in q_2.

If we define Person (x) with the following expression

$$\text{Person}(x) \equiv (\exists y)(\text{live}(x,y)),$$

then we can define the defined queries q_1' and q_2' corresponding to q_1 and q_2.

$$q_1' = \text{Person}(x) \wedge \neg\text{Live}(x,\text{London})$$

$$q_2' = \text{Person}(x) \wedge \text{Person}(y) \wedge (\text{Live}(x,\text{Paris}) \vee \text{Live}(y,\text{London}))$$

These queries are defined because their answers are the same in the two interpretations.

Until now, there has been no syntactic characterization of the set of all defined queries. The subset of evaluable queries includes the subset of "acceptable queries" defined by Artaud and Nicolas [1974], and the subset of "proper formulas" defined by Di Paola [1971]. Codd [1972] defined a set of WFFs of the Relational Calculus, named "range separable WFFs" and which are defined, corresponding to a subset of evaluable queries in FOPC. The new definition of evaluable queries, given below, also includes the subset of WFFs satisfying the range restricted property defined by Nicolas [1979].

Evaluable Queries

Restricted, unrestricted, positive and negative variables in a formula. In order to define evaluable queries, we have first to define restricted and unrestricted variables and, second, the positive and negative variables.

To simplify the definitions, we will use the following predicates:

Free(x,F) : x is free in the formula F
[Here, "free" has it usual meaning.]

Res(x,F) : x is restricted in the formula F

Unres(x,F) : x is unrestricted in the formula F

Pos(x,F) : x is positive in the formula F

Neg(x,F) : x is negative in the formula F

The purpose of defining the predicates Res, Unres, Pos and Neg is to generalize the following remarks to any formula.

It is easy to see that, if P_1 and P_2 are predicates, then the elementary formulae: $P_1(x) \vee P_2(y)$, $\neg P_2(x)$, $\forall x\ (P_2(x))$, and $\exists x\ (\neg P_2(x))$ are not defined, whereas: $P_1(x) \vee P_2(x)$, $P_1(x) \wedge \neg P_2(x)$, $\forall x\ (\neg P_1(x) \vee P_2(x))$ and $\exists x\ (P_1(x) \wedge \neg P_2(x))$ are defined. The reason is that in $P_1(x) \vee P_2(x)$ we have the same free variables in both operands of the v; in $P_1(x) \wedge \neg P_2(x)$ we have one argument of the $\wedge$ in which the free variable appears in a predicate not preceded by an $\neg$; in $\forall x\ (\neg P_1(x) \vee P_2(x))$ the universally quantified variable is restricted by the predicate P_1; and in $\exists x\ (P_1(x) \wedge P_2(x))$ the existentially quantified variable is restricted by $P_1(x)$.

Moreover, we distinguish the predicate Res (respectively Unres) from the predicate Pos (respectively Neg) in order to generalize the following remarks.

The formulae $P_1(a) \vee P_2(x)$ and $P_1(a) \wedge \neg P_2(x)$ are not defined, but the formula $(\exists x)(P_1(a) \vee P_2(x))$ and $\forall x\ (P_1(a) \wedge \neg P_2(x))$ are defined. That is the reason why we have to distinguish the constraints imposed on the free variables and on the quantified variables.

Definition 1

$\text{Res}(x_i,F) \Leftrightarrow \text{Free}(x_i,F)$ *and*

If $F = \neg F_1$ *then* $\text{Unres}(x_i,F_1)$

If $F = F_1 \wedge F_2$ *then* $\text{Res}(x_i,F_1)$ *or* $\text{Res}(x_i,F_2)$

If $F = F_1 \lor F_2$ *then* $Res(x_i, F_1)$ *and* $Res(x_i, F_2)$
If $F = \exists x_j F_1$ *or* $F = \forall x_j F_1$ *then* $Res(x_i, F_1)$
If $F = P(\bar{x}_1, \bar{x}_2, \ldots, \bar{x}_n)$ *then* $\exists j\; x_i = \bar{x}_j$. [1]

<u>Definition 2</u>

$Unres(x_i, F) \Leftrightarrow Free(x_i, F)$ *and*
If $F = \neg F_1$ *then* $Res(x_i, F_1)$
If $F = F_1 \land F_2$ *then* $Unres(x_i, F_1)$ *and* $Unres(x_i, F_2)$
If $F = F_1 \lor F_2$ *then* $Unres(x_i, F_1)$ *or* $Unres(x_i, F_2)$
If $F = \exists x_j F_1$ *or* $F = \forall x_j F_1$ *then* $Unres(x_i, F_1)$.

<u>Definition 3</u>

$Pos(x_i, F) \Leftrightarrow Free(x_i, F)$ *and*
If $F = \neg F_1$ *then* $Neg(x_i, F_1)$
If $F = F_1 \land F_2$ *then* $Pos(x_i, F_1)$ *or* $Pos(x_i, F_2)$
If $F = F_1 \lor F_2$ *then*
If $Free(x_i, F_1)$ *and* $Free(x_i, F_2)$ *then* $Pos(x_i, F_1)$ *and* $Pos(x_i, F_2)$
If $Free(x_i, F_1)$ *and not* $Free(x_i, F_2)$ *then* $Pos(x_i, F_1)$
If $F = \exists x_j F_1$ *or* $F = \forall x_j F_1$ *then* $Pos(x_i, F_1)$
If $F = P(\bar{x}_1, \bar{x}_2, \ldots, \bar{x}_n)$ *then* $\exists j\; x_i = \bar{x}_j$.

<u>Definition 4</u>

$Neg(x_i, F) \Leftrightarrow Free(x_i, F)$ *and*
If $F = \neg F_1$ *then* $Pos(x_i, F_1)$
If $F = F_1 \land F_2$ *then*
If $Free(x_i, F_1)$ *and* $Free(x_i, F_2)$ *then* $Neg(x_i, F_1)$ *and* $Neg(x_i, F_2)$
If $Free(x_i, F_1)$ *and not* $Free(x_i, F_2)$ *then* $Neg(x_i, F_1)$
If $F = F_1 \lor F_2$ *then* $Neg(x_i, F_1)$ *or* $Neg(x_i, F_2)$
If $F = \exists x_j F_1$ *or* $F = \forall x_j F_1$ *then* $Neg(x_i, F_1)$.

---

1 $\bar{x}_j$ can denote a constant or a variable.

In the definitions F_1 and F_2 play the same role, so that: $Free(x_i,F_2)$ and not $Free(x_i,F_1)$ can be deduced by symmetry.

Several properties concerning the predicates Res, Unres, Pos and Neg can be proved.

Property 1

A variable may be neither Restricted nor Unrestricted in a formula.

Proof: We have just to exhibit the following example: $F = P(x) \vee Q(y)$. In F, x and y are neither Restricted, nor Unrestricted.

Property 2

$Free(x_i,F) \Rightarrow Pos(x_i,F)$ or $Neg(x_i,F)$

Proof: We prove this property by induction on the height of the formulae.

Base Case: In the case where the height of the formula is equal to 1 we have $Free(x_i,F) \Rightarrow Pos(x_i,F)$, so that the induction hypothesis is true for n = 1.

Induction Hypothesis: Let h be the height of a formula. For each formula F if $h \leq n$ then $Free(x_i,F) \Rightarrow Pos(x_i,F)$ *or* $Neg(x_i,F)$.

Let n+1 be the height of the formula F.

If $F = \neg F_1$ *then* $Free(x_i,F) \Rightarrow Free(x_i,F_1)$

The height of F_1 is n therefore by the induction hypothesis we have: $Pos(x_i,F_1)$ *or* $Neg(x_i,F_1)$.

$Free(x_i,F_1)$ *and* $Pos(x_i,F_1) \Rightarrow Neg(x_i,\neg F_1)$
(by Definition 4)

$Free(x_i,F_1)$ *and* $Neg(x_i,F_1) \Rightarrow Pos(x_i,\neg F_1)$
(by Definition 3)

So we have $Pos(x,F)$ *or* $Neg(x,F)$

If $F = F_1 \wedge F_2$ *then* $Free(x_i,F) \Rightarrow Free(x_i,F_1)$ *or* $Free(x_i,F_2)$

If $Free(x_i,F_1)$ *then*

$Free(x_i,F_1) \Rightarrow Pos(x_i,F_1)$ *or* $Neg(x_i,F_1)$
(by the Induction Hypothesis)

If not $Neg(x_i,F_1)$ *then* $Pos(x_i,F_1)$

$Free(x_i,F)$ *and* $Pos(x_i,F_1) \Rightarrow Pos(x_i,F)$

(by Definition 3)

If $Neg(x_i,F_1)$ *then*

If not $Free(x_i,F_2)$ *then*

$Free(x_i,F_1)$ *and not* $Free(x_i,F_2)$ *and* $Neg(x_i,F_1)$ $\Rightarrow Neg(x_i,F)$

(by Definition 4)

If $Free(x_i,F_2)$ *then*

$Free(x_i,F_2) \Rightarrow Pos(x_i,F_2)$ *or* $Neg(x_i,F_2)$

(by the Induction Hypothesis)

If not $Pos(x_i,F_2)$ *then* $Neg(x_i,F_2)$

$Free(x_i,F_1)$ *and* $Free(x_i,F_2)$ *and* $Neg(x_i,F_1)$ *and* $Neg(x_i,F_2) \Rightarrow Neg(x_i,F)$

(by Definitions 3 and 4)

If $Pos(x_i,F_2)$ *then*

$Free(x_i,F)$ *and* $Pos(x_i,F_2) \Rightarrow Pos(x_i,F)$

(by Definition 3)

If not $Free(x_i,F_1)$ *then* $Free(x_i,F_2)$

$Free(x_i,F_2) \Rightarrow Pos(x_i,F_2)$ *or* $Neg(x_i,F_2)$

(by the Induction Hypothesis)

If $Pos(x_i,F_2)$ *then*

$Free(x_i,F)$ *and* $Pos(x_i,F_2) \Rightarrow Pos(x_i,F)$

(by Definition 3)

If not $Pos(x_i,F_2)$ *then* $Neg(x_i,F_2)$

not $Free(x_i,F_1)$ *and* $Free(x_i,F_2)$ *and* $Neg(x_i,F_2) \Rightarrow Neg(x_i,F)$

(by Definition 4)

Thus, in all cases, we have $Pos(x_i,F)$ or $Neg(x_i,F)$.
The same conclusion can be obtained in the cases of $F_1 \vee F_2$, $\exists x_j\, F_1$ and $\forall x_j\, F_1$ with similar proofs.

Property 3

$Res(x_i,F) \Rightarrow Pos(x_i,F)$.

Proof: The proof is by induction on the height of the formulae.

We consider first the base case.

Base Case: In the case where the height of the formula is equal to 1 we have $Res(x_i,F)$ and $Pos(x_i,F)$, as the induction hypothesis is true for $n = 1$.

Induction Hypothesis: For each formula if $h \leq n$ then

$$Res(x_i,F) \Rightarrow Pos(x_i,F)$$

Let n+1 be the height of the formula F.

If $F = F_1 \vee F_2$ *then*

$Res(x_i,F) \Rightarrow Res(x_i,F_1)$ *and* $Res(x_i,F_2)$ (Definition 1)

$Res(x_i,F_1) \Rightarrow Pos(x_i,F_1)$ (Induction Hypothesis)

$Res(x_i,F_2) \Rightarrow Pos(x_i,F_2)$ (Induction Hypothesis)

$Pos(x_i,F_1)$ *and* $Pos(x_i,F_2) \Rightarrow Pos(x_i,F)$ (Definition 3)

In all other cases we have the same definition of Res and Pos, therefore the property is true.

Property 4

$Unres(x_i,F) \Rightarrow Neg(x_i,F)$

Proof: $Unres(x_i,F) \Rightarrow Res(x_i,\neg F)$ (Definition 2)

$Res(x_i,\neg F) \Rightarrow Pos(x_i,\neg F)$ (Property 3)

$Pos(x_i,\neg F) \Rightarrow Neg(x_i,F)$

(Definitions 2 and 3).

Evaluable queries. The new definition of evaluable query is:

Definition 5

A query F is evaluable iff:

- for each free variable x_i of F, we have: $Res(x_i,F)$;
- for each existentially quantified variable, we have, for the subquery quantified F_1: $Pos(x_i,F_1)$;
- for each universally quantified variable, we have, for the subquery quantified F_1: $Neg(x_i,F_1)$.

In Demolombe [1979b] we proved, using the same method as in Demolombe [1979a], that these evaluable queries are defined queries.

Examples of evaluable queries are:

$$P(y) \wedge \exists x(Q(x) \vee R(y))$$

$$S(y) \wedge \exists x(P(x) \vee (R(y) \wedge Q(x)))$$

$$S(y) \wedge \forall x((\neg P(x) \quad R(y)) \vee Q(x))$$

$$\neg(P(x) \vee \neg T(x,y))$$

We will show later how to transform unevaluable queries into queries that are evaluable.

TRANSFORMATION OF QUERY ROOT

The idea is to compute, from a query F and from the domains associated with the predicates which appear in F, the domain of each variable of F. This computation is done by the function $D(x_i,F)$. Furthermore, we use the result of $D(x_i,F)$ to restrict the variable with an $\wedge$, in the case of free variables or existentially quantified variables, or with an $\neg$ _ $\vee$ _ , in the case of universally quantified variables.

For example, let us consider the predicates Father(x,y) and Mother(x,y), with the domain associated with each argument of each relation defined by:

$$\text{Father}(x,y) \rightarrow \text{Man}(x) \wedge \text{Child}(y)$$

$$\text{Mother}(x,y) \rightarrow \text{Woman}(x) \wedge \text{Child}(y)$$

If we consider now the formula:

$$F = \neg(\text{Father}(x,\text{John}) \vee \text{Mother}(x,\text{John}))$$

then the function D(x,F) will define the domain of x in F (according to the choice of the section Choice of the Function $D(x_i,F)$ as Union of Domains, as follows:

$$D(x,F) = \text{Man}(x) \vee \text{Woman}(x)$$

The formula F is ill defined because the range of x in F is not made explicit. But we can assign a precise meaning to F by restricting the variable x to the domain D(x,F). That is by transforming F into:

$$D(x,F) \wedge F = (\text{Man}(x) \vee \text{Woman}(x)) \wedge \neg(\text{Father}(x,\text{John}) \vee \text{Mother}(x,\text{John})) .$$

We will see later that from the definition of D, we have $\text{Res}(x_i,D(x_i,F))$, therefore we have:

$$\text{Res}(x_i,D(x_i,F) \wedge F)$$

$$\text{Unres}(x_i,\neg D(x_i,F) \vee F)$$

Thus we define the following transformation Tr which, when applied to all the variables of F, give an evaluable formula.

$$Tr(x_i,F) = \begin{cases} D(x_i,F) \wedge F & \textit{If } \mathrm{Free}(x_i,F) \textit{ and not } \mathrm{Res}(x_i,F) \\ F(F_1 | D(x_i,F_1) \wedge F_1) & \textit{If } F \text{ contains a subexpression} \\ & \exists x\ F_1 \textit{ and not } \mathrm{Pos}(x_i,F_1) \\ F(F_1 | \neg D(x_i,F_1) \vee F_1) & \textit{If } F \text{ contains a subexpression} \\ & \forall x\ F_1 \textit{ and not } \mathrm{Neg}(x_i,F_1) \\ F & \text{otherwise .} \end{cases}$$

Where $F(A|B)$ means that B is substituted for A in F. We now show how to choose the function $D(x_i,F)$.

Choice of Function $D(x_i,F)$ as Intersection of Domains

The function $D(x_i,F)$ computes the domain of x_i in F from its domains in each subformula of F.

If $F=\neg F_1$, we choose $D(x_i,\neg F_1)=D(x_i,F_1)$.

This choice may seem inconsistent with the choice made for the functions D and Δ in Demolombe [1979a]. However, the choices made for D and Δ correspond to the function of Module 2, which is quite different from that of Module 3.

Indeed, if we want to carry out a semantic check of queries such as $P(x) \wedge \neg Q(x)$ (Module 2), we can say that x is in the domain $P_1(x)$ of $P(x)$; but it would be wrong to say that x is also in the domain $Q_1(x)$ of $Q(x)$. This is because we have:

$$Q(x) \rightarrow Q_1(x),\quad P(x) \rightarrow P_1(x) \vdash P(x) \wedge \neg Q(x) \rightarrow P_1(x)$$

but we do not have:

$$Q(x) \rightarrow Q_1(x),\quad P(x) \rightarrow P_1(x) \vdash P(x) \wedge \neg Q(x) \rightarrow Q_1(x) \wedge P_1(x)$$

On the other hand, if we want to transform an unevaluable query into an evaluable query (Module 3), for example, $\neg P(x)$, we have to choose domains to restrict the variables. In this case, the most natural choice is to take the domain $P_1(x)$ of $P(x)$. This is the reason why we have chosen

$$D(x,\neg P(x)) = D(x,P(x)) = P_1(x)$$

The query $\neg P(x)$ is transformed into $P_1(x) \wedge \neg P(x)$.

We can then choose either $D(x_i,F_1 \wedge F_2)$ or $D(x_i,F_1 \vee F_2)$, but not both, because the operators $\neg$, $\wedge$ and $\vee$ are not independent.

In this section, we will first choose $D(x_i,F_1 \wedge F_2)$. We take $D(x_i,F_1 \wedge F_2) = D(x_i,F_1) \wedge D(x_i,F_2)$; that is, the domain of an $\wedge$ is the intersection of the domains of the operands. This corresponds to the choice made in MRPPS (McSkimin and Minker [1977]).

We can deduce the expression of $D(x_i,F_1 \vee F_2)$ from the expression of $D(x_i,F_1 \wedge F_2)$:

$$\begin{aligned} D(x_i,F_1 \vee F_2) &= D(x_i,\neg(\neg F_1 \wedge \neg F_2)) \\ &= D(x_i,\neg F_1 \wedge \neg F_2) \\ &= D(x_i,\neg F_1) \wedge D(x_i,\neg F_2) \\ &= D(x_i,F_1) \wedge D(x_i,F_2) \end{aligned}$$

So as to be homogeneous with the choice made for the $\wedge$, if F is an atomic formula, we will choose the domain of x_i to be the intersection of the domains associated with each occurrence of x_i in this atomic formula. The domain associated with the jth argument of P will be named $P_j(x)$.

Finally, the function D is formally defined by the following rule:

<u>Definition 6</u> (The function $D(x_i,F)$ as an intersection of domains)

If $\mathrm{Free}(x_i,F)$ *then*

If $F=\neg F_1$ *then* $D(x_i,\neg F_1)=D(x_i,F_1)$

If $F=F_1 \wedge F_2$ *then* $D(x_i,F_1 \wedge F_2)=D(x_i,F_1) \wedge D(x_i,F_2)$

If $F=F_1 \vee F_2$ *then* $D(x_i,F_1 \vee F_2)=D(x_i,F_1) \vee D(x_i,F_2)$

If $F=\exists x_j F_1$ *or* $F=\forall x_j F_1$ *then* $D(x_i,F)=D(x_i,F_1)$

If $F=P(\bar{x}_1,\bar{x}_2,\ldots,\bar{x}_n)$ *then*

$D(x_i,F)=P_{i_1}(x_i) \wedge P_{i_2}(x_i) \wedge \ldots \wedge P_{i_p}(x_i)$ with $\bar{x}_{i_j}=x_i$

If not $\mathrm{Free}(x_i,F)$ *then* $D(x_i,F)=I$

The constant I is a neutral element for the operators $\wedge$, $\vee$, $\neg$, that is, we have $\neg I=I$; $I \wedge F=F$; $I \vee F=F$.

As $D(x_i,F)$ is applied only to formulas in which x_i is free, we can never have the final result of D equal to I.

We can see that $D(x_i,F)$ represents the intersection of all the domains associated with all the x_i occurrences in F.

We call two formulas "equivalent", one of which can be obtained from the other, distributing, or factoring, the operators $\neg$, $\wedge$ and $\vee$. It is important that two "equivalent" unevaluable queries be transformed into two "equivalent" queries. The above remark shows that this condition is satisfied.

We will show, with examples, what the consequences are of the choices made for the function D.

Let us consider the relations:

$$T(x,y) : x \text{ teaches subject } y$$

$$L(x,y) : x \text{ learns subject } y$$

The associated domains are:

$$T_1(x)=\text{Prof}(x) \qquad T_2(x)=\text{Subject}(x)$$

$$L_1(x)=\text{Student}(x) \qquad L_2(x)=\text{Subject}(x)$$

We assume that the two domains Prof(x) and Student(x) overlap.

We will consider questions which are translated by the user from natural language into the FOPC language. During this translation the user may fail to make explicit the range of some variable, thus obtaining an ill-defined formula. Then we will see how the transformation Tr can be used to transform the formula into one that is well defined. For each query q_i, below, we give an English paraphrase which is not supposed to be what the user had in mind. Let us consider the query q_3.

"Who does not teach, nor learn mathematics?"

We assume that the user expresses the query by the following formula:

$$q_3=\neg T(x,\text{Math}) \wedge \neg L(x,\text{Math})$$

This formula is not evaluable and will be transformed into: $Tr(x,q_3)=D(x,q_3) \wedge q_3$. We have:

$$D(x,q_3)=D(x,\neg T(x,\text{Math})) \wedge D(x,\neg L(x,\text{Math}))$$

$$=D(x,T(x,\text{Math})) \wedge D(x,L(x,\text{Math}))$$

$$=\text{Prof}(x) \wedge \text{Student}(x)$$

Therefore, we have:

$$Tr(x,q_3)=\text{Prof}(x) \wedge \text{Student}(x) \wedge (\neg T(x,\text{Math}) \wedge \neg L(x,\text{Math})) .$$

This is represented in Figure 2.

We note that in case the domains Prof(x) and Student(x) are disjoint, the answer is the empty set. This fact may be surprising for the user if he knows people who do not learn and do not teach mathematics.

Let us consider the query q_4 : "Who does not teach or does not learn mathematics?" Assume that the user expresses the query by the following formula:

$$q_4 = \neg T(x,Math) \vee \neg L(x,Math)$$

This formula is not evaluable, and will be transformed into:

$$Tr(x,q_4) = D(x,q_4) \wedge q_4$$

We have:

$$\begin{aligned} D(x,q_4) &= D(x,\neg T(x,Math)) \wedge D(x,\neg L(x,Math)) \\ &= D(x,T(x,Math)) \wedge D(x,L(x,Math)) \\ &= Prof(x) \wedge Student(x) \end{aligned}$$

Therefore, we have:

$$Tr(x,q_4) = Prof(x) \wedge Student(x) \wedge (\neg T(x,Math) \vee \neg L(x,Math))$$

This is represented in Figure 3.

In this case, it is more surprising to give an empty answer when the domains Prof(x) and Student(x) are disjoint.

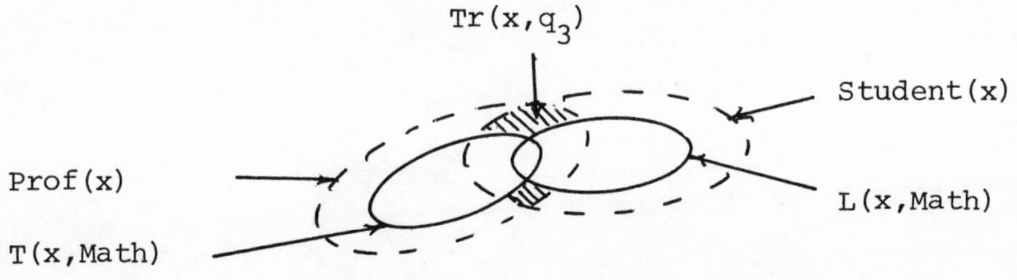

Figure 2. Diagram for the Query

$Prof(x) \wedge Student(x) \wedge (\neg T(x,Math) \wedge \neg L(x,Math))$.

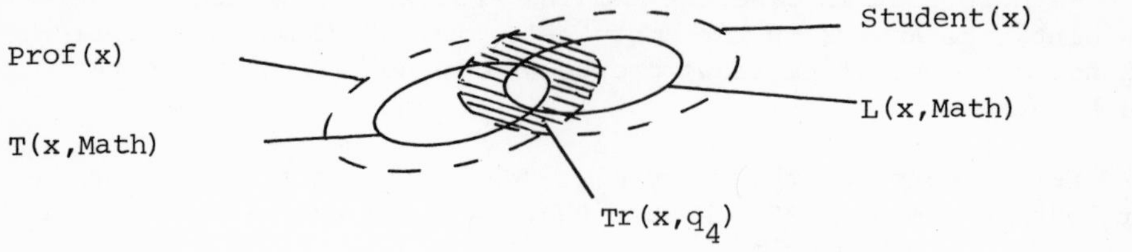

Figure 3. Diagram for the Query

$Prof(x) \wedge Student(x) \wedge (\neg T(x,Math) \vee \neg L(x,Math))$.

Note If we consider the queries $q_{41} = T(x,Math)$ and $q_{42} = L(x,Math)$, we have:

$Tr(x,q_{41}) = Prof(x) \wedge \neg T(x,Math)$ $\quad Tr(x,q_{42}) = Student(x) \wedge \neg L(x,Math)$

We can see that $q_4 = q_{41} \vee q_{42}$, while $Tr(x,q_4) \neq Tr(x,q_{41}) \vee Tr(x,q_{42})$

Finally, let us consider the query q_5. "Who are the professors where, for each subject they teach, there exists a student who does not learn the subject?" Assume that the user expresses the query by the following formula:

$$q_5 = (\forall x)(\exists x)(T(z,x) \wedge \neg L(y,x))$$

We call q_6 the formula: $q_6 = T(z,x) \wedge \neg L(y,x)$. The variable z is restricted in q_5, but x is not negative in $\exists y\ (q_6)$ and y is not positive in q_6. Therefore q_6 is not evaluable and must be transformed into q_7:

$$q_7 = Tr(x,Tr(y,q_5))$$

We have:

$$Tr(y,q_5) = \forall x\ \exists y\ (D(y,q_6) \wedge q_6)$$

$$Tr(x,Tr(y,q_5)) = \forall x(\ D(x,\exists y\ D(y,q_6) \wedge q_6) \vee (\exists y\ D(y,q_6) \wedge q_6))$$

$$\begin{aligned} D(y,q_6) &= D(y,T(z,x)) \wedge D(y,\neg L(y,x)) \\ &= I \wedge D(y,L(y,x)) \\ &= Student(y) \end{aligned}$$

Therefore we have:

$$\begin{aligned} D(x,\exists y\, D(y,q_6) \wedge q_6 &= D(x,\exists y\, \text{Student}(y) \wedge q_6) \\ &= D(x,\text{Student}(y) \wedge q_6) \\ &= D(x,\text{Student}(y)) \wedge D(x,T(z,x)) \\ &\qquad \wedge D(x,\neg L(y,x)) \\ &= I \wedge \text{Subject}(x) \wedge \text{Subject}(x) \\ &= \text{Subject}(x)\ . \end{aligned}$$

Finally, we have:

$$q_7 = \forall x (\neg \text{Subject}(x) \vee (\exists y (\text{Student}(y) \wedge T(z,x) \wedge \neg L(y,x))))$$

Choice of the Function $D(x_i,F)$ as Union of Domains

We will now study a second choice for the function $D(x_i,F)$. We will keep the previous choice concerning the operator $\neg$, that is $D(x_i,\neg F_1)=D(x_i,F_1)$, but for operator $\vee$, we choose:

$$D(x_i,F_1 \vee F_2)=D(x_i,F_1) \vee D(x_i,F_2)$$

We deduce from it:

$$\begin{aligned} D(x_i,F_1 \wedge F_2) &= D(x_i,\neg(\neg F_1 \vee \neg F_2)) \\ &= D(x_i,\neg F_1 \vee \neg F_2) \\ &= D(x_i,\neg F_1) \vee D(x_i,\neg F_2) \\ &= D(x_i,F_1) \vee D(x_i,F_2) \end{aligned}$$

In order to be consistent with previous choices, in the case F is an atomic formula, we assume that the domain of x_i in F is the union of the domains associated with each x_i occurrence in the atomic formula.

Finally, the function D is formally defined by the following rules:

<u>Definition 7</u> (The function $D(x_i,F)$ as the union of domains)

If $\text{Free}(x_i,F)$ *then*

If $F=\neg F_1$ *then* $D(x_i,\neg F_1)=D(x_i,F_1)$

If $F=F_1 \wedge F_2$ *then* $D(x_i,F_1 \wedge F_2)=D(x_i,F_1) \vee D(x_i,F_2)$

If $F=F_1 \vee F_2$ *then* $D(x_i,F_1 \vee F_2)=D(x_i,F_1) \vee D(x_i,F_2)$

If $F=\exists x_j F_1$ *or* $F=\forall x_j F_1$ *then* $D(x_i,F)=D(x_i,F_1)$

If $F=P(\bar{x}_1,\bar{x}_2,\ldots,\bar{x}_n)$ *then*

$$D(x_i,F)=P_{i_1}(x_1) \vee P_{i_2}(x_i) \vee \ldots \vee P_{i_p}(x_i) \text{ with } \bar{x}_{i_j}=x_i$$

If not $Free(x_i,F)$ *then* $D(x_i,F)=I$

<u>Notes</u>

$D(x_i,F)$ is the union of all the domains associated with all the occurrences of x_i in F. The consequence is that if F_1 and F_2 are "equivalent", then $D(x_i,F_1)=D(x_i,F_2)$.

It should be easy to prove by induction on the height of the formulas that x_i is the only free variable of $D(x_i,F)$; therefore, we have $D(x_i,D(x_j,F))=I$.

Using the same examples as in the section Choice of the Function $D(x_i,F)$ as Union of Domains, we examine the results of the transformation Tr.

For query q_3, we have:

$$D(x,q_3)=D(x,\neg T(x,Math)) \vee D(x,\neg L(x,Math))$$
$$=Prof(x) \vee Student(x)$$

Therefore, we have:

$$Tr(x,q_3)=(Prof(x) \vee Student(x)) \wedge (\neg T(x,Math) \wedge \neg L(x,Math))$$

This is shown in Figure 4:

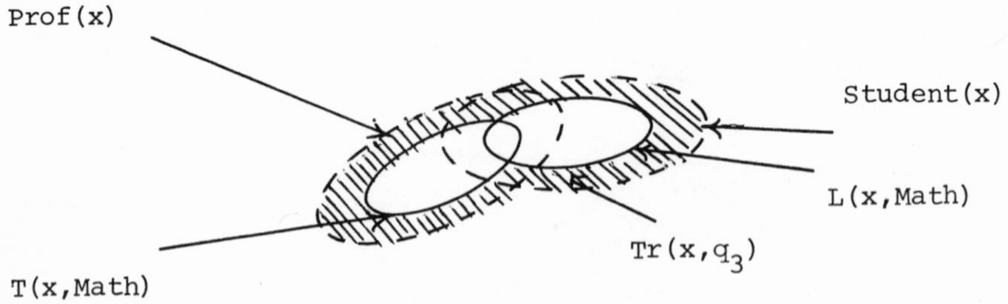

Figure 4. Diagram for the query $(Prof(x) \vee Student(x)) \wedge (\neg T(x,Math) \wedge \neg L(x,Math))$

For the query q_4, we have:

$$D(x,q_4)=D(x,\neg T(x,Math)) \vee D(x,\neg L(x,Math))$$
$$=Prof(x) \vee Student(x)$$

Therefore, we have:

$$Tr(x,q_4)=(Prof(x) \vee Student(x)) \wedge (\neg T(x,Math) \vee \neg L(x,Math))$$

This is shown in Figure 5.

NOTES

In the case of query q_3, we do not have the problem that arose in the section Choice of the Function $D(x_i,F)$ as Intersection of Domains, when Prof(x) and Student(x) are disjoint, but in the case of query q_4 the answer will be the union of Prof(x) and Student(x), and this, also may be surprising.

On the other hand, we have: $q_3=q_4 \wedge q_{42}$ while $Tr(x,q_3) \neq Tr(x,q_{41}) \wedge Tr(x,q_{42})$.

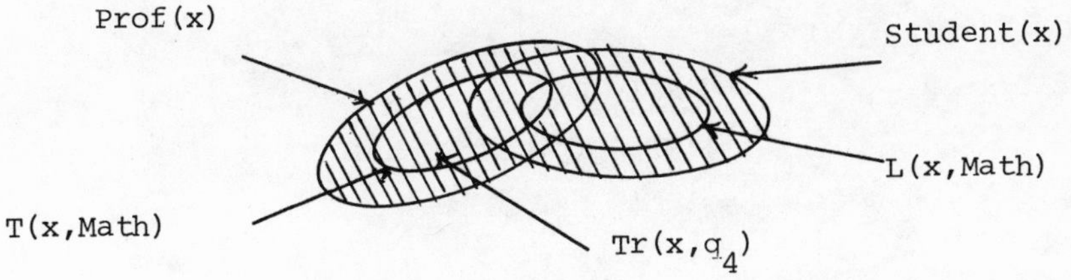

Figure 5. Diagram for the Query
$(Prof(x) \vee Student(x)) \wedge (\neg T(x,Math) \vee \neg L(x,Math))$

Commutativity of the Order of Transformations

When we have to apply several transformations to the same query, we have to verify that the result does not depend on the order in which the transformations are applied. We will prove that this condition is satisfied by the transformations Tr.

Let us consider query F, which contains the subquery:

$$f_1 = QyF_2(Q'xF_3)$$

where Q and Q'= ∃ or ∀ , and $Q'xF_3$ is a subquery of F_2. We suppose that we have to transform f_1 with regard to the variables x and y. If we apply first the transformation corresponding to y to F_2, we have:

$$f_2 = QyD(y, F_2(Q'xF_3)OF_2(Q'xF_3)$$

where O=∧ if Q=∃, and O=¬_∨_ if Q=∀. Furthermore, if we apply the transformation corresponding to x to F_3, we have:

$$f_3 = QyD(y, F_2(Q'xD(x, F_3)O'F_3))OF_2(Q'xD(x, F_3)O'F_3)$$

If we first apply the transformation corresponding to x to F_3, we have:

$$f_2' = QyF_2(Q'xD(x, F_3)O'F_3)$$

If we then apply the transformation corresponding to y to F_2, the result is:

$$f_3' = QyD(y, F_2(Q'xD(x, F_3)O'F_3)OF_2(Q'xD(x, F_3)O'F_3)$$

In conclusion, we have $f_3 = f_3'$. We may notice that:

$D(y, Q'xD(x, F3)O'F_3) =$

If O' = ∧ $\quad = Q'xD(y, D(x, F_3)) \wedge D(y, F_3)$

$= Q'xI \wedge D(y, F_3)$

$= Q'xD(y, F_3)$

$= D(y, Q'xF_3)$

If O'= ¬_∨_ $\quad = Q'xD(y, \neg D(x, F_3)) \wedge D(y, F_3)$

$= Q'xI \wedge D(y, F_3)$

$= Q'xb(y, F_3)$

$= D(y, Q'xF_3)$

Therefore, in all cases, we have:

$$D(y,Q'xD(x,F_3)O'F_3)=D(y,Q'xF_3)$$

Therefore, we have:

$$D(y,F_2(Q'xD(x,F_3)O'F_3))=D(y,F_2(Q'xF_3))$$

This result shows that the domain of y in F_2 does not depend on the fact that the transformation corresponding to x has been applied or not.

If x and y are two free variables of F, we have to compare Tr(x,Tr(y,F)) and Tr(y,Tr(x,F)). We have:

$$\begin{aligned} Tr(y,Tr(x,F)) &= D(y,Tr(x,F)) \wedge Tr(x,F) \\ &= D(y,D(x,F) \wedge F) \wedge D(x,F) \wedge F \\ &= D(y,D(x,F)) \wedge D(y,F) \wedge D(x,F) \wedge F \\ &= I \wedge D(y,F) \wedge D(x,F) \wedge F \\ &= D(y,F) \wedge D(x,F) \wedge F \end{aligned}$$

By symmetry with x and y, we have:

$$Tr(x,Tr(y,F))=D(x,F) \wedge D(y,F) \wedge F$$

Therefore, we have Tr(y,Tr(x,F))=Tr(x,Tr(y,F)). Similarly, we could show that if x and y are variables which must be negative then we have:

$$Tr(x,Tr(y,F))=Tr(y,Tr(x,F))=(\neg D(x,F)) \vee (\neg D(y,F)) \vee F$$

We can therefore conclude that, in all cases, the order of the transformation is irrelevant.

TRANSFORMATION OF QUERY LEAVES

The idea is to find a transformation which defines how the sub-queries of an unevaluable query are to be transformed so as to obtain an evaluable query. This transformation is applied until the leaves are reached, which are themselves, effectively, modified.

We define four transformations S_1, Σ_1, S_2, Σ_2, which transform the status of a variable in a query into restricted, unrestricted, positive or negative. These transformations are such that we have:

(a) $Res(x_i,S_1(x_i\ F))$ (b) $Unres(x_i, \Sigma_1(x_i,F))$

(c) $Pos(x_i,S_2(x_i,F))$ (d) $Neg(x_i, \Sigma_2(x_i,F))$

The transformations are defined according to the definitions of restricted, unrestricted, positive and negative variables such as those indicated below:

If not $\mathrm{Free}(x_i,F)$ *then* $S_1(x_i,F)=F \quad \Sigma_1(x_i,F)=F$

$S_2(x_i,F)=F \quad \Sigma_2(x_i,F)=F$

If $\mathrm{Free}(x_i,F)$ *then*

If $F=\neg F_1$ *then*

$$S_1(x_i,F)=\neg\Sigma_1(x_i,F_1)$$
$$\Sigma_1(x_i,F)=\neg S_1(x_i,F_1)$$
$$S_2(x_i,F)=\neg\Sigma_2(x_i,F_1)$$
$$\Sigma_2(x_i,F)=\neg S_2(x_i,F_1)$$

If $F=F_1 \wedge F_2$ *then*

If $\mathrm{Free}(x_i,F_1)$ *and* $\mathrm{Free}(x_i,F_2)$ *then*

$$S_1(x_1,F)=S_1(x_i,F_1) \wedge S_1(x_i,F_2) \quad (1)$$
$$\Sigma_1(x_i,F)=\Sigma_1(x_i,F_1) \wedge \Sigma_1(x_i,F_2)$$
$$S_2(x_i,F)=S_2(x_i,F_1) \wedge S_2(x_i,F_2) \quad (2)$$
$$\Sigma_2(x_i,F)=\Sigma_2(x_i,F_1) \wedge \Sigma_2(x_i,F_2)$$

If $\mathrm{Free}(x_i,F_1)$ *and not* $\mathrm{Free}(x_i,F_2)$ *then*

$$S_1(x_i,F)=S_1(x_i,F_1) \wedge F_2$$
$$\Sigma_1(x_i,F)=\Sigma_1(x_i,F_1) \wedge (\neg D(x_i,F_1) \vee F_2) \quad (5)$$
$$S_2(x_i,F)=S_2(x_i,F_1) \wedge F_2$$
$$\Sigma_2(x_i,F)=\Sigma_2(x_i,F_1) \wedge F_2$$

If $F=F_1 \vee F_2$ *then*

If $\mathrm{Free}(x_i,F_1)$ *and* $\mathrm{Free}(x_i,F_2)$ *then*

$$S_1(x_i,F)=S_1(x_i,F_1) \vee S_1(x_i,F_2)$$
$$\Sigma_1(x_i,F)=\Sigma_1(x_i,F_1) \vee \Sigma_1(x_i,F_2) \quad (3)$$
$$S_2(x_i,F)=S_2(x_i,F_1) \vee S_2(x_i,F_2)$$
$$\Sigma_2(x_i,F)=\Sigma_2(x_i,F_1) \vee \Sigma_2(x_i,F_2) \quad (4)$$

If $\mathrm{Free}(x_i,F_1)$ *and not* $\mathrm{Free}(x_i,F_2)$ *then*

$$S_1(x_i,F)=S_1(x_i,F_1) \vee (D(x_i,F_1) \wedge F_2) \quad (6)$$
$$\Sigma_1(x_i,F)=\Sigma_1(x_i,F_1) \vee F_2$$
$$S_2(x_i,F)=S_2(x_i,F_1) \vee F_2$$
$$\Sigma_2(x_i,F)=\Sigma_2(x_i,F_1) \vee F_2$$

If $F=\exists x_j F_1$ *then*

$$s(x_i,F)=\exists x_j s(x_i,F_1) \quad (\text{with } s=S_1,\ \Sigma_1,\ S_2 \text{ or } \Sigma_2)$$

If $F=\forall x_j F_1$ *then*

$$s(x_i,F)=\forall x_j s(x_i,F_1)$$

If $F=P(\bar{x}_1,\bar{x}_2,\ldots,\bar{x}_n)$ *then*

$$S_1(x_i,F)=P(\bar{x}_1,\bar{x}_2,\ldots,\bar{x}_n)$$
$$\Sigma_1(x_i,F)=\neg D(x_i,F) \vee P(\bar{x}_1,\bar{x}_2,\ldots,\bar{x}_n)$$
$$S_2(x_i,F)=P(\bar{x}_1,\bar{x}_2,\ldots,\bar{x}_n)$$
$$\Sigma_2(x_i,F)=\neg D(x_i,F) \vee P(\bar{x}_1,\bar{x}_2,\ldots,\bar{x}_n)$$

In some cases, the transformations impose unnecessary constraints on the subqueries. For example, if we have $F=F_1 \vee F_2$ and $\text{Free}(x_i,F_1)$ and $\text{Free}(x_i,F_2)$, it is sufficient to have $\text{Neg}(x_i,F_1)$ or $\text{Neg}(x_i,F_2)$ to have $\text{Neg}(x_i,F)$. Therefore, in this case, we could define Σ_2 as:

$$\Sigma_2(x_i,F)=\Sigma_2(x_i,F_1) \vee F_2$$

or

$$\Sigma_2(x_i,F)=F_1 \vee \Sigma_2(x_i,F_2)$$

We choose $\Sigma_2(x_i,F)= \Sigma_2(x_i,F_1)\vee \Sigma_2(x_i,F_2)$ because F_1 and F_2 play symmetrical roles. Rules (1), (2), (3) and (4) have been defined according to the above remark.

We choose rule (5) because, in this case, to have $\text{Unres}(x_i,F_1 \wedge F_2)$, it is necessary to have $\text{Unres}(x_i,F_1)$ and $\text{Unres}(x_i,F_2)$. However, we do not have x_i free in F_2; therefore, we transform F_2 into a formula in which x_i is free and unrestricted. The most natural way seems to be to introduce x_i with its domain into the nearest subquery of F_2, that is, F_1. Rule (6) has been chosen for the same reason. In cases (5) and (6), the transformation is not applied to the leaves but to an intermediate node. On the other hand, transformations S_1 and Σ_1 are not homomorphisms for the "equivalence" between queries because of rules (5) and (6).

Let us consider, for example, the queries:

$$F_1=(P(x,y) \vee Q(x,y)) \vee R(y)$$

$$F_2=P(x,y) \vee (Q(x,y) \vee R(y))$$

They are "equivalent", and the result of the transformations is:

$$F_1' = (P(x,y) \vee Q(x,y)) \vee (D(x,P(x,y) \vee Q(x,y)) \wedge R(y))$$

$$F_2' = P(x,y) \vee (Q(x,y) \vee (D(x,Q(x,y)) \wedge R(y)))$$

F_1' and F_2' are not equivalent.

Function D may be one of the transformations defined above. Finally, we can see that in some cases rules (5) and (6) lead to strange results. Let us consider a query which defines Professors and Subjects taught by them, such that the Subject satisfies a given condition C(y) or is Mathematics. If the user asks the question:

$$(T(x,y) \wedge C(y)) \vee T(x,Math)$$

the transformed question will be:

$$(T(x,y) \wedge C(y)) \vee (T(x,Math) \wedge Subject(y))$$

It does not correspond to the user's idea; a good translation would be:

$$T(x,y) \wedge (C(y) \vee y=Math)$$

which has a quite different meaning.

Because of these results, we could refuse to transform a query in cases (5) or (6). However, the transformed query should be submitted for the user's approval before eavluation, and for this reason, it is better not to interrupt the transformation process.

We will now examine, using the examples of the section Choice of the Function $D(x_i,F)$ as Intersection of Domains, the results of the transformations defined above.

For query q_3, we have:

$$\begin{aligned} S_1(x,q_3) &= S_1(x,\neg T(x,Math)) \wedge S_1(x,\neg L(x,Math)) \\ &= \neg\Sigma_1(x,T(x,Math)) \wedge \neg\Sigma_1(x,L(x,Math)) \\ &= \neg(\neg D(x,T(x,Math)) \vee T(x,Math)) \\ &\quad \wedge \neg(\neg D(x,L(x,Math)) \vee L(x,Math)) \\ &= Prof(x) \wedge \neg T(x,Math) \wedge Student(x) \wedge \neg L(x,Math) \end{aligned}$$

We have the same result as in the section Choice of the Function $D(x_i,F)$ as Intersection of Domains. For query q_4, we have:

$$S_1(x,q_4)=S_1(x,\neg T(x,Math)) \vee S_1(x,\neg L(x,Math))$$
$$=\neg\Sigma_1(x,T(x,Math)) \vee \neg\Sigma_1(x,L(x,Math))$$
$$=\neg(\neg D(x,T(x,Math)) \vee T(x,Math))$$
$$\vee\neg(\neg D(x,L(x,Math)) \vee L(x,Math))$$
$$=(Prof(x) \wedge \neg T(x,Math)) \vee (Student(x) \wedge \neg L(x,Math))$$

This is shown in Figure 6.

For query q_5, we have:

$$\forall x\Sigma_2(x,\exists y S_2(y,q_6))=\forall x\exists y\Sigma_2(x,S_2(y,q_6))$$
$$S_2(y,q_6)=S_2(y,T(z,x) \wedge \neg L(y,x))$$
$$=T(z,x) \wedge S_2(y,\neg L(y,x))$$
$$=T(z,x) \wedge \neg\Sigma_2(y,L(y,x))$$
$$=T(z,x) \wedge \neg(\neg Student(y) \vee L(y,x))$$
$$\Sigma_2(x,S_2(y,q_6))=\Sigma_2(x,T(z,x) \wedge \neg(\neg Student(y) \vee L(y,x)))$$
$$=(\neg Subject(x)\ T(z,x)) \wedge \neg\Sigma_2(x, Student(y) \vee L(y,x))$$
$$=(\neg Subject(x)\ T(z,x)) \wedge \neg(\neg Student(y) \vee S_2(x,L(y,x)))$$
$$=(\neg Subject(x)\ T(z,x)) \wedge \neg(\neg Student(y) \vee L(y,x))$$

Finally, we have:

$$\forall x\exists y(\neg Subject(x) \vee T(z,x)) \wedge \neg(\neg Student(y) \vee L(y,x))$$

This result is different from the result of the section TRANSFORMATION OF QUERY ROOT.

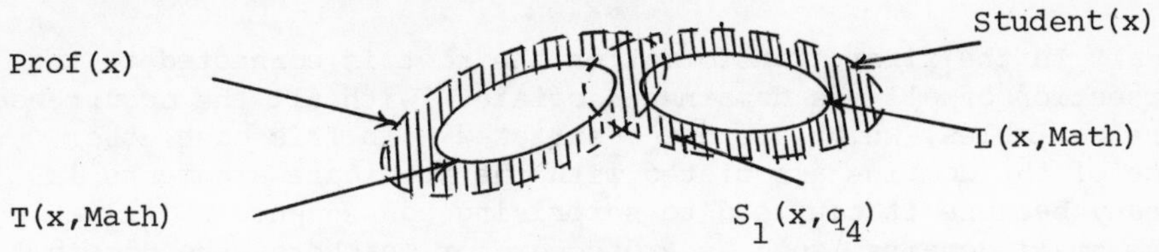

Figure 6. Diagram for the query

$(Prof(x) \wedge \neg T(x,Math) \vee (Student(x) \wedge \neg L(x,Math))$

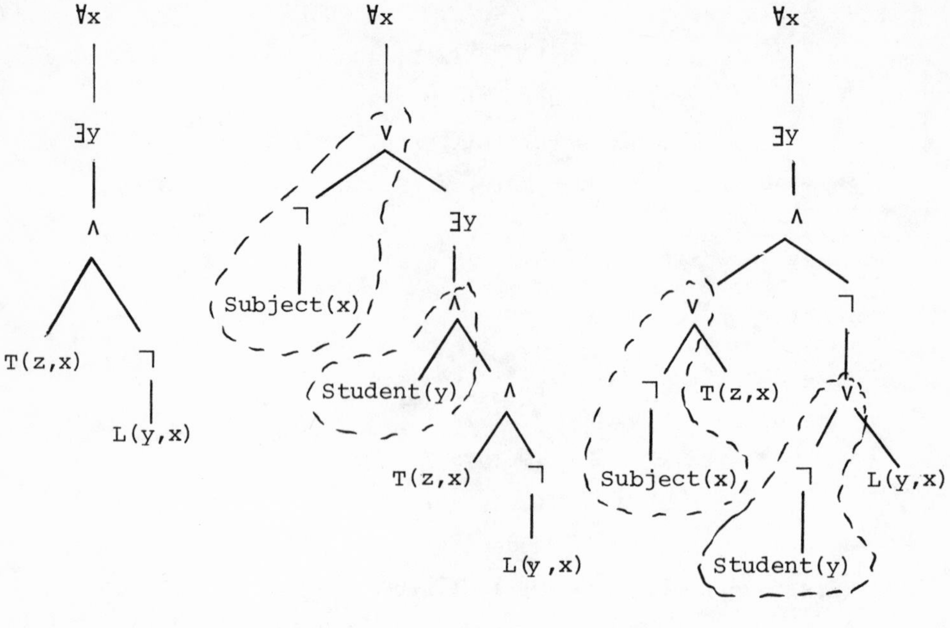

Query q_5 Query q_5 transformed by the root Ouery q_5 transformed by the leaves

Figure 7. Transformed Query

CONCLUSION

We have defined three different ways of transforming unevaluable queries into ones that are evaluable.

1. Two kinds of transformations modify the root of the tree representing the query.

a) In the first transformation the root is connected to the intersection of all the domains associated with all the occurrences of the variables, which are not restricted. In this case, the choice of the domains associated with the predicate arguments is not easy because it can lead to surprising consequences. If we choose small domains, such as Professors or Teachers, the domain of the variables in a given query may be too restricted. In some cases, it can be an empty set. If, in order to avoid this problem, we choose large domains, such as Persons, we may obtain, in the answers to some queries, elements which are irrelevant. For example, the query ┐Learn(x,Math) should be transformed into Person(x) ∧

¬Learn(x,Math). In the answer will appear not only the students who do not learn Mathematics, but also Teachers. This may not be the intention of the user.

Moreover, a query such as: ¬Father(x,John) ∧ ¬Mother(x,John) will be transformed into: Man(x) ∧ Woman(x) ∧ ¬Father(x,John) ∧ ¬Mother(x,John). This query will be rejected by the semantic check (module 2), because Man(x) and Woman(x) are disjoint. It is not obvious that this is the correct strategy.

b) In the second transformation the domain of a variable in a query is the union of its domain occurrences instead of the intersection. In this case, the problem we saw above cannot arise. For example, the last query is transformed into:

$$(\text{Man}(x) \vee \text{Woman}(x)) \wedge \neg\text{Father}(x,\text{John}) \wedge \neg\text{Mother}(x,\text{John}) .$$

However in the cases (a) and (b) the transformations D and Δ (defined in Demolombe [1979a]) which calculate the domains of the variables, in order to do a semantic check, thus resulting in rejection of wrong queries. For example the domain of x calculated by these transformations in the query: Father(x,John) ∧ Mother(x,John) will be Man(x) ∧ Woman(x), and even if in module 3 the transformations give the union of domains, in module 2 we obtain, for this query, the intersection of domains and this query will be rejected.

2. Finally, the third transformation modifies the leaves of the query. Figure 7 allows a comparison of this method with the previous one. In this case, the domain of a variable is not systematically the intersection or the union of the domains; it depends on the query structure and may be the union or the intersection. This method modifies the structure of the query as little as possible and it seems a good tradeoff. Unfortunately, in cases (5) and (6), it fails.

In conclusion, for each method, it is possible to find some example leading to unsatisfactory results and the choice of method will be more or less subjective. In this paper we have pointed out the advantages and disadvantages of each method. If the techniques described here were implemented as part of a query system, it would provide the user with a useful tool to permit him to revise his query, if so required.

ACKNOWLEDGEMENTS

The author wishes to thank A. Colmerauer and G. Zanon for many helpful discussions throughout this work.

REFERENCES

1. Artaud, A. and Nicolas, J. M. [1972] "Système d'Interrogation Expérimental SYNTEX. Logique des Interrogations, *Rapport DRME n° 70.368, Vol. 4,* 1972, 29-34.

2. Artaud, A. and Nicolas, J. M. [1974] An Experimental Query System: SYNTEX. *Proc. of IFIPS,* North Holland, 1974, 595-600.

3. Chang, C.L. [1978] DEDUCE 2: Further Investigations of Deduction in Relational Data Bases. In: *Logic and Data Base,* Plenum Press, New York City, 1978, 201-236.

4. Codd, E. F. [1972] "Relational Completeness of Data Base Sublanguages in Data Base Systems." In: *Courant Computer Science Symposium 6* (R. Rustin, Ed.), Prentice Hall, Englewood Cliffs, N. J., 1972,

5. Colmerauer, A. [1977] "An Interesting Natural Language Subset." *Preprints of the Workshop on Logic and Data Base,* Toulouse, France, Nov. 1977.

6. Demolombe, R. [1979a] "Semantic Checking of Questions Expressed in Predicate Calculus Language. *Proceedings of Very Large Data Bases,* Rio de Janairo, Brasil, Oct. 1979, 444-450.

7. Demolombe, R. [1979b] Démonstration du Fait que les Formules Evaluables sont Définies. *Rapport interne. LBD,* 1979, ONERA-CERF, Toulouse, France.

8. Di Paola, R. A. [1971] "The Relational Data File and the Decision Problem for Classes of Proper Formula," *Report R-661-PR,* Rand Corporation, Santa Monica, California, 1971.

9. Kuhns, J. L. [1970] "Interrogating a Relational Data File: Remarks on the Admissibility of Input Queries" *Report R-511-PR.* Rand Corporation, Santa Monica, California, 1970.

10. McSkimin, J.R. and Minker, J. [1977] "The Use of a Semantic Network in a Deductive Question-Answering System," Proceedings *IJCAI-77,* Cambridge, Mass., 1977, 50-58.

11. Minker, J. [1978] "An Experimental Relational Data Base System Based on Logic" In: *Logic and Data Bases* (H. Gallaire and J. Minker, Eds.), Plenum Press, New York, N.Y., 1978, 107-147.

12. Nicolas, J.M. [1979] "A Property of Logical Formulas Corresponding to Integrity Constraints on Data Base Relations. *Preprints of Workshop on "Formal Bases for Data Bases",* Toulouse.

13. Pique, J. F. [1978] "Interface entre le Francais et les Formules Logiques, Interrogation d'une Banque de Données. *Rapport de la Convention BNIST 291767,* Univ. de Marseille, 1978.

14. Pirotte, A. [1976] *Explicit Description of Entities and their Manipulation in Languages for the Relational Data Base Model.* Doctoral Thesis. Univ. of Bruxelles, 1976.

15. Reiter, R. [1977] "An Approach to Deductive Question-Answering," *Tech. Report BBN. N^{O} 3649,* Bolt, Beranek and Newman Corporation, Cambridge, Mass., 1977.

16. Reiter, R. [1978] "On Closed World Data Bases," In: *Logic and Data Bases* (H. Gallaire and J. Minker, Eds.), Plenum Press, New York, 1978, 55-76.

17. Reiter, R. [1971] "On the Integrity of Typed First Order Data Bases," This Volume.

ON THE FEASIBILITY OF INFORMATIVE ANSWERS

Jürgen M. Janas

Hochschule der Bundeswehr München

Federal Republic of Germany

ABSTRACT

In this chapter, we investigate the situation where a user's request for data cannot be answered in the desired way because the data base does not contain the data requested. We argue that in such a situation it is not sufficient to report to the user the fact that the query failed, without providing the deeper reasons for the failure; an informative answer to a failing query, however, will adjust the user's wrong assumptions about the contents of the data base and often will free him/her from the need of asking additional queries. We describe a formal method by means of which the reasons for the failure of a user's query expressed in a relational calculus based language may be inferred and reported to the user as answer; special attention is paid to the amount of computation required for this answer generation procedure. We then show that a wide class of integrity constraints of a data base may be used to further improve the inference process and that any abuse of informative answers for the deduction of confidential information may be prevented easily.

INTRODUCTION

The problem of how to supply an informative answer to a failing data base query has been investigated recently from several points of view, namely for queries to CODASYL type data bases (cf. Lee [1978a]), for queries expressed in a relational calculus based language (cf. Janas [1979b]), and for natural language queries (cf. Kaplan [1979]). In all cases, the starting point is that a data base query such as "Find all X which have the property Y" (where both X and Y may be composite) cannot be answered directly because there are no such X in the data base. Though an answer like, "There are no such X", is a correct answer in such a situation, it will not be very helpful for the user in many cases. An informative answer to such a query, however, collects the wrong assumptions which are inherent to the query and reports them to the user; an example for an informative answer to the question "Find all employees in the shoe department who are older than 55" would be: "There is no shoe department in the data base."

The advantage of informative user interfaces in the sense of the above explanation is twofold: On the one hand the computational costs for solving a problem with the assistance of the data base will be reduced since after a query has failed the user no longer has to ask additional queries to detect the reasons for the failure; on the other hand the user will be more likely to accept such a system because it responds to him in a more natural way. However, the feasibility of supplying informative answers to the user depends on whether there are satisfying answers to the following two questions:

i) What is the amount of computation required for obtaining an informative answer?

ii) Can we guarantee that an informative answer does not contain any information to which the user has no access rights?

The second question needs a short explanation. We assume that access control is performed for every query entered by the user; since generating an informative answer includes the computation of certain subqueries of the user's query, we have to make sure that these subqueries do not cross the borders of the user's access rights. The rest of this paper will be devoted to these two questions.

In detail, we shall give a summary of the procedure for inferring an informative answer to a given data base query and thereby investigate the costs for obtaining such an informative answer. In the section, INFORMATIVE ANSWERS AND INTEGRITY CONSTRAINTS, we shall examine the implications of a wide class of integrity constraints for the answer generation procedure; it will be shown how incorporating integrity constraints further contributes to the efficiency of this procedure. The section, INFORMATIVE ANSWERS AND DATA SECURITY, deals with the problem of the security and privacy of data. We shall start by demonstrating that — unless certain precautions are taken — a user may abuse informative answers to deduce confidential information to which he has no access rights; then we shall show that the respective precautions can be taken easily.

HOW TO INFER INFORMATIVE ANSWERS

In this section, we shall describe the procedure for obtaining informative answers to data base queries. All examples within this section refer to the following data base according to the relational model of data (cf. Codd [1970]):

EMP (*NAME*, AGE, SAL, DN)

DEPT(*DNO*,DNAME, MAN)

CAR (*LIP*, OWN, COL)

An employee (EMP) has a name (NAME), an age (AGE), and a salary (SAL) and works for a department (DEPT) which is identified by a department number (DNO or DN respectively) and which has a department name (DNAME) and a manager (MAN) who in turn is an employee. Moreover there are cars (CAR) which have a license plate (LIP), a color (COL), and an owner (OWN) who again is an employee identified by his name. The primary key attributes of the relations are italicized. The queries are expressed in a relational calculus based language which is very similar to the data sublanguage ALPHA (cf. Codd [1971b]). The essential constituents of our query language are the so-called qualification expressions which describe the sets of data to be retrieved; a qualification expression consists of one or more terms which are combined by means of the usual logical symbols. A query is written as a set of data items which satisfy the qualification expression; thus, e.g.,

(2.1) $$\{x \mid ((x.AGE<30) \wedge (x.SAL>25{,}000))\}$$

is a query for all employees who are younger than 30 and earn more than $25,000. Note that the variables occurring in the qualification expression are implicitly typed, i.e. ,for each variable the relation it refers to may be uniquely determined since all of the attributes in our data base are named differently. As a consequence of this typing of the variables, every admissible qualification expression is range-separable (cf. Codd [1971a]), i.e., a wide class of qualification expressions which do not produce meaningful queries are excluded (for a more detailed discussion of the problem of how to characterize meaningful queries see also Demolombe [1979a, 1979b], Reiter [1981], McSkimin and Minker [1977]). The advantage of the set notation is that we may use the same notation also to express negative answers to queries: If B is the set which represents the query "Find all X with the property Y" then "B = Ø" represents the answer "There are no X which have the property Y". There is one important difference between the qualification expressions in ALPHA and those to be used in our query language: A qualification expression in our query language has to be a "coherent expression"; coherent expressions are defined by means of "connected expressions".

An expression χ is called a *connected expression* if each of the bound variables in χ is connected with at least one free variable in χ via a join term or a chain of join terms. By *join term* we mean a term which contains two different variables; the notions "free variable" and "bound variable" are in full agreement with their use in predicate logic. Queries formed from unconnected expressions do not make very much sense as one can see from the example

$$\{x \mid ((x.AGE<30) \wedge \exists y(y.COL='red'))\} \qquad (2.2)$$

which means "Find all employees who are younger than 30 and there is a red car in the data base"; in particular, if the answer is "none" one does not know whether this is due to the fact that there are no red cars or that there are no employees who are younger than 30. An expression χ is called a *coherent expression* if each of the conjuncts of the disjunctive prenex normal form of χ (cf. Chang and Lee [1973]) is a connected expression. The following expression is connected but not coherent:

$$((x.AGE<30) \wedge \exists y((x.NAME=y.OWN) \vee (y.COL='red'))) \qquad (2.3)$$

since the disjunctive prenex normal form of (2.3)

$$\exists y(((x.AGE<30) \wedge (y.OWN=x.NAME)) \vee ((x.AGE<30) \wedge (y.COL='red'))) \qquad (2.4)$$

contains a conjunct which is not connected, namely

$$((x.AGE<30) \wedge (y.COL='red')) \qquad (2.5)$$

Just as in the example of (2.2), the query corresponding to (2.3) would not make very much sense.

The basic idea for the inference of an informative answer to a failing query B_0 is to compute the direct, i.e., immediately subordinate subqueries of the original query and see whether they fail or not. The direct subqueries of a given query are essentially obtained by removing one occurrence of a term from the qualification expression of the given query (disjunctive queries have to be treated differently as we shall see below). It can be shown that if the direct subqueries $B_1, B_2, \ldots, B_n$ $(n > 0)$ of the query B_0 fail then

$$B_1 = \emptyset \wedge B_2 = \emptyset \wedge \ldots \wedge B_n = \emptyset$$

is a more informative answer than "$B_0 = \emptyset$" because B_0 (now regarded as a set) is a subset of each of the B_i $(1 \leq i \leq n)$. Since these

B_i ($1 \leq i \leq n$) are queries themselves they may be in turn substituted by their failing direct subqueries. If all the direct subqueries of some B_j ($0 \leq j \leq n$) have positive answers, then the (partial) answer "$B_j = \emptyset$" cannot be decomposed further into a more informative answer. The direct subqueries of

(2.6) $C_0 = \{x \mid (((.AGE>55) \wedge (x.SAL>25,000)) \wedge (x.DN=E605))\}$

are

(2.7) $C_1 = \{x \mid ((x.AGE>55) \wedge (x.SAL>25,000))\}$

(2.8) $C_2 = \{x \mid ((x.AGE>55 \wedge (x.DN=E605))\}$

(2.9) $C_3 = \{x \mid ((x.SAL>25,000) \wedge (x.DN=E605))\}$

and each of these queries has in turn two direct subqueries out of the following three queries:

(2.10) $C_4 = \{x \mid (x.AGE>55)\}$

(2.11) $C_5 = \{x \mid (x.SAL>25,000)\}$

(2.12) $C_6 = \{x \mid (x.DN=E605)\}$

We may represent this situation by means of a directed graph (see Figure 1) whose nodes correspond to the queries and which contains an edge from A to B iff B is a direct subquery of A.

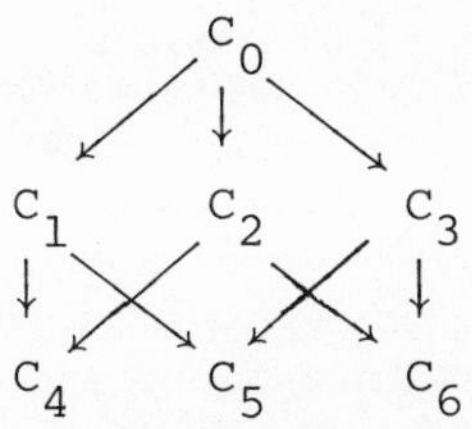

Figure 1. Graphical Representation of the Relationship Between Query (2.6) and its Subqueries

Let us now assume that C_0, C_1, C_2, and C_4 fail while C_3, C_5, and C_6 do not. Then an informative answer to the query C_0 is obtained in the following way: The answer "$C_0 = \emptyset$" first will be replaced by "$C_1 = \emptyset \wedge C_2 = \emptyset$" which then will be replaced by "$C_4 = \emptyset$". So the final answer to C_0 (i.e., find all employees who are older than 55 and earn more than \$25,000 and work for the department with department number E605) would be "There are no employees who are older than 55". An answer obtained in this way always implies the correct direct answer to the user's query.

It should be noted that informative answers to failing data base queries are meaningful only under the closed world assumption (cf. Reiter [1978]). The closed world assumption means that the knowledge about the domain represented in the data base is complete whereas the open world assumption assumes that there may be gaps in that knowledge. Under the open world assumption, e.g., the fact that "there are no blue cars in the data base" does not necessarily imply the fact that "there are no employees in the data base who own a blue car" because it is possible that the fact that some employee owns a blue car is not represented in the data base. Therefore, under the open world assumption, informative answers would not actually contain any additional information.

If each of the terms in the qualification expression of a query may be eliminated thus yielding a proper direct subquery, then (as observed in Lee [1978b]) the total number of subqueries of a given query is $2^n - 2$ where n is the number of terms in the qualification expression of that query. Though this is not an average number but only the upper bound for the number of subqueries which have to be computed in order to find an informative answer to a certain query and though n usually will be comparatively small, every effort has to be made to reduce the number of subqueries which have to be computed. One possibility to reduce this number results from our postulation that the qualification expression of a proper query has to be coherent: If elimination of a certain term from a qualification expression yields a noncoherent expression, then the query corresponding to this noncoherent expression may be neglected in the further process of inferring the informative answer. Noncoherent expressions are frequently obtained when eliminating a join term from a coherent expression. Thus the query

(2.13) $$\{x \mid ((x.COL='red') \land \exists y((y.NAME=x.OWN) \land \exists z((z.DNO=y.DN) \land (z.DNAME='shoe'))))\}$$

(find all red cars which are owned by employees who work for the shoe department) has only two instead of four direct subqueries, namely:

(2.14) $$\{x \mid ((x.COL='red') \land \exists y((y.NAME=x.OWN) \land \exists z(z.DNO=y.DN)))\}$$

(2.15) $$\{x \mid \exists y((y.NAME=x.OWN) \land \exists z((z.DNO=y.DN) \land (z.DNAME='shoe')))\}$$

The full benefit of our restriction to coherent expressions for a query like (2.13) is illustrated by the following diagrams:

Figure 2 shows the directed graph which represents the relationship between (2.13) and its subqueries in the case where noncoherent expressions are allowed, whereas Figure 3 shows the same situation under the restriction to coherent expressions. The number of admissible subqueries of (2.13) and thereby the average amount of computation required to give an informative answer to (2.13) is reduced considerably due to this restriction.

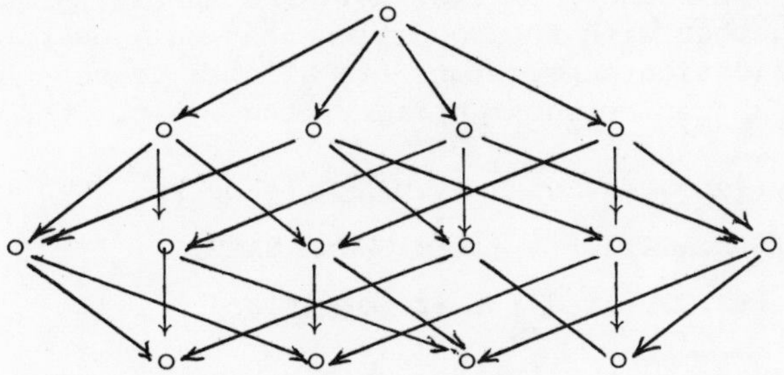

Figure 2. Graphical Representation of the Relationship Between Query (2.13) and its Subqueries Without Restriction to Coherent Queries

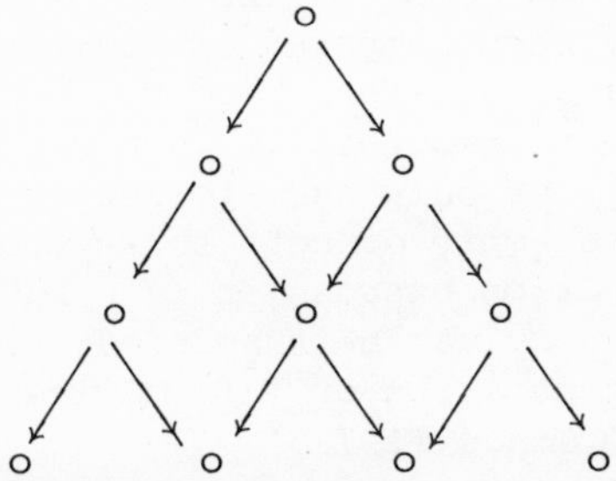

Figure 3. Graphical Representation of the Relationship Between Query (2.13) and its Subqueries Under the Restriction to Coherent Queries

Another way to reduce the number of admissible subqueries results from a special treatment of queries which are disjunctive at the top level, i.e., which have a qualification expression of the form (A V B) where A and B are expressions; we define that the only direct subqueries of such a query are those which have the qualification expressions A or B respectively. Therefore if a query is disjunctive at the top level and if its query expression contains n terms, then the number of its admissible subqueries is $2^k + 2^l - 4$ (instead of $2^n - 2$) where k and l are the numbers of terms in A or B respectively ($k + l = n$). Note that this special treatment of disjunction at the top level has consequences also for queries which contain a disjunction somewhere else in the qualification expression: Among the subqueries of such a query there will be a query which contains this disjunction at the top level of its qualification expression and the set of its subqueries is contained in the set of subqueries of the original query. Moreover there are certain restrictions concerning the removal of terms from disjunctive subexpressions of a qualification expression that will not be discussed here for reasons of brevity. The special treatment of disjunction together with the condition that only queries with coherent qualification expressions are allowed decreases the number of admissible subqueries substantially; thus, e.g., the query:

$$\text{(2.16)} \quad \{x \mid (\exists y((y.DNO=x.DN) \wedge (y.DNAME='shoe')) \wedge ((x.AGE<20) \vee \exists z((z.OWN=x.NAME) \wedge ((z.COL='red') \vee (z.COL='blue')))))\}$$

(find all employees in the shoe department who are younger than 20 or own a car which is red or blue) has only 14 admissible subqueries instead of 62 (= 2^6 - 2) subqueries.

If a certain subquery is required during the process of inferring an informative answer, this does not necessarily mean that this subquery has in fact to be computed, because many of the subqueries of a query have already been computed in order to find out that the original query failed and therefore need not be evaluated again. Finally it has to be mentioned that it is not necessary to compute the subqueries properly, we only need to know whether the corresponding sets of data are empty or not; so as soon as one data item satisfying the qualification expression of a subquery is found, evaluation of this subquery may be suspended. For a more thorough discussion of how the generation of informative answers may be implemented we refer to Janas [1979a].

INFORMATIVE ANSWERS AND INTEGRITY CONSTRAINTS

In this section, we shall examine the implications of integrity constraints for the answer generation procedure. We shall consider static integrity constraints only (i.e., integrity constraints which are conditions for the correctness of a state of the data base) since dynamic integrity constraints (i.e., integrity constraints which are conditions for the correctness of a transition from one state of the data base to another) have no implications for data base queries whatsoever.

A wide class of static integrity constraints that a data base may be subject to can be expressed by means of expressions which do not contain any free variables; thus the integrity constraint

(3.1) For every car which is in the data base, the owner of that car has to be in the data base too.

may be expressed as

(3.2) $$\forall x \; \exists y \; (x.OWN = y.NAME)$$

Obviously integrity constraints of arbitrary complexity may be stated and a complex integrity constraint cannot always be decomposed into several simpler constraints such that the simple constraints in combination are logically equivalent to the original one; thus, e.g., the constraint

(3.3) $$\exists x((x.AGE>60) \wedge (x.SAL>50,000))$$

would not be represented correctly if it were decomposed into

(3.4) $$\exists x(x.AGE>60)$$

and

(3.5) $$\exists x(x.SAL>50,000)$$

Nevertheless we shall restrict our further considerations to integrity constraints which contain one term only because we believe that the more complex integrity constraints which cannot be decomposed are rarely used for simplifying queries.

The general idea is to transform the qualification expression e of a query into a different expression e' such that the integrity constraints of the data base imply the logical equivalence of e and e'. Obviously, we are interested only in those transformations that produce expressions e' which are "simpler" than their corresponding original expressions e; in particular, this criterion is met if e' results from e by deleting a certain subexpression from e. In this section, we study the transformations that result from integrity constraints which contain one term only and investigate the circumstances under which they may be applied to query expressions. According to the structure of their expressions, we distinguish six types of integrity constraints. For the following, we shall assume the relations R and R' and the attributes A, A_1, A_2 (all from R), and B (from R'); moreover let v be an attribute value of A and ω a relational operator, i.e., $\omega \in \{=,<,\leq,>,\geq\}$.

The simplest sort of integrity constraint has the following form.

(3.6) $$\exists x(x.A \; \omega \; v) \quad \text{or} \quad \exists x(x.A_1 \; \omega \; x.A_2)$$

Integrity constraints of this type are very weak and therefore hardly ever will be used in practice. If, e.g., ω is $\neq$, then (3.6) means that there has to be at least one tuple from R which does not have the value v on attribute A (or for which the values of attribute A_1 and A_2 do not agree). A term which occurs in an integrity constraint of type (3.6) cannot be eliminated from a query expression without changing the meaning of the query because we restricted ourselves to coherent query expressions.

The next type of integrity constraint we consider is

$$\forall x\ (x.A\ \omega\ v) \quad \text{or} \quad \forall x\ (x.A_1\ \omega\ x.A_2) \tag{3.7}$$

Though in the case where ω is = this means that tuples from R have a constant value v on attribute A (or totally agree on the attributes A_1 and A_2), there are many meaningful instances of constraints of this type mainly if $\omega \in \{<, \leq, >, \geq\}$. Obviously a term τ which occurs in an integrity constraint of type (3.7) does not restrict the set of tuples from R in any way when τ is part of some query expression χ. Since χ has to be a coherent expression, it must contain a subexpression of one of the following forms

$$(\alpha \wedge \tau) \quad \text{or} \quad (\tau \wedge \alpha) \tag{3.8}$$

$$(\alpha \vee \tau) \quad \text{or} \quad (\tau \vee \alpha) \tag{3.9}$$

where α is an arbitrary expression. A subexpression of type (3.8) may be replaced in χ by the expression α without changing the meaning of the query. A subexpression of type (3.9) even may be deleted from χ; in this latter case even a subexpression

$$(\alpha_1 \vee \ldots \vee \alpha_k \vee \tau \vee \alpha_{k+1} \vee \ldots \vee \alpha_\ell)\ ,\quad 0 \leq k \leq \ell,\quad \ell \geq 1 \tag{3.10}$$

may be deleted from χ (where χ is written without any unnecessary parentheses). Note that if we have an integrity constraint

$$\forall x\ (x.A\ \omega\ v) \quad \text{with} \quad \omega \in \{<, >, \leq, \geq\} \tag{3.11}$$

then the above even applies to all terms

$$\tau = (x.A\ \omega\ v') \tag{3.12}$$

with $v\ \omega\ v'$. The following two types of integrity constraints again hardly ever will be used in practice.

$$\exists x\ \forall y\ (x.A\ \omega\ y.B) \tag{3.13}$$

$$\exists x\ \exists y\ (x.A\ \omega\ y.B) \tag{3.14}$$

Thus, e.g., if ω is = in (3.13), then this implies that the tuples from R' have a constant value on attribute B. A term which occurs in an integrity constraint of either type (3.13) or (3.14) must not be removed from a query expression because otherwise the meaning of that query would be changed; again this is a consequence of our restriction to coherent query expressions.

A very frequently occurring type of integrity constraint is

(3.15) $$\forall x\, \exists y\ (x.A\ \omega\ y.B)$$

An example for this type is the integrity constraint (3.2). A join term which occurs in an integrity constraint of type (3.15) may be deleted from a query expression χ without changing the meaning of the query if each of the following conditions is fulfilled:

(a) y does not occur in any other term of χ.
(b) y is existentially quantified in χ.
(c) Either the quantifier of x precedes the quantifier of y in χ or x is free in χ.

According to this definition, the term from (3.2) may be deleted from

(3.16) $$\{x \mid ((x.COL='red') \wedge \exists y(x.OWN=y.NAME))\}$$

(find all red cars which are owned by an employee) but it must not be deleted from

(3.17) $$\{y \mid \exists x((x.OWN=y.NAME) \wedge (x.COL='red'))\}$$

(find all employees who own a red car) nor from

(3.18) $$\{x \mid \exists y((x.OWN=y.NAME) \wedge (y.AGE<30))\}$$

(find all cars which are owned by an employee who is younger than 30). This seems to be quite reasonable because (3.16) is equivalent in meaning to

(3.19) $$\{x \mid (x.COL='red')\}$$

whereas (3.17) is not equivalent to

(3.20) $$\{y \mid \exists x(x.COL='red')\}$$

and (3.18) is not equivalent to

(3.21) $$\{x \mid \exists y(y.AGE<30)\}$$

Finally there are integrity constraints of the following type.

(3.22) $$\forall x\, \forall y\ (x.A\ \omega\ y.B)$$

Indeed (3.22) does not make much sense if ω is = (all tuples from R and R' would have to have the same value on the attributes A and B) but for $\omega \in \{<, \leq, >, \geq\}$ there are many meaningful applications. A join term which is contained in an integrity constraint of type (3.22) may be removed from a query expression χ unless both x and y occur in other terms of χ.

Since terms from constraints of type (3.7) may be removed under any circumstances, we shall assume that they have been deleted already from the original query (a warning should be given to the user in such a situation); thus integrity constraints of type (3.7) reduce the number of admissible subqueries only indirectly. This is different for integrity constraints of type (3.15) and (3.22); it is possible (and in fact occurs very frequently) that a term from such a constraint must not be removed from the qualification expression of the original query because not all of the conditions are fulfilled but may be removed from the qualification expression of one or more of its subqueries. Thus the qualification expression of the respective subquery is simplifed and thereby the number of its admissible subqueries is reduced; this in turn means that the number of admissible subqueries of the original query is reduced.

If we assume the integrity constraint

(3.23) $$\forall x \; \exists y \; (x.DN = y.DNO)$$

i.e., for every employee there is a department he works for, then this further reduces the number of admissible subqueries of (2.16) from 14 to 11: The subquery

(3.24) $$\{x \mid (\exists y(y.DNO=x.DN) \wedge ((x.AGE<20) \vee \exists z((z.OWN=x.NAME) \wedge ((z.COL='red') \vee (z.COL='blue')))))\}$$

is equivalent in meaning to

(3.25) $$\{x \mid ((x.AGE<20) \vee \exists z((z.OWN=x.NAME) \wedge ((z.COL='red') \vee (z.COL='blue'))))\}$$

the subquery

(3.26) $$\{x \mid (\exists y(y.DNO=x.DN) \wedge ((x.AGE<20) \vee \exists z(z.OWN=x.NAME)))\}$$

is equivalent in meaning to

(3.27) $$\{x \mid ((x.AGE < 20) \vee \exists z(z.OWN = x.NAME))\}$$

and finally the subquery

$$\{x \mid \exists y(y.DNO=x.DN)\} \tag{3.28}$$

is no longer meaningful since its qualification expression no longer restricts the set of all employees in any way.

It should be mentioned that this technique of query simplification by means of integrity constraints may be useful also in the context of decomposition of queries to a distributed data base: Hopefully a distributed data base will be divided into parts according to a set of criteria; these criteria may be expressed as integrity constraints to the respective parts of the data base. The different parts of a query that are addressed to different parts of the data base then may be simplified according to the corresponding sets of integrity constraints.

INFORMATIVE ANSWERS AND DATA SECURITY

So far we have tacitly assumed that a user always should be given an informative answer; we did not consider that such an answer might contain information to which the user has no access rights. As we have seen, an informative answer always consists of one or more statements of the form "The set of data described by the property Y is empty"; therefore one might think that informative answers could be given to the user unhesitatingly even if Y describes a set of data the user is not authorized to retrieve. Though it is true that one single such answer hardly ever will convey any useful information, a set of such answers may be used to infer confidential attribute values. In general, such a behavior is known as deduction of confidential information by inference (cf. Denning and Denning [1979]). In the remainder of this section we shall demonstrate how informative answers may be used to infer confidential information and then discuss methods to prevent this kind of abuse of informative answers.

Suppose that the manager of a department is authorized to retrieve data about the employees from his own department but not about employees from any other department; moreover, let us assume that the manager of the shoe department wants to find out the salary of Mr. Brown who works in the food department. For this purpose, he may start with the following query

$$\{x \mid (((x.NAME='Brown') \wedge (x.SAL>25{,}000)) \wedge \exists y((y.DNO=x.DN) \wedge (y.DNAME='shoe')))\} \tag{4.1}$$

(find all employees named Brown who work in the shoe department and earn more than \$25,000). Obviously the questioner is allowed to ask this query because it refers to employees from the shoe department only; however, there is no employee named Brown in the shoe department (because there is an employee named Brown in the food department and NAME is the primary key attribute of the EMP relation) and therefore an informative answer to this query will be inferred. Among the subqueries of (4.1) that will be formed in order to find the informative answer, there has to be the following query (if we presume that every employee works for some department):

$$\{x \mid ((x.NAME='Brown') \land (x.SAL>25{,}000))\} \tag{4.2}$$

i.e., find all employees named Brown who earn more than $25,000. If the informative answer contains the statement "There are no employees named Brown who earn more than $25,000" or even "There are no employees who earn more than $25,000", then Mr. Brown from the food department does not earn more than $25,000; if, however, the informative answer contains none of these statements then Mr. Brown earns more than $25,000. From here on it is well known how the manager of the shoe department has to choose new values for the attribute SAL in (4.1) in order to find out the exact salary of Mr. Brown very quickly.

In fact, this is a very simple example but the same technique may be applied also in more complex situations; e.g., a snooper need not know the value of the primary key attribute of the tuple he is interested in, it is sufficient that he knows an arbitrary expression by means of which the tuple in question is characterized uniquely. We do not claim that this method will succeed in finding any desired attribute value, yet already our simple example indicates that we must not supply the user with informative answers in an utterly uncontrolled way. Since the user obtains confidential information by inference, one might assume that inference controls are the right tools for preventing this kind of abuse. However, inference controls (for an overview cf. Denning and Denning [1979]) either would endanger the correctness of the informative answers or would be only a partial solution. Instead we shall examine two sorts of access controls with regard to their appropriateness for preventing the deduction of confidential information by means of informative answers.

A very evident and also very powerful method for access control is query modification (cf. Stonebraker and Wong [1974]). The idea of this method is that every query is modified by linking a constraint expression to its qualification expression; such a constraint expression is characteristic of the particular user and describes a set of data the user is allowed to retrieve. An example for a constraint expression (which describes the access rights of the manager of the shoe department) is:

(4.3) $\exists$y((y.DNO=x.DN) $\wedge$ (y.DNAME='shoe'))

Clearly informative answers would be safe from any abuse of the described kind if we first compute the admissible subqueries from the user's unmodified query and then modify their qualification expressions by the respective constraint expressions. Note, however, that different subqueries may require different constraint expressions; so for every subquery first the applicable constraint expression must be determined and then this constraint expression has to be fitted in the qualification expression. Thus this method may become rather expensive.

Another way to ensure that a user will not violate his access rights is to submit each query to a series of tests. A much simplified sequence of such tests (for a more detailed sequence see Date [1975]) might look like this.

(T1) Are all relations mentioned in the qualification expression of the query unconditionally accessible to the user?

(T2) Is there a relation mentioned in the qualification expression of the query unconditionally prohibited to the user?

(T3) Are all attributes mentioned in the qualification expression of the query unconditionally accessible to the user?

(T4) Is there an attribute mentioned in the qualification expression of the query unconditionally prohibited to the user?

(T5) Are all combinations of attributes mentioned in the qualification expression of the query unconditionally accessible to the user?

(T6) Is there a combination of attributes mentioned in the qualification expression of the query unconditionally prohibited to the user?

(T7) For each combination of attributes which is not unconditionally accessible to the user, is there a subexpression of the query which constrains the values of the participating attributes to lie within ranges accessible to the user?

For a given query, these tests are performed one after another until there is a test which gives the result YES; then the query either is permitted (if the successful test was (T1), (T3), (T5), or (T7)) or is rejected (if the successful test was (T2), (T4), or (T6) or if all (T1) through (T7) did not succeed).

When we have to infer an informative answer to query Q, we know that Q has passed the test sequence successfully and we know which test succeeded. If, e.g., (T3) succeeded for Q, then all of the subqueries may be computed without any further testing; this is due to the fact that the set of all attributes which occur in the subquery is a subset of the set of attributes occurring in Q: Since all attributes of the original query are unconditionally accessible, so are all attributes of the subquery. Similar statements can be made in the cases where the succeeding test for Q is either (T1) or (T5). If Q was permitted because of (T7), however, then the subexpression whose existence is postulated in (T7) need not be a subexpression of the qualification expression of a subquery Q'; moreover the qualification expression of the subquery Q' does not necessarily contain all the relations which occur in the qualification expression of Q; this also holds for the attributes and combinations of attributes occurring in the qualification expression of Q'. Therefore, if Q was permitted because of (T7) then a subquery Q' has to be submitted to the sequence of tests in the same way as Q. Note, however, that if Q was permitted because of (T7) and a subquery Q' of Q was permitted because of(T1), (T3), or (T5) then all subqueries of Q' may be computed without any further tests.

For our example, we might assume that the relations CAR and DEPT and the attributes NAME and DN from the relation EMP are unconditionally accessible to the manager of the shoe department and that the attributes AGE and SAL are accessible to him only if they appear in a qualification expression which contains (4.3) as a subexpression. Query (4.1) then would be permitted because of (T7) and the "sensitive subexpression" would be (4.3). Among the subqueries, (4.2) would be rejected because of (T7) since it does not contain (4.3) whereas, e.g.,

(4.4) $\{x \mid ((x.NAME='Brown') \wedge \exists y((y.DNO=x.DN) \wedge (y.DNAME='shoe')))\}$

would be permitted. The procedure for obtaining an informative answer then may be modified in the following way: An answer "$B_0 = \emptyset$" to a user's query may be substituted by the answer

$$B_1 = \emptyset \wedge B_2 = \emptyset \wedge \dots \wedge B_n = \emptyset$$

where B_i are those of the direct subqueries of B_0 which fail themselves and which are permitted for that particular user. This guarantees that deduction of confidential information by means of informative answers will no longer be possible.

CONCLUSION

In this paper, we have investigated the feasibility of supplying informative answers to the user of a data base. We started by giving a recapitulation of the procedure by means of which informative answers are obtained; special attention was paid to the computational costs involved. Next we examined the influence of integrity constraints on the process of generating informative answers; it turned out that less subqueries have to be computed in order to give an informative answer if integrity constraints are considered. Finally we showed that informative answers must not be given to the user in an utterly uncontrolled way and suggested two methods which select only those answer constituents that may be given to the user unhesitatingly. Summarizing we can say that neither efficiency nor security prohibit the practical application of informative answers; thus informative answers should be used in order to make data base query systems act more naturally.

ACKNOWLEDGEMENT

I wish to thank Michael Aschenbrenner, formerly of Technische Universität München, who first suggested examining informative answers from the viewpoint of data security.

REFERENCES

1. Chang, C.-L. and R. C. T. Lee [1973] *Symbolic Logic and Mechanical Theorem Proving*, Academic Press, New York, 1973.

2. Codd, E. F. [1970] "A Relational Model of Data for Large Shared Data Banks." *Communications ACM 13*, 6 (1970), 377-387.

3. Codd, E. F. [1971a] "Relational Completeness of Data Base Sublanguages." In *Courant Computer Science Symposia, Vol. 6, Data Base Systems* (R. Rustin, Ed.) Prentice Hall, Englewood Cliffs, New Jersey, 1972.

4. Codd, E. F. [1971b]. "A Database Sublanguage Founded on the Relational Calculus." In *Proc. 1971 SIGFIDET Workshop*, ACM, New York, 1971, 35-68.

5. Date, C. J. [1975] *An Introduction to Database Systems*, Addison-Wesley Publishing Co., Reading Mass., 1975.

6. Demolombe, R. [1979a] "Semantic Checking of Questions Expressed in Predicate Calculus Language." In *Proc. 5th Int. Conf. on Very Large Data Bases*. Rio de Janeiro, 1979, 444-450.

7. Demolombe, R. [1979b] "Assigning Meaning to Ill-defined Queries Expressed in Predicate Calculus Language." In *Preprints of the Workshop on Formal Bases for Data Bases*. Toulouse, 1979, 21.1-21.26.

8. Denning, D. E. and P. J. Denning [1979] "Data Security", *ACM Computing Surveys 11*, 3 (1979), 227-249.

9. Janas, J. M. [1979a] "How to not Say Nil — Improving Answers to Failing Queries in Data Base Systems." In *Proc. 6th Int. Joint Conf. on Artificial Intelligence*. Tokyo, 1979, 429-434.

10. Janas, J. M. [1979b] "Towards More Informative User Inferfaces." In *Proc. 5th Int. Conf. on Very Large Data Bases*. Rio de Janeiro, 1979, 17-23.

11. Kaplan, S. J. [1979] "Cooperative Responses from a Portable Natural Language Data Base Query System." Ph.D. Thesis, Dept. of Computer and Information Sciences, University of Pennsylvania, 1979.

12. Lee, R. M. [1978a] "Conversational Aspects of Database Interactions." In *Proc. 4th Int. Conf. on Very Large Data Bases*. Berlin, 1978, 392-399.

13. Lee R. M. [1978b] "Algorithmic Analysis for Informative Failure in the Relational Calculus." Working Paper 78-10-08, Dept. of Decision Sciences, University of Pennsylvania, 1978.

14. McSkimin, J. R. and J. Minker [1977] "The Use of a Semantic Network in a Deduction Question Answering System." In *Proc. 5th Int. Joint Conf. on Artificial Intelligence*. Cambridge, MA, 1977, 50-58.

15. Reiter, R. [1978] "On Closed World Data Bases." In *Logic and Data Bases* (H. Gallaire and J. Minker, Eds.) Plenum Press, New York, 1978, 55-76.

16. Reiter, R. [1981] "On the Integrity of Typed First Order Data Bases." In *Advances in Data Base Theory — Volume 1*, (H. Gallaire, J. Minker and J. M. Nicolas, Eds.), Plenum Press, New York, 1981, 137-157.

17. Stonebraker, M. and E. Wong [1974]. "Access Control in a Relational Data Base Management System by Query Modification." In *Proc. ACM 1974*, 1974, 180-186.

NAME INDEX

SUBJECT INDEX

LIST OF REFEREES

The editors are indebted to the referees for their detailed reading and constructive comments. Every article was reviewed by at least three reviewers. The quality of each article has been enhanced over the original submission due to their efforts.

W. W. Armstrong	Université de Montréal, Canada
F. Bancilhon	INRIA, France
C. Beeri	Hebrew University, Israel
J. Biskup	Technische Hochschule Aachen, Federal Republic of Germany
M. Brodie	University of Maryland, USA
A. Colmerauer	Université de Marseille, France
C. Delobel	Université de Grenoble, France
R. Demolombe,	CERT, France
M. van Emden	University of Waterloo, Canada
R. Fagin	IBM, USA
H. Gallaire	ENSAE-CERT, France
J. Grant	Towson State University, USA
J. M. Janas	Hochschule der Bundeswehr München, Federal Republic of Germany
P. Kandzia	Christian Albrechts Universität, Federal Republic of Germany

C. Kellogg	SDC, USA
H. J. Klein	Christian Albrechts Universität, Federal Republic of Germany
R. A. Kowalski	Imperial College of London, Great Britain
M. LaCroix	Philips Research, Belgium
M. Leonard	Université de Genève, Switzerland
W. Lipski, Jr.	Polish Academy of Science, Poland
D. Maier	State University of New York, Stony Brook, USA
A. Mendelzon	IBM, USA
J. Minker	University of Maryland, USA
J. M. Nicolas	ONERA-CERT, France
P. Paolini	IEE Politecnico di Milano, Italy
J. Paredaens	Universitaire Instelling Antwerpen, Belgium
E. Pichet	Université de Grenoble, France
J. F. Pique	Université de Marseille, France
A. Pirotte	Philips Research, Belgium
R. Reiter	University of British Columbia, Canada
J. Rissanen	IBM, USA
Y. Sagiv	University of Illinois, USA
S. A. Tarnlund	University of Upsala, Sweden
L. Travis	University of Wisconsin, USA
M. Vardi	Weizmann Institute, Israel
D. Warren	University of Edinburgh, Great Britain
G. Zanon	CERT, France

ADDRESSES OF CONTRIBUTING AUTHORS

C. Beeri
Department of Computer Science
Institute of Mathematics
The Hebrew University
of Jerusalem
Jerusalem, Israel

J. Biskup
Lehrstuhl für Angewandte
Mathematik/INSB Informatik
RWTH Aachen
Templergraben 55
D-5100 Aachen
Federal Republic of Germany

C. L. Chang
IBM Research Laboratory-K54/282
5600 Cottle Road
San Jose, California 95193
USA

A. Colmerauer
Groupe d'Intelligence
Artificielle
Université d'Aix
Marseille II
Marseille Luminy
70, Route Léon Lachamp
13009 Marseille
France

R. Demolombe
ONERA-CERT
Department d'Informatique
2, Avenue Edouard Belin
31055 Toulouse Cedex
France

M. van Emden
Department of Computer Science
University of Waterloo
Waterloo, Ontario, Canada

H. Gallaire
ENSAE
BP 4032
31005 Toulouse Cedex, FRANCE

J. Grant
Towson State University
Department of Mathematics
and Computer Science
Towson, Maryland 21204 USA

J. M. Janas
Fachbereich Informatik
Hochschule der Bundeswehr-München
Werner-Heisenberg-Weg 39
D-8014-Neubiberg
Federal Republic of Germany

D. Janssens
Universiteit Antwerpen
Department Wiskunde
Univeriteitsplein 1
B 2610 WILRIJK
Belgium

C. Kellogg
System Development Corporation
Research & Development Division
2500 Colorado Avenue
Santa Monica, California 94406 USA

T. S. E. Maibaum
Department of Computer Science
University of Waterloo
Waterloo, Ontario, Canada

D. Maier
Department of Computer Science
State University of New York
Stonybrook, New York 11794 USA

M. A. Melkanoff
Computer Science Department
University of California, UCLA
Los Angeles, California 90024 USA

A. O. Mendelzon
University of Toronto
Department of Computer Science
Toronto, Canada H55 1A7

J. Minker
Department of Computer Science
University of Maryland
College Park, Maryland 20742 USA

J. M. Nicolas
ONERA-CERT
Department d'Informatique
2, Avenue Edouard Belin
31055 Toulouse Cedex France

J. Paredaens
Universiteit Antwerpen
Department Wiskunde
Universiteitsplein 1
B 2610 WILRIJK Belgium

J. F. Pique
Groupe d'Intelligence Artificielle
Université d'Aix Marseille II
Marseille Luminy
70, Route Léon Lachamp
13009 Marseille France

R. Reiter
Department of Computer Science
University of British Columbia
Vancouver BCV GT 1 W5 Canada

F. Sadri
Computer Science Department
Stanford University
Stanford, California 94305 USA

A. M. Silva
Computer Science Department
University of California, UCLA
Los Angeles, California 90024 USA

L. Travis
Department of Computer Science
University of Wisconsin
Madison, Wisconsin USA

J. D. Ullman
Computer Science Department
Stanford University
Stanford, California 94305 USA

M. Y. Vardi
Department of Computer Science
Institute of Mathematics
The Hebrew University of Jerusalem
Jerusalem, Israel